A TRAMP ABROAD

THE OXFORD MARK TWAIN
Shelley Fisher Fishkin, Editor

The Celebrated Jumping Frog of Calaveras County, and Other Sketches
Introduction: Roy Blount Jr.
Afterword: Richard Bucci

The Innocents Abroad
Introduction: Mordecai Richler
Afterword: David E. E. Sloane

Roughing It
Introduction: George Plimpton
Afterword: Henry B. Wonham

The Gilded Age
Introduction: Ward Just
Afterword: Gregg Camfield

Sketches, New and Old
Introduction: Lee Smith
Afterword: Sherwood Cummings

The Adventures of Tom Sawyer
Introduction: E. L. Doctorow
Afterword: Albert E. Stone

A Tramp Abroad
Introduction: Russell Banks
Afterword: James S. Leonard

A Tramp Abroad

Mark Twain

FOREWORD

SHELLEY FISHER FISHKIN

INTRODUCTION

RUSSELL BANKS

AFTERWORD

JAMES S. LEONARD

New York   Oxford

OXFORD UNIVERSITY PRESS

1996

OXFORD UNIVERSITY PRESS

Oxford   New York

Athens, Auckland, Bangkok, Bogotá, Bombay
Buenos Aires, Calcutta, Cape Town, Dar es Salaam
Delhi, Florence, Hong Kong, Istanbul, Karachi
Kuala Lumpur, Madras, Madrid, Melbourne
Mexico City, Nairobi, Paris, Singapore
Taipei, Tokyo, Toronto
and associated companies in
Berlin, Ibadan

Copyright © 1996 by
Oxford University Press, Inc.
Introduction © 1996 by Russell Banks
Afterword © 1996 by James S. Leonard
Illustrators and Illustrations in Mark Twain's First
American Editions © 1996 by Beverly R. David and
Ray Sapirstein
Reading the Illustrations in A Tramp Abroad
© 1996 by Beverly R. David and Ray Sapirstein
Text design by Richard Hendel
Composition: David Thorne

Published by
Oxford University Press, Inc.
198 Madison Avenue, New York,
New York 10016

Library of Congress
Cataloging-in-Publication Data

Twain, Mark, 1835–1910.
A tramp abroad / by Mark Twain; with an
introduction by Russell Banks and an afterword by
James Leonard.
p. cm. — (The Oxford Mark Twain)
1. Twain, Mark, 1835–1910—Journeys—Europe.
2. Europe—Description and travel. I. Title.
II. Series: Twain, Mark, 1835–1910. Works. 1996.
PS1321.A1 1996
818'.403—dc20
[B]
96-17032
CIP
ISBN 0-19-510137-5 (trade ed.)
ISBN 0-19-511408-6 (lib. ed.)
ISBN 0-19-509088-8 (trade ed. set)
ISBN 0-19-511345-4 (lib. ed. set)

9 8 7 6 5 4 3 2 1

Printed in the United States of America
on acid-free paper

FRONTISPIECE
Samuel L. Clemens is seen here seated at his
writing desk in 1880, the year *A Tramp Abroad*
was published. (Courtesy, The Mark Twain Project,
The Bancroft Library)

CONTENTS

EDITOR'S NOTE

The Oxford Mark Twain consists of twenty-nine volumes of facsimiles of the first American editions of Mark Twain's works, with an editor's foreword, new introductions, afterwords, notes on the texts, and essays on the illustrations in volumes with artwork. The facsimiles have been reproduced from the originals unaltered, except that blank pages in the front and back of the books have been omitted, and any seriously damaged or missing pages have been replaced by pages from other first editions (as indicated in the notes on the texts).

In the foreword, introduction, afterword, and essays on the illustrations, the titles of Mark Twain's works have been capitalized according to modern conventions, as have the names of characters (except where otherwise indicated). In the case of discrepancies between the title of a short story, essay, or sketch as it appears in the original table of contents and as it appears on its own title page, the title page has been followed. The parenthetical numbers in the introduction, afterwords, and illustration essays are page references to the facsimiles.

FOREWORD

Shelley Fisher Fishkin

S amuel Clemens entered the world and left it with Halley's Comet, little dreaming that generations hence Halley's Comet would be less famous than Mark Twain. He has been called the American Cervantes, our Homer, our Tolstoy, our Shakespeare, our Rabelais. Ernest Hemingway maintained that "all modern American literature comes from one book by Mark Twain called *Huckleberry Finn.*" President Franklin Delano Roosevelt got the phrase "New Deal" from *A Connecticut Yankee in King Arthur's Court. The Gilded Age* gave an entire era its name. "The future historian of America," wrote George Bernard Shaw to Samuel Clemens, "will find your works as indispensable to him as a French historian finds the political tracts of Voltaire."[1]

There is a Mark Twain Bank in St. Louis, a Mark Twain Diner in Jackson Heights, New York, a Mark Twain Smoke Shop in Lakeland, Florida. There are Mark Twain Elementary Schools in Albuquerque, Dayton, Seattle, and Sioux Falls. Mark Twain's image peers at us from advertisements for Bass Ale (his drink of choice was Scotch), for a gas company in Tennessee, a hotel in the nation's capital, a cemetery in California.

Ubiquitous though his name and image may be, Mark Twain is in no danger of becoming a petrified icon. On the contrary: Mark Twain lives. *Huckleberry Finn* is "the most taught novel, most taught long work, and most taught piece of American literature" in American schools from junior high to the graduate level.[2] Hundreds of Twain impersonators appear in theaters, trade shows, and shopping centers in every region of the country.[3] Scholars publish hundreds of articles as well as books about Twain every year, and he is the subject of daily exchanges on the Internet. A journalist somewhere in the world finds a reason to quote Twain just about every day. Television series such as *Bonanza, Star Trek: The Next Generation,* and *Cheers* broadcast episodes that feature Mark Twain as a character. Hollywood screenwriters regularly produce movies inspired by his works, and writers of mysteries and science fiction continue to weave him into their plots.[4]

A century after the American Revolution sent shock waves throughout Europe, it took Mark Twain to explain to Europeans and to his countrymen alike what that revolution had wrought. He probed the significance of this new land and its new citizens, and identified what it was in the Old World that America abolished and rejected. The founding fathers had thought through the political dimensions of making a new society; Mark Twain took on the challenge of interpreting the social and cultural life of the United States for those outside its borders as well as for those who were living the changes he discerned.

Americans may have constructed a new society in the eighteenth century, but they articulated what they had done in voices that were largely inter-changeable with those of Englishmen until well into the nineteenth century. Mark Twain became the voice of the new land, the leading translator of what and who the "American" was — and, to a large extent, is. Frances Trollope's *Domestic Manners of the Americans,* a best-seller in England, Hector St. John de Crèvecoeur's *Letters from an American Farmer,* and Tocqueville's *Democracy in America* all tried to explain America to Europeans. But Twain did more than that: he allowed European readers to *experience* this strange "new world." And he gave his countrymen the tools to do two things they had not quite had the confidence to do before. He helped them stand before the cultural icons of the Old World unembarrassed, unashamed of America's lack of palaces and shrines, proud of its brash practicality and bold inventiveness, unafraid to reject European models of "civilization" as tainted or corrupt. And he also helped them recognize their own insularity, boorishness, arrogance, or ignorance, and laugh at it — the first step toward transcending it and becoming more "civilized," in the best European sense of the word.

Twain often strikes us as more a creature of our time than of his. He appreciated the importance and the complexity of mass tourism and public relations, fields that would come into their own in the twentieth century but were only fledgling enterprises in the nineteenth. He explored the liberating potential of humor and the dynamics of friendship, parenting, and marriage. He narrowed the gap between "popular" and "high" culture, and he meditated on the enigmas of personal and national identity. Indeed, it would be difficult to find an issue on the horizon today that Twain did not touch on somewhere in his work. Heredity versus environment? Animal rights? The boundaries of gender? The place of black voices in the cultural heritage of the United States? Twain was there.

With startling prescience and characteristic grace and wit, he zeroed in on many of the key challenges — political, social, and technological — that would face his country and the world for the next hundred years: the challenge of race relations in a society founded on both chattel slavery and ideals of equality, and the intractable problem of racism in American life; the potential of new technologies to transform our lives in ways that can be both exhilarating and terrifying — as well as unpredictable; the problem of imperialism and the difficulties entailed in getting rid of it. But he never lost sight of the most basic challenge of all: each man or woman's struggle for integrity in the face of the seductions of power, status, and material things.

Mark Twain's unerring sense of the right word and not its second cousin taught people to pay attention when he spoke, in person or in print. He said things that were smart and things that were wise, and he said them incomparably well. He defined the rhythms of our prose and the contours of our moral map. He saw our best and our worst, our extravagant promise and our stunning failures, our comic foibles and our tragic flaws. Throughout the world he is viewed as the most distinctively American of American authors — and as one of the most universal. He is assigned in classrooms in Naples, Riyadh, Belfast, and Beijing, and has been a major influence on twentieth-century writers from Argentina to Nigeria to Japan. The Oxford Mark Twain celebrates the versatility and vitality of this remarkable writer.

The Oxford Mark Twain reproduces the first American editions of Mark Twain's books published during his lifetime.[5] By encountering Twain's works in their original format — typography, layout, order of contents, and illustrations — readers today can come a few steps closer to the literary artifacts that entranced and excited readers when the books first appeared. Twain approved of and to a greater or lesser degree supervised the publication of all of this material.[6] The Mark Twain House in Hartford, Connecticut, generously loaned us its originals.[7] When more than one copy of a first American edition was available, Robert H. Hirst, general editor of the Mark Twain Project, in cooperation with Marianne Curling, curator of the Mark Twain House (and Jeffrey Kaimowitz, head of Rare Books for the Watkinson Library of Trinity College, Hartford, where the Mark Twain House collection is kept), guided our decision about which one to use.[8] As a set, the volumes also contain more than eighty essays commissioned especially for The Oxford Mark Twain, in which distinguished contributors reassess Twain's achievement as a writer and his place in the cultural conversation that he did so much to shape.

Each volume of The Oxford Mark Twain is introduced by a leading American, Canadian, or British writer who responds to Twain — often in a very personal way — as a fellow writer. Novelists, journalists, humorists, columnists, fabulists, poets, playwrights — these writers tell us what Twain taught them and what in his work continues to speak to them. Reading Twain's books, both famous and obscure, they reflect on the genesis of his art and the characteristics of his style, the themes he illuminated, and the aesthetic strategies he pioneered. Individually and collectively their contributions testify to the place Mark Twain holds in the hearts of readers of all kinds and temperaments.

Scholars whose work has shaped our view of Twain in the academy today have written afterwords to each volume, with suggestions for further reading. Their essays give us a sense of what was going on in Twain's life when he wrote the book at hand, and of how that book fits into his career. They explore how each book reflects and refracts contemporary events, and they show Twain responding to literary and social currents of the day, variously accepting, amplifying, modifying, and challenging prevailing paradigms. Sometimes they argue that works previously dismissed as quirky or eccentric departures actually address themes at the heart of Twain's work from the start. And as they bring new perspectives to Twain's composition strategies in familiar texts, several scholars see experiments in form where others saw only formlessness, method where prior critics saw only madness. In addition to elucidating the work's historical and cultural context, the afterwords provide an overview of responses to each book from its first appearance to the present.

Most of Mark Twain's books involved more than Mark Twain's words: unique illustrations. The parodic visual send-ups of "high culture" that Twain himself drew for *A Tramp Abroad*, the sketch of financial manipulator Jay Gould as a greedy and sadistic "Slave Driver" in *A Connecticut Yankee in King Arthur's Court*, and the memorable drawings of Eve in *Eve's Diary* all helped Twain's books to be sold, read, discussed, and preserved. In their essays for each volume that contains artwork, Beverly R. David and Ray Sapirstein highlight the significance of the sketches, engravings, and photographs in the first American editions of Mark Twain's works, and tell us what is known about the public response to them.

The Oxford Mark Twain invites us to read some relatively neglected works by Twain in the company of some of the most engaging literary figures of our time. Roy Blount Jr., for example, riffs in a deliciously Twain-like manner on "An Item Which the Editor Himself Could Not Understand," which may well rank as one of the least-known pieces Twain ever published. Bobbie Ann Mason celebrates the "mad energy" of Twain's most obscure comic novel, *The American Claimant*, in which the humor "hurtles beyond tall tale into simon-pure absurdity."[9] Garry Wills finds that *Christian Science* "gets us very close to the heart of American culture." Lee Smith reads "Political Economy" as a sharp and funny essay on language. Walter Mosley sees "The Stolen White Elephant," a story "reduced to a series of ridiculous telegrams related by an untrustworthy narrator caught up in an adventure that is as impossible as it is ludicrous," as a stunningly compact and economical satire of a world we still recognize as our own. Anne Bernays returns to "The Private History of a Campaign That Failed" and finds "an antiwar manifesto that is also confession, dramatic monologue, a plea for understanding and absolution, and a romp that gradually turns into atrocity even as we watch." After revisiting Captain Stormfield's heaven, Frederik Pohl finds that there "is no imaginable place more pleasant to spend eternity." Indeed, Pohl writes, "one would almost be willing to die to enter it."

While less familiar works receive fresh attention in The Oxford Mark Twain, new light is cast on the best-known works as well. Judith Martin ("Miss Manners") points out that it is by reading a court etiquette book that Twain's pauper learns how to behave as a proper prince. As important as etiquette may be in the palace, Martin notes, it is even more important in the slums.

> That etiquette is a sorer point with the ruffians in the street than with the proud dignitaries of the prince's court may surprise some readers. As in our own streets, etiquette is always a more volatile subject among those who cannot count on being treated with respect than among those who have the power to command deference.

And taking a fresh look at *Adventures of Huckleberry Finn,* Toni Morrison writes,

> much of the novel's genius lies in its quiescence, the silences that pervade it and give it a porous quality that is by turns brooding and soothing. It lies in . . . the subdued images in which the repetition of a simple word, such as "lonesome," tolls like an evening bell; the moments when nothing is said, when scenes and incidents swell the heart unbearably precisely because unarticulated, and force an act of imagination almost against the will.

Engaging Mark Twain as one writer to another, several contributors to The Oxford Mark Twain offer new insights into the processes by which his books came to be. Russell Banks, for example, reads *A Tramp Abroad* as "an important revision of Twain's incomplete first draft of *Huckleberry Finn,* a second draft, if you will, which in turn made possible the third and final draft." Erica Jong suggests that *1601,* a freewheeling parody of Elizabethan manners and mores, written during the same summer Twain began *Huckleberry Finn*, served as "a warm-up for his creative process" and "primed the pump for other sorts of freedom of expression." And Justin Kaplan suggests that "one of the transcendent figures standing behind and shaping" *Joan of Arc* was Ulysses S. Grant, whose memoirs Twain had recently published, and who, like Joan, had risen unpredictably "from humble and obscure origins" to become a "military genius" endowed with "the gift of command, a natural eloquence, and an equally natural reserve."

As a number of contributors note, Twain was a man ahead of his times. *The Gilded Age* was the first "Washington novel," Ward Just tells us, because "Twain was the first to see the possibilities that had eluded so many others." Commenting on *The Tragedy of Pudd'nhead Wilson,* Sherley Anne Williams observes that "Twain's argument about the power of environment in shaping character runs directly counter to prevailing sentiment where the negro was concerned." Twain's fictional technology, wildly fanciful by the standards of his day, predicts developments we take for granted in ours. DNA cloning, fax machines, and photocopiers are all prefigured, Bobbie Ann Mason tells us, in *The American Claimant.* Cynthia Ozick points out that the "telelectrophonoscope" we meet in "From the 'London Times' of 1904" is suspiciously like what we know as "television." And Malcolm Bradbury suggests that in the "phrenophones" of "Mental Telegraphy" "the Internet was born."

Twain turns out to have been remarkably prescient about political affairs as well. Kurt Vonnegut sees in *A Connecticut Yankee* a chilling foreshadowing (or perhaps a projection from the Civil War) of "all the high-tech atrocities which followed, and which follow still." Cynthia Ozick suggests that "The Man That Corrupted Hadleyburg," along with some of the other pieces collected under that title — many of them written when Twain lived in a Vienna ruled by Karl Lueger, a demagogue Adolf Hitler would later idolize — shoot up moral flares that shed an eerie light on the insidious corruption, prejudice, and hatred that reached bitter fruition under the Third Reich. And Twain's portrait in this book of "the dissolving Austria-Hungary of the 1890s," in Ozick's view, presages not only the Sarajevo that would erupt in 1914 but also "the disintegrated components of the former Yugoslavia" and "the *fin-de-siècle* Sarajevo of our own moment."

Despite their admiration for Twain's ambitious reach and scope, contributors to The Oxford Mark Twain also recognize his limitations. Mordecai Richler, for example, thinks that "the early pages of *Innocents Abroad* suffer from being a tad broad, proffering more burlesque than inspired satire," perhaps because Twain was "trying too hard for knee-slappers." Charles Johnson notes that the Young Man in Twain's philosophical dialogue about free will and determinism (*What Is Man?*) "caves in far too soon," failing to challenge what through late-twentieth-century eyes looks like "pseudoscience" and suspect essentialism in the Old Man's arguments.

Some contributors revisit their first encounters with Twain's works, recalling what surprised or intrigued them. When David Bradley came across "Fenimore Cooper's Literary Offences" in his college library, he "did not at first realize that Twain was being his usual ironic self with all this business about the 'nineteen rules governing literary art in the domain of romantic fiction,' but by the time I figured out there was no such list outside Twain's own head, I had decided that the rules made *sense*. . . . It seemed to me they were a pretty good blueprint for writing — Negro writing included." Sherley Anne Williams remembers that part of what attracted her to *Pudd'nhead Wilson* when she first read it thirty years ago was "that Twain, writing at the end of the nineteenth century, could imagine negroes as characters, albeit white ones, who actually thought for and of themselves, whose actions were the product of their thinking rather than the spontaneous ephemera of physical instincts that stereotype assigned to blacks." Frederik Pohl recalls his first reading of *Huckleberry Finn* as "a watershed event" in his life, the first book he read as a child in which "bad people" ceased to exercise a monopoly on doing "bad things." In *Huckleberry Finn* "some seriously bad things — things like the possession and mistreatment of black slaves, like stealing and lying, even like killing other people in duels — were quite often done by people who not only thought of themselves as exemplarily moral but, by any other standards I knew how to apply, actually *were* admirable citizens." The world that

Tom and Huck lived in, Pohl writes, "was filled with complexities and con-
tradictions," and resembled "the world I appeared to be living in myself."

Other contributors explore their more recent encounters with Twain, explaining why they have revised their initial responses to his work. For Toni
Morrison, parts of *Huckleberry Finn* that she "once took to be deliberate eva-
sions, stumbles even, or a writer's impatience with his or her material," now
strike her "as otherwise: as entrances, crevices, gaps, seductive invitations
flashing the possibility of meaning. Unarticulated eddies that encourage diving into the novel's undertow — the real place where writer captures reader."
One such "eddy" is the imprisonment of Jim on the Phelps farm. Instead of
dismissing this portion of the book as authorial bungling, as she once did,
Morrison now reads it as Twain's commentary on the 1880s, a period that
"saw the collapse of civil rights for blacks," a time when "the nation, as well as
Tom Sawyer, was deferring Jim's freedom in agonizing play." Morrison believes that Americans in the 1880s were attempting "to bury the combustible
issues Twain raised in his novel," and that those who try to kick Huck Finn
out of school in the 1990s are doing the same: "The cyclical attempts to remove the novel from classrooms extend Jim's captivity on into each generation of readers."

Although imitation-Hemingway and imitation-Faulkner writing contests
draw hundreds of entries annually, no one has ever tried to mount a faux-
Twain competition. Why? Perhaps because Mark Twain's voice is too much
a part of who we are and how we speak even today. Roy Blount Jr. suggests
that it is impossible, "at least for an American writer, to parody Mark Twain.
It would be like doing an impression of your father or mother: he or she is already there in your voice."

Twain's style is examined and celebrated in The Oxford Mark Twain by
fellow writers who themselves have struggled with the nuances of words, the
structure of sentences, the subtleties of point of view, and the trickiness of
opening lines. Bobbie Ann Mason observes, for example, that "Twain loved
the sound of words and he knew how to string them by sound, like different
shades of one color: 'The earl's barbaric eye,' 'the Usurping Earl,' 'a double-

dyed humbug.'" Twain "relied on the punch of plain words" to show writers how to move beyond the "wordy romantic rubbish" so prevalent in nineteenth-century fiction, Mason says; he "was one of the first writers in America to deflower literary language." Lee Smith believes that "American writers have benefited as much from the way Mark Twain opened up the possibilities of first-person narration as we have from his use of vernacular language." (She feels that "the ghost of Mark Twain was hovering someplace in the background" when she decided to write her novel *Oral History* from the standpoint of multiple first-person narrators.) Frederick Busch maintains that "A Dog's Tale" "boasts one of the great opening sentences" of all time: "My father was a St. Bernard, my mother was a collie, but I am a Presbyterian." And Ursula Le Guin marvels at the ingenuity of the following sentence that she encounters in *Extracts from Adam's Diary*.

. . . This made her sorry for the creatures which live in there, which she calls fish, for she continues to fasten names on to things that don't need them and don't come when they are called by them, which is a matter of no consequence to her, as she is such a numskull anyway; so she got a lot of them out and brought them in last night and put them in my bed to keep warm, but I have noticed them now and then all day, and I don't see that they are any happier there than they were before, only quieter.[10]

Le Guin responds,

Now, that is a pure Mark-Twain-tour-de-force sentence, covering an immense amount of territory in an effortless, aimless ramble that seems to be heading nowhere in particular and ends up with breathtaking accuracy at the gold mine. Any sensible child would find that funny, perhaps not following all its divagations but delighted by the swing of it, by the word "numskull," by the idea of putting fish in the bed; and as that child grew older and reread it, its reward would only grow; and if that grown-up child had to write an essay on the piece and therefore earnestly studied and pored over this sentence, she would end up in unmitigated admiration of its vocabulary, syntax, pacing, sense, and rhythm, above all the beautiful timing of the last two words; and she would, and she does, still find it funny.

The fish surface again in a passage that Gore Vidal calls to our attention, from *Following the Equator*: "'The Whites always mean well when they take human fish out of the ocean and try to make them dry and warm and happy and comfortable in a chicken coop,' which is how, through civilization, they did away with many of the original inhabitants. Lack of empathy is a principal theme in Twain's meditations on race and empire."

Indeed, empathy — and its lack — is a principal theme in virtually all of Twain's work, as contributors frequently note. Nat Hentoff quotes the following thoughts from Huck in *Tom Sawyer Abroad*:

I see a bird setting on a dead limb of a high tree, singing with its head tilted back and its mouth open, and before I thought I fired, and his song stopped and he fell straight down from the limb, all limp like a rag, and I run and picked him up and he was dead, and his body was warm in my hand, and his head rolled about this way and that, like his neck was broke, and there was a little white skin over his eyes, and one little drop of blood on the side of his head; and laws! I could n't see nothing more for the tears; and I hain't never murdered no creature since that war n't doing me no harm, and I ain't going to.[11]

"The Humane Society," Hentoff writes, "has yet to say anything as powerful — and lasting."

Readers of The Oxford Mark Twain will have the pleasure of revisiting Twain's Mississippi landmarks alongside Willie Morris, whose own lower Mississippi Valley boyhood gives him a special sense of connection to Twain. Morris knows firsthand the mosquitoes described in *Life on the Mississippi* — so colossal that "two of them could whip a dog" and "four of them could hold a man down"; in Morris's own hometown they were so large during the flood season that "local wags said they wore wristwatches." Morris's Yazoo City and Twain's Hannibal shared a "rough-hewn democracy . . . complicated by all the visible textures of caste and class, . . . harmless boyhood fun and mischief right along with . . . rank hypocrisies, churchgoing sanctimonies, racial hatred, entrenched and unrepentant greed."

For the West of Mark Twain's *Roughing It*, readers will have George Plimpton as their guide. "What a group these newspapermen were!" Plimpton writes about Twain and his friends Dan De Quille and Joe Goodman in Virginia City, Nevada. "Their roisterous carryings-on bring to mind the kind of frat-house enthusiasm one associates with college humor magazines like the *Harvard Lampoon*." Malcolm Bradbury examines Twain as "a living example of what made the American so different from the European." And Hal Holbrook, who has interpreted Mark Twain on stage for some forty years, describes how Twain "played" during the civil rights movement, during the Vietnam War, during the Gulf War, and in Prague on the eve of the demise of Communism.

Why do we continue to read Mark Twain? What draws us to him? His wit? His compassion? His humor? His bravura? His humility? His understanding of who and what we are in those parts of our being that we rarely open to view? Our sense that he knows we can do better than we do? Our sense that he knows we can't? E. L. Doctorow tells us that children are attracted to *Tom Sawyer* because in this book "the young reader confirms his own hope that no matter how troubled his relations with his elders may be, beneath all their disapproval is their underlying love for him, constant and steadfast." Readers in general, Arthur Miller writes, value Twain's "insights into America's always uncertain moral life and its shifting but everlasting hypocrisies"; we appreciate the fact that he "is not using his alienation from the public illusions of his hour in order to reject the country implicitly as though he could live without it, but manifestly in order to correct it." Perhaps we keep reading Mark Twain because, in Miller's words, he "wrote much more like a father than a son. He doesn't seem to be sitting in class taunting the teacher but standing at the head of it challenging his students to acknowledge their own humanity, that is, their immemorial attraction to the untrue."

Mark Twain entered the public eye at a time when many of his countrymen considered "American culture" an oxymoron; he died four years before a world conflagration that would lead many to question whether the contradiction in terms was not "European civilization" instead. In between he worked in journalism, printing, steamboating, mining, lecturing, publishing, and editing, in virtually every region of the country. He tried his hand at humorous sketches, social satire, historical novels, children's books, poetry, drama, science fiction, mysteries, romance, philosophy, travelogue, memoir, polemic, and several genres no one had ever seen before or has ever seen since. He invented a self-pasting scrapbook, a history game, a vest strap, and a gizmo for keeping bed sheets tucked in; he invested in machines and processes designed to revolutionize typesetting and engraving, and in a food supplement called "Plasmon." Along the way he cheerfully impersonated himself and prior versions of himself for doting publics on five continents while playing out a charming rags-to-riches story followed by a devastating riches-to-rags story followed by yet another great American comeback. He had a long-running real-life engagement in a sumptuous comedy of manners, and then in a real-life tragedy not of his own design: during the last fourteen years of his life almost everyone he ever loved was taken from him by disease and death.

Mark Twain has indelibly shaped our views of who and what the United States is as a nation and of who and what we might become. He understood the nostalgia for a "simpler" past that increased as that past receded — and he saw through the nostalgia to a past that was just as complex as the present. He recognized better than we did ourselves our potential for greatness and our potential for disaster. His fictions brilliantly illuminated the world in which he lived, changing it — and us — in the process. He knew that our feet often danced to tunes that had somehow remained beyond our hearing; with perfect pitch he played them back to us.

My mother read *Tom Sawyer* to me as a bedtime story when I was eleven. I thought Huck and Tom could be a lot of fun, but I dismissed Becky Thatcher as a bore. When I was twelve I invested a nickel at a local garage sale in a book that contained short pieces by Mark Twain. That was where I met Twain's Eve. Now, *that's* more like it, I decided, pleased to meet a female character I could identify *with* instead of against. Eve had spunk. Even if she got a lot wrong, you had to give her credit for trying. "The Man That Corrupted

Hadleyburg" left me giddy with satisfaction: none of my adolescent reveries of getting even with my enemies were half as neat as the plot of the man who got back at that town. "How I Edited an Agricultural Paper" set me off in uncontrollable giggles.

People sometimes told me that I looked like Huck Finn. "It's the freckles," they'd explain — not explaining anything at all. I didn't read *Huckleberry Finn* until junior year in high school in my English class. It was the fall of 1965. I was living in a small town in Connecticut. I expected a sequel to *Tom Sawyer*. So when the teacher handed out the books and announced our assignment, my jaw dropped: "Write a paper on how Mark Twain used irony to attack racism in *Huckleberry Finn*."

The year before, the bodies of three young men who had gone to Mississippi to help blacks register to vote — James Chaney, Andrew Goodman, and Michael Schwerner — had been found in a shallow grave; a group of white segregationists (the county sheriff among them) had been arrested in connection with the murders. America's inner cities were simmering with pent-up rage that began to explode in the summer of 1965, when riots in Watts left thirty-four people dead. None of this made any sense to me. I was confused, angry, certain that there was something missing from the news stories I read each day: the why. Then I met Pap Finn. And the Phelpses.

Pap Finn, Huck tells us, "had been drunk over in town" and "was just all mud." He erupts into a drunken tirade about "a free nigger . . . from Ohio — a mulatter, most as white as a white man," with "the whitest shirt on you ever see, too, and the shiniest hat; and there ain't a man in town that's got as fine clothes as what he had."

> . . . they said he was a p'fessor in a college, and could talk all kinds of languages, and knowed everything. And that ain't the wust. They said he could *vote*, when he was at home. Well, that let me out. Thinks I, what is the country a-coming to? It was 'lection day, and I was just about to go and vote, myself, if I warn't too drunk to get there; but when they told me there was a State in this country where they'd let that nigger vote, I drawed out. I says I'll never vote agin. Them's the very words I said. . . . And to see the

cool way of that nigger — why, he wouldn't a give me the road if I hadn't shoved him out o' the way.[12]

Later on in the novel, when the runaway slave Jim gives up his freedom to nurse a wounded Tom Sawyer, a white doctor testifies to the stunning altruism of his actions. The Phelpses and their neighbors, all fine, upstanding, well-meaning, churchgoing folk,

> agreed that Jim had acted very well, and was deserving to have some notice took of it, and reward. So every one of them promised, right out and hearty, that they wouldn't curse him no more.
>
> Then they come out and locked him up. I hoped they was going to say he could have one or two of the chains took off, because they was rotten heavy, or could have meat and greens with his bread and water, but they didn't think of it.[13]

Why did the behavior of these people tell me more about why Watts burned than anything I had read in the daily paper? And why did a drunk Pap Finn railing against a black college professor from Ohio whose vote was as good as his own tell me more about white anxiety over black political power than anything I had seen on the evening news?

Mark Twain knew that there was nothing, absolutely *nothing*, a black man could do — including selflessly sacrificing his freedom, the only thing of value he had — that would make white society see beyond the color of his skin. And Mark Twain knew that depicting racists with chilling accuracy would expose the viciousness of their world view like nothing else could. It was an insight echoed some eighty years after Mark Twain penned Pap Finn's rantings about the black professor, when Malcolm X famously asked, "Do you know what white racists call black Ph.D.'s?" and answered, "'*Nigger!*'"[14]

Mark Twain taught me things I needed to know. He taught me to understand the raw racism that lay behind what I saw on the evening news. He taught me that the most well-meaning people can be hurtful and myopic. He taught me to recognize the supreme irony of a country founded in freedom that continued to deny freedom to so many of its citizens. Every time I hear of another effort to kick Huck Finn out of school somewhere, I recall everything that Mark Twain taught *this* high school junior, and I find myself jumping into the fray.[15] I remember the black high school student who called CNN during the phone-in portion of a 1985 debate between Dr. John Wallace, a black educator spearheading efforts to ban the book, and myself. She accused Dr. Wallace of insulting her and all black high school students by suggesting they weren't smart enough to understand Mark Twain's irony. And I recall the black cameraman on the *CBS Morning News* who came up to me after he finished shooting another debate between Dr. Wallace and myself. He said he had never read the book by Mark Twain that we had been arguing about — but now he really wanted to. One thing that puzzled him, though, was why a white woman was defending it and a black man was attacking it, because as far as he could see from what we'd been saying, the book made whites look pretty bad.

As I came to understand *Huckleberry Finn* and *Pudd'nhead Wilson* as commentaries on the era now known as the nadir of American race relations, those books pointed me toward the world recorded in nineteenth-century black newspapers and periodicals and in fiction by Mark Twain's black contemporaries. My investigation of the role black voices and traditions played in shaping Mark Twain's art helped make me aware of their role in shaping all of American culture.[16] My research underlined for me the importance of changing the stories we tell about who we are to reflect the realities of what we've been.[17]

Ever since our encounter in high school English, Mark Twain has shown me the potential of American literature and American history to illuminate each other. Rarely have I found a contradiction or complexity we grapple with as a nation that Mark Twain had not puzzled over as well. He insisted on taking America seriously. And he insisted on *not* taking America seriously: "I think that there is but a single specialty with us, only one thing that can be called by the wide name 'American,'" he once wrote. "That is the national devotion to ice-water."[18]

Mark Twain threw back at us our dreams and our denial of those dreams, our greed, our goodness, our ambition, and our laziness, all rattling around together in that vast echo chamber of our talk — that sharp, spunky American talk that Mark Twain figured out how to write down without robbing it of its energy and immediacy. Talk shaped by voices that the official arbiters of "culture" deemed of no importance — voices of children, voices of slaves, voices of servants, voices of ordinary people. Mark Twain listened. And he made us listen. To the stories he told us, and to the truths they conveyed. He still has a lot to say that we need to hear.

Mark Twain lives — in our libraries, classrooms, homes, theaters, movie houses, streets, and most of all in our speech. His optimism energizes us, his despair sobers us, and his willingness to keep wrestling with the hilarious and horrendous complexities of it all keeps us coming back for more. As the twenty-first century approaches, may he continue to goad us, chasten us, delight us, berate us, and cause us to erupt in unrestrained laughter in unexpected places.

NOTES

1. Ernest Hemingway, *Green Hills of Africa* (New York: Charles Scribner's Sons, 1935), 22. George Bernard Shaw to Samuel L. Clemens, July 3, 1907, quoted in Albert Bigelow Paine, *Mark Twain: A Biography* (New York: Harper and Brothers, 1912), 3:1398.

2. Allen Carey-Webb, "Racism and *Huckleberry Finn*: Censorship, Dialogue and Change," *English Journal* 82, no. 7 (November 1993):22.

3. See Louis J. Budd, "Impersonators," in J. R. LeMaster and James D. Wilson, eds., *The Mark Twain Encyclopedia* (New York: Garland Publishing Company, 1993), 389-91.

4. See Shelley Fisher Fishkin, "Ripples and Reverberations," part 3 of *Lighting Out for the Territory: Reflections on Mark Twain and American Culture* (New York: Oxford University Press, 1996).

5. There are two exceptions. Twain published chapters from his autobiography in the *North American Review* in 1906 and 1907, but this material was not published in book form in Twain's lifetime; our volume reproduces the material as it appeared in the *North American Review*. The other exception is our final volume, *Mark Twain's Speeches*, which appeared two months after Twain's death in 1910.

An unauthorized handful of copies of *1601* was privately printed by an Alexander Gunn of Cleveland at the instigation of Twain's friend John Hay in 1880. The first American edition authorized by Mark Twain, however, was printed at the United States Military Academy at West Point in 1882; that is the edition reproduced here.

It should further be noted that four volumes — *The Stolen White Elephant and Other Detective Stories, Following the Equator and Anti-imperialist Essays, The Diaries of Adam and Eve,* and *1601, and Is Shakespeare Dead?* — bind together material originally published separately. In each case the first American edition of the material is the version that has been reproduced, always in its entirety. Because Twain constantly recycled and repackaged previously published works in his collections of short pieces, a certain amount of duplication is unavoidable. We have selected volumes with an eye toward keeping this duplication to a minimum.

Even the twenty-nine-volume Oxford Mark Twain has had to leave much out. No edition of Twain can ever claim to be "complete," for the man was too prolix, and the file drawers of both ephemera and as yet unpublished texts are deep.

6. With the possible exception of *Mark Twain's Speeches*. Some scholars suspect Twain knew about this book and may have helped shape it, although no hard evidence to that effect has yet surfaced. Twain's involvement in the production process varied greatly from book to book. For a fuller sense of authorial intention, scholars will continue to rely on the superb definitive editions of Twain's works produced by the Mark Twain Project at the University of California at Berkeley as they become available. Dense with annotation documenting textual emendation and related issues, these editions add immeasurably to our understanding of Mark Twain and the genesis of his works.

7. Except for a few titles that were not in its collection. The American Antiquarian Society in Worcester, Massachusetts, provided the first edition of *King Leopold's Soliloquy*; the Elmer Holmes Bobst Library of New York University furnished the 1906–7 volumes of the *North American Review* in which *Chapters from My Autobiography* first appeared; the Harry Ransom Humanities Research Center at the University of Texas at Austin made their copy of the West Point edition of *1601* available; and the Mark Twain Project provided the first edition of *Extract from Captain Stormfield's Visit to Heaven*.

8. The specific copy photographed for Oxford's facsimile edition is indicated in a note on the text at the end of each volume.

9. All quotations from contemporary writers in this essay are taken from their introductions to the volumes of The Oxford Mark Twain, and the quotations from Mark Twain's works are taken from the texts reproduced in The Oxford Mark Twain.

10. *The Diaries of Adam and Eve*, The Oxford Mark Twain [hereafter OMT] (New York: Oxford University Press, 1996), p. 33.

11. *Tom Sawyer Abroad*, OMT, p. 74.

12. *Adventures of Huckleberry Finn*, OMT, p. 49–50.

13. Ibid., p. 358.

14. Malcolm X, *The Autobiography of Malcolm X*, with the assistance of Alex Haley (New York: Grove Press, 1965), p. 284.

15. I do not mean to minimize the challenge of teaching this difficult novel, a challenge for which all teachers may not feel themselves prepared. Elsewhere I have developed some concrete strategies for approaching the book in the classroom, including teaching it in the context of the history of American race relations and alongside books by black writers. See Shelley Fisher Fishkin, "Teaching *Huckleberry Finn,*" in James S. Leonard, ed., *Making Mark Twain Work in the Classroom* (Durham: Duke University Press, forthcoming). See also Shelley Fisher Fishkin, *Was Huck Black? Mark Twain and African-American Voices* (New York: Oxford University Press, 1993), pp. 106–8, and a curriculum kit in preparation at the Mark Twain House in Hartford, containing teaching suggestions from myself, David Bradley, Jocelyn Chadwick-Joshua, James Miller, and David E. E. Sloane.

16. See Fishkin, *Was Huck Black?* See also Fishkin, "Interrogating 'Whiteness,' Complicating 'Blackness': Remapping American Culture," in Henry Wonham, ed., *Criticism and the Color Line: Desegregating American Literary Studies* (New Brunswick: Rutgers UP, 1996, pp. 251–90 and in shortened form in *American Quarterly* 47, no. 3 (September 1995):428–66.

17. I explore the roots of my interest in Mark Twain and race at greater length in an essay entitled "Changing the Story," in Jeffrey Rubin-Dorsky and Shelley Fisher Fishkin, eds., *People of the Book: Thirty Scholars Reflect on Their Jewish Identity* (Madison: U of Wisconsin Press, 1996), pp. 47–63.

18. "What Paul Bourget Thinks of Us," *How to Tell a Story and Other Essays*, OMT, p. 197.

INTRODUCTION
Russell Banks

For me, for years the most intriguing character in *A Tramp Abroad* was not Samuel Clemens' garrulous, curmudgeonly traveler, Mark Twain. Not that I wasn't charmed, like most readers, by the world-famous Yankee author playing cat and mouse with his considerable fame and fortune and the by-then venerable tradition of the account of the European Grand Tour. Who wouldn't be? A tongue-in-cheek travelogue written for those of his countrymen who had stayed home and had no intention of ever taking the tour themselves and who wished perhaps to feel virtuous about that decision, its ideal reader was probably an American who at bottom wanted someone knowledgeable to tell him that a journey through Germany, Switzerland, and Italy wasn't really worth all the considerable expense and trouble. It's a nonfiction genre that Clemens had simultaneously parodied and extended with his earlier, immensely popular *Innocents Abroad*, whose narrator was essentially a younger, less affluent, unknown, but no less crankily opinionated version of the narrator of this, its companion volume; and indeed, most readers remember more of Twain and his hard-nosed opinions of his fellow Americans from both accounts than they do of the foreign lands and peoples that he visited. Which was, no doubt, as he intended.

But generally, I myself preferred the man and his opinions as I read them in his Mississippi writings and in his great works of fiction. In fact, in *A Tramp Abroad*, it was Mark Twain's traveling companion that I most remembered — the mysterious Mr. Harris. This is not to say that Mark Twain as traveler and narrator was not great good company. Quite the opposite. Given the choice, unless I preferred traveling in silence, I would far rather make my way through Germany and across the Alps into Italy, as he does in *A Tramp Abroad*, with Mr. Twain at my side than anyone else on this planet. Here, as everywhere in his work, Clemens' first person narrator is one of the most fluent, humorous, allusive, and utterly seductive talkers imaginable, so that the worst thing he can do to you as a reader or listener is go silent on you.

One always, on closing a book narrated by Mark Twain, misses most his *voice*. With the possible exception of Huckleberry Finn's, it's the sly, sardonic, confiding voice of Mark Twain, Clemens' other great talker, that is the most characteristically American voice in our entire literature. We recognize it at once, joyfully, as if waking to the voice of a favorite member of our immediate family — dear, rumpled Uncle Mark, smelling of cigar smoke and port, speaking in funny accents and making up parodies jokes and tall tales on the spot, but always switching to the somber side at just the right moment to catch our laughter out and restore to the conversation, or more properly, to the monologue, an appropriate dignity and seriousness, so that we might by the end of it feel respected by this brilliant, witty man, and understood. Twain makes us feel more intelligent than we are, more honest, and less patient with hypocrisy, cant, and greed. Who could wish for more from a narrator? Or from a relative? Or friend?

But even so, in *A Tramp Abroad*, which I first read nearly thirty years ago and whose actual itinerary in the intervening years I mostly forgot, it was not the narrator but his companion, his sidekick, who somehow engaged me in a continuing way and whom I remembered most clearly. It was the character of Mr. Harris, the anxious, often hapless, American gentleman who acts in turn, and sometimes simultaneously, as the narrator's foil, fool, goad, guide, and all-purpose straight man, that fascinated me. Mr. Twain was everywhere in the account precisely the man he appeared to be, but that Mr. Harris was a bit of a mystery, a character who was deliberately foregrounded and present but was somehow not quite accounted for. Who was that utterly decent, if slightly humorless, fellow without profession or family who finally showed up at the narrator's side in chapter 10 but seemed nonetheless to have been there, practically unmentioned, from the start of Twain's tramp weeks earlier? Strangely, for the longest time, Mr. Harris is but a shadow of Mr. Twain — his unacknowledged second in the dueling society chapters, his overlooked and evidently silent dining companion in the Heidelberg chapters, and his ignored, no doubt politely deferential roommate in the Schloss Hotel. Then, once he's properly acknowledged and more or less formally introduced to us, as if Mr. Twain had suddenly remembered that we may not have noticed yet his shy traveling companion, he's everywhere. He plays Butch Cassidy to Twain's Sundance, Sancho to his Quixote, Tonto to his Lone Ranger, Hardy to his Laurel. And yes, Tom to his Huck.

A Tramp Abroad, however, is not fictional film, romance, poem, or myth; it's a presumably nonfictional account of a fraternal pair of Yankee *bourgeois gentilhommes* on a lengthy peripatetic journey abroad, composed after the fact by the more entertaining of the pair. For all its humorous asides, exaggerations, tall tales, and fantastical, obviously invented digressions, the story itself is *real*. Is fact. It's a (more or less) truthful description of a journey undertaken by the author and his friend (actually, there was a considerable entourage along — Mrs. Clemens, their daughters, Susy and Clara, a companion for Mrs. Clemens, and two servants — but not a one of them is even mentioned in the book). Yet in spite of these and other omissions of fact and the more than a few "stretchers" that fill out the narrative, there is an implicit, underlying contract with the reader, an assurance that this journey actually took place and that it went approximately as described. We are expected to believe that it was not invented out of whole cloth in Sam Clemens' study back in Hartford, Connecticut. And thus, if the narrator, Mr. Mark Twain, is for all intents and purposes a real and even well-known citizen of these United States, then perhaps Mr. Harris, his companion, is an equally real, if less well-known, citizen of these United States.

And indeed, just as the bourgeois Connecticut Yankee Mark Twain is a literary stand-in for the Missouri native Samuel Clemens, who grew up poor and marginalized on the banks of the Mississippi River, his roommate and erstwhile hiking, rafting, and carriage companion in Germany, Switzerland, and

Italy in the summer and fall of 1878, the hapless Mr. Harris, is a convenient, teasing disguise for the Reverend Joseph Twichell, pastor of the Asylum Hill Congregational Church of Hartford.

This is common knowledge among Twain scholars, of course. It was not at all known to me, however, until about eight years ago, when my wife-to-be, surnamed Twichell, let it slip in conversation, not without a certain justifiable pride, that her great-grandfather was admired in the family for having been, among other things, Samuel Clemens' best friend and the minister who married him to his beloved Livy and presided over the burials of all the Clemenses, even that of the Great Man himself. Furthermore, Great-grandfather Twichell had traveled to Europe with him, at Clemens' expense, and had been immortalized as Mr. Harris in *A Tramp Abroad*. There was more, of course — trips to Bermuda, to the Adirondacks, to Boston and New York, with letters and even photographs to prove it.

Naturally, as a fiction writer myself and a lifelong devotee of Twain's work, I was delighted by this unexpected proximity to the man and his inner circle of Hartford friends, even if only by dint of marriage and coming four genera-tions too late. I remembered reading somewhere that Clemens took immense pleasure in staying up over good cigars and old brandy with his Hartford cronies, telling stories, singing songs, and reciting his more scabrous and scatological works, even including *1601* and the heretical *Extracts from Adam's Diary*. Reverend Twichell was among those cronies, and what, I won-dered, did the good reverend make of the reckless humor, the anger, and the darkness of those works? He must have been quite a tolerant and to my mind a wise reverend. Certainly, he was less decorous, less conformist, less obtuse than poor Mr. Harris.

In *A Tramp Abroad*, Mr. Harris (to be honest, I can only think of him now as Reverend Twichell, my great-grandfather-in-law) is pictured quite literally in numerous illustrations, some drawn by Twain himself in a deliberately (and comically) amateurish hand, as a tall, scrawny character, a figure sug-gesting the schoolmaster Ichabod Crane, which happens nicely to match Twain's verbal portrait — timid, awkward, somewhat insecure, and in blunt contrast to our irreverent illustrator and narrator, sensibly conformist. My wife possesses a photograph of Clemens and Reverend Twichell, however, which gives the lie to Twain's portraiture. The two stand on the top deck of a steamship, the wind blowing their large white moustaches back like smoke from a chimney, and the inscription written below, evidently by someone in the Twichell family, says, "Bermuda Bound!" They look gleeful and mischievous, a couple of happy runaways, and the tall, athletically built Twichell looks quite as capable of outrageous behavior as his somewhat shorter friend.

Also, from a written account less interested in literary effect than Twain's version in *A Tramp Abroad* and more concerned perhaps with literal truth, one gets a revealing glimpse of the actual man behind Harris. In a February 1876 issue of the *Essex County Republican* (New York) there is a delightful description by the famous Adirondack guide Orson "Mountain" Phelps of a climb up Mount Colvin with Charles Dudley Warner, Dr. Horace Bushnell, and the Reverend Joseph Twichell: "Mr. Twichell strides off with more than an average pair of legs supporting the frame of a man in every respect," declares the mountaineer. "He is a thorough go-ahead man, vehement and impressive, sometimes amounting to rashness. He has a clear, powerful voice, which makes him an interesting public speaker."

Hardly the Mr. Harris we have come to know in *A Tramp Abroad*. But he is the sort of man we would expect Sam Clemens to feel comfortable with — "a thorough go-ahead man, vehement and impressive, sometimes amounting to rashness," a man as likely as Clemens was to long for escape from the confines of Hartford respectability and High Victorian family life, which surely must have felt stifling at times to both men. It's an old male dodge, and not just in America (its earliest literary representation in the western world is probably the Homeric one) — the hunter-gatherer's dream of leaving the women, children, and servants behind and lighting out for the territory with his best male friend. And though it's usually portrayed as a young man's quest for knowledge of the wider world, with hopes of gaining in the process a bit of actual wisdom and an ultimate truth or two, it's no less attractive a fantasy for a middle-aged man, especially one who, like Clemens and possibly like

Reverend Twichell as well, had recently been running a little low on the inspiration and force that had shaped his life and made him, in his own eyes and in the eyes of his community, successful.

It's a painful conflict treated too seldom these days with the sympathy it deserves. Each man's success had provided him with the very bourgeois respectability that, while making him usefully accountable to family, friends, and the community at large, had also made him feel trapped, perhaps a little angry and resentful, and for all his hard-won social power, whether as writer or reverend, surprisingly impotent. So it should come as no surprise that Clemens' main literary obsession during these years was a fictional story narrated in vernacular American English by a marginalized, homeless Southern boy with an escaped slave for his companion, the two of them drifting down the Mississippi River on a raft. And it should come as no surprise that he was finding himself unable to finish it.

Clemens, like many writers, characteristically put his narrative material through three intimately linked stages before finally abandoning the material and moving on to the next book. He was first an anecdotalist, then a journalist/memoirist, and finally an artist. One thinks of how Melville processed and transformed his experiences in the South Seas; or Thoreau and Emerson, moving from private conversation and journal to sermon, pamphlet, and Athenaeum stump speech on to personal essay or poem; or Stephen Crane's three-stage transformation of his war experiences; or, in the twentieth century, Ernest Hemingway on big game hunting, fishing, bullfighting, and also war; and even some contemporary writers, like Norman Mailer. I don't think of it as a peculiarly American sequence or as strictly a habit of male writers, but it may be both, at least for realists for whom a public life, as warrior, sailor, preacher, or journalist, is a given.

It's a process I observed firsthand early. As a very young writer, I came to know personally another American realist, Nelson Algren, then in his early fifties. I was at that time eager to learn how a real writer worked, and in particular to see how a man who seemed no more extraordinary than I had somehow managed to transform the dross of his everyday life into the pure gold of narrative art. And it was with Algren that for the first time I observed this triple-jump sequence, leading from personal anecdote to popular journalistic account to literary fiction. Algren, perhaps like Mark Twain a hundred years earlier, liked to regale his listeners into the night (over cigarettes and whiskey, instead of cigars and brandy) with stories of his adventures in underground Chicago, Hanoi, Paris, and New York. I was present at several of these sessions in the early 1960s, and a few months later would open a magazine or a new Algren book of nonfiction (*Hemingway All the Way*, for instance, Algren's own version of *A Tramp Abroad*), and there would be the same story, told more efficiently this time and more powerfully and with a sharper point to the humor than I'd heard in conversation. Then, after a year or two had passed, I would read yet a third, the fictional, version of the story, in his collection *The Neon Wilderness*, for example, and by now all that remained of the original oral version was the psychological truth of it and the mythic infrastructure, neither of which I had noticed before.

It's a useful technique, or procedure, to take one's fact-based fictional material out for a trial run, as it were, so long as in the process of telling it to one's cronies or writing it up in a nonfictional form one doesn't drain it of its dramatic meaning and structure or weaken its ties to one's deepest emotional life, leaving it useless for art, void of all passion and freshness of perception or thought, flat, rehearsed, prepackaged. It's a risky business for an author. One has to husband one's small store of stories carefully, nurturing them often for years in the darkness of silence and solitude, before they can be understood and felt deeply enough to flower as art. But Sam Clemens, for whom silence and solitude seem to have been anathema, was especially skilled at the procedure. It is an elaborate mode of public revision, actually — inventing large segments of one's life, one's travel in particular, which is one of the more easily controlled, or willed, aspects of one's life, to provide material for late-night or dinner-table storytelling, even as one is compiling and organizing the material for a nonfiction book already under contract, which book must later provide the basis for a work of literary fiction.

And in the case of *A Tramp Abroad*, published in 1880, that latter work would turn out to be Twain's masterpiece, *Adventures of Huckleberry Finn*, published in 1885, after having been started and then several times abandoned in frustration and artistic unsureness, most recently in 1879–80, not long after Clemens returned from Germany. *A Tramp Abroad*, then, might well be read as an important revision of Twain's incomplete first draft of *Huckleberry Finn*, a second draft, if you will, which in turn made possible the third and final draft, from which, as Hemingway noted, all American literature lies in direct descent. Read this way, any number of episodes in *A Tramp Abroad* can be seen not simply as prefiguring similar episodes in *Huckleberry Finn* but as trial runs, drafts, and sketches that, once told, once set down on the page, helped Twain reimagine his long-shelved story. The idyllic raft trip on the Neckar (with Harris and crew aboard) and its unexpected, violent crash are obvious examples, but the careful reader can spot many other parallels, similarities, and suggestive formal and linguistic templates that connect the two books.

Finally, however, for me, the most intriguing parallel remains the sweetly symmetrical, interlocking pair of triangles through which Clemens/Twain/Huck is fraternally tied to Twichell/Harris/Tom. Both Clemens and Twichell, like Twain and Harris, and like Huck and Tom, were American males clearly blessed with the gift of friendship, of giving it and of receiving and holding on to it. And thus, perhaps because of my own somewhat recently acquired familial ties to Twichell, *A Tramp Abroad*, of all Clemens' books, has turned out to be the most personally revealing of the literary genius himself, that secretive and very private man who lived his entire life ducking behind a complex series of overlapping and often conflicting public personae. Through stacked layers of irony and elaborate literary subterfuge, self-mockery, broad humor, grotesque exaggeration, and ventriloquism, Samuel Clemens managed always in his greatest works to reveal indirectly his impassioned, often enraged heart. His solitary heart. But for me, moreso than anywhere else, in *A Tramp Abroad* he unveils as well his abiding commitment to that bottom-line, most democratic of virtues, fraternity, which, surely, all through his turbulent middle and late years, soothed and calmed that heart.

A TRAMP ABROAD

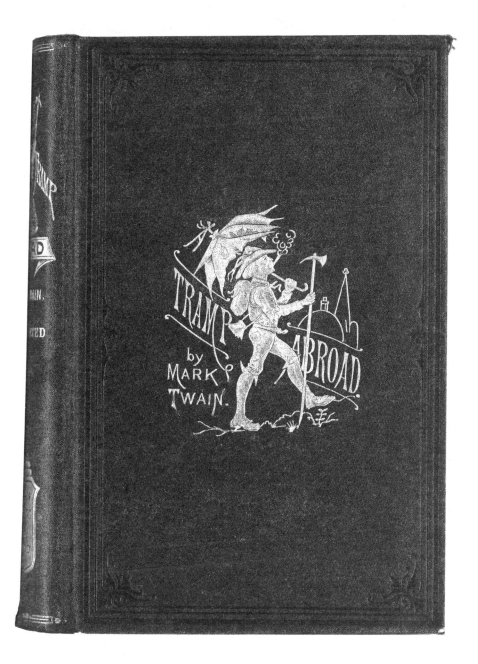

TRAMP ABROAD

by MARK TWAIN.

TITIAN'S MOSES.

A TRAMP ABROAD;

ILLUSTRATED BY W. FR. BROWN, TRUE WILLIAMS, B. DAY AND OTHER
ARTISTS—WITH ALSO THREE OR FOUR PICTURES MADE BY
THE AUTHOR OF THIS BOOK, WITHOUT OUTSIDE HELP;
IN ALL

THREE HUNDRED AND TWENTY-EIGHT ILLUSTRATIONS.

BY
MARK TWAIN,
(SAMUEL L. CLEMENS.)

(SOLD BY SUBSCRIPTION ONLY.)

HARTFORD, CONN.:
AMERICAN PUBLISHING COMPANY.
CHATTO & WINDUS, LONDON.
1880.

ILLUSTRATIONS.

ILLUSTRATIONS. vii

CONTENTS.

CHAPTER VII.

CHAPTER VIII.

CHAPTER IX.

CHAPTER X.

CHAPTER XI.

CHAPTER XII.

CHAPTER XXXIII.

CHAPTER XXXIV.

CHAPTER XXXV.

CHAPTER XXXVI.

CHAPTER XXXVII.

CHAPTER XXXVIII.

CHAPTER XXXIX.

CHAPTER XL.

CHAPTER XLI.

CHAPTER XLII.

CHAPTER XLIII.

CHAPTER XLIV.

THE AUTHOR'S MEMORIES.

CHAPTER I.

ONE day it occurred to me that it had been many years since the world had been afforded the spectacle of a man adventurous enough to undertake a journey through Europe on foot. After much thought, I decided that I was a person fitted to furnish to mankind this spectacle. So I determined to do it. This was in March, 1878.

I looked about me for the right sort of person to accompany me in the capacity of agent, and finally hired a Mr. Harris for this service.

It was also my purpose to study art while in Europe. Mr. Harris was in sympathy with me in this. He was as much of an enthusiast in art as I was, and not less anxious to learn to paint. I desired to learn the German language; so did Harris.

Toward the middle of April we sailed in the *Holsatia*, Capt. Brandt, and had a very pleasant trip indeed.

After a brief rest at Hamburg, we made preparations for a long pedestrian trip southward in the soft spring weather, but at the last moment we changed the program, for private reasons, and took the express train.

We made a short halt at Frankfort-on-the-Main, and found it an interesting city. I would have liked to visit the birthplace of Guttenberg, but it could not be done, as no memorandum of the site of the house has been kept. So we spent

17

an hour in the Goethe mansion instead. The city permits this house to belong to private parties, instead of gracing and dignifying herself with the honor of possessing and protecting it.

Frankfort is one of the sixteen cities which have the distinction of being the place where the following incident occurred. Charlemagne, while chasing the Saxons, (as *he* said,) or being chased by them, (as *they* said,) arrived at the bank of the river at dawn, in a fog. The enemy were either before him or behind him ; but in any case he wanted to get across, very badly. He would have given anything for a guide, but none was to be had. Presently he saw a deer, followed by her young, approach the water. He watched her, judging that she would seek a ford, and he was right. She waded over, and the army followed. So a great Frankish victory or defeat was gained or avoided ; and in order to commemorate the episode, Charlemagne commanded a city to be built there, which he named Frankfort,—the ford of the Franks. None of the other cities where this event happened were named from it. This is good evidence that Frankfort was the first place it occurred at.

Frankfort has another distinction,—it is the birthplace of the German alphabet : or at least of the German word for alphabet,—*Buchstaben.* They say that the first movable types were made on birch sticks,—*Buchstabe,*—hence the name.

I was taught a lesson in political economy in Frankfort. I had brought from home a box containing a thousand very cheap cigars. By way of experiment, I stepped into a little shop in a queer old back street, took four gaily decorated boxes of wax matches and three cigars, and laid down a silver piece worth 48 cents. The man gave me 43 cents change.

In Frankfort everybody wears clean clothes, and I think we noticed that this strange thing was the case in Hamburg too, and in the villages along the road. Even in the narrowest and poorest and most ancient quarters of Frankfort neat and clean clothes were the rule. The little children of both sexes were nearly always nice enough to take into a body's lap. And as for the uniforms of the soldiers, they were newness and brightness carried to perfection. One could never detect a smirch or a grain of dust upon them. The street car conductors and drivers wore pretty uniforms which seemed to be just out of the bandbox, and their manners were as fine as their clothes.

In one of the shops I had the luck to stumble upon a book which has charmed me nearly to death. It is entitled " The Legends of the Rhine from Basle to Rotterdam, by F. J. Kiefer ; Translated by L. W. Garnham, B. A."

All tourists *mention* the Rhine legends,—in that sort of way which quietly pretends that the mentioner has been familiar with them all his life, and that the reader cannot possibly be ignorant of them,—but no tourist ever *tells* them. So this little book fed me in a very hungry place ; and I, in my turn, intend to feed my reader, with one or two little lunches from the same larder. I shall not mar Garnham's translation by meddling with its English ; for the most toothsome thing about it is its quaint fashion of building English sentences on the German plan,—and punctuating them according to no plan at all.

In the chapter devoted to " Legends of Frankfort," I find the following :

" THE KNAVE OF BERGEN."

" In Frankfort at the Romer was a great mask-ball, at the coronation festival, and in the illuminated saloon, the clanging music invited to dance, and splendidly appeared the rich toilets and charms of the ladies, and the festively costumed Princes and Knights. All seemed pleasure, joy, and roguish gayety, only one of the numerous guests had a gloomy exterior ; but exactly the black armor in which he walked about excited general attention, and his tall figure, as well as the noble propriety of his movements, attracted especially the regards of the ladies. Who the Knight was? Nobody could guess, for his Vizier was well closed, and nothing made him recognizable. Proud and yet modest he advanced to the Empress ; bowed on one knee before her seat, and begged

for the favor of a waltz with the Queen of the festival.   And
she allowed his request.   With light and graceful steps he
danced through the long saloon, with the sovereign who
thought never to have found a more dexterous and excellent
dancer.   But also by the grace of his manner, and fine con-

versation he knew to win the
Queen, and she graciously accord-
ed him a second dance for which
he begged, a third, and a fourth,
as well as others were not refused
him.   How all regarded the happy
dancer, how many envied him the
high favor; how increased curiosity, who the masked knight could be.

Also the Emperor became more
and more excited with curiosity, and with great suspense one
awaited the hour, when according

THE BLACK KNIGHT.

to mask-law, each masked guest must make himself known.
This moment came, but although all others had unmasked;
the secret knight still refused to allow his features to be seen,
till at last the Queen driven by curiosity, and vexed at the
obstinate refusal; commanded him to open his Vizier.   He

OPENING HIS VIZIER.

opened it, and none of the high ladies and knights knew
him.   But from the crowded spectators, 2 officials advanced,

who recognized the black dancer, and horror and terror spread in the saloon, as they said who the supposed knight was. It was the executioner of Bergen. But glowing with rage, the King commanded to seize the criminal and lead him to death, who had ventured to dance, with the queen ; so disgraced the Empress, and insulted the crown. The culpable threw himself at the feet of the Emperor, and said,—

" ' Indeed I have heavily sinned against all noble guests assembled here, but most heavily against you my sovereign and my queen. The Queen is insulted by my haughtiness equal to treason, but no punishment even blood, will not be able to wash out the disgrace,

THE ENRAGED EMPEROR.

which you have suffered by me. Therefore oh King! allow me to propose a remedy, to efface the shame, and to render it as if not done. Draw your sword and knight me, then I will throw down my gauntlet, to every one who dares to speak disrespectfully of my king.

" The Emperor was surprised at this bold proposal, however it appeared the wisest to him ; " You are a knave he replied after a moment's consideration, however your advice is good, and displays prudence, as your offense shows adventurous courage. Well then, and gave him the knight-stroke, so I raise you to nobility, who begged for grace for your offence now kneels before me, rise as knight ; knavish you have acted, and Knave of Bergen shall you be called henceforth, and gladly the Black knight rose ; three cheers were given in honor of the Emperor, and loud cries of joy testified the approbation with which the Queen danced still once with the Knave of Bergen.

CHAPTER II.

WE stopped at a hotel by the railway station. Next morning, as we sat in my room waiting for breakfast to come up, we got a good deal interested in something which was going on over the way, in front of another hotel. First, the personage who is called the *portier*, (who is not the *porter*, but is a sort of first-mate of a hotel,) * appeared at the door in a spick and span new blue cloth uniform, decorated with shining brass buttons, and with bands of gold lace around his cap and wristbands; and he wore white gloves, too. He shed an official glance upon the situation, and then began to give orders. Two women servants came out with pails and brooms and brushes, and gave the sidewalk a thorough scrubbing; meanwhile two others scrubbed the four marble steps which led up to the door; beyond these we could see some men-servants taking up the carpet of the grand staircase. This carpet was carried away and the last grain of dust beaten and banged and swept out of it; then brought back and put down again. The brass stair rods received an exhaustive polishing and were returned to their places. Now a troop of servants brought pots and tubs of blooming plants and formed them into a beautiful jungle about the door and the base of the staircase. Other servants

---

*·See Appendix A.   22

adorned all the balconies of the various stories with flowers and banners; others ascended to the roof and hoisted
a great flag on a staff there. Now came some more chamber-
maids and retouched the sidewalk, and afterwards wiped the
marble steps with damp cloths and finished by dusting them

THT PORTIER.

off with feather brushes. Now
a broad black c a r p e t was
brought out and laid down the
marble steps and out across the
sidewalk t o t h e curbstone.
The *portier* cast his eye along
it, and found it was not absolutely straight; he commanded
it to be straightened; the servants made the effort,—made
several efforts, in fact,— but the
portier was not satisfied. He
finally had it taken up, and
then he put it down himself
and got it right.

At this stage of the proceedings, a narrow bright red carpet
was unrolled and stretched from
the top of the marble steps to
the curbstone, along the center
of the black carpet. This red
p a t h cost the *portier* more
trouble than even the black one had done. But he patiently
fixed and re-fixed it until it was exactly right and lay precisely
in the middle of the black carpet. In New York these performances would have gathered a mighty crowd of curious
and intensely interested spectators; but here it only captured
an audience of half-a-dozen little boys, who stood in a row
across the pavement, some with their school knapsacks on
their backs and their hands in their pockets, others with arms
full of bundles, and all absorbed in the show. Occasionally

one of them skipped irreverently over the carpet and
took up a position on the other side. This always visibly
annoyed the *portier*.

ONE OF THOSE BOYS.

Now came a waiting
interval. The landlord,
in plain clothes, a n d
bareheaded, placed him-
self on the bottom mar-
ble step, abreast the
portier, who stood on
the other end of the
same steps; six or eight
waiters, gloved, bare-
headed, a n d wearing
their whitest linen, their whitest cravats, and their finest swallow-tails, grouped themselves about these chiefs, but leaving
the carpet-way clear. Nobody moved or spoke any more
but only waited.

In a short time the shrill piping of a coming train was
heard, and immediately groups of people began to gather in
the street. Two or three open carriages arrived, and deposited some maids of honor and some male officials at the
hotel. Presently another open carriage brought the Grand
Duke of Baden, a stately man in uniform, who wore the
handsome brass-mounted, steel-spiked helmet of the army on
his head. Last came the Empress of Germany and the Grand
Duchess of Baden in a close carriage; these passed through
the low-bowing groups of servants and disappeared in the
hotel, exhibiting to us only the backs of their heads, and then
the show was over.

It appears to be as difficult to land a monarch as it is to
launch a ship.

But as to Heidelberg. The weather was growing pretty
warm,—very warm, in fact. So we left the valley and took
quarters at the Schloss Hotel, on the hill, above the Castle.

Heidelberg lies at the mouth of a narrow gorge—a gorge
the shape of a shepherd's crook; if one looks up it he

SCHLOSS HOTEL, HEIDELBERG.

perceives that it is about straight, for a mile and a half, then makes a sharp curve to the right and disappears. This gorge, —along whose bottom pours the swift Neckar,—is confined between (or cloven through) a couple of long, steep ridges, a thousand feet high and densely wooded clear to their summits, with the exception of one section which has been shaved and put under cultivation. These ridges are chopped off at the mouth of the gorge and form two bold and conspicuous headlands, with Heidelberg nestling between them; from their bases spreads away the vast dim expanse of the Rhine valley, and into this expanse the Neckar goes wandering in shining curves and is presently lost to view.

Now if one turns and looks up the gorge once more, he will see the Schloss hotel on the right, perched on a precipice overlooking the Neckar,—a precipice which is so sumptuously cushioned and draped with foliage that no glimpse of the rock appears. The building seems very airily situated. It has the appearance of being on a shelf half way up the wooded mountain side; and as it is remote and isolated, and very white, it makes a strong mark against the lofty leafy rampart at its back.

This hotel had a feature which was a decided novelty; and one which might be adopted with advantage by any house which is perched in a commanding situation. This feature may be described as a series of glass-enclosed parlors *clinging to the outside of the house*, one against each and every bedchamber and drawing-room. They are like long, narrow, high-ceiled bird-cages hung against the building. My room was a corner room, and had two of these things, a north one and a west one.

From the north cage one looks up the Neckar gorge; from the west one he looks down it. This last affords the most extensive view, and it is one of the loveliest that can be imagined, too. Out of a billowy upheaval of vivid green foliage, a rifle-shot removed, rises the huge ruin of Heidelberg Castle, * with empty window arches, ivy-mailed battlements, moldering towers—the Lear of inanimate nature,—

* See Appendix B.

deserted, discrowned, beaten by the storms, but royal still, and beautiful. It is a fine sight to see the evening sunlight

IN MY CAGE.

suddenly strike the leafy declivity at the Castle's base and dash up it and drench it as with a luminous spray, while the adjacent groves are in deep shadow.

Behind the Castle swells a great dome-shaped hill, forest-clad, and beyond that a nobler and loftier one. The Castle looks down upon the compact brown-roofed town; and from the town two picturesque old bridges span the river. Now the view broadens; through the gateway of the sentinel headlands you gaze out over the wide Rhine plain, which stretches away, softly and richly tinted, grows gradually and dreamily indistinct, and finally melts imperceptibly into the remote horizon.

I have never enjoyed a view which had such a serene and satisfying charm about it as this one gives.

The first night we were there, we went to bed and to sleep early; but I awoke at the end of two or three hours, and lay a comfortable while listening to the soothing patter of the rain against the balcony windows. I took it to be

HEIDELBERG CASTLE.

rain, but it turned out to be only the murmur of the restless Neckar, tumbling over her dikes and dams far below, in
the gorge. I got up and went into the west balcony and
saw a wonderful sight. Away down on the level, under the
black mass of the Castle, the town lay, stretched along the
river, its intricate cobweb of streets jeweled with twinkling
lights; there were rows of lights on the bridges; these flung
lances of light upon the water, in the black shadows of the
arches; and away at the extremity of all this fairy spectacle
blinked and glowed a massed multitude of gas jets which
seemed to cover acres of ground; it was as if all the dia-
monds in the world had been spread out there. I did not
know before, that a half mile of sextuple railway tracks could
be made such an adornment.

One thinks Heidelberg by day—with its surroundings—is
the last possibility of the beautiful; but when he sees Heidelberg by night, a fallen Milky Way, with that glittering
railway constellation pinned to the border, he requires time
to consider upon the verdict.

One never tires of poking about in the dense woods that
clothe all these lofty Neckar hills to their tops. The great
deeps of a boundless forest have a beguiling and impressive
charm in any country; but German legends and fairy tales
have given these an added charm. They have peopled all
that region with gnomes, and dwarfs, and all sorts of mysterious and uncanny creatures. At the time I am writing of,
I had been reading so much of this literature that sometimes
I was not sure but I was beginning to believe in the gnomes
and fairies as realities.

One afternoon I got lost in the woods about a mile from
the hotel, and presently fell into a train of dreamy thought
about animals which talk, and kobolds, and enchanted folk,
and the rest of the pleasant legendary stuff; and so, by stim-
ulating my fancy, I finally got to imagining I glimpsed small
flitting shapes here and there down the columned aisles of the
forest. It was a place which was peculiarly meet for the
occasion. It was a pine wood, with so thick and soft a carpet

of brown needles that one's footfall made no more sound
than if he was treading on wool; the tree-trunks were as
round and straight and smooth as pillars, and stood close
together; they were bare of branches to a point about twenty-
five feet above ground, and from there upward so thick with
boughs that not a ray of sunlight could pierce through. The
world was bright with sunshine outside, but a deep and mellow twilight reigned in there, and also a silence so profound
that I seemed to hear my own breathings.

When I had stood ten minutes, thinking and imagining,
and getting my spirit in tune with the place, and in the right
mood to enjoy the supernatural, a raven suddenly uttered a
hoarse croak over my head. It made me start; and then I
was angry because I started. I looked up, and the creature
was sitting on a limb right over me, looking down at me. I
felt something of the same sense of humiliation and injury
which one feels when he finds that a human stranger has
been clandestinely inspecting him in his privacy and mentally commenting upon him. I eyed the raven, and the raven
eyed me. Nothing was said during some seconds. Then
the bird stepped a little way along his limb to get a better
point of observation, lifted his wings, stuck his head far
down below his shoulders toward me, and croaked again—a
croak with a distinctly insulting expression about it. If he
had spoken in English he could not have said any more
plainly than he did say in raven, " Well, what do *you* want
here ? " I felt as foolish as if I had been caught in some
mean act by a responsible being, and reproved for it. However, I made no reply; I would not bandy words with a raven.
The adversary waited a while, with his shoulders still lifted,
his head thrust down between them, and his keen bright eye
fixed on me; then he threw out two or three more insults,
which I could not understand, further than that I knew a
portion of them consisted of language not used in church.

I still made no reply. Now the adversary raised his head
and called. There was an answering croak from a little
distance in the wood,—evidently a croak of inquiry. The

HEIDELBURG CASTLE, RIVER FRONTAGE.

adversary explained with enthusiasm, and the other raven
dropped everything and came.   The two sat side by side on
the limb and discussed me as freely and offensively as two

THE RETREAT.

great naturalists might discuss a new kind of bug.   The
thing became more and more embarrassing.   They called in
another friend.   This was too much.   I saw that they had
the advantage of me, and so I concluded to get out of the
scrape by walking out of it.   They enjoyed my defeat as
much as any low white people could have done.   They cra-
ned their necks and laughed at me, (for a raven *can* laugh,
just like a man,) they squalled insulting remarks after me as
long as they could see me.   They were nothing but ravens
—I knew that,—what they thought about me could be a
matter of no consequence,—and yet when even a raven
shouts after you, " What a hat ! " " O, pull down your vest ! "
and that sort of thing, it hurts you and humiliates you, and
there is no getting around it with fine reasoning and pretty
arguments.

Animals talk to each other, of course. There can be no question about that; but I suppose there are very few people who can understand them. I never knew but one man who could. I knew he could, however, because he told me so himself. He was a middle-aged, simple-hearted miner who had lived in a lonely corner of California, among the woods and mountains, a good many years, and had studied the ways of his only neighbors, the beasts and the birds, until he believed he could accurately translate any remark which they made. This was Jim Baker. According to Jim

Baker, some animals have only a limited education, and use only very simple words, and scarcely ever a comparison or a flowery figure; whereas, certain other animals have a large vocabulary, a fine command of language and a ready and fluent delivery; consequently these latter talk a great deal; they like it; they are conscious of their talent, and they enjoy "showing off."

Baker said, that after long and careful observation, he had come to the conclusion that the blue-jays were the best talkers he had found among birds and beasts. Said he:—

"There's more *to* a blue-jay than any other creature. He has got more moods, and more different kinds of feelings than other creature; and mind you, whatever a blue-jay feels, he can put into language. And no mere commonplace language, either, but rattling, out-and-out book-talk—and bristling with metaphor, too—just bristling! And as for command of language—why *you* never see a blue-jay get stuck for a word. No man ever did. They just boil out of him! And another thing: I've noticed a good deal, and there's no bird, or cow, or anything that uses as good grammar as a blue-jay. You may say a cat uses good grammar. Well, a cat does—but you let a cat get excited, once; you let a cat get to pulling fur with another cat on a shed, nights, and you'll hear grammar that will give you the lockjaw. Ignorant people think it's the *noise* which fighting cats make that is so aggravating, but it ain't so; it's the sickening grammar they use. Now I've never heard a jay use bad grammar but very seldom; and when they do, they are as ashamed as a human; they shut right down and leave.

"You may call a jay a bird. Well, so he is, in a measure —because he's got feathers on him, and don't belong to no church, perhaps; but otherwise he is just as much a human as you be. And I'll tell you for why. A jay's gifts, and instincts, and feelings, and interests, cover the whole ground. A jay hasn't got any more principle than a Congressman. A jay will lie, a jay will steal, a jay will deceive, a jay will betray; and four times out of five, a jay will go back on his solemnest promise. The sacredness of an obligation is a thing which you can't cram into no blue-jay's head. Now on top of all this, there's another thing: a jay can out-swear any gentleman in the mines. You think a cat can swear. Well, a cat can; but you give a blue-jay a subject that calls for his reserve-powers, and where is your cat? Don't talk to *me*—I know too much about this thing. And there's yet another thing: in the one little particular of scolding—just good, clean, out-and-out scolding—a blue-jay can lay over anything, human or divine. Yes, sir, a jay is everything that a man is. A jay can cry, a jay can laugh, a jay can fee shame, a jay can reason and plan and discuss, a jay likes gossip and scandal, a jay has got a sense of humor, a jay knows when he is an ass just as well as you do—maybe better. If a jay ain't human, he better take in his sign, that's all. Now I'm going to tell you a perfectly true fact about some blue-jays."

CHAPTER III.

"WHEN I first begun to understand jay language correctly, there was a little incident happened here.
Seven years ago, the last man in this region but me, moved
away. There stands his house,—been empty ever since; a
log house, with a plank roof—just one big room, and no
more; no ceiling—nothing between the rafters and the floor.
Well, one Sunday morning I was sitting out here in front of
my cabin, with my cat, taking the sun, and looking at the blue
hills, and listening to the leaves rustling so lonely in the
trees, and thinking of the home away yonder in the States,
that I hadn't heard from in thirteen years, when a blue jay lit
on that house, with an acorn in his mouth, and says, ' Hello,
I reckon I've struck something.' When he spoke, the acorn
dropped out of his mouth and rolled down the roof, of course,
but he didn't care; his mind was all on the thing he had
struck. It was a knot-hole in the roof. He cocked his head
to one side, shut one eye and put the other one to the hole,
like a ' possum looking down a jug; then he glanced up
with his bright eyes, gave a wink or two with his wings—
which signifies gratification, you understand,—and says, ' It
looks like a hole, it's located like a hole,—blamed if I don't
believe it *is* a hole!'

"Then he cocked his head down and took another look; he
glances up perfectly joyful, this time; winks his wings and

38

his tail both, and says, ' O, no, this ain't no fat thing, I reckon! If I ain't in luck!—why it's a perfectly elegant hole!' So he flew down and got that acorn, and fetched it up and dropped it in, and was just tilting his head back, with the heavenliest smile on his face, when all of a sudden he was paralyzed into a listening attitude and that smile faded gradually out of his countenance like breath off'n a razor, and the queerest look of surprise took its place. Then he says, ' Why I didn't hear it fall!' He cocked his eye at the hole again, and took a long look; raised up and shook his head; stepped around to the other side of the hole and took another look from that side; shook his head again. He studied a while, then he just went into the *details*—walked round and round the hole and spied into it from every point of the compass. No use. Now he took a thinking attitude on the comb of the roof and scratched the back of his head with his right foot a minute, and finally says, ' Well, it's too many for *me*, that's certain; must be a mighty long hole; however, I ain't got no time to fool around here, I got to 'tend to business; I reckon it's all right—chance it, anyway.'

" So he flew off and fetched another acorn and dropped it in, and tried to flirt his eye to the hole quick enough to see what become of it, but he was too late. He held his eye there as much as a minute; then he raised up and sighed, and says, ' Consound it, I don't seem to understand this thing, no way; however, I'll tackle her again.' He fetched another acorn, and done his level best to see what become of it, but he couldn't. He says, ' Well, *I* never struck no such a hole as this, before; I'm of the opinion it's a totally new kind of a hole.' Then he begun to get mad. He held in for a spell, walking up and down the comb of the roof and shaking his head and muttering to himself; but his feelings got the upper hand of him, presently, and he broke loose and cussed himself black in the face. I never see a bird take on so about a little thing. When he got through he walks to the hole and looks in again for half a minute; then he says, ' Well, you're a long hole, and a deep hole,

3

and a mighty singular hole altogether—but I've started in to fill you, and I'm d—d if I *don't* fill you, if it takes a hundred years!'

"And with that, away he went. You never see a bird work so since you was born. He laid into his work like a nigger, and the way he hove acorns into that hole for about two hours and a half was one of the most exciting and astonishing spectacles I e v e r struck. He never stopped to take a look any more—he just hove 'em in a n d went for more. Well at last he could hardly flop his wings, he was so tuckered out. He comes a-drooping down, once more, sweating like an ice-pitcher, drops his acorn in and says, '*Now* I guess I've got the bulge on you by this time!' So he bent down for a look. If you'll believe me, when his head come up again he was just pale with rage. He says, 'I've shoveled acorns enough i n there t o keep the family thirty years, and if I can see a sign of one of 'em I wish I may land in a museum with a belly full of s a w d u s t in two minutes!'

"He j u s t had strength enough to crawl up on to the comb and lean his back

"A BLUE FLUSH ABOUT IT."

agin the chimbly, and then he collected his impressions and begun to free his mind. I see in a second that what I had mistook for profanity in the mines was only just the rudiments, as you may say.

" Another jay was going by, and heard him doing his devotions, and stops to inquire what was up. The sufferer told him the whole circumstance, and says, 'Now yonder's the hole, and if you don't believe me, go and look for yourself.' So this fellow went and looked, and comes back and says, 'How many did you say you put in there?' 'Not any less than two tons,' says the sufferer. The other jay went and looked again. He couldn't seem to make it out, so he raised a yell, and three more jays come. They all examined the hole, they all made the sufferer tell it over again, then they all discussed it, and got off as many leather-headed opinions about it as an average crowd of humans could have done.

"They called in more jays; then more and more, till pretty soon this whole region 'peared to have a blue flush about it. There must have been five thousand of them; and such another jawing and disputing and ripping and cussing, you never heard. Every jay in the whole lot put his eye to the hole and delivered a more chuckle-headed opinion about the mystery than the jay that went there before him. They examined the house all over, too. The door was standing half open, and at last one old jay happened to go and light on it and look in. Of course that knocked the mystery galley-west in a second. There lay the acorns, scattered all over the floor. He flopped his wings and raised a whoop. 'Come here!' he says, 'Come here, everybody; hang'd if this fool hasn't been trying to fill up a house with acorns!' They all came a-swooping down like a blue cloud, and as each fellow lit on the door and took a glance, the whole absurdity of the contract that that first jay had tackled hit him home and he fell over backwards suffocating with laughter, and the next jay took his place and done the same.

"Well, sir, they roosted around here on the house-top and the trees for an hour, and guffawed over that thing like human beings. It ain't any use to tell me a blue-jay hasn't got a sense of humor, because I know better. And memory, too. They brought jays here from all over the United States to look down that hole, every summer for three years Other birds too. And they could all see the point, except an owl that come from Nova Scotia to visit the Yo Semite, and he took this thing in on his way back. He said he couldn't see anything funny in it. But then he was a good deal disappointed about Yo Semite, too."

CHAPTER IV.

THE summer semester was in full tide; consequently the most frequent figure in and about Heidelberg was the student. Most of the students were Germans, of course, but the representatives of foreign lands were very numerous. They hailed from every corner of the globe,—for instruction is cheap in Heidelberg, and so is living, too. The Anglo-American Club, composed of British and American students, had twenty-five members, and there was still much material left to draw from.

Nine-tenths of the Heidelberg students wore no badge or uniform; the other tenth wore caps of various colors, and belonged to social organizations called " corps." There were five corps, each with a color of its own; there were white caps, blue caps, and red, yellow, and green ones. The famous duel-fighting is confined to the " corps" boys. The "*kneip*" seems to be a specialty of theirs, too. Kneips are held, now and then, to celebrate great occasions,—like the election of a beer king, for instance. The solemnity is simple; the five corps assemble at night, and at a signal they all fall loading themselves with beer, out of pint-mugs, as fast as possible, and each man keeps his own count,—usually by laying aside a lucifer match for each mug he empties. The election is soon decided. When the candidates can hold no more, a count is instituted and the one who has drank the

43

greatest number of pints is proclaimed king. I was told that the last beer king elected by the corps,—or by his own capabilities,—emptied his mug seventy-five times. No stomach

THE BEER KING.

could hold all that quantity at one time, of course,—but there are ways of frequently creating a vacuum, which those who have been much at sea will understand.

One sees so many students abroad at all hours, that he presently begins to wonder if they ever have any working hours. Some of them have, some of them haven't. Each can choose for himself whether he will work or play; for German university life is a very free life; it seems to have no restraints. The student does not live in the college buildings, but hires his own lodgings, in any locality he prefers, and he takes his meals when and where he pleases. He goes to bed when it suits him, and does not get up at all unless he wants to. He is not entered at the university for any particular length of time; so he is likely to change about. He passes no examination upon entering college. He merely pays a trifling fee of five or ten dollars, receives a card entitling him to the privileges of the university, and that is the end of it. He is now ready for business,—or play, as he shall prefer. If he elects to work, he finds a large list of lectures to choose from. He selects the subjects which he will study, and enters his name for these studies; but he can skip attendance.

The result of this system is, that lecture-courses upon specialties of an unusual nature are often deliverd to very slim audiences, while those upon more practical and every-day matters of education are delivered to very large ones. I

THE LECTURER'S AUDIENCE.

heard of one case where, day after day, the lecturer's audience consisted of three students,—and always the same three. But one day two of them remained away. The lecturer began as usual,—

"Gentlemen,"—

—then, without a smile, he corrected himself, saying,—

"Sir,"—

—and went on with his discourse.

It is said that the vast majority of the Heidelberg students are hard workers, and make the most of their opportunities; that they have no surplus means to spend in dissipation, and no time to spare for frolicking. One lecture follows right on the heels of another, with very little time for the student to get out of one hall and into the next; but the industrious

INDUSTRIOUS STUDENTS.

ones manage it by going on a trot. The professors assist them in the saving of their time by being promptly in their little boxed-up pulpits when the hours strike, and as promptly out again when the hour finishes. I entered an empty lecture room one day just before the clock struck. The place had simple, unpainted pine desks and benches for about 2oo persons.

About a minute before the clock struck, a hundred and fifty students swarmed in, rushed to their seats, immediately spread open their note-books and dipped their pens in the ink. When the clock began to strike, a burly professor entered, was received with a round of applause, moved swiftly down the center aisle, said "Gentlemen," and began to talk as he climbed his pulpit steps; and by the time he had arrived in his box and faced his audience, his lecture was well under way and all the pens were going. He had no notes, he talked with prodigious rapidity and energy for an hour,—then the students began to remind him in certain well understood ways that his time was up; he seized his hat, still talking, proceeded swiftly down his pulpit steps, got out the last word of his discourse as he struck the floor; everybody rose respectfully, and he swept rapidly, down the

aisle and disappeared.   An instant rush for some other lecture
room followed, and in a minute I was alone with the empty
benches once more.

Yes, without doubt, idle students are not the rule.   Out
of eight hundred in the town, I knew the faces of only about
fifty; but these I saw everywhere, and daily.   They walked
about the streets and the wooded hills, they drove in cabs,
they boated on the river, they sipped beer and coffee, after-

noons, in the Schloss
gardens.   A good
many of them wore
the colored caps of
the corps.   They were
finely and fashionably
dressed, their manners
were quite superb, and
they led an easy, care-
less, comfortable life.
If a dozen of them sat
together, and a lady
or a gentleman passed
whom one of them
knew and saluted, they
all rose to their feet

IDLE STUDENT.   and took off their caps.

The members of a corps always received a fellow-member
in this way, too; but they paid no attention to members of
other corps; they did not seem to see them.   This was not
a discourtesy; it was only a part of the elaborate and rigid
corps-etiquette.

There seems to be no chilly distance existing between the
German students and the professor; but on the contrary, a
companionable intercourse, the opposite of chilliness and
reserve.   When the professor enters a beer hall in the evening where students are gathered together, these rise up and
take off their caps, and invite the old gentleman to sit with
them and partake.   He accepts, and the pleasant talk and

the beer flow for an hour or two, and by and by the professor, properly charged and comfortable, gives a cordial good

night, while the students stand bowing and uncovered ; and then he moves on his h a p p y way homew a r d with all his vast cargo of learning afloat in his hold. Nobody finds fault or f e e l s outraged; no harm has been done.

COMPANIONABLE INTERCOURSE.

It seemed to be a part of corps-etiquette to keep a dog or so, too. I mean a corps-dog,—the common property of the organization, like the corps-steward or head servant; then there are other dogs, owned by individuals.

On a summer afternoon in the Castle gardens, I have seen six students march solemnly into the grounds, in single file, each carrying a bright Chinese parasol and leading a prodigious dog by a string. It was a very imposing spectacle. Sometimes there would be about as many dogs around the

AN IMPOSING SPECTACLE.

pavilion as students ; and of all breeds and of all degrees of beauty and ugliness. These dogs had a rather dry time of it; for they were tied to the benches and had no amusement for an hour or two at a time except what they could get out of pawing at the gnats, or trying to sleep and not succeeding. However, they got a lump of sugar occasionally—they were fond of that.

It seemed right and proper that students should indulge in dogs; but every body else had them, too,—old men and young ones, old women and nice young ladies. If there is one spectacle that is unpleasanter than another, it is that of an elegantly dressed young lady towing a dog by a string. It is said to be the sign and symbol of blighted love. It seems to me that some other way of advertising it might be devised, which would be just as conspicuous and yet not so trying to the proprieties.

It would be a mistake to suppose that the easy-going pleasure-seeking student carries an empty head. Just the contrary.

AN ADVERTISMENT.

He has spent nine years in the Gymnasium, under a system

which allowed him no freedom, but vigorously compelled him to work like a slave. Consequently he has left the gymnasium with an education which is so extensive and complete, that the most a university can do for it is to perfect some of its profounder specialties. It is said that when a pupil leaves the gymnasium, he not only has a comprehensive education, but he *knows* what he knows,—it is not befogged with uncertainty, it is burnt into him so that it will stay. For instance, he does not merely read and write Greek, but speaks it; the same with the Latin. Foreign youth steer clear of the gymnasium; its rules are too severe. They go to the university to put a mansard roof on their whole general education; but the German student already has his mansard roof, so he goes there to add a steeple in the nature of some specialty, such as a particular branch of law, or medicine, or philology—like international law, or diseases of the eye, or special study of the ancient Gothic tongues. So this German attends only the lectures which belong to the chosen branch, and drinks his beer and tows his dog around and has a general good time the rest of the day. He has been in rigid bondage so long that the large liberty of university life is just what he needs and likes and thoroughly appreciates; and as it cannot last forever, he makes the most of it while it does last, and so lays up a good rest against the day that must see him put on the chains once more and enter the slavery of official or professional life.

CHAPTER V.

ONE day in the interest of science my agent obtained permission to bring me to the students' dueling place. We crossed the river and drove up the bank a few hundred yards, then turned to the left, entered a narrow alley, followed it a hundred yards and arrived at a two-story public house; we were acquainted with its outside aspect, for it was visible from the hotel. We went up stairs and passed into a large whitewashed apartment which was perhaps fifty feet long, by thirty feet wide and twenty or twenty-five high. It was a well lighted place. There was no carpet. Across one end and down both sides of the room extended a row of tables, and at these tables some fifty or seventy-five students* were sitting.

Some of them were sipping wine, others were playing cards, others chess, other groups were chatting together, and many were smoking cigarettes while they waited for the coming duels. Nearly all of them wore colored caps; there were white caps, green caps, blue caps, red caps, and bright yellow ones; so, all the five corps were present in strong force. In the windows at the vacant end of the room stood six or eight long, narrow-bladed swords with large protecting guards for the hand, and outside was a man at work sharpening

---

* See Appendix C.

others on a grindstone. He understood his business; for when a sword left his hand one could shave himself with it.

It was observable that the young gentlemen neither bowed to nor spoke with students whose caps differed in color from their own. This did not mean hostility, but only an armed neutrality. It was considered that a person could strike harder in the duel, and with a more earnest in-terest, if he had never been in a condition of comradeship with his antagonist; therefore, comradeship between the corps was not per-mitted. At intervals the presidents of the five corps have a cold official intercourse with each other, but nothing further. For example when the regular duel-ing day of one of the corps approaches, its

"UNDERSTANDS HIS BUSINESS."

president calls for volunteers from among the membership to offer battle; three or more respond,—but there must not be less than three; the president lays their names before the other presidents, with the request that they furnish antagonists for these challengers from among their corps. This is promptly done. It chanced that the present occa-sion was the battle day of the Red Cap Corps. They were the challengers, and certain caps of other colors had volun-teered to meet them. The students fight duels in the room which I have described, *two days in every week during seven and a half or eight months in every year.* This custom has continued in Germany two hundred and fifty years.

To return to my narrative. A student in a white cap met us and introduced us to six or eight friends of his who also wore white caps, and while we stood conversing, two strange looking figures were led in from another room. They were students panoplied for the duel. They were bare-headed; their eyes were protected by iron goggles which projected an inch or more, the leather straps of which bound their ears flat against their heads; their necks were wound around and around with thick wrappings which a sword could not cut through; from chin to ankle they were padded thoroughly against injury; their arms were bandaged and re-bandaged, layer upon layer, until they looked like solid black logs. These weird apparitions had been handsome youths, clad in fashionable attire, fifteen minutes before, but now they did not resemble any beings one ever sees unless in nightmares. They strode along, with their arms projecting straight out from their bodies; they did not hold them out

THE OLD SURGEON.

themselves, but fellow students walked beside them and gave the needed support.

There was a rush for the vacant end of the room, now, and we followed and got good places. The combatants were placed face to face, each with several members of his own corps about him to assist; two seconds, well padded, and with swords in their hands, took near stations; a student belonging to neither of the opposing corps placed himself in a good position to umpire the combat; another student stood by with a watch and a memorandum-book to keep record of the time and the number and nature of the wounds; a gray haired surgeon was present with his lint, his bandages and his instruments. After a moment's pause the duelists saluted the umpire respectfully, then one after another the several officials stepped forward, gracefully removed their caps and saluted him also, and returned to their places. Everything was ready, now; students stood crowded together in the foreground, and others stood behind them on chairs and tables. Every face was turned toward the center of attraction.

The combatants were watching each other with alert eyes;

THE FIRST WOUND.

a perfect stillness, a breathless interest reigned. I felt that I was going to see some wary work. But not so. The instant the word was given, the two apparitions sprang forward and began to rain blows down upon each other with such lightning rapidity that I could not quite tell whether I saw the swords or only the flashes they made in the air; the rattling din of these blows, as they struck steel or paddings was something wonderfully stirring, and they were struck with such terrific force that I could not understand why the opposing sword was not beaten down under the assault. Presently, in the midst of the sword-flashes, I saw a handful of hair skip into the air as if it had lain loose on the victim's head and a breath of wind had puffed it suddenly away.

The seconds cried "Halt!" and knocked up the combatant's swords with their own. The duelists sat down; a student-official stepped forward, examined the wounded head and touched the place with a sponge once or twice; the surgeon came and turned back the hair from the wound—and revealed a crimson gash two or three inches long, and proceeded to bind an oval piece of leather and a bunch of lint over it; the tally-keeper stepped up and tallied one for the opposition in his book.

Then the duelists took position again; a small stream of blood was flowing down the side of the injured man's head, and over his shoulder and down his body to the floor, but he did not seem to mind this. The word was given, and they plunged at each other as fiercely as before; once more the blows rained and rattled and flashed; every few moments the quick-eyed seconds would notice that a sword was bent—then they called "Halt!" struck up the contending weapons, and an assisting student straightened the bent one.

The wonderful turmoil went on—presently a bright spark sprung from a blade, and that blade, broken in several pieces, sent one of its fragments flying to the ceiling. A new sword was provided, and the fight proceeded. The exercise was tremendous, of course, and in time the fighters began to show great fatigue. They were allowed to rest a moment, every little while; they got other rests by wounding each other, for then they could sit down while the doctor applied the lint and bandages. The law is that the battle must continue fifteen minutes if the men can hold out; and as the pauses do not count, this duel was protracted to twenty or thirty minutes, I judged. At last it was decided that the men were too much wearied to do battle longer. They were led away drenched with crimson from head to foot. That was a good fight, but it could not count, partly because it did not last the lawful fifteen minutes, (of actual fighting,) and partly because neither man was disabled by his wounds. It was a drawn battle, and corps-law requires that drawn battles shall be re-fought as soon as the adversaries are well of their hurts.

4

During the conflict, I had talked a little, now and then, with a young gentleman of the white cap corps and he had mentioned that he was to fight next,—and had also pointed out his challenger, a young gentleman who was leaning against the opposite wall smoking a cigarette and restfully observing the duel then in progress.

My acquaintanceship with a party to the coming contest had the effect of giving me a kind of personal interest in it; I naturally wished he might win, and it was the reverse of pleasant to learn that he probably would not, because although he was a notable swordsman, the challenger was held to be his superior.

The duel presently began and in the same furious way which had marked the previous one. I stood close by, but could not tell which blows told and which did not, they fell and vanished so like flashes of light. They all seemed to tell; the swords always bent over the opponents' heads, from the forehead back over the crown, and seemed to touch, all the way; but it was not so,—a protecting blade, invisible to me, was always interposed between. At the end of ten seconds each man had struck twelve or fifteen blows, and warded off twelve or fifteen, and no harm done; then a sword became disabled, and a short rest followed whilst a new one was brought. Early in the next round the white corps student got an ugly wound on the side of his head and gave his opponent one like it. In the third round the latter received another bad wound in the head, and the former had his under-lip divided. After that, the white corps student gave many severe wounds, but got none of consequence in return. At the end of five minutes from the beginning of the duel the surgeon stopped it; the challenging party had suffered such injuries that any addition to them might be dangerous. These injuries were a fearful spectacle, but are better left undescribed. So, against expectation, my acquaintance was the victor.

CHAPTER VI.

THE third duel was brief and bloody. The surgeon stopped it when he saw that one of the men had received such bad wounds that he could not fight longer without endangering his life.

The fourth duel was a tremendous encounter; but at the end of five or six minutes the surgeon interfered once more: another man so severely hurt as to render it unsafe to add to his harms. I watched this engagement as I had watched the others,—with rapt interest and strong excitement, and with a shrink and a shudder for every blow that laid open a cheek or a forehead; and a conscious paling of my face when I occasionally saw a wound of a yet more shocking nature inflicted. My eyes were upon the loser of this duel when he got his last and vanquishing wound,—it was in his face and it carried away his—but no matter, I must not enter into details. I had but a glance, and then turned quickly away, but I would not have been looking at all if I had known what was coming. No, that is probably not true; one thinks he would not look if he knew what was coming, but the interest and the excitement are so powerful that they would doubtless conquer all other feelings; and so, under the fierce exhilaration of the clashing steel, he would yield and look, after all. Sometimes spectators of these duels faint,—and it does seem a very reasonable thing to do, too.

57

Both parties to this fourth duel were badly hurt; so much so that the surgeon was at work upon them nearly or quite an hour,—a fact which is suggestive. But this waiting interval was not wasted in idleness by the assembled students. It was past noon; therefore they ordered their landlord, down stairs, to send up hot beefsteaks, chickens, and such things, and these they ate, sitting comfortably at the several tables, whilst they chatted, disputed and laughed. The door to the surgeon's room stood open, meantime, but the cutting, sewing, splicing and bandaging going on in there in plain view, did not seem to disturb any one's appetite. I went in and saw the surgeon labor a while, but could not enjoy it; it was much less trying, to see the wounds given and received than to see them mended; the stir and turmoil, and the music of the steel, were wanting, here,—one's nerves were wrung by this grisly spectacle, whilst the duel's compensating pleasurable thrill was lacking.

Finally the doctor finished, and the men who were to fight the closing battle of the day came forth. A good many dinners were not completed, yet, but no matter, they could be eaten cold, after the battle; therefore everybody crowded forward to see. This was not a love duel, but a "satisfaction" affair. These two students had quarreled, and were here to settle it. They did not belong to any of the corps, but they were furnished with weapons and armor, and permitted to fight here by the five corps as a courtesy. Evidently these two young men were unfamiliar with the dueling ceremonies, though they were not unfamiliar with the sword. When they were placed in position they thought it was time to begin,—and they did begin, too, and with a most impetuous energy, without waiting for anybody to give the word. This vastly amused the spectators, and even broke down their studied and courtly gravity and surprised them into laughter. Of course the seconds struck up the swords and started the duel over again. At the word, the deluge of blows began, but before long the surgeon once more interfered,—for the only reason which ever permits him to interfere,—and the

THE CASTLE COURT.

day's war was over. It was now two in the afternoon, and I had been present since half past nine in the morning. The field of battle was indeed a red one by this time; but some sawdust soon righted that. There had been one duel before I arrived. In it one of the men received many injuries, while the other one escaped without a scratch.

I had seen the heads and faces of ten youths gashed in every direction by the keen two-edged blades, and yet had not seen a victim wince, nor heard a moan, or detected any fleeting expression which confessed the sharp pain the hurts were inflicting. This was good fortitude, indeed. Such endurance is to be expected in savages and prize-fighters, for they are born and educated to it; but to find it in such perfection in these gently bred and kindly natured young fellows is matter for surprise. It was not merely under the excitement of the sword-play that this fortitude was shown; it was shown in the surgeon's room where an uninspiring quiet reigned, and where there was no audience. The doctor's manipulations brought out neither grimaces nor moans. And in the fights it was observable that these lads hacked and slashed with the same tremendous spirit, after they were covered with streaming wounds, which they had shown in the beginning.

The world in general looks upon the college duels as very farcical affairs: true, but considering that the college duel is fought by boys; that the swords are real swords; and that the head and face are exposed, it seems to me that it is a farce which has quite a grave side to it. People laugh at it mainly because they think the student is so covered up with armor that he cannot be hurt. But it is not so; his eyes and ears are protected, but the rest of his face and head are bare. He can not only be badly wounded, but his life is in danger; and he would sometimes lose it but for the interference of the surgeon. It is not intended that his life shall be endangered. Fatal accidents are possible, however. For instance, the student's sword may break, and the **end of it fly** up behind his antagonist's ear and cut an artery which could not be reached if the sword remained whole. This has happened, sometimes, and death has resulted on the spot. Formerly the student's armpits were not protected,—and at that time the swords were pointed, whereas they are blunt, now; so an artery in the armpit was sometimes cut, and death followed. Then in the days of sharp-pointed swords, a spectator was an occasional victim,—the end of a broken sword flew five or ten feet and buried itself in his neck or his heart, and death ensued instantly. The student duels in Germany occasion two or three deaths every year, now, but this arises only from the carelessness of the wounded men; they eat or drink imprudently, or commit excesses in the way of over-exertion; inflammation sets in and gets such a headway that it cannot be arrested. Indeed there is blood and pain and danger enough about the college duel to entitle it to a considerable degree of respect.

All the customs, all the laws, all the details, pertaining to the student duel are quaint and naive. The grave, precise, and courtly ceremony with which the thing is conducted, invests it with a sort of antique charm.

This dignity, and these knightly graces suggest the tournament, not the prize fight. The laws are as curious as they are strict. For instance, the duelist may step forward from the line he is placed upon, if he chooses, but never back of it. If he steps back of it, or even leans back, it is considered that he did it to avoid a blow or contrive an advantage; so he is dismissed from his corps in disgrace. It would seem but natural to step from under a descending sword unconsciously, and against one's will and intent,—yet this unconsciousness is not allowed. Again: if under the sudden anguish of a wound the receiver of it makes a grimace, he falls some degrees in the estimation of his fellows; his corps are ashamed of him; they call him " hare foot," which is the German equivalent for chicken-hearted.

CHAPTER VII.

IN addition to the corps laws, there are some corps-usages which have the force of laws.

Perhaps the president of a corps notices that one of the membership who is no longer an exempt,—that is a freshman,—has remained a sophomore some little time without volunteering to fight; some day, the president, instead of calling for volunteers, will *appoint* this sophomore to measure swords with a student of another corps; he is free to decline—everybody says so,—there is no compulsion. This is all true,—but I have not heard of any student who *did* decline. He would naturally rather retire from the corps than decline; to decline, and still remain in the corps would make him unpleasantly conspicuous, and properly so, since he knew, when he joined, that his main business, as a member, would be to fight. No, there is no law against declining,—except the law of custom, which is confessedly stronger than written law, everywhere.

The ten men whose duels I had witnessed did not go away when their hurts were dressed, as I had supposed they would, but came back, one after another, as soon as they were free of the surgeon, and mingled with the assemblage in the dueling room. The white-cap student who won the second fight witnessed the remaining three, and talked with us during the intermissions. He could not talk very well, because his opponent's sword had cut his under lip in two,

and then the surgeon had sewed it together and overlaid it
with a profusion of white plaister patches; neither could he

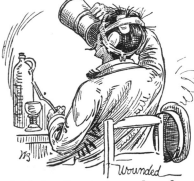

Wounded

eat easily, still he contrived to accomplish a s l o w
and troublesome luncheon
w h i l e the last duel was
preparing. The man who
was the worst hurt of all,
played chess while waiting
to see this engagement. A
good part of his face was
covered with patches and
bandages, and all the rest
of his head was covered and concealed by them. It is said
that the student likes to appear on the street and in other
public places in this kind of array, and that this predilec-
tion often keeps him out when exposure to rain or sun is

FAVORITE STREET COSTUME.

a positive danger for him.
Newly bandaged students
are a very common specta-
cle in the public gardens
of Heidelberg. It is also
said that t h e student is
glad to get wounds in the
f a c e , because the scars
they leave will show so
well there; and it is also
s a i d t h a t these face-
wounds are so prized that
youths have even b e e n
known to pull them apart from time to time and put red
wine in them to make them heal badly and leave as ugly a
scar as possible. It does not look reasonable, but it is
roundly asserted and maintained, nevertheless; I am sure of
one thing,—scars are plenty enough in Germany, among
the young men; and very grim ones they are, too. They
criss-cross the face in angry red welts, and are permanent

and ineffaceable. Some of these scars are of a very strange
and dreadful aspect; and the effect is striking when several
such accent the milder ones, which form a city map on a
man's face; they suggest
the "burned district"
then.

We had often noticed
that many of the students
wore a colored silk band
or ribbon diagonally
across their breasts. It
transpired that this sig-
nifies that the wearer
has fought three duels
in which a decision was
reached—duels in which
he either whipped or
was whipped,—for

INEFFACEABLE SCARS.

drawn battles do not count.* After a student has received
his ribbon, he is "free;" he can cease from fighting, without reproach,—except some one insult him; his president
cannot appoint him to fight; he can volunteer if he wants
to, or remain quiescent if he prefers to do so. Statistics
show that he does *not* prefer to remain quiescent. They
show that the duel has a singular fascination about it somewhere, for these free men, so far from resting upon the privilege of the badge, are always volunteering. A corps student
told me it was of record that Prince Bismarck fought thirty-
two of these duels in a single summer term when he was in

* FROM MY DIARY.—Dined in a hotel a few miles up the Neckar, in a room
whose walls were hung all over with framed portrait-groups of the Five
Corps; some were recent, but many antedated photography, and were pictured in lithography—the dates ranged back to forty or fifty years ago.
Nearly every individual wore the ribbon across his breast. In one portrait-
group representing (as each of these pictures did) an entire Corps, I took
pains to count the ribbons: there were twenty-seven members, and twenty-
one of them wore that significant badge.

college. So he fought twenty-nine after his badge had given him the right to retire from the field.

The statistics may be found to possess interest in several particulars. Two days in every week are devoted to dueling. The rule is rigid that there must be three duels on each of these days; there are generally more, but there cannot be fewer. There were six the day I was present; sometimes there are seven or eight. It is insisted that eight duels a week,—four for each of the two days,—is too low an average to draw a calculation from, but I will reckon from that basis, preferring an under-statement to an over-statement of the case. This requires about four hundred and eighty or five hundred duelists in a year,—for in summer the college term is about three and a half months, and in winter it is four months and sometimes longer. Of the seven hundred and fifty students in the university at the time I am writing of, only eighty belonged to the five corps, and it is only these corps that do the dueling; occasionally other students borrow the arms and battle-ground of the five corps in order to settle a quarrel, but this does not happen every dueling day.* Consequently eighty youths furnish the material for some two hundred and fifty duels a year. This average gives six fights a year to each of the eighty. This large work could not be accomplished if the badge-holders stood upon their privilege and ceased to volunteer.

Of course where there is so much fighting, the students make it a point to keep themselves in constant practice with the foil. One often sees them, at the tables in the Castle grounds, using their whips or canes to illustrate some new sword trick which they have heard about; and between the duels, on the day whose history I have been writing, the swords were not always idle; every now and then we heard a succession of the keen hissing sounds which the sword makes

---

*They have to borrow the arms because they could not get them elsewhere or otherwise. As I understand it, the public authorities, all over Germany, allow the five corps to keep swords, but *do not allow them to use them*. This law is rigid; it is only the execution of it that is lax.

when it is being put through its paces in the air, and this informed us that a student was practicing. Necessarily this unceasing attention to the art develops an expert occasionally. He becomes famous in his own university, his renown spreads to other universities. He is invited to Göttingen, to fight with a Göttingen expert; if he is victorious, he will be invited to other colleges, or those colleges will send their experts to him. Americans and Englishmen often join one or another of the five corps. A year or two ago, the principal Heidelberg expert was a big Kentuckian; he was invited to the various universities and left a wake of victory behind him all about Germany; but at last a little student in Strasburg defeated him. There was formerly a student in Heidelberg who had picked up somewhere and mastered a peculiar trick of cutting up under instead of cleaving down from above. While the trick lasted he won in sixteen successive duels in his own university; but by that time observers had discovered what his charm was, and how to break it, therefore his championship ceased.

The rule which forbids social intercourse between members of different corps is strict. In the dueling house, in the parks, on the street, and anywhere and everywhere that students go, caps of a color group themselves together. If all the tables in a public garden were crowded but one, and that one had two red-cap students at it and ten vacant places, the yellow caps, the blue caps, the white caps and the green caps, seeking seats, would go by that table and not seem to see it, nor seem to be aware that there was such a table in the grounds. The student by whose courtesy we had been enabled to visit the dueling place, wore the white cap,— Prussian Corps. He introduced us to many white caps but to none of another color. The corps etiquette extended even to us, who were strangers, and required us to group with the white corps only, and speak only with the white corps, while we were their guests, and keep aloof from caps of the other colors. Once I wished to examine some of the swords, but an American student said, "It would not be quite polite; these now in the windows all have red hilts or blue; they will bring in some with white hilts presently, and those you can handle freely." When a sword was broken in the first duel, I wanted a piece of it; but its hilt was the wrong color, so it was considered best and politest to await a properer season. It was brought to me after the room was cleared, and I will now make a "life-size" sketch of it by tracing a line around it with my pen, to show the width of the weapon. The length of these swords is about three feet, and they are quite heavy. One's disposition to cheer, during the course of the duels or at their close, was naturally strong, but corps etiquette forbade any demonstrations of this sort. However brilliant a contest or a victory might be, no sign or sound betrayed that any one was moved. A dignified gravity and repression were maintained at all times.

When the dueling was finished and we were ready to go, the gentlemen of the Prussian Corps to whom we had been introduced took off their caps in the courteous German way, and also shook hands; their brethren of the same order took off their caps and bowed, but without shaking hands; the gentlemen of the other corps treated us just as they would have treated white caps,—they fell apart, apparently unconsciously, and left us an unobstructed pathway, but did not seem to see us or know we were there. If we had gone thither the following week as guests of another corps, the white caps, without meaning any offense would have observed the etiquette of their order and ignored our presence.

PIECE OF SWORD.

[How strangely are comedy and tragedy blended in this life! I had not been home a full half hour, after witnessing those playful sham-duels, when circumstances made it necessary for me to get ready immediately to assist personally at a real one—a duel with no effeminate limitations in the matter of results, but a battle to the death. An account of it, in the next chapter, will show the reader that duels between boys, for fun and duels between men in earnest, are very different affairs.]

CHAPTER VIII.

MUCH as the modern French duel is ridiculed by certain smart people, it is in reality one of the most dangerous institutions of our day. Since it is always fought in the open air the combatants are nearly sure to catch cold. M. Paul de Cassagnac, the most inveterate of the French duelists, has suffered so often in this way that he is at last a confirmed invalid; and the best physician in Paris has expressed the opinion that if he goes on dueling for fifteen or twenty years more,—unless he forms the habit of fighting in a comfortable room where damps and draughts cannot intrude,—he will eventually endanger his life. This ought to moderate the talk of those people who are so stubborn in maintaining that the French duel is the most health-giving of recreations because of the open-air exercise it affords. And it ought also to moderate that foolish talk about French duelists and socialist-hated monarchs being the only people who are immortal.

But it is time to get at my subject. As soon as I heard of the late fiery outbreak between M. Gambetta and M. Fourtou in the French Assembly, I knew that trouble must follow. I knew it because a long personal friendship with M. Gambetta had revealed to me the desperate and implacable nature of the man. Vast as are his physical proportions, I knew that the thirst for revenge would penetrate to the remotest frontiers of his person.

69

I did not wait for him to call on me, but went at once to him. As I expected, I found the brave fellow steeped in a profound French calm. I say French calm, because French calmness and English calmness have points of difference. He

FRENCH CALM.

was moving swiftly back and forth among the *débris* of his furniture, now and then staving chance fragments of it across the room with his foot; grinding a constant g r i s t o f curses through his set teeth; and halting every little while to deposit another handful of his hair on the pile which he had been building of it on the table.

He threw his arms around my neck, bent me over his stomach to his breast, kissed me on both cheeks, hugged me four or five times, and then placed me in his own arm-chair. As soon as I had got well again, we began business at once.

I said I supposed he would wish me to act as his second, and he said, "Of course." I said I must be allowed to act under a French name, so that I might be shielded from obloquy in my country, in case of fatal results. He winced here, probably at the suggestion that dueling was not regarded with respect in America. However, he agreed to my requirement. This accounts for the fact that in all the newspaper reports M. Gambetta's second was apparently a Frenchman.

First, we drew up my principal's will. I insisted upon this, and stuck to my point. I said I had never heard of a man in his right mind going out to fight a duel without first making his will. He said he had never heard of a man in his right mind doing anything of the kind. When he had finished the will, he wished to proceed to a choice of his "last words." He wanted to know how the following words, as a dying exclamation, struck me :—

" I die for my God, for my country, for freedom of speech, for progress, and the universal brotherhood of man ! "

I objected that this would require too lingering a death ; it was a good speech for a consumptive, but not suited to the exigencies of the field of honor. We wrangled over a good many ante-mortem outbursts, but I finally got him to cut his obituary down to this, which he copied into his memorandum book, purposing to get it by heart :—

" I DIE THAT FRANCE MAY LIVE."

I said that this remark seemed to lack relevancy ; but he said relevancy was a matter of no consequence in last words, what you wanted was thrill.

The next thing in order was the choice of weapons. My principal said he was not feeling well, and would leave that and the other details of the proposed meeting to me. Therefore I wrote the following note and carried it to M. Fourtou's friend :—

" SIR : M. Gambetta accepts M. Fourtou's challenge, and authorizes me to propose Plessis-Piquet as the place of meeting ; to-morrow morning at daybreak as the time ; and axes as the weapons. I am, sir, with great respect,

MARK TWAIN."

M. Fourtou's friend read this note, and shuddered. Then he turned to me, and said, with a suggestion of severity in his tone :—

"Have you considered, sir, what would be the inevitable result of such a meeting as this ? "

"Well, for instance, what *would* it be ? "

"Bloodshed ! "

"That's about the size of it," I said. "Now, if it is a fair question, what was your side proposing to shed ? "

THE CHALLENGE ACCEPTED.

I had him, there. He saw he had made a blunder, so he hastened to explain it away. He said he had spoken jestingly. Then he added that he and his principal would enjoy axes, and indeed prefer them, but such weapons were barred by the French code, and so I must change my proposal.

I walked the floor, turning the thing over in my mind, and finally it occurred to me that Gatling guns at fifteen paces would be a likely way to get a verdict on the field of honor. So I framed this idea into a proposition.

But it was not accepted. The code was in the way again. I proposed rifles; then double-barreled shot-guns; then, Colt's navy revolvers. These being all rejected, I reflected a while, and sarcastically suggested brick-bats at three quarters of a mile. I always hate to fool away a humorous thing on a person who has no perception of humor; and it filled me with bitterness when this man went soberly away to submit the last proposition to his principal.

He came back presently and said his principal was charmed with the idea of brick-bats at three quarters of a mile, but must decline on account of the danger to disinterested parties passing between. Then I said:—

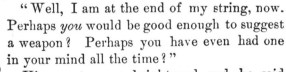

"Well, I am at the end of my string, now. Perhaps *you* would be good enough to suggest a weapon? Perhaps you have even had one in your mind all the time?"

His countenance brightened, and he said with alacrity,—

"Oh, without doubt, monsieur!"

So he fell to hunting in his pockets,— pocket after pocket, and he had plenty of them,— muttering all the while, "Now, what could I have done with them?"

At last he was successful. He fished out of his vest pocket a couple of little things which I carried to the light and ascertained to be pistols. They were single-barreled and silver-mounted, and very dainty and pretty. I was not able to speak for emotion. I silently hung one of them on my watch chain, and returned

A SEARCH.

the other. My companion in crime now unrolled a postage-stamp containing several cartridges, and gave me one of them. I asked if he meant to signify by this that our men were to be allowed but one shot apiece. He replied that the French code permitted no more. I then begged him to go on and suggest a distance, for my mind was growing weak and confused under the strain which had been put upon it. He named sixty-five yards. I nearly lost my patience. I said,—

"Sixty-five yards, with these instruments? Squirt-guns would be deadlier at fifty. Consider, my friend, you and I are banded together to destroy life, not make it eternal."

But with all my persuasions, all my arguments, I was only able to get him to reduce the distance to thirty-five yards; and even this concession he made with reluctance, and said with a sigh,—

"I wash my hands of this slaughter; on your head be it."

There was nothing for me but to go home to my old lion-heart and tell my humiliating story. When I entered, M. Gambetta was laying his last lock of hair upon the altar. He sprang toward me, exclaiming,

W.F B

HE SWOONED PONDEROUSLY.

"You have made the fatal arrangements,—I see it in your eye!"

"I have."

His face paled a trifle, and he leaned upon the table for support. He breathed thick and heavily for a moment or two, so tumultuous were his feelings; then he hoarsely whispered,—

"The weapon, the weapon! Quick! what is the weapon?"

"This!" and I displayed that silver-mounted thing. He cast but one glance at it, then swooned ponderously to the floor.

5

When he came to, he said mournfully,—

"The unnatural calm to which I have subjected myself has told upon my nerves. But away with weakness! I will confront my fate like a man and a Frenchman."

He rose to his feet, and assumed an attitude which for sublimity has never been approached by man, and has seldom been surpassed by statues. Then he said, in his deep bass tones,—

"Behold, I am calm, I am ready; reveal to me the distance."

"Thirty-five yards."...............

I could not lift him up, of course; but I rolled him over,

I ROLLED HIM OVER.

and poured water down his back. He presently came to, and said,—

"Thirty-five yards, —without a rest? But why ask? Since murder was that man's intention, why should he palter with small details? But mark you one thing: in my fall the world shall see how the chivalry of France meets death."

After a long silence he asked,—

"Was nothing said about that man's family standing up with him, as an offset to my bulk? But no matter; I would not stoop to make such a suggestion; if he is not noble enough to suggest it himself, he is welcome to this advantage, which no honorable man would take."

He now sank into a sort of stupor of reflection, which lasted some minutes; after which he broke silence with,—

"The hour,—what is the hour fixed for the collision?"

"Dawn, to-morrow."

He seemed greatly surprised, and immediately said,—

"Insanity! I never heard of such a thing. Nobody is abroad at such an hour."

"That is the reason I named it. Do you mean to say you want an audience?"

"It is no time to bandy words. I am astonished that M. Fourtou should ever have agreed to so strange an innovation. Go at once and require a later hour."

I ran down stairs, threw open the front door, and almost plunged into the arms of M. Fourtou's second. He said,—

"I have the honor to say that my principal strenuously objects to the hour chosen, and begs you will consent to change it to half past nine."

"Any courtesy, sir, which it is in our power to extend is at the service of your excellent principal. We agree to the proposed change of time."

"I beg you to accept the thanks of my client." Then he turned to a person behind him, and said, "You hear M. Noir, the hour is altered to half past nine." Whereupon M. Noir bowed, expressed his thanks, and went away. My accomplice continued:—

"If agreeable to you, your chief surgeons and ours shall proceed to the field in the same carriage, as is customary."

"It is entirely agreeable to me, and I am obliged to you for mentioning the surgeons, for I am afraid I should not have thought of them. How many shall I want? I suppose two or three will be enough?"

"Two is the customary number for each party. I refer to 'chief' surgeons; but considering the exalted positions occupied by our clients, it will be well and decorous that each of us appoint several consulting surgeons, from among the highest in the profession. These will come in their own private carriages. Have you engaged a hearse?"

"Bless my stupidity, I never thought of it! I will attend to it right away. I must seem very ignorant to you; but you must try to overlook that, because I have

THE ONE I HIRED.

never had any experience of such a swell duel as this before

I have had a good deal to do with duels on the Pacific coast, but I see now that they were crude affairs. A hearse,— sho! we used to leave the elected lying around loose, and let anybody cord them up and cart them off that wanted to. Have you anything further to suggest?"

"Nothing, except that the head undertakers shall ride together, as is usual. The subordinates and mutes will go on foot, as is also usual. I will see you at eight o'clock in the morning, and we will then arrange the order of the procession. I have the honor to bid you a good day."

I returned to my client, who said, "Very well; at what hour is the engagement to begin?"

"Half past nine."

"Very good indeed. Have you sent the fact to the newspapers?"

"*Sir!* If after our long and intimate friendship you can for a moment deem me capable of so base a treachery"—

"Tut, tut! What words are these, my dear friend? Have I wounded you? Ah, forgive me; I am overloading you with labor. Therefore go on with the other details, and drop this one from your list. The bloody-minded Fourtou will be sure to attend to it. Or I myself—yes, to make certain, I will drop a note to my journalistic friend, M. Noir"—

"Oh, come to think, you may save yourself the trouble; that other second has informed M. Noir."

"H'm! I might have known it. It is just like that Fourtou, who always wants to make a display."

At half past nine in the morning the procession approached the field of Plessis-Piquet in the following order: first came our carriage,—nobody in it but M. Gambetta and myself; then a carriage containing M. Fourtou and his second; then a carriage containing two poet-orators who did not believe in God, and these had MS. funeral orations projecting from their breast pockets; then a carriage containing the head surgeons and their cases of instruments; then eight private carriages containing consulting surgeons; then a hack con-

THE MARCH TO THE FIELD.

taining a coroner; then the two hearses; then a carriage containing the head undertakers; then a train of assistants and mutes on foot; and after these came plodding through the fog a long procession of camp followers, police, and citizens generally. It was a noble turn-out, and would have made a fine display if we had had thinner weather.

There was no conversation. I spoke several times to my principal, but I judge he was not aware of it, for he always referred to his note-book and muttered absently, " I die that France may live."

Arrived on the field, my fellow-second and I paced off the thirty-five yards, and then drew lots for choice of position. This latter was but an ornamental ceremony, for all choices were alike in such weather. These preliminaries being ended, I went to my principal and asked him if he was ready. He spread himself out to his full width, and said in a stern voice, " Ready! Let the batteries be charged."

The loading was done in the presence of duly constituted witnesses. We considered it best to perform this delicate service with the assistance of a lantern, on account of the state of the weather. We now placed our men.

At this point the police noticed that the public had massed themselves together on the right and left of the field; they therefore begged a delay, while they should put these poor people in a place of safety. The request was granted.

The police having ordered the two multitudes to take positions behind the duelists, we were once more ready. The weather growing still more opaque, it was agreed between myself and the other second that before giving the fatal signal we should each deliver a loud whoop to enable the combatants to ascertain each other's whereabouts.

I now returned to my principal, and was distressed to observe that he had lost a good deal of his spirit. I tried my best to hearten him. I said, "Indeed, sir, things are not as bad as they seem. Considering the character of the weapons, the limited number of shots allowed, the generous distance, the impenetrable solidity of the fog, and the added fact that one of the combatants is one-eyed and the other cross-eyed and near-sighted, it seems to me that this conflict need not necessarily be fatal. There are chances that both of you may survive. Therefore, cheer up; do not be down-hearted."

This speech had so good an effect that my principal imme-diately stretched forth his hand and said, "I am myself again; give me the weapon."

I laid it, all lonely and forlorn, in the centre of the vast solitude of his palm. He gazed at it and shuddered. And

THE POST OF DANGER.

still mournfully contempla-ting it, he murmured, in a broken voice,—

"Alas, it is not death I dread but mutilation."

I heartened him once more, and with such success that he presently s a i d, "Let the tragedy begin. Stand at my back; do not desert me in this solemn hour, my friend."

I gave him my promise. I now assisted him to point his pistol toward the spot where I judged his adversary to be standing, and cautioned him to listen well and further guide himself by my fellow second's whoop. Then I propped myself against M. Gambetta's back, and raised a rousing "Whoop-ee!" This was answered from out the far distances of the fog, and I immediately shouted,—

"One,—two,—three,—*fire!*"

Two little sounds like *spit' spit!* broke upon my ear, and in the same instant I was crushed to the earth under a mountain of flesh. Bruised as I was, I was still able to catch a faint accent from above, to this effect,—

"I die for . . . for . . . perdition take it, what *is* it I die for? . . . oh, yes,—FRANCE! I die that France may live!"

The surgeons swarmed around with their probes in their hands, and applied their microscopes to the whole area of M.

Gambetta's person, with the happy result of finding nothing
in the nature of a wound. Then a scene ensued which was
in every way gratifying and inspiriting.

The two gladiators fell upon each other's necks, with floods
of proud and happy tears; that other second embraced me;
the surgeons, the orators, the undertakers, the police, every-

THE RECONCILIATION.

body embraced, everybody congratulated, everybody cried,
and the whole atmosphere was filled with praise and with
joy unspeakable.

It seemed to me then that I would rather be a hero of a
French duel than a crowned and sceptred monarch.

When the commotion had somewhat subsided, the body of
surgeons held a consultation, and after a good deal of debate
decided that with proper care and nursing there was reason
to believe that I would survive my injuries. My internal
hurts were deemed the most serious, since it was apparent
that a broken rib had penetrated my left lung, and that
many of my organs had been pressed out so far to one side
or the other of where they belonged, that it was doubtful if
they would ever learn to perform their functions in such remote and unaccustomed localities. They then set my left

arm in two places, pulled my right hip into its socket again, and re-elevated my nose. I was an object of great interest, and even admiration; and many sincere and warm-hearted persons had themselves introduced to me, and said they were proud to know the only man who had been hurt in a French duel in forty years.

I was placed in an ambulance at the very head of the procession; and thus with gratifying *éclat* I was marched into

AN OBJECT OF ADMIRATION.

Paris, the most conspicuous figure in that great spectacle, and deposited at the hospital.

The cross of the Legion of Honor has been conferred upon me. However, few escape that distinction.

Such is the true version of the most memorable private conflict of the age.

I have no complaints to make against any one. I acted for myself, and I can stand the consequences. Without boasting, I think I may say I am not afraid to stand before a modern French duelist, but as long as I keep in my right mind I will never consent to stand behind one again.

CHAPTER IX.

ONE day we took the train and went down to Mannheim to see King Lear played in German. It was a mistake. We sat in our seats three whole hours and never understood anything but the thunder and lightning; and even that was reversed to suit German ideas, for the thunder came first and the lightning followed after.

The behavior of the audience was perfect. There were no rustlings, or whisperings, or other little disturbances; each act was listened to in silence, and the applauding was done after the curtain was down. The doors opened at half past four, the play began promptly at half past five, and within two minutes afterward all who were coming were in their seats, and quiet reigned. A German gentleman in the train had said that a Shaksperian play was an appreciated treat in Germany and that we should find the house filled. It was true; all the six tiers were filled, and remained so to the end, —which suggested that it is not only balcony people who like Shakspeare in Germany, but those of the pit and the gallery, too.

Another time, we went to Mannheim and attended a shivaree,—otherwise an opera,—the one called Lohengrin. The banging and slamming and booming and crashing were something beyond belief. The racking and pitiless pain of it remains stored up in my memory alongside the memory of

83

the time that I had my teeth fixed. There were circumstances which made it necessary for me to stay through the
four hours to the end, and I staid; but the recollection of

WAGNER.

that long, dragging, re-
lentless season of suffering
is indestructible. T o
have to endure it in silence.
and sitting still, made it
all the harder. I was in a
railed compartment. with
eight or ten strangers, of
the two sexes, and this
compelled repression ; yet
at times the pain was so
exquisite t h a t I c o u l d
hardly keep the tears back.

At those times, as the howlings and wailings and shriekings
of the singers, and the ragings and roarings and explosions
of the vast orchestra rose higher and higher, and wilder and

wilder, and fiercer and fiercer, I
could have cried if I had been alone.
Those strangers would not have
been surprised to see a man do such
a thing who was being gradually
skinned, but they would have marveled at it here, and made remarks
about it no doubt, whereas there was
nothing in the present case which
was an advantage over being
skinned. There was a wait of half

RAGING.

an hour at the end of the first act, and I could have gone
out and rested during that time, but I could not trust myself
to do it, for I felt that I should desert and stay out. There
was another wait of half an hour toward nine o'clock, but I
had gone through so much by that time that I had no spirit
left, and so had no desire but to be let alone.

I do not wish to suggest that the rest of the people there were like me, for indeed they were not. Whether it was that they naturally liked that noise, or whether it was that they had learned to like it by getting used to it, I did not at that time know; but they did like it,—this was plain enough. While it was going on they sat and looked as rapt and grateful as cats do when one strokes their backs; and whenever the curtain fell they rose to their feet, in one solid mighty multitude, and the air was snowed thick with waving handkerchiefs, and

ROARING.

hurricanes of applause swept the place. This was not comprehensible to me. Of course there were many people there who were not under compulsion to stay; yet the tiers were as full at the close as they had been at the beginning. This showed that the people liked it.

SHRIEKING.

It was a curious sort of a play. In the matter of costumes and scenery it was fine and showy enough; but there was not much action. That is to say, there was not much really done, it was only talked about; and always violently. It was what one might call a narrative play. Everybody had a narrative and a grievance, and none were reasonable about it but all in an offensive and ungovernable state. There was little of that sort of customary thing where the tenor and the soprano stand down by the footlights, warbling, with blended voices, and keep holding out their arms toward each other and drawing them back and spreading both hands over first one breast and then the other with a shake and a pressure,—no it was, every rioter for himself

A CUSTOMARY THING.

and no blending. Each sang his indictive narrative in turn, accompanied by the whole orchestra of sixty instruments, and when this had continued for some time, and one was hoping they might come to an understanding and modify the noise, a great chorus composed entirely of maniacs would suddenly break forth, and then during two minutes, and sometimes three, I lived over again all that I had suffered the time the orphan asylum burned down.

We only had one brief little season of heaven and heaven's sweet ecstasy and peace during all this long and diligent and acrimonious reproduction of the other place. This was while a gorgeous procession of people marched around and around, in the third act, and sang the Wedding Chorus. To my untutored ear that was music,—almost divine music. While my seared soul was steeped in the healing balm of those gracious sounds, it seemed to me that I could almost re-suffer the torments which had gone before, in order to be so healed again. There is where the deep ingenuity of the operatic idea is betrayed. It deals so largely in pain that its scattered delights are prodigiously augmented by the contrasts. A pretty air in an opera is prettier there than it could be anywhere else, I suppose, just as an honest man in politics shines more than he would elsewhere.

I have since found out that there is nothing the Germans like so much as an opera. They like it, not in a mild and moderate way, but with their whole hearts. This is a legitimate result of habit and education. Our nation will like the opera, too, by and by, no doubt. One in fifty of those who attend our operas likes it already, perhaps, but I think a good many of the other forty-nine go in order to learn to like it, and the rest in order to be able to talk knowingly about it. The latter usually hum the airs while they are being sung, so that their neighbors may perceive that they have been to operas before. The funerals of these do not occur often enough.

ONE OF THE REST.

A gentle, old-maidish person and a sweet young girl of seventeen sat right in front of us that night at the Mannheim opera. These people talked, between the acts, and I understood them, though I understood nothing that was uttered on the distant stage. At first they were guarded in their talk, but after they had heard my agent and me conversing in English they dropped their reserve and I picked up many of their little confidences; no, I mean many of *her* little confidences,—meaning the elder party,— for the young girl only listened, and gave assenting nods, but never said a word. How pretty she was, and how sweet she was! I wished she would speak. But evidently she was absorbed in her own thoughts, her own young-girl dreams, and found a dearer pleasure in silence. But she was not dreaming sleepy dreams, —no, she was awake, alive, alert, she could not sit still a moment. She was an enchanting study. Her gown was of a soft white silky stuff that clung to her round young figure like a fish's skin, and it was rippled over with the gracefullest little fringy films of lace; she had deep, tender eyes, with long, curved lashes; and she had peachy cheeks, and a dimpled chin, and such a dear little dewy rosebud of a mouth; and she was so dove-like, so pure, and so gracious, so sweet and bewitching. For long hours I did mightily wish she would speak. And at last she did; the red lips parted, and out leaped her thought, —and with such a guileless and pretty enthusiasm, too: "Auntie, I just *know* I've got five hundred fleas on me!"

That was probably over the average. Yes, it must have been very much over the average. The average at that time in the Grand Duchy of Baden was forty-five to a young per-

son, (when alone,) according to the official estimate of the Home Secretary for that year; the average for older people was shifty and indeterminable, for whenever a wholesome young girl came into the presence of her elders she immediately lowered their average and raised her own. She became a sort of contribution box. This dear young thing in the theatre had been sitting there unconsciously taking up

A CONTRIBUTION BOX.

a collection. Many a skinny old being in our neighborhood was the happier and the restfuller for her coming.

In that large audience, that night, there were eight very conspicuous people. These were ladies who had their hats or bonnets on. What a blessed thing it would be if a lady could make herself conspicuous in our theatres by wearing her hat. It is not usual in Europe to allow ladies and gentle men to take bonnets, hats, over coats, canes or umbrellas into the auditorium, but in Mannheim this rule was not enforced be- cause the audiences were large- ly made up of people from a distance, and among these were always a few timid ladies who were afraid that if they had to go into an ante-room to get their things when the play was over, they would miss their train. But the great mass of those who came from a distance always

CONSPICUOUS.

ran the risk and took the chances, preferring the loss of the train to a breach of good manners and the discomfort of being unpleasantly conspicuous during a stretch of three or four hours.

CHAPTER X.

THREE or four hours. That is a long time to sit in one place, whether one be conspicuous or not, yet some of Wagner's operas bang along for six whole hours on a stretch! But the people sit there and enjoy it all, and wish it would last longer. A German lady in Munich told me that a person could not like Wagner's music at first, but must go through the deliberate process of learning to like it,—then he would have his sure reward; for when he had learned to like it he would hunger for it and never be able to get enough of it. She said that six hours of Wagner was by no means too much. She said that this composer had made a complete revolution in music and was burying the old masters one by one. And she said that Wagner's operas differed from all others in one notable respect, and that was that they were not merely spotted with music here and there, but were *all* music, from the first strain to the last. This surprised me. I said I had attended one of his insurrections, and found hardly *any* music in it except the Wedding Chorus. She said Lohengrin was noisier than Wagner's other operas, but that if I would keep on going to see it I would find by and by that it was all music, and therefore would then enjoy it. I *could* have said, " But would you advise a person to deliberately practice having the toothache in the pit of his stomach for a couple of years in order that he might then come to enjoy it?" But I reserved that remark.

This lady was full of the praises of the head-tenor who had performed in a Wagner opera the night before, and went on to enlarge upon his old and prodigious fame, and how many honors had been lavished upon him by the princely houses of Germany. Here was another surprise. I had attended that very opera, in the person of my agent, and had made close and accurate observations. So I said:

"Why madam, *my* experience warrants me in stating that that tenor's voice is not a voice at all, but only a shriek,— the shriek of a hyena."

"That is very true," she said; "he cannot sing now; it is already many years that he has lost his voice, but in other times he sang, yes, divinely! So whenever he comes, now, you shall see, yes, that the theatre will not hold the people. *Jawohl bei Gott!* his voice is *wunderschön* in that past time."

I said she was discovering to me a kindly trait in the Germans which was worth emulating. I said that over the water we were not quite so generous; that with us, when a singer had lost his voice and a jumper had lost his legs, these parties ceased to draw. I said I had been to the opera in Hanover, once,

ONLY A SHRIEK.

and in Mannheim once, and in Munich, (through my authorized agent,) once, and this large experience had nearly persuaded me that the Germans *preferred* singers who couldn't sing. This was not such a very extravagant speech, either, for that burly Mannheim tenor's praises had been the talk of all Heidelberg for a week before his performance took place,—yet his voice was like the distressing noise which a nail makes when you screech it across a window pane. I said so to Heidelberg friends the next day, and they said, in

6

the calmest and simplest way, that that was very true, but that in earlier times his voice *had* been wonderfully fine. And the tenor in Hanover was just another example of this sort. The English-speaking German gentleman who went with me to the opera there was brimming with enthusiasm over that tenor. He said:—

"*Ach Gott !* a great man ! You shall see him. He is so celebrate in all Germany,—and he has a pension, yes, from the government. He not obliged to sing, now, only twice every year; but if he not sing twice each year they take him his pension away."

Very well, we went. When the renowned old tenor appeared, I got a nudge and an excited whisper :—

"Now you see him !"

But the "celebrate" was an astonishing disappointment to me. If he had been behind a screen I should have supposed they were performing a surgical operation on him. I looked at my friend,—to my great surprise he seemed intoxicated with pleasure, his eyes were dancing with eager delight. When the curtain at last fell, he burst into the stormiest applause, and kept it up,—as did the whole house,—until the afflictive tenor had come three times before the curtain to make his bow. While the glowing enthusiast was swabbing the perspiration from his face, I said :—

"HE ONLY CRY."

"I don't mean the least harm, but really, now, do you think he can sing ?"

"Him ? *No ! Gott im Himmel, aber*, how he has been able to sing twenty-five years ago ? " [Then pensively.] "*Ach*, no, *now* he not sing any more, he only cry. When he think he sing, now, he not sing at all, no, he only make like a cat which is unwell."

Where and how did we get the idea that the Germans

are a stolid, phlegmatic race? In truth they are widely removed from that. They are warm-hearted, emotional, impulsive, enthusiastic, their tears come at the mildest touch, and it is not hard to move them to laughter. They are the very children of impulse. We are cold and self-contained, compared to the Germans. They hug and kiss and cry and shout and dance and sing; and where we use one loving, petting expression they pour out a score. Their language is full of endearing diminutives; nothing that they love escapes the application of a petting diminutive,—neither the house, nor the dog, nor the horse, nor the grandmother, nor any other creature, animate or inanimate.

In the theatres at Hanover, Hamburg, and Mannheim, they had a wise custom. The moment the curtain went up, the lights in the body of the house went down. The audience sat in the cool gloom of a deep twilight, which greatly enhanced the glowing splendors of the stage. It saved gas, too, and people were not sweated to death.

When I saw King Lear played, nobody was allowed to see a scene shifted; if there was nothing to be done but slide a forest out of the way and expose a temple beyond, one did not see that forest split itself in the middle and go shrieking away, with the accompanying disenchanting spectacle of the hands and heels of the impelling impulse,—no, the curtain was always dropped for an instant,—one heard not the least movement behind it,—but when it went up, the next instant, the forest was gone. Even when the stage was being entirely re-set, one heard no noise. During the whole time that King Lear was playing, the curtain was never down two minutes at any one time. The orchestra played until the curtain was ready to go up for the first time, then they departed for the evening. Where the stage-waits never reach two minutes there is no occasion for music. I had never seen this two-minute business between acts but once before, and that was when the " Shaughran " was played at Wallack's.

I was at a concert in Munich one night, the people were

streaming in, the clock-hand pointed to seven, the music
struck up, and instantly all movement in the body of the
house ceased,—nobody was standing, or walking up the aisles
or fumbling with a seat, the stream of incomers had suddenly
dried up at its source. I listened undisturbed to a piece of
music that was fifteen minutes long,—always expecting some
tardy ticket-holders to come crowding past my knees, and
being continuously and pleasantly disappointed,—but when
the last note was struck, here came the stream again. You
see, they had made those late comers wait in the comfortable
waiting-parlor from the time the music had begun until it
was ended.

It was the first time I had ever seen this sort of crimi-
nals denied the privilege of destroying the comfort of a
house full of their betters. Some of these were pretty
fine birds, but no matter, they had to tarry outside in the

LATE COMERS CARED FOR.

long parlor under the inspection of a double rank of liveried footmen and waiting-maids who supported the two walls

with their backs and held the wraps and traps of their masters and mistresses on their arms.

We had no footmen to hold our things, and it was not permissible to take them into the concert room; but there were some men and women to take charge of them for us. They gave us checks for them and charged a fixed price, payable in advance,—five cents.

In Germany they always hear one thing at an opera which has never yet been heard in America, perhaps,—I mean the closing strain of a fine solo or duet. We always smash into it with an earthquake of applause. The result is that we rob ourselves of the sweetest part of the treat; we get the whisky, but we don't get the sugar in the bottom of the glass.

Our way of scattering applause along through an act seems to me to be better than the Mannheim way of saving it all up till the act is ended. I do not see how an actor can forget himself and portray hot passion before a cold still audience. I should think he would feel foolish. It is a pain to me to this day, to remember how that old German Lear raged and wept and howled around the stage, with never a response from that hushed house, never a single outburst till the act was ended. To me there was something unspeakably uncomfortable in the solemn dead silences that always followed this old person's tremendous outpourings of his feelings. I could not help putting myself in his place,—I thought I knew how sick and flat he felt during those silences, because I remembered a case which came under my observation once, and which,—but I will tell the incident:

One evening on board a Mississippi steamboat, a boy of ten years lay asleep in a berth,—a long, slim-legged boy, he was, encased in quite a short shirt; it was the first time he had ever made a trip on a steamboat, and so he was troubled, and scared, and had gone to bed with his head filled with impending snaggings, and explosions, and conflagrations, and sudden death. About ten o'clock some twenty ladies were sitting around about the ladies' saloon, quietly reading, sewing, embroidering, and so on, and among them sat a sweet, benignant old dame with round spectacles on her nose and her busy knitting-needles in her hands. Now all of a sudden, into the midst of this peaceful scene burst that slim-shanked boy in the brief shirt, wild-eyed, erect-haired, and shouting,

EVIDENTLY DREAMING.

"Fire, fire! *jump and run, the boat's afire and there ain't a minute to lose!*" All those ladies looked sweetly up and smiled, nobody stirred, the old lady pulled her spectacles down, looked over them, and said, gently,—

"But you mustn't catch cold, child. Run and put on your breast-pin, and then come and tell us all about it."

It was a cruel chill to give to a poor little devil's gushing vehemence. He was expecting to be a sort of hero—the creator of a wild panic—and here everybody sat and smiled a mocking smile, and an old woman made fun of his bugbear. I turned and crept humbly away—for I was that boy—and never even cared to discover whether I had dreamed the fire or actually seen it.

I am told that in a German concert or opera, they hardly ever encore a song; that though they may be dying to hear it again, their good breeding usually preserves them against requiring the repetition.

Kings may encore; that is quite another matter; it delights everybody to see that the king is pleased; and as to the actor encored, his pride and gratification are simply boundless. Still, there are circumstances in which even a royal encore—

But it is better to illustrate. The King of Bavaria is a poet, and has a poet's eccentricities—with the advantage over all other poets of being able to gratify them, no matter what form they may take. He is fond of the opera, but not fond of sitting in the presence of an audience; therefore, it has sometimes occurred, in Munich, that when an opera has been concluded and the players were getting off their paint and finery, a command has come to them to get their paint and finery on again. Presently the king would arrive, solitary and alone, and the players would begin at the beginning and do the entire opera over again with only that one individual in the vast solemn theatre for audience. Once he took an odd freak into his head. High up and out of sight, over the prodigious stage of the court theatre is a maze of interlacing water-pipes, so pierced that in case of fire, innumerable little thread-like streams of water can be caused to descend; and in case of need, this discharge can be augmented to a pouring flood. American managers might make a note of that. The King was sole audience. The opera proceeded, it was a piece with a storm in it; the mimic thunder began to mutter, the mimic wind began to wail and sough, and the mimic rain to patter. The King's interest rose higher and higher; it developed into enthusiasm. He cried out,—

"It is good, very good indeed! But I will have real rain! Turn on the water!"

The manager pleaded for a reversal of the command; said it would ruin the costly scenery and the splendid costumes, but the king cried,—

"No matter, no matter, I will have real rain! Turn on the water?"

So the real rain was turned on and began to descend in gossamer lances to the mimic flower beds and gravel walks of the stage.   The richly-dressed actresses and actors tripped

"TURN ON MORE RAIN."

about singing bravely and pretending not to mind it.   The
King was delighted,—his enthusiasm grew higher.   He cried
out,—

"Bravo, bravo!   More thunder! more lightning! turn on
more rain!"

The thunder boomed, the lightning glared, the storm-
winds raged, the deluge poured down.   The mimic royalty
on the stage, with their soaked satins clinging to their bodies,
slopped around ankle deep in water, warbling their sweetest
and best, the fiddlers under the eaves of the stage sawed
away for dear life, with the cold overflow spouting down the
backs of their necks, and the dry and happy King sat in his
lofty box and wore his gloves to ribbons applauding.

"More yet!" cried the King; "more yet,—let loose all the
thunder, turn on all the water!   I will hang the man that
raises an umbrella!"

When this most tremendous and effective storm that had
ever been produced in any theatre was at last over, the
King's approbation was measureless.   He cried,—

"Magnificent, magnificent!   *Encore!*   Do it again!"

But the manager succeeded in persuading him to recall the encore, and said the company would feel sufficiently rewarded and complimented in the mere fact that the encore was desired by his Majesty, without fatiguing him with a repetition to gratify their own vanity.

During the remainder of the act the lucky performers were those whose parts required changes of dress; the others were a soaked, bedraggled and uncomfortable lot, but in the last degree picturesque. The stage scenery was ruined, trap-doors were so swollen that they wouldn't work for a week afterward, the fine costumes were spoiled, and no end of minor damages were done by that remarkable storm.

It was a royal idea—that storm—and royally carried out. But observe the moderation of the king: he did not insist upon his encore.

HARRIS ATTENDING THE OPERA.

If he had been a gladsome, unreflecting American opera-audience, he probably would have had his storm repeated and repeated until he drowned all those people.

CHAPTER XI.

THE summer days passed pleasantly in Heidelberg. We had a skilled trainer, and under his instructions we were getting our legs in the right condition for the contemplated pedestrian tours; we were well satisfied with the progress which we had made in the German language*, and more than satisfied with what we had accomplished in Art. We had had the best instructors in drawing and painting in Germany,—Hämmerling, Vogel, Müller, Dietz and Schumann. Hämmerling taught us landscape painting, Vogel taught us figure drawing, Müller taught us to do still-life, and Dietz and Schumann gave us a finishing course in two specialties,—battle-pieces and shipwrecks. Whatever I am in Art I owe to these men. I have something of the manner of each and all of them; but they all said that I had also a manner of my own, and that it was conspicuous. They said there was a marked individuality about my style,—insomuch that if I ever painted the commonest type of a dog, I should be sure to throw a something into the aspect of that dog which would keep him from being mistaken for the creation of any other artist. Secretly I wanted to believe all these kind sayings, but I could not; I was afraid that my masters' partiality for me, and pride in me, biased their judgment. So I resolved to make a test. Privately, and unknown to any one, I painted my great picture, "Heidelberg Castle

---

* See Appendix D for information concerning this fearful tongue.

100

Illuminated,"—my first really important work in oils,—and
had it hung up in the midst of a wilderness of oil pictures in
the Art Exhibition, with no name attached to it. To my
great gratification it was instantly recognized as mine. All
the town flocked to see it, and people even came from neighboring localities to visit it. It made more stir than any other
work in the Exhibition. But the most gratifying thing of

PAINTING MY GREAT PICTURE.

all, was, that chance strangers, passing through, who had not
heard of my picture, were not only drawn to it, as by a lode-
stone, the moment they entered the gallery, but always took
it for a " Turner."

Mr. Harris was graduated in Art about the same time with
myself, and we took a studio together. We waited awhile
for some orders; then as time began to drag a little, we

concluded to make a pedestrian tour. After much considera.
tion, we determined on a trip up the shores of the beautiful
Neckar to Heilbronn. Apparently nobody had ever done
that. There were ruined castles on the overhanging cliffs
and crags all the way; these were said to have their legends,
like those on the Rhine, and what was better still, they had
never been in print. There was nothing in the books about
that lovely region; it had been neglected by the tourist, it
was virgin soil for the literary pioneer.

Meantime the knapsacks, the rough walking suits and the
stout walking shoes which we had ordered, were finished and
brought to us. A Mr. X. and a young Mr. Z. had agreed to go
with us. We went around, one evening and bade good-bye
to our friends, and afterwards had a little farewell banquet
at the hotel. We got to bed early, for we wanted to make
an early start, so as to take advantage of the cool of the
morning.

We were out of bed at break of day, feeling fresh and
vigorous, and took a hearty breakfast, then plunged down
through the leafy arcades of the Castle grounds, toward the
town. What a glorious summer morning it was, and how
the flowers did pour out their fragrance, and how the birds
did sing! It was just the time for a tramp through the
woods and mountains.

We were all dressed alike: broad slouch hats, to keep the
sun off; gray knapsacks; blue army shirts; blue overalls;
leathern gaiters buttoned tight from knee down to ankle;
high-quarter coarse shoes snugly laced. Each man had an
opera glass, a canteen, and a guide-book case slung over his
shoulder, and carried an alpen-stock in one hand and a sun
umbrella in the other. Around our hats were wound many
folds of soft white muslin, with the ends hanging and flapping
down our backs,—an idea brought from the Orient and used
by tourists all over Europe. Harris carried the little watch-
like machine called a " pedometer," whose office is to keep
count of a man's steps and tell how far he has walked. Everybody stopped to admire our costumes and give us a hearty:

"Pleasant march to you!"

When we got down town I found that we could go by rail to within five miles of Heilbronn. The train was just starting, so we jumped aboard and went tearing away in splendid spirits. It was agreed all around that we had done wisely, because it would be just as enjoyable to walk *down* the Neckar as up it, and it could not be needful to walk both ways. There were some nice German people in our compartment. I got to talking some pretty private matters

OUR START. (BY HARRIS.)

presently, and Harris became nervous; so he nudged me and said,—

"Speak in German,—these Germans may understand English."

I did so, and it was well I did; for it turned out that there was not a German in that party who did not understand English perfectly. It is curious how wide-spread our language is in Germany. After a while some of those folks got out and a German gentleman and his two young daughters got in. I spoke in German to one of the latter several times, but without result. Finally she said,—

'Ich verstehe nur Deutch und Englische,"—or words to that effect. That is, "I don't understand any language but German and English."

And sure enough, not only she but her father and sister spoke English. So after that we had all the talk we wanted; and we wanted a good deal, for they were very agreeable people. They were greatly interested in our costumes; especially the alpenstocks, for they had not seen any before.

They said that the Neckar road was perfectly level, so we must be going to Switzerland or some other rugged country; and asked us if we did not find the walking pretty fatiguing in such warm weather. But we said no.

We reached Wimpfen,—I think it was Wimpfen,—in about three hours, and got out, not the least tired; found a good hotel and ordered beer and dinner,—then took

AN UNKNOWN COSTUME.

a stroll through the venerable old village. It was very picturesque and tumble-down, and dirty and interesting. It had queer houses five hundred years old, in it and a military tower, 115 feet high, which had stood there more than ten centuries. I made a little sketch of it. I kept a copy, but gave the original to the Burgomaster. I think the original was better than the copy, because it had more windows in it and the grass stood up better and had a brisker look. There was none around the tower though; I composed the grass myself, from studies I made in a field by Heidelberg in Hämmerling's time. The man on top, looking at the view, is apparently too large, but I found he could not be made smaller, conveniently. I wanted him there, and I wanted him visible, so I thought out a way to manage it; I composed the picture from two points of view; the spectator is to observe the man from about where that flag is, and he must observe the tower itself from the ground. This harmonizes the seeming discrepancy.

Near an old Cathedral, under a shed, were three crosses of stone,—mouldy and damaged things, bearing life-size stone figures. The two thieves were dressed in the fanciful court costumes of the middle of the sixteenth century, while the Savior was nude, with the exception of a cloth around the loins.

THE TOWER.

We had dinner under the green trees in a garden belonging to the hotel and overlooking the Neckar; then, after a smoke, we went to bed. We had a refreshing nap, then got up about three in the afternoon and put on our panoply. As we tramped gaily out at the gate of the town, we overtook a peasant's cart, partly laden with odds and ends of cabbages and similar vegetable rubbish, and drawn by a

SLOW BUT SURE.

small cow and a smaller donkey yoked together. It was a pretty slow concern, but it got us into Heilbronn before dark, —five miles, or possibly it was seven.

We stopped at the very same inn which the famous old robber knight and rough fighter, Götz von Berlichingen, abode in after he got out of captivity in the Square Tower of Heilbronn between three hundred and fifty and four hundred years ago. Harris and I occupied the same room which he had occupied and the same paper had not all peeled off the walls yet. The furniture was quaint old carved stuff, full four hundred years old, and some of the smells were over a thousand. There was a hook in the wall, which the landlord said the terrific old Götz used to hang his iron hand on when he took it off to go to bed. This room was very large,—it might be called immense,—and it was on the first floor; which means it was in the second story, for in Europe the houses are so high that they do not count the first story, else they would get tired climbing before they got to the top. The wall paper was a fiery red, with huge gold figures in it, well smirched by time, and it covered all the doors. These doors fitted so snugly and continued the figures of the paper so unbrokenly, that when they were closed one had to go feeling and searching along the wall to find them. There was a stove in the corner,—one of those tall, square, stately white porcelain things that looks like a monument and keeps you thinking of death when you ought to be enjoying your travels. The windows looked out on a little alley, and over that into a stable and some poultry and pig yards in the rear of some tenement houses. There were the customary two beds in the room, one in one end of it, the other in the other, about an old-fashioned brass-mounted, single-barreled pistol-shot apart. They were fully as narrow as the usual German bed, too, and had the German bed's ineradicable habit of spilling the blankets on the floor every time you forgot yourself and went to sleep.

A round-table as large as King Arthur's stood in the centre of the room; while the waiters were getting ready to serve our dinner on it we all went out to see the renowned clock on the front of the municipal buildings.

CHAPTER XII.

THE *Rathhaus,* or municipal building, is of the quaintest and most picturesque Middle-Age architecture. It has a massive portico and steps, before it, heavily balustraded, and adorned with life-size rusty iron knights in complete armor. The clock-face on the front of the building is very large and of curious pattern. Ordinarily a gilded angel strikes the hour on a big bell with a hammer; as the striking ceases, a life-size figure of Time raises its hour-glass and turns it; two golden rams advance and butt each other; a gilded cock lifts its wings; but the main features are two great angels, who stand on each side of the dial with long horns at their lips; it was said that they blew melodious blasts on these horns every hour,—but they did not do it for us. We were told, later, that they blew only at night, when the town was still.

Within the *Rathhaus* were a number of huge wild boar's heads, preserved, and mounted on brackets along the wall; they bore inscriptions telling who killed them and how many hundred years ago it was done. One room in the building was devoted to the preservation of ancient archives. There they showed us no end of aged documents; some were signed by Popes, some by Tilly and other great Generals, and one was a letter written and subscribed by Götz von Berlichingen in Heilbronn in 1519 just after his release from the Square Tower.

7   107

This fine old robber-knight was a devoutly and sincerely religious man, hospitable, charitable to the poor, fearless in fight, active, enterprising, and possessed of a large and generous nature. He had in him a quality which was rare in that rough time,—the quality of being able to overlook moderate injuries, and of being able to forgive and forget mortal ones as soon as he had soundly trounced the authors of them. He was prompt to take up any poor devil's quarrel and risk his neck to right him. The common folk held him dear, and his memory is still green in ballad and tradition. He used to go on the highway and rob rich wayfarers; and other times he would swoop down from his high castle on the hills of the Neckar and capture passing cargoes of merchandize. In his memoirs he piously thanks the Giver of all Good for remembering him in his needs and delivering sundry such cargoes into his hands at times when only special providences could have relieved him. He was a doughty warrior and found a deep joy in battle. In an assault upon a stronghold in Bavaria when he was only twenty-three years old, his right hand was shot away, but he was so interested in the fight that he did not observe it for a while. He said that the iron hand which was made for him afterward, and which he wore for more than half a century, was nearly as clever a member as the fleshy one had been. I was glad to get a fac-simile of the letter written by this fine old German Robin Hood, though I was not able to read it. He was a better artist with his sword than with his pen.

We went down by the river and saw the Square Tower. It was a very venerable structure, very strong, and very unornamental. There was no opening near the ground. They had to use a ladder to get into it, no doubt.

We visited the principal church, also,—a curious old structure, with a tower-like spire adorned with all sorts of grotesque images. The inner walls of the church were placarded with large mural tablets of copper, bearing engraved inscriptions celebrating the merits of old Heilbronn worthies of two or three centuries ago, and also bearing rudely painted effigies

THE ROBBER CHIEF.

of themselves and their families tricked out in the queer costumes of those days. The head of the family sat in the foreground, and beyond him extended a sharply receding and diminishing row of sons; facing him sat his wife, and beyond her extended a long row of diminishing daughters. The family was usually large, but the perspective bad.

Then we hired the hack and the horse which Götz von Berlichingen used to use, and drove several miles into the country to visit the place called *Weibertreu,*—Wife's Fidelity I suppose it means. It was a feudal castle of the Middle Ages. When we reached its neighborhood we found it was beautifully situated, but on top of a mound, or hill, round and tolerably steep, and about two hundred feet high. Therefore, as the sun was blazing hot, we did not climb up there, but took the place on trust, and observed it from a distance while the horse leaned up against a fence and rested. The place has no interest except that which is lent it by its legend, which is a very pretty one—to this effect:

THE LEGEND.

In the Middle Ages, a couple of young dukes, brothers, took opposite sides in one of the wars, the one fighting for the Emperor, the other against him. One of them owned the castle and village on top of the mound which I have been speaking of, and in his absence his brother came with his knights and soldiers and began a siege. It was a long and tedious business, for the people made a stubborn and faithful defense. But at last their supplies ran out and starvation began its work; more fell by hunger than by the missiles of the enemy. They by and by surrendered, and begged for charitable terms. But the beleaguering prince was so incensed against them for their long resistance that he said he would spare none but the women and children,—all the men should be put to the sword without exception, and all their goods destroyed. Then the women came and fell on their knees and begged for the lives of their husbands.

"No," said the prince, not a man of them shall escape alive; you yourselves, shall go with your children into house-

less and friendless banishment; but that you may not starve
I grant you this one grace, that each woman may bear with
her from this place as much of her most valuable property
as she is able to carry.

Very well, presently the gates swung open and out filed
those women carrying their *husbands* on their shoulders.
The besiegers, furious at the trick, rushed forward to slaughter the men, but the Duke step-
ped between and said,—

"No, put up your swords,—
a prince's word is inviolable."

When we got back to the
hotel, King Arthur's Round
Table was ready for us in its
white drapery, and the head
waiter and his first assistant, in
swallow-tails and white cravats,
brought in the soup and the
hot plates at once.

Mr. X. had ordered the dinner, and when the wine came
on, he picked up a bottle,
glanced at the label, and then
turned to the grave, the melancholy, the sepulchral head
waiter and said it was not the
sort of wine he had asked for.
The head waiter picked up the
bottle, cast his undertaker-eye
on it and said,—

W.F.B.

AN HONEST MAN.

"It is true; I beg pardon."
Then he turned on his subordinate and calmly said, "Bring
another label."

At the same time he slid the present label off with his
hand and laid it aside; it had been newly put on, its paste
was still wet. When the new label came, he put it on; our
French wine being now turned into German wine, according

to desire, the head waiter went blandly about his other
duties, as if the working of this sort of miracle was a common and easy thing to him.

Mr. X. said he had not known, before, that there were
people honest enough to do this miracle in public, but he
was aware that thousands upon thousands of labels were
imported into America from Europe every year, to enable
dealers to furnish to their customers in a quiet and inex-
pensive way, all the different kinds of foreign wines they
might require.

THE TOWN BY NIGHT.

We took a turn
around the town, after
dinner, and found it
fully as interesting in
the moonlight as it had
been in the day time.
The streets were nar-
row and roughly paved,
and there was not a
sidewalk or a street
lamp anywhere. The
dwellings were centu-
ries old, and vast
enough for hotels.
They widened all the
way up; the stories
projected further and
further forward and
aside as they ascended,
and the long rows
of lighted windows,
filled with little bits of panes, curtained with figured white
muslin and adorned outside with boxes of flowers, made a
pretty effect. The moon was bright, and the light and
shadow very strong; and nothing could be more picturesque
than those curving streets, with their rows of huge high
gables leaning far over toward each other in a friendly

gossipping way, and the crowds below drifting through the alternating blots of gloom and mellow bars of moonlight. Nearly everybody was abroad, chatting, singing, romping, or massed in lazy comfortable attitudes in the doorways.

In one place there was a public building which was fenced about with a thick, rusty chain, which sagged from post to post in a succession of low swings. The pavement, here, was made of heavy blocks of stone. In the glare of the moon a party of barefooted*children were swinging on those chains and having a noisy good time. They were not the

GENERATIONS OF BARE FEET.

first ones who had done that; even their great-great-grand-fathers had not been the first to do it when they were children. The strokes of the bare feet had worn grooves inches deep in the stone flags; it had taken many generations of swinging children to accomplish that. Everywhere in the town were the mould and decay that go with antiquity, and evidence it; but I do not know that anything else gave us so vivid a sense of the old age of Heilbronn as those foot-worn grooves in the paving stones.

CHAPTER XIII.

WHEN we got back to the hotel I wound and set the pedometer and put it in my pocket, for I was to carry it next day and keep record of the miles we made. The work which we had given the instrument to do during the day which had just closed, had not fatigued it perceptibly.

We were in bed by ten, for we wanted to be up and away on our tramp homeward with the dawn. I hung fire, but Harris went to sleep at once. I hate a man who goes to sleep at once; there is a sort of indefinable something about it which is not exactly an insult, and yet is an insolence; and one which is hard to bear, too. I lay there fretting over this injury, and trying to go to sleep; but the harder I tried, the wider awake I grew. I got to feeling very lonely in the dark, with no company but an undigested dinner. My mind got a start by and by, and began to consider the beginning of every subject which has ever been thought of; but it never went further than the beginning; it was touch and go; it fled from topic to topic with a frantic speed. At the end of an hour my head was in a perfect whirl and I was dead tired, fagged out.

The fatigue was so great that it presently began to make some head against the nervous excitement; while imagining myself wide awake, I would really doze into momentary

114

unconsciousnesses, and come suddenly out of them with a
physical jerk which nearly
wrenched my joints apart,
—the delusion of the in-
stant being that I was tumbling backwards over a precipice. After I had fallen
over eight or nine preci-
pices and thus found out
that one half of my brain
had been asleep eight or
n i n e times without the
wide-awake, hard-working
other half suspecting it,
the periodical unconsciousnesses began to extend their
spell gradually over more
of my brain-territory, and
at last I sank into a drowse
which grew deeper and
deeper and was doubtless
just on the very point of
becoming a solid, blessed,
dreamless stupor, when,
—what was that ?

My dulled faculties drag-
ged themselves partly back
to life and took a receptive
attitude. Now out of an
immense, a limitless dis-
tance, came a something
which grew and grew, and
approached, and presently
was recognizable as a sound,

OUR BEDROOM.

—it had rather seemed to be a feeling, before. This sound
was a mile away, now—perhaps it was the murmur of a storm ;
and now it was nearer,—not a quarter of a mile away ; was

it the muffled rasping and grinding of distant machinery? No, it came still nearer; was it the measured tramp of a marching troop? But it came nearer still, and still nearer, —and at last it was right in the room: it was merely a mouse gnawing the wood-work. So I had held my breath all that time for such a trifle.

Well, what was done could not be helped; I would go to sleep at once and make up the lost time. That was a thoughtless thought. Without intending it,—hardly knowing it,—I fell to listening intently to that sound, and even unconsciously counting the strokes of the mouse's nutmeg-grater. Presently I was deriving exquisite suffering from this employment, yet maybe I could have endured it if the mouse had attended steadily to his work; but he did not do that; he stopped every now and then, and I suffered more while waiting and listening for him to begin again than I did while he was gnawing. Along at first I was mentally offering a reward of five,—six,—seven,—ten— dollars for that mouse; but toward the last I was offering rewards which were entirely beyond my means. I close-reefed my ears,—that is to say, I bent the flaps of them down and furled them into five or six folds, and pressed them against the hearing-orifice,—but it did no good: the faculty was so sharpened by nervous excitement that it was become a microphone and could hear through the overlays without trouble.

My anger grew to a frenzy. I finally did what all persons before me have done, clear back to Adam, —resolved to throw something. I reached down and got my walking shoes, then sat up in bed and listened, in order to exactly locate the noise. But I couldn't do it; it was as unlocatable as a cricket's noise; and where one thinks that that is, is always the very place where it isn't. So I presently hurled a shoe at random, and with a vicious vigor. It struck the wall over Harris's head and fell down on him; I had not imagined I could throw so far. It woke Harris, and I was

glad of it until I found he was not angry ; then I was sorry.
He soon went to sleep again, which pleased me ; but straightway the mouse began again, which roused my temper once
more. I did not
want to wake Har-
ris a second time,
but t h e gnawing
continued until I
w a s compelled to
throw the o t h e r
shoe. This time I
broke a mirror,—
there were two in
the room,—I g o t
the largest one, of
course. H a r r i s
woke again, but did
not complain, and
I was sorrier than

PRACTICING.

ever. I resolved that I would suffer all possible torture
before I would disturb him a third time.

The mouse eventually retired, and by and by I was sinking to sleep, when a clock began to strike ; I counted, till it
was done, and was about to drowse again when another
clock began ; I counted ; then the two great Rathhaus clock
angels began to send forth soft, rich, melodious blasts from
their long trumpets. I had never heard anything that was so
lovely, or weird, or mysterious,—but when they got to blowing the quarter-hours, they seemed to me to be overdoing
the thing. Every time I dropped off for a moment, a new
noise woke me. Each time I woke I missed my coverlet, and
had to reach down to the floor and get it again.

At last all sleepiness forsook me. I recognized the fact
that I was hopelessly and permanently wide awake. Wide
awake, and feverish and thirsty. When I had lain tossing
there as long as I could endure it, it occurred to me that it

would be a good idea to dress and go out in the great square
and take a refreshing wash in the fountain, and smoke and
reflect there until the remnant of the night was gone.

I believed I could dress in the dark without waking Harris.
I had banished my shoes after the mouse, but my slippers
would do for a summer night. So I rose softly, and gradually got on everything,—down to one sock. I couldn't
seem to get on the track of that sock, any way I could fix it.
But I had to have it; so I went down on my hands and
knees, with one slipper on and the other in my hand, and

PAWING AROUND.

began to paw gently around and rake the floor, but with no
success. I enlarged my circle, and went on pawing and
raking. With every pressure of my knee, how the floor
creaked! and every time I chanced to rake against any article, it seemed to give out thirty-five or thirty-six times more
noise than it would have done in the day time. In those
cases I always stopped and held my breath till I was sure
Harris had not awakened,—then I crept along again. I
moved on and on, but I could not find the sock; I could not
seem to find anything but furniture. I could not remember

that there was much furniture in the room when I went to bed, but the place was alive with it now,—especially chairs, —chairs everywhere,—had a couple of families moved in, in the meantime? And I never could seem to *glance* on one of those chairs, but always struck it full and square with my head. My temper rose, by steady and sure degrees, and as I pawed on and on, I fell to making vicious comments under my breath.

Finally, with a venomous access of irritation, I said I would leave without the sock; so I rose up and made straight for the door,—as I supposed,—and suddenly confronted my dim spectral image in the unbroken mirror. It startled the breath out of me, for an instant; it also showed me that I was lost, and had no sort of idea where I was. When I realized this, I was so angry that I had to sit down on the floor and take hold of something to keep from lifting the roof off with an explosion of opinion. If there had been only one mirror, it might possibly have helped to locate me; but there were two, and two were as bad as a thousand; besides these were on opposite sides of the room. I could see the dim blur of the windows, but in my turned-around condition they were exactly where they ought not to be, and so they only confused me instead of helping me.

I started to get up, and knocked down an umbrella; it made a noise like a pistol-shot when it struck that hard, slick carpetless floor; I grated my teeth and held my breath, —Harris did not stir. I set the umbrella slowly and carefully on end against the wall, but as soon as I took my hand away, its heel slipped from under it, and down it came again with another bang. I shrunk together and listened a moment in silent fury,—no harm done, everything quiet. With the most painstaking care and nicety I stood the umbrella up once more, took my hand away, and down it came again.

I have been strictly reared, but if it had not been so dark and solemn and awful there in that lonely vast room, I do believe I should have said something then which could not be put into a Sunday School book without injuring the sale of it. If my reasoning powers had not been already sapped dry by my harassments, I would have known better than to try to set an umbrella on end on one of those glassy German floors in the dark; it can't be done in the daytime without four failures to one success. I had one comfort, though, —Harris was yet still and silent,—he had not stirred.

The umbrella could not locate me,—there were four standing around the room, and all alike. I thought I would feel along the wall and find the door in that way. I rose up and began this operation, but raked down a picture. It was not a large one, but it made noise enough for a panorama. Harris gave out no sound, but I felt that if I experimented any further with the pictures I should be sure to wake him. Better give up trying to get out. Yes, I would find King Arthur's Round Table once more,—I had already found it several times,—and use it for a base of departure on an exploring tour for my bed; if I could find my bed I could then find my water pitcher; I would quench my raging thirst and turn in. So I started on my hands and knees, because I could go faster that way, and with more confidence, too, and not knock down things. By and by I found the table,—with my head,—rubbed the bruise a little, then rose up and started, with hands abroad and fingers spread, to balance myself. I found a chair; then the wall; then another chair; then a sofa; then an alpenstock, then another sofa; this confounded me, for I had thought there was only one sofa. I hunted up the table again and took a fresh start; found some more chairs.

It occurred to me, now, as it ought to have done before, that as the table was round, it was therefore of no value as a base to aim from; so I moved off once more, and at random among the wilderness of chairs and sofas,—wandered off into unfamiliar regions, and presently knocked a candlestick off a mantel-piece; grabbed at the candlestick and knocked off a lamp; grabbed at the lamp and knocked off a water-pitcher with a rattling crash, and thought to myself, "I've found you at last,—I judged I was close upon you." Harris shouted "murder," and "thieves," and finished with "I'm abso-

lutely drowned."

The crash had roused the house. Mr. X. pranced in, in his long night garment, with a candle, young Z. after him with another candle; a procession swept in at another door, with candles and lanterns,— landlord and two German guests in their nightgowns, and a chambermaid in hers.

I looked around; I was at Harris's bed, a Sabbath day's journey from my own. There

A NIGHT'S WORK.

was only one sofa; it was against the wall; there was only one chair where a body could get at it,—I had been revolving around it like a planet, and colliding with it like a comet half the night.

I explained how I had been employing myself, and why. Then the landlord's party left, and the rest of us set about our preparations for breakfast, for the dawn was ready to break. I glanced furtively at my pedometer, and found I had made 47 miles. But I did not care, for I had come out for a pedestrian tour anyway.

CHAPTER XIV.

WHEN the landlord learned that I and my agent were artists, our party rose perceptibly in his esteem; we rose still higher when he learned that we were making a pedestrian tour of Europe.

He told us all about the Heidelberg road, and which were the best places to avoid and which the best ones to tarry at; he charged me less than cost for the things I broke in the night; he put up a fine luncheon for us and added to it a quantity of great light-green plums, the pleasantest fruit in Germany; he was so anxious to do us honor that he would not allow us to walk out of Heilbronn, but called up Götz von Berlichingen's horse and cab and made us ride.

I made a sketch of the turn-out. It is not a Work, it is only what artists call a "study"—a thing to make a finished picture from. This sketch has several blemishes in it; for instance, the wagon is not traveling as fast as the horse is. This is wrong. Again, the person trying to get out of the way is too small; he is out of perspective, as we say. The two upper lines are not the horse's back, they are the reins; —there seems to be a wheel missing—this would be correct-ed in a finished Work, of course. That thing flying out be-hind is not a flag, it is a curtain. That other thing up there is the sun, but I didn't get enough distance on it. I do not

122

remember, now, what that thing is that is in front of the man who is running, but I think it is a haystack or a woman. This study was exhibited in the Paris Salon of 1879, but did not take any medal; they do not give medals for studies.

We discharged the carriage at the bridge. The river was full of logs,—long, slender, barkless pine logs,—a n d we leaned on the rails of the bridge and watched the men put them together into rafts. These rafts were of a shape and construction to suit the crookedness and extreme narrowness of the N e c k a r. They were from 50 to 1 0 0 yards long, and they gradually tapered from a 9-log breadth at their sterns, to a 3-l o g breadth at their bow-ends. The main part of the steering is done at the bow, with a pole; the 3-log breadth there furnishes r o o m for only the steersman, for these little logs are not larger around than an average young lady's waist. The connections of the several sections of the raft are slack and pliant, so that the raft may be readily bent into any sort of curve required by the shape of the river.

The Neckar is in many places so narrow that a person can

8

throw a dog across it, if he has one ; when it is also sharply curved in such places, the raftsman has to do some pretty nice snug piloting to make the turns.   The river is not always allowed to spread over its whole bed,—which is as much as 30, and sometimes 40, yards wide,—but is split into three equal bodies of water, by stone dikes which throw the main volume, depth, and current, into the central one.   In low water these neat narrow-edged dikes project four or five inches above the surface, like the comb of a submerged roof, but in high water they are overflowed.   A hatful of rain makes high water in the Neckar, and a basketful produces an overflow.

There are dikes abreast the Schloss Hotel, and the current is violently swift at that point.   I used to sit for hours in my glass cage, watching the long, narrow rafts slip along through the central channel, grazing the right-bank dike and aiming carefully for the middle arch of the stone bridge below ; I watched them in this way, and lost all this time hoping to see one of them hit the bridge-pier and wreck itself some- time or other, but was always disappointed.   One was smash- ed there one morning, but I had just stepped into my room a moment to light a pipe, so I lost it.

While I was looking down upon the rafts that morning in Heilbronn, the dare-devil spirit of adventure came suddenly upon me, and I said to my comrades,—

" *I* am going to Heidelberg on a raft. Will you venture with me ? "

Their faces paled a little, but they assented with as good a grace as they could.   Harris wanted **to** cable his mother, —thought it his duty to do that, as he was all she had in this world,—so, while he attended to this, I went down to the longest and finest raft and hailed the captain with a hearty " Ahoy, shipmate ! " which put us upon pleasant terms at once, and we entered upon business.   I said we were on a pedestrian tour to Heidelberg, and would like to take passage with him.   I said this partly through young Z, who spoke German very well, and partly through Mr. X, who spoke it

peculiarly. I can *understand* German as well as the maniac
that invented it, but I *talk* it best through an interpreter.

The captain hitched up his trowsers, then shifted his quid
thoughtfully. Presently he said just what I was expecting
he would say,—that he had no license to carry passengers,

THE CAPTAIN.

and therefore was afraid the law would be after him in case
the matter got noised about or any accident happened. So
I *chartered* the raft and the crew and took all the responsi-
bilities on myself.

With a rattling song the starboard watch bent to their work and hove the cable short, then got the anchor home, and our bark moved off with a stately stride, and soon was bowling along at about two knots an hour.

Our party were grouped amidships. At first the talk was a little gloomy, and ran mainly upon the shortness of life, the uncertainty of it, the perils which beset it, and the need and wisdom of being always prepared for the worst; this shaded off into low-voiced references to the dangers of the deep, and kindred matters; but as the gray east began to redden and the mysterious solemnity and silence of the dawn to give place to the joy-songs of the birds, the talk took a cheerier tone, and our spirits began to rise steadily.

Germany, in the summer, is the perfection of the beautiful, but nobody has understood, and realized, and enjoyed the utmost possibilities of this soft and peaceful beauty unless he has voyaged down the Neckar on a raft. The motion of a raft is the needful motion; it is gentle, and gliding, and smooth, and noiseless; it calms down all feverish activities, it soothes to sleep all nervous hurry and impatience; under its restful influence all the troubles and vexations and sorrows that harass the mind vanish away, and existence becomes a dream, a charm, a deep and tranquil ecstasy. How it contrasts with hot and perspiring pedestrianism, and dusty and deafening railroad rush, and tedious jolting behind tired horses over blinding white roads!

We went slipping silently along, between the green and fragrant banks, with a sense of pleasure and contentment that grew, and grew, all the time. Sometimes the banks were over-hung with thick masses of willows that wholly hid the ground behind; sometimes we had noble hills on one hand, clothed densely with foliage to their tops, and on the other hand open levels blazing with poppies, or clothed in the rich blue of the corn-flower; sometimes we drifted in the shadow of forests, and sometimes along the margin of long stretches of velvety grass, fresh and green and bright, a tireless charm to the eye. And the birds!—they were everywhere; they swept back and forth across the river constantly, and their jubilant music was never stilled.

It was a deep and satisfying pleasure to see the sun create the new morning, and gradually, patiently, lovingly, clothe it on with splendor after splendor, and glory after glory, till the miracle was complete. How different is this marvel observed from a raft, from what it is when one observes it through the dingy windows of a railway station in some wretched village while he munches a petrified sandwich and waits for the train.

CHAPTER. XV.

MEN and women and cattle were at work in the dewy fields by this time. The people often stepped aboard the raft, as we glided along the grassy shores, and gossiped with us and with the crew for a hundred yards or so, then stepped ashore again, refreshed by the ride.

Only the men did this; the women were too busy. The women do all kinds of work on the continent. They dig, they hoe, they reap, they sow, they bear monstrous burdens on their backs, they shove similar ones long distances on wheelbarrows, they drag the cart when there is no dog or lean cow to drag it,—and when there is, they assist the dog or cow. Age is no matter,—the older the woman, the stronger she is, apparently. On the farm a woman's duties are not defined,—she does a little of everything; but in the towns it is different, there she only does certain things, the men do the rest. For instance, a hotel chambermaid has nothing to do but make beds and fires in fifty or sixty rooms, bring towels and candles, and fetch several tons of water up several flights of stairs, a hundred pounds at a time, in prodigious metal pitchers. She does not have to work more than eighteen or twenty hours a day, and she can always get down on her knees and scrub the floors of halls and closets when she is tired and needs a rest.

As the morning advanced and the weather grew hot, we took off our outside clothing and sat in a row along the edge of the raft and enjoyed the scenery, with our sun umbrellas over our heads and our legs dangling in the water. Every

"A DEEP AND TRANQUIL ECSTASY."

now and then we plunged in and had a swim. Every projecting grassy cape had its joyous group of naked children, the boys to themselves and the girls to themselves, the latter usually in care of some motherly dame who sat in the shade of a tree with her knitting. The little boys swam out to us, sometimes, but the little maids stood knee deep in the water and stopped their splashing and frolicking to inspect the raft with their innocent eyes as it drifted by. Once we turned a corner suddenly and surprised a slender girl of twelve years or upwards, just stepping into the water. She had not time to run, but she did what answered just as well; she promptly drew a lithe young willow bough athwart her white body with one hand, and then contemplated us with a simple and untroubled interest. Thus she stood while we glided by. She was a pretty creature, and she and her willow bough made a very pretty picture, and one which could not offend the modesty of the most fastidious spectator. Her white skin had a low bank of fresh green willows for background and effective contrast,—for she stood against them,—and

"WHICH ANSWERED JUST AS WELL."

above and out of them projected the eager faces and white shoulders of two smaller girls.

Towards noon we heard the inspiriting cry,—

"Sail ho!"

"Where away?" shouted the captain.

"Three points off the weather bow!"

We ran forward to see the vessel. It proved to be a steamboat,—for they had begun to run a steamer up the Neckar, for the first time in May. She was a tug, and one of very peculiar build and aspect. I had often watched her from the hotel, and wondered how she propelled herself, for apparently she had no propeller or paddles. She came churning along, now, making a deal of noise of one kind and another, and aggravating it every now and then by blowing a hoarse whistle. She had nine keel-boats hitched on behind and following after her in a long, slender rank. We met her in a narrow place, between dikes, and there was hardly room for us both in the cramped passage. As she went grinding and groaning by, we perceived the secret of her moving impulse. She did not drive herself up the river with paddles or propeller, she pulled herself by hauling on a great chain. This chain is laid in the bed of the river and is only fastened at the two ends. It is seventy miles long. It comes in over the boat's bow, passes around a drum, and is payed out astern. She pulls on that chain, and so drags herself up the river or down it. She has neither bow nor stern, strictly speaking, for she has a long-bladed rudder on each end and she never turns around. She uses both rudders all the time, and they are powerful enough to enable her to turn to the right or the left and steer around curves, in spite of the strong resistance of the chain. I would not have believed that that impossible thing could be done; but I saw it done, and therefore I know that there is one impossible thing which *can* be done. What miracle will man attempt next?

We met many big keel boats on their way up, using sails, mule power, and profanity—a tedious and laborious business. A wire rope led from the foretop mast to the file of mules on the tow-path a hundred yards ahead, and by dint of much banging and swearing and urging, the detachment of drivers managed to get a speed of two or three miles an hour out of the mules against the stiff current. The Neckar has always been used as a canal, and thus has given employment to a great many men and animals; but now that this steamboat is able, with a small crew and a bushel or so of coal, to take nine keel boats farther up the river in one hour than thirty men and thirty mules can do it in two, it is believed that the old-fashioned towing industry is on its death-bed. A second steamboat began work in the Neckar three months after the first one was put in service.

At noon we stepped ashore and bought some bottled beer and got some chickens cooked, while the raft waited; then

we immediately put to sea again, and had our dinner while
the beer was cold and the chickens hot. There is no pleasanter place for such a meal than a raft that is gliding down
the winding Neckar past green meadows and wooded hills,
and slumbering villages, and craggy heights graced with
crumbling towers and battlements.

In one place we saw a nicely dressed German gentleman

LIFE ON A RAFT.

without any spectacles. Before I could come to anchor he
had got away. It was a great pity. I so wanted to make
a sketch of him. The captain comforted me for my loss,
however, by saying that the man was without any doubt a
fraud who had spectacles, but kept them in his pocket in
order to make himself conspicuous.

Below Hassmersheim we passed Hornberg, Götz von Berlichingen's old castle. It stands on a bold elevation 200 feet
above the surface of the river; it has high vine-clad walls
enclosing trees, and a peaked tower about 75 feet high.
The steep hillside, from the castle clear down to the water's
edge, is terraced, and clothed thick with grape vines. This
is like farming a mansard roof. All the steeps along that
part of the river which furnish the proper exposure, are given
up to the grape. That region is a great producer of Rhine
wines. The Germans are exceedingly fond of Rhine wines;

they are put up in tall, slender bottles, and are considered a pleasant beverage. One tells them from vinegar by the label.

The Hornberg hill is to be tunneled, and the new railway will pass under the castle.

THE CAVE OF THE SPECTRE.

Two miles below Hornberg castle is a cave in a low cliff, which the captain of the raft said had once been occupied by a beautiful heiress of Hornberg,—the Lady Gertrude,—in the old times. It was seven hundred years ago. She had a number of rich and noble lovers and one poor and obscure

one, Sir Wendel Lobenfeld. With the native chuckleheadedness of the heroine of romance, she preferred the poor and obscure lover. With the native sound judgment of the father of a heroine of romance, the von Berlichingen of that day shut his daughter up in his donjon keep, or his oubliette, or his culverin, or some such place,

LADY GERTRUDE.

and resolved that she should stay there until she selected a husband from among her rich and noble lovers. The latter visited her and persecuted her with their supplications, but without effect, for her heart was true to her poor despised Crusader, who was fighting in the Holy Land. Finally she resolved that she would endure the attentions of the rich lovers no longer; so one stormy night she escaped and went down the river and hid herself in the cave on the other side. Her father ransacked the country for her, but found not a trace of her. As the days went by, and still no tidings of her came, his conscience began to torture him, and he caused proclamation to be made that if she were yet living and would return, he would oppose her no longer, she might marry whom she would. The months dragged on, all hope forsook the old man, he ceased from his customary pursuits and pleasures, he devoted himself to pious works, and longed for the deliverance of death.

Now just at midnight, every night, the lost heiress stood in the mouth of her cave, arrayed in white robes, and sang a little love ballad which her Crusader had made for her. She judged that if he came home alive the superstitious peasants would tell him about the ghost that sang in the cave, and that as soon as they described the ballad he would know that none but he and she knew that song, therefore he would suspect that she was alive, and would come and find her. As time went on, the people of the region became sorely distressed about the Spectre of the Haunted Cave. It was said that ill luck of one kind or another always overtook any one who had the misfortune to hear that song. Eventually, every calamity that happened thereabouts was laid at the door of that music. Consequently no boatman would consent to pass the cave at night; the peasants shunned the place, even in the daytime.

But the faithful girl sang on, night after night, month after month, and patiently waited; her reward must come at last. Five years dragged by, and still, every night at midnight, the plaintive tones floated out over the silent land, while the distant boatmen and peasants thrust their fingers into their ears and shuddered out a prayer.

And now came the Crusader home, bronzed and battle-scarred, but bringing a great and splendid fame to lay at the feet of his bride. The old lord of Hornberg received him as a son, and wanted him to stay by him and be the comfort and blessing of his age; but the tale of that young girl's devotion to him and its pathetic consequences, made a changed man of the knight. He could not enjoy his well earned rest. He said his heart was broken, he would give the remnant of his life to high deeds in the cause of humanity, and so find a worthy death and a blessed reunion with the brave true

MOUTH OF THE CAVERN.

heart whose love had more honored him than all his victories
in war.

When the people heard this resolve of his, they came and
told him there was a pitiless dragon in human disguise in the
Haunted Cave, a dread creature which no knight had yet
been bold enough to face, and begged him to rid the land of
its desolating presence. He said he would do it. They told
him about the song, and when he asked what song it was,
they said the memory of it was gone, for nobody had been
hardy enough to listen to it for the past four years and more.

Towards midnight the Crusader came floating down the
river in a boat, with his trusty cross-bow in his hands. He
drifted silently through the dim reflections of the crags and
trees, with his intent eyes fixed upon the low cliff which he
was approaching. As he drew nearer, he discerned the black
mouth of the cave. Now,—is that a white figure? Yes.
The plaintive song begins to well forth and float away over

A FATAL MISTAKE.

meadow and river,—the cross-bow is slowly raised to position,
a steady aim is taken, the bolt flies straight to the mark,—
the figure sinks down, still singing, the knight takes the wool

out of his ears, and recognizes the old ballad,—too late ! Ah, if he had only not put the wool in his ears !

The Crusader went away to the wars again, and presently fell in battle, fighting for the Cross. Tradition says that during several centuries the spirit of the unfortunate girl sang nightly from the cave at midnight, but the music carried no curse with it; and although many listened for the mysterious sounds, few were favored, since only those could hear them who had never failed in a trust. It is believed that the singing still continues, but it is known that nobody has heard it during the present century.

Bird waiting for a Fish, a
common Spectacle.
(Perspective of Bird not correct.)

Raft coming down between stone Dikes.

Raft curving itself through
crooked piece of River. (Merely
a study not a finished
picture.)

BANNING ON THE NECKAR.

CHAPTER XVI.

AN ANCIENT LEGEND OF THE RHINE.

THE last legend reminds one of the "Lorelei"—a legend of the Rhine. There is a song called "The Lorelei."

Germany is rich in folk-songs, and the words and airs of several of them are peculiarly beautiful,—but "The Lorelei" is the people's favorite. I could not endure it at first but by and by it began to take hold of me, and now there is no tune which I like so well.

It is not possible that it is much known in America, else I should have heard it there. The fact that I never heard it there, is evidence that there are others in my country who have fared likewise ; therefore, for the sake of these, I mean to print the words and the music in this chapter. And I will refresh the reader's memory by printing the legend of the Lorelei too. I have it by me in the "Legends of the Rhine," done into English by the wildly gifted Garnham, Bachelor of Arts. I print the legend partly to refresh my own memory, too, for I have never read it before.

THE LEGEND.

Lore, (two syllables,) was a water nymph who used to sit on a high rock called Ley or Lei (pronounced like our word *lie*) in the Rhine, and lure boatmen to destruction in a furious rapid which marred the channel at that spot. She so bewitched them with her plaintive songs and her wonderful beauty that they forgot everything else to gaze up at her,

140

and so they presently drifted among the broken reefs and were
lost.

In those old, old times, the count Bruno lived in a great
castle near there with his son the count Hermann, a youth of
twenty.   Hermann had heard
a great deal about the beautiful Lore, and had finally fallen
very deeply in love with her
without having yet seen her.
So he used to wander to the
neighborhood of the Lei,
evenings, with his Zither and
" Express his Longing in low
Singing," as Garnham says.
On one of these occasions,
"suddenly there hovered
around the top of the rock a
brightness of unequaled clearness and color, which, in in-
creasingly smaller circles
thickened, was the enchanting
figure of the beautiful Lore.
" An unintentional cry of

THE LORELEI.

Joy escaped the Youth, he let his Zither fall, and with extended arms he called out the name of the enigmatical Being, who
seemed to stoop lovingly to him and beckon to him in a
friendly manner; indeed, if his ear did not deceive him, she
called his name with unutterable sweet Whispers, proper to
love.   Beside himself with delight the youth lost his Senses
and sank senseless to the earth."

After that he was a changed person.   He went dreaming
about, thinking only of his fairy and caring for naught else
in the world.   " The old count saw with affliction this changement in his son," whose cause he could not divine, and tried
to divert his mind into cheerful channels, but to no purpose.
Then the old count used authority.   He commanded the

youth to betake himself to the camp.   Obedience was promised.   Garnham says:

"It was on the evening before his departure, as he wished still once to visit the Lei and offer to the Nymph of the Rhine his Sighs, the tones of his Zither, and his Songs.   He went, in his boat, this time accompanied by a faithful squire, down the stream.   The moon shed her silvery light over the whole Country; the steep bank mountains appeared in the most fantastical shapes, and the high oaks on either side bowed their Branches on Hermann's passing.   As soon as he approached the Lei, and was aware of the surf-waves, his attendant was seized with an inexpressible Anxiety and he begged permission to land; but the Knight swept the strings of his Guitar and sang:

> "Once I saw thee in dark night,
>   In supernatural Beauty bright;
> Of Light-rays, was the Figure wove,
>   To share its light, locked-hair strove.

> "Thy Garment color wave-dove,
>   By thy hand the sign of love,
> Thy eyes sweet enchantment,
>   Raying to me, oh! entrancement.

> "O, wert thou but my sweetheart,
>   How willingly thy love to part!
> With delight I should be bound
>   To thy rocky house in deep ground."

That Hermann should have gone to that place at all, was not wise; that he should have gone with such a song as that in his mouth was a most serious mistake.   The Lorelei did not "call his name in unutterable sweet Whispers" this time. No, that song naturally worked an instant and thorough "changement" in her; and not only that, but it stirred the bowels of the whole afflicted region round about there,— for,—

"Scarcely had these tones sounded, everywhere there began tumult and sound, as if voices above and below the water.   On the Lei rose flames, the Fairy stood above, as that time, and beckoned with her right hand clearly and urgently to the infatuated Knight, while with a staff in her left she called the waves to her service. They began to mount heavenward; the boat was upset, mocking every exertion; the waves rose to the gunwale, and splitting on the

hard stones, the Boat broke into Pieces. The youth sank into the depths, but the squire was thrown on shore by a powerful wave."

The bitterest things have been said about the Lorelei during many centuries, but surely her conduct upon this occasion entitles her to our respect. One feels drawn tenderly toward her and is moved to forget her many crimes and remember only the good deed that crowned and closed her career.

" The Fairy was never more seen; but her enchanting tones

THE LOVER'S FATE.

have often been heard. In the beautiful, refreshing, still nights of spring, when the moon pours her silver light over the Country, the listening shipper hears from the rushing of the waves, the echoing Clang of a wonderfully charming voice, which sings a song from the crystal castle, and with sorrow and fear he thinks on the young Count Hermann, seduced by the Nymph."

Here is the music, and the German words by Heinrich Heine. This song has been a favorite in Germany for forty years, and will remain a favorite always, maybe:

Lorelei.

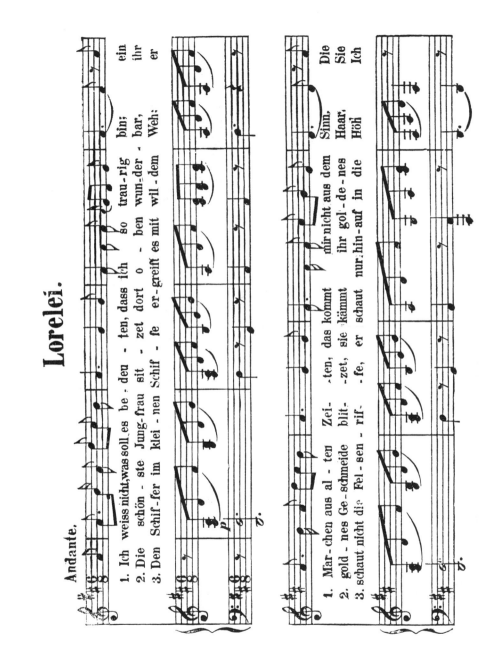

Andante.

1. Ich weiss nicht, was soll es be - deu - ten, dass ich so trau-rig bin;
2. Die schön - ste Jung-frau sit - zet dort o - ben wun-der - bar,
3. Den Schif - fer im klei - nen Schif - fe er - greift es mit wil - dem Weh:

1. Mär - chen aus al - ten Zei - ten, das kommt mir nicht aus dem Sinn. Die
2. gold - nes Ge - schmeide blit - zet, sie kämmt ihr gol - de - nes Haar, Sie
3. schaut nicht die Fel - sen - rif - fe, er schaut nur hin - auf in die Höh' Ich

ein
ihr
er

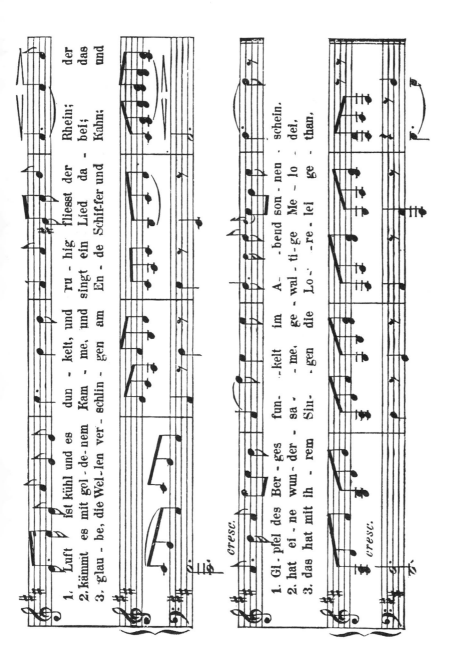

1. Luft ist kühl und es dun - kelt, und ru - hig fliesst der Rhein; der
2. kämmt es mit gol - de - nem Kam - me, und singt ein Lied da - bei; das
3. glau - be, die Wel - len ver - schlin - gen am En - de Schif-fer und Kahn; und

1. Gi - pfel des Ber - ges fun - kelt im A - bend son - nen - schein.
2. hat ei - ne wun - der - sa - me, ge - wal - ti - ge Me - lo - dei,
3. das hat mit ih - rem Sin - gen die Lo - re - lei ge - than,

I have a prejudice against people who print things in a foreign language and add no translation. When I am the reader, and the author considers me able to do the translating myself, he pays me quite a nice compliment,—but if he would do the translating for me I would try to get along without the compliment.

If I were at home, no doubt I could get a translation of this poem, but I am abroad and can't; therefore I will make a translation myself. It may not be a good one, for poetry is out of my line, but it will serve my purpose,—which is, to give the un-German young girl a jingle of words to hang the tune on until she can get hold of a good version, made by some one who is a poet and knows how to convey a poetical thought from one language to another.

THE LORELEI.

I cannot divine what it meaneth,
  This haunting nameless pain:
A tale of the bygone ages
  Keeps brooding through my brain:

The faint air cools in the gloaming,
  And peaceful flows the Rhine,
The thirsty summits are drinking
  The sunset's flooding wine;

The loveliest maiden is sitting
  High-throned in yon blue air,
Her golden jewels are shining,
  She combs her golden hair;

She combs with a comb that is golden,
  And sings a weird refrain
That steeps in a deadly enchantment
  The list'ner's ravished brain:

The doomed in his drifting shallop,
  Is tranced with the sad sweet tone,
He sees not the yawning breakers,
  He sees but the maid alone:

The pitiless billows engulf him!—
  So perish sailor and bark;
And this, with her baleful singing,
  Is the Lorelei's grewsome work.

I have a translation by Garnham, Bachelor of Arts, in the
"Legends of the Rhine," but it would not answer the purpose I mentioned above, because the measure is too nobly
irregular; it don't fit the tune snugly enough; in places it
hangs over at the ends too far, and in other places one runs
out of words before he gets to the end of a bar. Still, Garnham's translation has high merits, and I am not dreaming of
leaving it out of my book. I believe this poet is wholly
unknown in America and England; I take peculiar pleasure
in bringing him forward because I consider that I discovered
him:

THE LORELEI.

Translated by L. W. Garnham, B. A.

I do not known what it signifies.
   That I am so sorrowful?
A fable of old Times so terrifies,
   Leaves my heart so thoughtful.

The air is cool and it darkens,
   And calmly flows the Rhine;
The summit of the mountain hearkens
   In evening sunshine line.

The most beautiful Maiden entrances
   Above wonderfully there,
Her beautiful golden attire glances,
   She combs her golden hair.

With golden comb so lustrous,
   And thereby a song sings,
It has a tone so wondrous,
   That powerful melody rings.

The shipper in the little ship
   It effects with woes sad might;
He does not see the rocky clip,
   He only regards dreaded height.

I believe the turbulent waves
   Swallow at last shipper and boat;
She with her singing craves
   All to visit her magic moat.

No translation could be closer. He has got in all the facts;

and in their regular order too.   There is not a statistic want
ing.   It is as succinct as an invoice.   That is what a translation ought to be; it should exactly reflect the thought of the
original.   You can't *sing* "Above wonderfully there," because
it simply won't go to the tune, without damaging the singer;
but it is a most clingingly exact translation of *Dort oben wun-
derbar*,—fits it like a blister.   Mr. Garnham's reproduction
has other merits,—a hundred of them,—but it is not necessary
to point them out.   They will be detected.

No one with a specialty can hope to have a monopoly of
it.   Even Garnham has a rival.   Mr. X. had a small pamphlet
with him which he had bought while on a visit to Munich.
It was entitled "A Catalogue of Pictures in the Old Pin-
acotek," and was written in a peculiar kind of English.   Here
are a few extracts:

"It is not permitted to make use of the work in question
to a publication of the same contents as well as to the pirated
edition of it."

"An evening landscape.   In the foreground near a pond
and a group of white beeches is leading a footpath animated
by travelers."

"A learned man in a cynical and torn dress holding an
open book in his hand."

"St. Bartholomew and the Executioner with the knife to
fulfill the martyr."

"Portrait of a young man.   A long while this picture was
thought to be Bindi Altoviti's portrait; now somebody will
again have it to be the self-portrait of Raphael."

"Susan bathing, surprised by the two old man.   In the
background the lapidation of the condemned."

("Lapidation" is good; it is much more elegant than
"stoning.")

"St. Rochus sitting in a landscape with an angel who looks
at his plague-sore, whilst the dog the bread in his mouth
attents him."

"Spring.   The Goddess Flora, sitting.   Behind her a
fertile valley perfused by a river."

"A beautiful bouquet animated by May-bugs, etc."

"A warrior in armor with a gypseous pipe in his hand leans against a table and blows the smoke far away of himself."

"A Dutch landscape along a navigable river which perfuses it till to the background."

"Some peasants singing in a cottage. A woman lets drink a child out of a cup."

"St. John's head as a boy,—painted in fresco on a brick." (Meaning a tile.)

"A young man of the Riccio family, his hair cut off right at the end, dressed in black with the same cap. Attributed to Raphael, but the signation is false."

"The Virgin holding the Infant. Is very painted in the manner of Sassoferrato."

"A Larder with greens and dead game animated by a cook-maid and two kitchen-boys."

However, the English of this catalogue is at least as happy as that which distinguishes an inscription upon a certain picture in Rome,—to wit :

"Revelations-View. St. John in Patterson's Island."

But meantime the raft is moving on.

CHAPTER XVII.

A MILE or two above Eberbach we saw a peculiar ruin projecting above the foliage which clothed the peak of a high and very steep hill. This ruin consisted of merely a couple of crumbling masses of masonry which bore a rude resemblance to human faces; they leaned forward and touched foreheads, and had the look of being absorbed in conversation. This ruin had nothing very imposing or picturesque about it, and there was no great deal of it, yet it was called the " Spectacular Ruin."

LEGEND OF THE " SPECTACULAR RUIN."

The captain of the raft, who was as full of history as he could stick, said that in the Middle Ages a most prodigious fire-breathing dragon used to live in that region, and made more trouble than a tax collector. He was as long as a railway train, and had the customary impenetrable green scales all over him. His breath bred pestilence and conflagration, and his appetite bred famine. He ate men and cattle impartially, and was exceedingly unpopular. The German emperor of that day made the usual offer : he would grant to the destroyer of the dragon, any one solitary thing he might ask for ; for he had a surplusage of daughters, and it was customary for dragon-killers to take a daughter for pay.

So the most renowned knights came from the four corners of the earth and retired down the dragon's throat one after the other. A panic arose and spread. Heroes grew cautious. The procession ceased. The dragon became more destructive than ever. The people lost all hope of succor, and fled to the mountains for refuge.

At last Sir Wissenschaft, a poor and obscure knight, out of a far country, arrived to do b a t t l e with the m o n s t e r. A pitiable object, he was, with his a r m o r hanging in rags about him, and his strange shaped knapsack strapped upon his back. Everybody turned up their noses at him, and some openly jeered him. But he was calm. He simply enquired if the emperor's offer was still in force. The emperor said it was,—but charitably advised him to go and hunt hares and not endanger so precious a life as his in an attempt which had brought death to so many of the world's most illustrious heroes.

THE UNKNOWN KNIGHT.

But this tramp only asked,—"Were any of these heroes men of science?" This raised a laugh, of course, for science was despised in those days. But the tramp was not in the least ruffled. He said he might be a little in advance of his age, but no matter,—science would come to be honored, some time or other. He said he would march against the dragon in the morning. Out of compassion, then, a decent spear was offered him, but he declined, and said, "spears were useless to men of science." They allowed him to sup in the servants' hall, and gave him a bed in the stables.

When he started forth in the morning, thousands were gathered to see. The emperor said,—

"Do not be rash, take a spear, and leave off your knapsack."

But the tramp said,—

"It is not a knapsack," and moved straight on.

The dragon was waiting and ready. He was breathing forth vast volumes of sulphurous smoke and lurid blasts of flame. The ragged knight stole warily to a good position, then he unslung his cylindrical knapsack,—which was simply the common fire-extinguisher known to modern times,—and the first chance he got he turned on his hose and shot the dragon square in the center of his cavernous mouth. Out went the fires in an instant, and the dragon curled up and died.

This man had brought brains to his aid. He had reared dragons from the egg, in his laboratory, he had watched over them like a mother, and patiently studied them and experimented upon them while they grew. Thus he had found out that fire was the life principle of a dragon; put out the dragon's fires and it could make steam no longer, and must die. He could not put out a fire with a spear, therefore he invented the extinguisher.

THE EMBRACE.

The dragon being dead, the emperor fell on the hero's neck and said,—

"Deliverer, name your request," at the same time beckoning out behind with his heel for a detachment of his daughters to form and advance. But the tramp gave them no observance. He simply said,—

"My request is, that upon me be conferred the monopoly of the manufacture and sale of spectacles in Germany."

The emperor sprang aside and exclaimed,—

"This transcends all the impudence I ever heard! A

modest demand, by my halidome! Why didn't you ask for the imperial revenues at once, and be done with it?"

But the monarch had given his word, and he kept it. To everybody's surprise, the unselfish monopolist immediately reduced the price of spectacles to such a degree that a great and crushing burden was removed from the nation. The emperor, to commemorate this generous act, and to testify his appreciation of it, issued a decree commanding everybody to buy this benefactor's spectacles and wear them, whether they needed them or not.

So originated the wide-spread custom of wearing spectacles in Germany; and as a custom once established in these old lands is imperishable, this one remains universal in the Empire to this day. Such is the legend of the monopolist's once stately and sumptuous castle, now called the "Spectacular Ruin."

On the right bank, two or three miles below the Spectacular Ruin, we passed by a noble pile of castellated buildings overlooking the water from the crest of a lofty elevation. A stretch of two hundred yards of the high front wall was heavily draped with ivy, and out of the mass of buildings within rose three picturesque old towers. The place was in fine order, and was inhabited by a family of princely rank. This castle had its legend, too, but I should not feel justified in repeating it because I doubted the truth of some of its minor details.

Along in this region a multitude of Italian laborers were blasting away the frontage of the hills to make room for the new railway. They were fifty or a hundred feet above the river. As we turned a sharp corner they began to wave signals and shout warnings to us to look out for the explosions. It was all very well to warn us, but what could *we* do? You can't back a raft up stream, you can't hurry it down stream, you can't scatter out to one side when you haven't any room to speak of, you won't take to the perpendicular cliffs on the other shore when they appear to be blasting there

too. Your resources are limited, you see. There is simply
nothing for it but to watch and pray.

For some hours we had been making three and a half or
four miles an hour and we were still making that. We had
been dancing right along until those men began to shout;
then for the next ten minutes it seemed to me that I had
never seen a raft go so slowly. When the first blast went
off we raised our sun-umbrellas and waited for the result.

PERILOUS POSITION.

No harm done; none of the stones fell in the water. Another blast followed, and another and another. Some of the
rubbish fell in the water just astern of us.

We ran that whole battery of nine blasts in a row, and it
was certainly one of the most exciting and uncomfortable
weeks I ever spent, either aship or ashore. Of course we frequently manned the poles and shoved earnestly for a second
or so, but every time one of those spurts of dust and *débris*
shot aloft every man dropped his pole and looked up to get
the bearings of his share of it. It was very busy times
along there for a while. It appeared certain that we must
perish, but even that was not the bitterest thought; no, the

abjectly unheroic nature of the death,—that was the sting,
—that and the bizarre wording of the resulting obituary:
"*Shot with a rock, on a raft.*"   There would be no poetry
written about it.   None *could* be written about it.   Example:

> *Not* by war's shock, or war's shaft,—
> *Shot*, with a rock, on a raft.

No poet who valued his reputation would touch such a
theme as that.   I should be distinguished as the only "distinguished dead" who went down to the grave unsonneted,
in 1878.

But we escaped, and I have never regretted it.   The last
blast was a peculiarly strong one, and after the small rubbish
was done raining around us and we were just going to shake
hands over our deliverance, a later and larger stone came
down amongst our little group of pedestrians and wrecked
an umbrella.   It did no other harm, but we took to the water
just the same.

It seems that the heavy work in the quarries and the new
railway gradings is done mainly by Italians.   That was a
revelation.   We have the notion in our country that Italians
never do heavy work at all, but confine themselves to the
lighter arts, like organ-grinding, operatic singing, and assassi-
nation.   We have blundered, that is plain.

All along the river, near every village, we saw little station houses for the future railway.   They were finished and
waiting for the rails and business.   They were as trim and
snug and pretty as they could be.   They were always of
brick or stone; they were of graceful shape, they had vines
and flowers about them already, and around them the grass
was bright and green, and showed that it was carefully
looked after.   They were a decoration to the beautiful landscape, not an offense.   Wherever one saw a pile of gravel, or
a pile of broken stone, it was always heaped as trimly and
exactly as a new grave or a stack of cannon balls; nothing
about those stations, or along the railroad or the wagon road
was allowed to look shabby or be unornamental.   The keeping

a country in such beautiful order as Germany exhibits, has a wise practical side to it, too, for it keeps thousands of people in work and bread who would otherwise be idle and mischievous.

As the night shut down, the captain wanted to tie up, but I thought maybe we might make Hirschhorn, so we went on. Presently the sky became overcast, and the captain came aft looking uneasy. He cast his eye aloft, then shook his head, and said it was coming on to blow. My party wanted to land at once,—therefore I wanted to go on. The captain said we ought to shorten sail, anyway, out of common prudence. Consequently the larboard watch was ordered to lay in his pole. It grew quite dark, now, and the wind began to rise. It wailed through the swaying branches of the trees, and swept our decks in fitful gusts. Things were taking on an ugly look. The captain shouted to the steersman on the forward log,—

" How's she heading ? "

The answer came faint and hoarse from far forward :

" Nor'-east-and-by-nor',——east-by-east, half-east, sir."

" Let her go off a point ! "

"Ay-aye, sir ! "

" What water have you got ? "

" Shoal, sir. Two foot large, on the stabboard, two and a half scant on the labboard ! "

" Let her go off another point ! "

"Ay-aye, sir ! "

" Forward, men, all of you ! Lively, now ! Stand by to crowd her round the weather corner ! "

"Ay-aye, sir ! "

Then followed a wild running and trampling and hoarse shouting, but the forms of the men were lost in the darkness and the sounds were distorted and confused by the roaring of the wind through the shingle-bundles. By this time the sea was running inches high, and threatening every moment to engulf the frail bark. Now came the mate hurrying aft, and said, close to the captain's ear, in a low, agitated voice,—

"Prepare for the worst, sir,—we have sprung a leak!"

"Heavens! where?"

"Right aft the second row of logs."

"Nothing but a miracle can save us! Don't let the men know, or there will be a panic and mutiny! Lay her in shore and stand by to jump with the stern-line the moment she touches. Gentlemen, I must look to you to second my endeavors in this hour of peril. You have hats,—go forrard and bail for your lives!"

Down swept another mighty blast of wind, clothed in spray and thick darkness. At such a moment as this, came from

THE RAFT IN A STORM.

away forward that most appalling of all cries that are ever heard at sea,—

"*Man overbóard!*"

The captain shouted,—

"Hard a-port! Never mind the man! Let him climb aboard or wade ashore!"

Another cry came down the wind,—

"Breakers ahead!"

"Where away?"

"Not a log's length off her port fore-foot!"

We had groped our slippery way forward, and were now

10

bailing with the frenzy of despair, when we heard the mate's terrified cry, from far aft,—

"Stop that dashed bailing, or we shall be aground!"

But this was immediately followed by the glad shout,—

" Land aboard the starboard transom!"

"Saved!" cried the captain. "Jump ashore and take a turn around a tree and pass the bight aboard!"

The next moment we were all on shore weeping and embracing for joy, while the rain poured down in torrents. The captain said he had been a mariner for forty years on the Neckar, and in that time had seen storms to make a man's

ALL SAFE ON SHORE.

cheek blanch and his pulses stop, but he had never, never seen a storm that even approached this one. How familiar that sounded! For I have been at sea a good deal and have heard that remark from captains with a frequency accordingly.

We framed in our minds the usual resolution of thanks and admiration and gratitude, and took the first opportunity to vote it, and put it in writing and present it to the captain, with the customary speech.

We tramped through the darkness and the drenching

summer rain full three miles, and reached "The Naturalist Tavern" in the village of Hirschhorn just an hour before midnight, almost exhausted from hardship, fatigue and terror. I can never forget that night.

The landlord was rich, and therefore could afford to be crusty and disobliging; he did not at all like being turned out of his warm bed to open his house for us. But no matter, his household got up and cooked a quick supper for us, and we brewed a hot punch for ourselves, to keep off consumption. After supper and punch we had an hour's soothing smoke while we fought the naval battle over again and voted the resolutions; then we retired to exceedingly neat and pretty chambers up stairs that had clean, comfortable beds in them with heir-loom pillow-cases most elaborately and tastefully embroidered by hand.

Such rooms and beds and embroidered linen are as frequent in German village inns as they are rare in ours. Our villages are superior to German villages in more merits, excellencies, conveniences and privileges than I can enumerate, but the hotels do not belong in the list.

"The Naturalist Tavern" was not a meaningless name; for all the halls and all the rooms were lined with large glass cases which were filled with all sorts of birds and animals, glass-eyed, ably stuffed, and set up in the most natural and eloquent and dramatic attitudes. The moment we were abed, the rain cleared away and the moon came out. I dozed off to sleep while contemplating a great white stuffed owl which was looking intently down on me from a high perch with the air of a person who thought he had met me before but could not make out for certain.

But young Z. did not get off so easily. He said that as he was sinking deliciously to sleep, the moon lifted away the shadows and developed a huge cat, on a bracket, dead and stuffed, but crouching, with every muscle tense, for a spring, and with its glittering glass eyes aimed straight at him. It made Z. uncomfortable. He tried closing his own eyes, but

that did not answer, for a natural instinct kept making him
open them again to see if the cat was still getting ready to
launch at him,—which she always was.   He tried turning

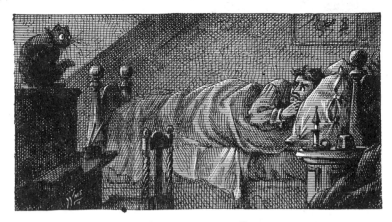

"IT WAS THE CAT."

his back, but that was a failure; he knew the sinister eyes
were on him still.   So at last he had to get up, after an hour
or two of worry and experiment, and set the cat out in the
hall.   So he won, that time.

CHAPTER XVIII.

IN the morning we took breakfast in the garden, under the trees, in the delightful German summer fashion. The air was filled with the fragrance of flowers and wild animals; the living portion of the menagerie of the "Naturalist Tavern" was all about us. There were great cages populous with fluttering and chattering foreign birds, and other great cages and greater wire pens, populous with quadrupeds, both native and foreign. There were some free creatures, too, and quite sociable ones they were. White rabbits went loping about the place, and occasionally came and sniffed at our shoes and shins; a fawn, with a red ribbon on its neck, walked up and examined us fearlessly; rare breeds of chickens and doves begged for crumbs, and a poor old tailless raven hopped about with a humble, shame-faced mien which said, "Please do not notice my exposure,—think how you would feel in my circumstances, and be charitable." If he was observed too much, he would retire behind something and stay there until he judged the party's interest had found another object. I never have seen another dumb creature that was so morbidly sensitive. Bayard Taylor, who could interpret the dim reasonings of animals, and understood their moral natures better than most men, would have found some way to make this poor old chap forget his troubles for a while,

BREAKFAST IN THE GARDEN.

but we had not his kindly art, and so had to leave the raven to his griefs.

After breakfast we climbed the hill and visited the ancient castle of Hirschhorn, and the ruined church near it. There were some curious old bas-reliefs leaning against the inner walls of the church,—sculptured lords of Hirschhorn in complete armor, and ladies of Hirschhorn in the picturesque court costumes of the Middle Ages. These things are suffering damage and passing to decay, for the last Hirschhorn has been dead two hundred years, and there is nobody now who cares to preserve the family relics. In the chancel was a twisted stone column, and the captain told us a legend about it, of course, for in the matter of legends he could not seem to restrain himself; but I do not repeat his tale because there was nothing plausible about it except that the Hero wrenched this column into its present screw-shape with his hands,—just one single wrench. All the rest of the legend was doubtful.

But Hirschhorn is best seen from a distance, down the river. Then the clustered brown towers perched on the green hilltop, and the old battlemented stone wall stretching up and over the grassy ridge and disappearing in the leafy sea beyond, make a picture whose grace and beauty entirely satisfy the eye.

We descended from the church by steep stone stairways which curved this way and that down narrow alleys between the packed and dirty tenements of the village. It was a quarter well stocked with deformed, leering, unkempt and uncombed idiots, who held out hands or caps and begged piteously. The people of the quarter were not all idiots, of course, but all that begged seemed to be, and were said to be.

I was thinking of going by skiff to the next town, Neckar-steinach; so I ran to the river side in advance of the party and asked a man there if he had a boat to hire. I suppose I must have spoken High-German,—Court German,—I intended it for that, anyway,—so he did not understand me. I turned and twisted my question around and about, trying to strike that man's average, but failed. He could not make out what I wanted. Now Mr. X. arrived, faced this same man, looked him in the eye, and emptied this sentence on him, in the most glib and confident way:

" Can man boat get here ? "

The mariner promptly understood and promptly answered. I can comprehend why he was able to understand that particular sentence, because by mere accident all the words in it except " get " have the same sound and the same meaning in German that they have in English ; but how he managed to understand Mr. X.'s next remark puzzled me. I will insert it, presently. X. turned away a moment, and I asked the mariner if he could not find a board, and so construct an additional seat. I spoke in the purest German, but I might as well have spoken in the purest Choctaw for all the good it did. The man tried his best to understand me ; he tried, and kept on trying, harder and harder, until I saw it was really of no use, and said,—

" There, don't strain yourself,—it is of no consequence."

EASILY UNDERSTOOD.

Then X. turned to him and crisply said,—

" Machen Sie a flat board."

I wish my epitaph may tell the truth about me if the man did not answer up at once, and say he would go and borrow a board as soon as he had lit the pipe which he was filling.

We changed our mind about taking a boat, so we did not have to go. I have given Mr. X.'s two remarks just as he made them. Four of the five words in the first one were English, and that they were also German was only accidental, not intentional ; three out of the five words in the second remark were English, and English only, and the two German ones did not mean anything in particular, in such a connection.

X. always spoke English, to Germans, but his plan was to turn the sentence wrong end first and upside down, according to German construction, and sprinkle in a German word without any essential meaning to it, here and there, by way of flavor. Yet he always made himself understood. He could make those dialect-speaking raftsmen understand him, sometimes, when even young Z. had failed with them ; and young Z. was a pretty good German scholar. For one thing, X. always spoke with such confidence,—perhaps that helped.

And possibly the raftsmen's dialect was what is called *platt-Deutch*, and so they found his English more familiar to their ears than another man's German. Quite indifferent students of German can read Fritz Reuter's charming platt-Deutch tales with some little facility because many of the words are English. I suppose this is the tongue which our Saxon ancestors carried to England with them. By and by I will inquire of some other philologist.

However, in the meantime it had transpired that the men employed to caulk the raft had found that the leak was not a leak at all, but only a crack between the logs,—a crack which belonged there, and was not dangerous, but had been magnified into a leak by the disordered imagination of the mate. Therefore we went aboard again with a good degree of confidence, and presently got to sea without accident. As we swam smoothly along between the enchanting shores, we fell to swapping notes about manners and customs in Germany and elsewhere.

As I write, now, many months later, I perceive that each of us, by observing and noting and inquiring, diligently and day by day, had managed to lay in a most varied and opulent stock of misinformation. But this is not surprising; it is very difficult to get accurate details in any country.

For example, I had the idea, once, in Heidelberg, to find out all about those five student-corps. I started with the White-cap corps. I began to inquire of this and that and the other citizen, and here is what I found out:

1. It is called the Prussian Corps, because none but Prussians are admitted to it.

2. It is called the Prussian Corps for no particular reason. It has simply pleased each corps to name itself after some German State.

3. It is not named the Prussian Corps at all, but only the White Cap Corps.

4. Any student can belong to it who is a German by birth.

5. Any student can belong to it who is European by birth.

6. Any European-born student can belong to it, except he be a Frenchman.

7. Any student can belong to it, no matter where he was born.

8. No student can belong to it who is not of noble blood.

9. No student can belong to it who cannot show three full generations of noble descent.

10. Nobility is not a necessary qualification.

11. No moneyless student can belong to it.

12. Money qualification is nonsense—such a thing has never been thought of.

I got some of this information from students themselves, —students who did not belong to the corps. I finally went to headquarters,—to the White Caps,—where I would have gone in the first place if I had been acquainted. But even at headquarters I found difficulties; I perceived that there were things about the White Cap Corps which one member knew and another one didn't. It was natural; for very few members of any organization know *all* that can be known about it. I doubt if there is a man or a woman in Heidelberg who would not answer promptly and confidently three out of every five questions about the White Cap Corps which a stranger might ask; yet it is a very safe bet that two of the three answers would be incorrect every time.

There is one German custom which is universal,—the bowing courteously to strangers when sitting down at table or rising up from it. This bow startles a stranger out of his self-possession, the first time it occurs, and he is likely to fall over a chair or something, in his embarrassment, but it pleases him nevertheless. One soon learns to expect this bow and be on the lookout and ready to return it; but to learn to lead off and make the initial bow one's self is a difficult matter for a diffident man. One thinks, "If I rise to go, and tender my bow and these ladies and gentlemen take it into their heads to ignore the custom of their nation, and not return it, how shall I feel, in case I survive to feel anything." Therefore he is afraid to venture. He sits out the dinner, and makes the strangers rise first and originate the bowing. A table d'hote dinner is a tedious affair for a man who seldom touches anything after the three first courses; therefore I used to do some pretty dreary waiting because of my fears. It took me months to assure myself that those fears were groundless, but I did assure myself at last by experimenting diligently through my agent. I made Harris get up and bow and leave; invariably his bow was returned, then I got up and bowed myself and retired.

Thus my education proceeded easily and comfortably for me, but not for Harris. Three courses of a table d'hote dinner were enough for me, but Harris preferred thirteen.

Even after I had acquired full confidence, and no longer needed the agent's help, I sometimes encountered difficulties. Once at Baden Baden I nearly lost a train because

EXPERIMENTING THROUGH HARRIS.

I could not be sure that three young ladies opposite me at table, were Germans, since I had not heard them speak; they might be American, they might be English, it was not safe to venture a bow; but just as I had got that far with my thought, one of them began a German remark, to my great relief and gratitude; and before she had got out her third word, our bows had been delivered and graciously returned, and we were off.

There is a friendly something about the German character which is very winning. When Harris and I were making a pedestrian tour through the Black Forest, we stopped at a little country inn for dinner one day; two young ladies and a young gentleman entered and sat down opposite us. They were pedestrians, too. Our knapsacks were strapped upon our backs, but they had a sturdy youth along to carry theirs for them. All parties were hungry, so there was no talking. By and by the usual bows were exchanged, and we separated.

As we sat at a late breakfast in the hotel at Allerheiligen, next morning, these young people entered and took places near us without observing us; but presently they saw us and at once bowed and smiled; not ceremoniously, but with the gratified look of people who have found acquaintances where they were expecting strangers. Then they spoke of the weather and the roads. We also spoke of the weather and the roads. Next, they said they had had an enjoyable walk, notwithstanding the weather. We said that that had been our case, too. Then they said they had walked thirty English miles the day before, and asked how many we had walked. I could not lie, so I told Harris to do it. Harris told them we had made thirty English miles, too. That was true; we had "made" them, though we had had a little assistance here and there.

After breakfast they found us trying to blast some information out of the dumb hotel clerk about routes, and observing that we were not succeeding pretty well, they went and got their maps and things, and pointed out and explained our course so clearly that even a New York detective could have followed it. And when we started they spoke out a hearty good-bye and wished us a pleasant journey. Perhaps they were more generous with us than they might have been with native wayfarers because we were a forlorn lot and in a strange land; I don't know; I only know it was lovely to be treated so.

Very well, I took an American young lady to one of the

fine balls in Baden-Baden, one night, and at the entrance-
door up stairs we were halted by an official,—something about
Miss Jones's dress was not according to rule; I don't remember what it was, now; something was wanting,—her back
hair, or a shawl, or a fan, or a shovel, or something. The
official was ever so polite, and ever so sorry, but the rule was
strict, and he could not let us in. It was very embarrassing,

AT THE BALL-ROOM DOOR.

for many eyes were on us. But now a richly dressed girl
stepped out of the ball-room, inquired into the trouble, and
said she could fix it in a moment. She took Miss Jones to
the robing-room, and soon brought her back in regulation
trim, and then we entered the ball-room with this benefactress
unchallenged.

Being safe, now, I began to puzzle through my sincere but
ungrammatical thanks, when there was a sudden mutual
recognition,—the benefactress and I had met at Allerheiligen.
Two weeks had not altered her good face, and plainly her
heart was in the right place yet, but there was such a difference between these clothes and the clothes I had seen her in
before, when she was walking thirty miles a day in the Black

Forest, that it was quite natural that I had failed to recognize her sooner. I had on *my* other suit, too, but my German would betray me to a person who had heard it once, anyway. She brought her brother and sister, and they made our way smooth for that evening.

Well,—months afterward, I was driving through the streets of Munich in a cab with a German lady, one day, when she said,—

"There that is Prince Ludwig and his wife, walking along there."

Everybody was bowing to them,—cabmen, little children, and everybody else,—and they were returning all the bows and overlooking nobody, when a young lady met them and made a deep curtsy.

"That is probably one of the ladies of the court," said my German friend.

I said,—

"She is an honor to it, then. I know her. I don't know her name, but I know *her*. I have known her at Allerheiligen and Baden-Baden. She ought to be an Empress, but she may be only a Duchess; it is the way things go in this world."

If one asks a German a civil question, he will be quite sure to get a civil answer. If you stop a German in the street and ask him to direct you to a certain place, he shows no sign of feeling offended. If the place be difficult to find, ten to one the man will drop his own matters and go with you and show you. In London, too, many a time, strangers have walked several blocks with me to show me my way. There is something very real about this sort of politeness. Quite often, in Germany, shopkeepers who could not furnish me the article I wanted, have sent one of their employes with me to show me a place where it could be had.

CHAPTER XIX.

HOWEVER, I wander from the raft. We made the port
of Neckarsteinach in good season, and went to the hotel
and ordered a trout dinner, the same to be ready against
our return from a two-hour pedestrian excursion to the village and castle of Dilsberg, a mile distant, on the other side
of the river. I do not mean that we proposed to be two
hours making two miles,—no, we meant to employ most of
the time in inspecting Dilsberg.

For Dilsberg is a quaint place. It is most quaintly and
picturesquely situated, too. Imagine the beautiful river before you; then a few rods of brilliant green sward on its
opposite shore; then a sudden hill,—no preparatory gently-
rising slopes, but a sort of instantaneous hill,—a hill two
hundred and fifty or three hundred feet high, as round as a
bowl, with the same taper upward that an inverted bowl has,
and with about the same relation of height to diameter that
distinguishes a bowl of good honest depth,—a hill which is
thickly clothed with green bushes,—a comely, shapely hill,
rising abruptly out of the dead level of the surrounding
green plains, visible from a great distance down the bends of
the river, and with just exactly room on the top of its head
for its steepled and turreted and roof-clustered cap of architecture, which same is tightly jammed and compacted within the perfectly round hoop of the ancient village wall.

There is no house outside the wall on the whole hill, **or** any vestige of a former house; all the houses are inside the wall, but there isn't room for another one. It is really a finished town, and has been finished a very long time. There is no space between the wall and the first circle of buildings; no, the village wall is itself the rear wall of the first circle of buildings, and the roofs jut a little over the wall and thus furnish it with eaves. The general level of the massed roofs is gracefully broken and relieved by the dominating towers of the ruined castle

DILSBERG.

and the tall spires of a couple of churches; so, from a distance Dilsberg has rather more the look of a king's crown than a cap. That lofty green eminence and its quaint cornet form quite a striking picture, you may be sure, in the flush of the evening sun.

We crossed over in a boat and began the ascent by a narrow, steep path which plunged us at once into the leafy deeps of the bushes. But they were not cool deeps by any means, for the sun's rays were weltering hot and there was little or no breeze to temper them. As we panted up the sharp ascent, we met brown, bareheaded and

OUR ADVANCE ON DILSBERG.

barefooted boys and girls, occasionally, and sometimes men; they came upon us without warning, they gave us good-day, flashed out of sight in the bushes, and were gone as suddenly and mysteriously as they had come. They were bound for the other side of the river to work. This path had been traveled by many generations of these people. They have always gone down to the valley to earn their bread, but they have always climbed their hill again to eat it, and to sleep in their snug town.

It is said that the Dilsbergers do not emigrate much; they find that living up there above the world, in their peaceful nest, is pleasanter than living down in the troublous world. The seven hundred inhabitants are all blood-kin to each other, too; they have always been blood-kin to each other for fifteen hundred years; they are simply one large family, and they like the home folks better than they like strangers, hence they persistently stay at home. It has been said that for ages Dilsberg has been merely a thriving and diligent idiot-factory. I saw no idiots there, but the captain said, "Because of late years the government has taken to lugging them off to asylums and otherwheres; and government wants to cripple the factory, too, and is trying to get these Dilsbergers to marry out of the family, but they don't like to."

The captain probably imagined all this, as modern science denies that the intermarrying of relatives deteriorates the stock.

Arrived within the wall, we found the usual village sights and life. We moved along a narrow, crooked lane which had been paved in the Middle Ages. A strapping, ruddy girl was beating flax or some such stuff in a little bit of a goods-box of a barn, and she swung her flail with a will,—if it was a flail; I was not farmer enough to know what she was at; a frowsy, barelegged girl was herding half a dozen geese with a stick,—driving them along the lane and keeping them out of the dwellings; a cooper was at work

11

in a shop which I know he did not make so large a thing
as a hogshead in, for there was not room. In the front
rooms of dwellings girls and women were cooking or spinning, and ducks and chickens were waddling in and out,
over the threshold, picking up chance crumbs and holding

INSIDE THE TOWN.

pleasant converse; a very old and wrinkled man sat asleep
before his door, with his chin upon his breast and his extin-
guished pipe in his lap; soiled children were playing in the
dirt everywhere along the lane, unmindful of the sun.

Except the sleeping old man, everybody was at work, but
the place was very still and peaceful, nevertheless; so still
that the distant cackle of the successful hen smote upon the
ear but little dulled by intervening sounds. That commonest of village sights was lacking here,—the public pump,
with its great stone tank or trough of limpid water, and its
group of gossiping pitcher-bearers; for there is no well or
fountain or spring on this tall hill; cisterns of rain water are
used.

Our alpenstocks and muslin tails compelled attention, and
as we moved through the village we gathered a considerable
procession of little boys and girls, and so went in some state
to the castle. It proved to be an extensive pile of crumbling

walls, arches and towers, massive, properly grouped for picturesque effect, weedy, grass-grown, and satisfactory. The children acted as guides; they walked us along the top of the highest wall, then took us up into a high tower and showed us a wide and beautiful landscape, made up of wavy distances of woody hills, and a nearer prospect of undulating expanses of green lowlands, on the one hand, and castle-graced crags and ridges on the other, with the shining curves of the Neckar flowing between. But the principal show, the chief pride of the children, was the ancient and empty well in the grass-grown court of the castle. Its massive stone curb stands up three or four feet above ground, and is whole and uninjured. The children said that in the Middle Ages this well was four hundred feet deep, and furnished all the village with an abundant supply of water, in war and peace. They said that in that old day its bottom was below the level of the Neckar, hence the water supply was inexhaustible.

But there were some who believed it had never been a well at all, and was never deeper than it is now,—eighty feet; that at that depth a subterranean passage branched from it and descended gradually to a remote place in the valley, where it opened into somebody's cellar or other hidden recess, and that the secret of this locality is now lost. Those who hold this belief say that herein lies the explanation that Dilsberg, besieged by Tilly and many a soldier before him, was never taken: after the longest and closest sieges the besiegers were astonished to perceive that the besieged were as fat and hearty as ever, and as well furnished with munitions of war,—therefore it must be that the Dilsbergers had been bringing these things in through the subterranean passage all the time.

The children said that there was in truth a subterranean outlet down there, and they would prove it. So they set a great truss of straw on fire and threw it down the well, while we leaned on the curb and watched the glowing mass descend. It struck bottom and gradually burned out. No

smoke came up. The children clapped their hands and said,—

"You see! Nothing makes so much smoke as burning straw— now where did the smoke go to, if there is no subterranean outlet?"

THE OLD WELL.

So it seemed quite evident that the subterranean outlet indeed existed. But the finest thing within the ruin's limits was a noble linden, which the children said was four hundred years old, and no doubt it was. It had a mighty trunk and a mighty spread of limb and foliage. The limbs near the ground were nearly the thickness of a barrel.

That tree had witnessed the assaults of men in mail,—how remote such a time seems, and how ungraspable is the fact that real men ever did fight in real armor!—and it had seen the time when these broken arches and crumbling battlements were a trim and strong and stately fortress, fluttering its gay banners in the sun, and peopled with vigorous humanity,—how impossibly long ago that seems!—and here it stands yet, and possibly may still be standing here, sunning itself and dreaming its historical dreams, when to-day shall have been joined to the days called "ancient."

Well, we sat down under the tree to smoke, and the captain delivered himself of his legend:

THE LEGEND OF DILSBERG CASTLE.

It was to this effect. In the old times there was once a great company assembled at the castle, and festivity ran high. Of course there was a haunted chamber in the castle, and

one day the talk fell upon that. It was said that whoever
slept in it would not wake again for fifty years. Now when
a young knight named Conrad von Geisberg heard this, he
said that if the castle were his he would destroy that chamber, so that no foolish person might have the chance to bring
so dreadful a misfortune upon himself and afflict such as
loved him with the memory of it. Straightway the company
privately laid their heads together to contrive some way to
get this superstitious young man to sleep in that chamber.
And they succeeded—in this way. They persuaded his be-
trothed, a lovely mischievous young creature, niece of the
lord of the castle, to help them in their plot. She presently
took him aside and had speech with him. She used all her
persuasions, but could not shake him; he said his belief was
firm that if he should sleep there he would wake no more for
fifty years, and it made him shudder to think of it. Catharina
began to weep. This was a better argument; Conrad could
not hold out against it. He yielded and said she should have
her wish if she would only smile and be happy again. She
flung her arms about his neck, and the kisses she gave him
showed that her thankfulness and her pleasure were very real.
Then she flew to tell the company her success, and the applause she received made her glad and proud she had undertaken her mission, since all alone she had accomplished what
the multitude had failed in.

At midnight, that night, after the usual feasting, Conrad
was taken to the haunted chamber and left there. He fell
asleep, by and by.

When he awoke again and looked about him, his heart
stood still with horror! The whole aspect of the chamber
was changed. The walls were mouldy and hung with ancient
cobwebs; the curtains and beddings were rotten; the furniture was rickety and ready to fall to pieces. He sprang out
of bed, but his quaking knees sunk under him and he fell to
the floor.

" This is the weakness of age," he said.

He rose and sought his clothing. It was clothing no lon‧ger. The colors were gone, the garments gave way in many

"SEND HITHER THE LORD ULRICH."

places while he was put‧ting them on. He tied, shuddering, into the corridor, and along it to the great hall. Here he was met by a middle-aged stranger of a kind countenance, who stop‧ped and gazed at him with surprise. Conrad said:—

"Good sir, will you send hither the lord Ulrich?"

The stranger looked puzzled a moment, then said,—

"The lord Ulrich?"

"Yes,—if you will be so good."

The stranger called,—"Wilhelm!" A young serving man came, and the stranger said to him,—

"Is there a lord Ulrich among the guests?"

"I know none of the name, so please your honor."

Conrad said, hesitatingly,—

"I did not mean a guest, but the lord of the castle, sir.

The stranger and the servant exchanged wondering glan‧ces. Then the former said,—

"I am the lord of the castle."

"Since when, sir?"

"Since the death of my father, the good lord Ulrich, more than forty years ago."

Conrad sank upon a bench and covered his face with his hands while he rocked his body to and fro and moaned. The stranger said in a low voice to the servant,—

"I fear me this poor old creature is mad. Call some one."

In a moment several people came, and grouped themselves about, talking in whispers. Conrad looked up and scanned

the faces about him wistfully. Then he shook his head and
said, in a grieved voice,—

" No, there is none among ye that I know. I am old and
alone in the world. They are dead and gone these many
years that cared for me. But sure, some of these aged ones
I see about me can tell me some little word or two concerning them."

Several bent and tottering men and women came nearer
and answered his questions about each former friend as he
mentioned the names. This one they said had been dead ten
years, that one twenty, another thirty. Each succeeding
blow struck heavier and heavier. At last the sufferer said,—

" There is one more, but I have not the courage to,—O,
my lost Catharina ! "

One of the old dames said,—

" Ah, I knew her well, poor soul. A misfortune overtook
her lover, and she died of sorrow nearly fifty years ago. She
lieth under the linden tree without the court."

Conrad bowed his head and said—

" Ah why did I ever wake ! And so she died of grief for
me, poor child. So young, so sweet, so good ! She never
wittingly did a hurtful thing in all the little summer of her
life. Her loving debt shall be repaid—for I will die of grief
for her."

His head drooped upon his breast. In a moment there
was a wild burst of joyous laughter, a pair of round young
arms were flung about Conrad's neck and a sweet voice
cried,—

" There, Conrad mine, thy kind words kill me,—the farce
shall go no further ! Look up, and laugh with us,—'twas
all a jest ! "

And he did look up, and gazed, in a dazed wonderment,—
for the disguises were stripped away, and the aged men and
women were bright and young and gay again. Catharina's
happy tongue ran on,—

" 'Twas a marvelous jest, and bravely carried out. They

gave you a heavy sleeping draught before you went to bed, and in the night they bore you to a ruined chamber where all had fallen to decay, and placed these rags of clothing by you. And when your sleep was spent and you came forth, two strangers, well instructed in their parts, were here to meet you; and all we, your friends, in our disguises, were close at hand, to see and hear, you may be sure. Ah, 'twas

"LEAD ME TO HER GRAVE."

a gallant jest! Come, now, and make thee ready for the pleasures of the day. How real was thy misery for the moment, thou poor lad! Look up and have thy laugh, now!"

He looked up, searched the merry faces about him in a dreamy way, then sighed and said,—

"I am aweary, good strangers, I pray you lead me to her grave."

All the smiles vanished away, every cheek blanched, Catharina sunk to the ground in a swoon.

All day the people went about the castle with troubled faces, and communed together in undertones. A painful hush pervaded the place which had lately been so full of cheery life. Each in his turn tried to arouse Conrad out of his hallucination and bring him to himself; but all the answer any got was a meek, bewildered stare, and then the words,—

"Good stranger, I have no friends, all are at rest these many years; ye speak me fair, ye mean me well, but I know ye not; I am alone and forlorn in the world,—prithee lead me to her grave."

During two years Conrad spent his days, from the early morning till the night, under the linden tree, mourning over the imaginary grave of his Catharina. Catharina was the only company of the harmless madman. He was very friendly toward her because, as he said, in some ways she reminded him of his Catharina whom he had lost "fifty years ago." He often said,—

UNDER THE LINDEN.

"She was so gay, so happy-hearted,—but you never smile; and always when you think I am not looking, you cry."

When Conrad died, they buried him under the linden, according to his directions, so that he might rest "near his poor Catharina." Then Catharina sat under the linden alone, every day and all day long, a great many years, speaking to no one, and never smiling; and at last her long repentance was rewarded with death, and she was buried by Conrad's side.

Harris pleased the captain by saying it was a good legend; and pleased him further by adding,—

"Now that I have seen this mighty tree, vigorous with its four hundred years, I feel a desire to believe the legend for *its* sake; so I will humor the desire, and consider that the tree really watches over those poor hearts and feels a sort of human tenderness for them."

We returned to Neckarsteinach, plunged our hot head into the trough at the town pump, and then went to the hotel and ate our trout dinner in leisurely comfort, in the garden, with the beautiful Neckar flowing at our feet, the quaint Dilsberg looming beyond, and the graceful towers and battlements of a couple of medieval castles (called the "Swallow's Nest"* and "The Brothers") assisting the rugged scenery of a bend of the river down to our right.

AN EXCELLENT PILOT—ONCE!

We got to sea in season to make the eight-mile run to Heidelberg before the night shut down. We sailed by the hotel in the mellow glow of sunset, and came slashing down with the mad current into the narrow passage between the dikes. I believed I could shoot the bridge myself, so I went to the forward triplet of logs and relieved the pilot of his pole and his responsibility.

We went tearing along in a most exhilarating way, and i performed the delicate duties of my office very well indeed for a first attempt; but perceiving presently, that I really was going to shoot the bridge itself instead of the archway under it, I judiciously stepped ashore. The next moment I

---

*The seeker after information is referred to Appendix E for our Captain's legend of the "Swallow's Nest" and "The Brothers."

had my long coveted desire: I saw a raft wrecked. It hit the pier in the center and went all to smash and scatteration like a box of matches struck by lightning.

I was the only one of our party who saw this grand sight; the others were attitudinizing, for the benefit of the long rank of young ladies who were promenading on the bank, and so they lost it. But I helped to fish them out of the river, down below the bridge, and then described it to them as well as I could. They were not interested, though. They said they were wet and

SCATTERATION

felt ridiculous and did not care anything for descriptions of scenery. The young ladies, and other people, crowded around and showed a great deal of sympathy, but that did not help matters; for my friends said they did not want sympathy, they wanted a back alley and solitude.

CHAPTER XX.

NEXT morning brought good news,—our trunks had arrived from Hamburg at last. Let this be a warning to the reader. The Germans are very conscientious, and this trait makes them very particular. Therefore if you tell a German you want a thing done immediately, he takes you at your word; he thinks you mean what you say; so he does that thing immediately—according to his idea of immediately—which is about a week; that is, it is a week if it refers to the building of a garment, or it is an hour and a half if it refers to the cooking of a trout. Very well; if you tell a German to send your trunk to you by "slow freight," he takes you at your word; he sends it by "slow freight," and you cannot imagine how long you will go on enlarging your admiration of the expressiveness of that phrase in the German tongue, before you get that trunk. The hair on my trunk was soft and thick and youthful, when I got it ready for shipment in Hamburg; it was baldheaded when it reached Heidelberg. However, it was still sound, that was a comfort, it was not battered in the least; the baggagemen seemed to be conscientiously careful, in Germany, of the baggage intrusted to their hands. There was nothing now in the way of our departure, therefore we set about our preparations.

Naturally my chief solicitude was about my collection of Keramics. Of course I could not take it with me, that would

184

be inconvenient, and dangerous besides. I took advice, but the best bric-a-brackers were divided as to the wisest course to pursue; some said pack the collection and warehouse it;

ETRUSCAN
TEAR-JUG.

others said try to get it into the Grand Ducal Museum at Mannheim for safe keeping. So I divided the collection, and followed the advice of both parties. I set aside, for the Museum, those articles which were the most frail and precious. Among these was my Etruscan tear-jug. I have made a little sketch of it here; that thing creeping up the side is not a bug, it is a hole. I bought this tear-jug of a dealer in antiquities for four hundred and fifty dollars. It is very rare. The man said the Etruscans used to keep tears or something in these things, and that it was very hard to get hold of a broken one, now. I also set aside my Henri II plate. See sketch from my pencil; it is in the main correct, though I think I have foreshortened one end of it a little too much, perhaps. This is very fine and rare; the shape is exceedingly beautiful and unusual. It has wonderful decorations on it, but I am not able to reproduce them. It cost more than the tear-jug, as the dealer said there was not another plate just like it in the world. He said there was much false Henri II ware around, but that the genuineness of this piece was unquestionable. He showed me its pedigree, or its history if you please; it was a document which traced this plate's movements all the way down from its birth,—showed who bought it, from whom, and what he paid for it—from the first buyer down to me, whereby I saw that it had gone steadily up from thirty-five cents to seven hundred dollars. He said that the whole Keramic world would be informed that it was now in my possession and would make a note of it, with the price paid.

HENRI II PLATE.

Old Blue China.

I also set apart my exquisite specimen of Old Blue China. This is considered to be the finest example of Chinese art now in existence; I do not refer to the bastard Chinese art of modern times but that noble & pure & genuine art which flourished under the fostering & appreciative care of the Emperors of the Chung-a Lung-Fung dynasty. —

There were Masters in those days, but alas, it is not so now. Of course the main preciousness of this piece lies in its color; it is that old sensuous, pervading, ramifying, interpolating, transboreal blue which is the despair of modern art. The little sketch which I have made of this gem cannot and does not do it justice, since I have been obliged to leave out the color. But I've got the expression though.

However, I must not be frittering away the reader's time with these details. I did not intend to go into any detail at all, at first, but it is the failing of the true keramiker, or the true devotee in any department of brick-a-brackery, that once he gets his tongue or his pen started on his darling theme, he cannot well stop until he drops from exhaustion. He has no more sense of the flight of time than has any other lover when talking of his sweetheart. The very "marks" on the bottom of a piece of rare crockery are able to throw me into a gibbering ecstasy; and I could forsake a drowning relative to help dispute about whether the stopple of a departed Buon Retiro scent-bottle was genuine or spurious.

Many people say that for a male person, bric-a-brac hunting is about as robust a business as making doll-clothes, or decorating Japanese pots with decalcomanie butterflies would be. and these people fling mud at that elegant Englishman, Byng, who wrote a book called "The Bric-a-Brac Hunter," and make fun of him for chasing around after what they choose to call "his despicable trifles;" and for "gushing" over these trifles; and for exhibiting his "deep infantile delight" in what they call his "tuppenny collection of beggarly trivialities;" and for beginning his book with a picture of himself, seated, in a "sappy, self-complacent attitude, in the midst of his poor little ridiculous bric-a-brac junk shop."

It is easy to say these things; it is easy to revile us, easy to despise us; therefore, let these people rail on; they cannot feel as Byng and I feel,—it is their loss, not ours. For my part I am content to be a brick-a-bracker and a keramiker,

—more, I am proud to be so named. I am proud to know that I lose my reason as immediately in the presence of a rare jug with an illustrious mark on the bottom of it, as if I had just emptied that jug. Very well; I packed and stored a part of my collection, and the rest of it I placed in the care of the Grand Ducal Museum in Mannheim, by permission. My Old Blue China Cat remains there yet. I presented it to that excellent institution.

A REAL ANTIQUE.

I had but one misfortune with my things. An egg which I had kept back from breakfast that morning, was broken in packing. It was a great pity. I had shown it to the best connoisseurs in Heidelberg, and they all said it was an antique. We spent a day or two in farewell visits, and then left for Baden-Baden. We had a pleasant trip of it, for the Rhine valley is always lovely. The only trouble was that the trip was too short. If I remember rightly it only occupied a couple of hours, therefore I judge that the distance was very little, if any, over fifty miles. We quitted the train at Oos, and walked the entire remaining distance to Baden-Baden, with the exception of a lift of less than an hour which we got on a passing wagon, the weather being exhaustingly warm. We came into town on foot.

BRIC-A-BRAC SHOP.

One of the first persons we encountered, as we walked up the street, was the Rev. Mr. ——, an old friend from America,—a lucky encounter, indeed, for his is a most gentle, refined and sensitive nature, and his company and companionship are a genuine refreshment. We knew he had been in Europe sometime, but were not at all expecting to run across him. Both parties burst forth into loving enthusiasms, and Rev. Mr. —— said,—

"I have got a brim-full reservoir of talk to pour out on you, and an empty one ready and thirsting to receive what you have got; we will sit up till midnight and have a good satisfying interchange, for I leave here early in the morning." We agreed to that, of course.

I had been vaguely conscious, for a while, of a person who was walking in the street abreast of us; I had glanced furtively at him once or twice, and noticed that he was a fine, large, vigorous young fellow, with an open, independent countenance, faintly shaded with a pale and even almost imperceptible crop of early down, and that he was clothed from head to heel in cool and enviable, snow-white linen. I thought I had also noticed, that his head had a sort of listening tilt to it. Now about this time the Rev. Mr. —— said,—

"The side-walk is hardly wide enough for three, so I will walk behind; but keep the talk going, keep the talk going, there's no time to lose, and you may be sure I will do my share." He ranged himself behind us, and straightway that stately snow-white young fellow closed up to the side-walk alongside him, fetched him a cordial slap on the shoulder with his broad palm, and sung out with a hearty cheeriness,—

"*Americans*, for two-and-a-half and the money up! *Hey?*"

The Reverend winced, but said mildly,—

"Yes,—we are Americans."

"Lord love you, you can just bet that's what *I* am, every time! Put it there!"

He held out his Sahara of a palm, and the Reverend laid his diminutive hand in it, and got so cordial a shake that we heard his glove burst under it.

12

"Say, didn't I put you up right?"

"O, yes."

"Sho! I spotted you for *my* kind the minute I heard your clack. You been over here long?"

"About four months. Have you been over long?"

"PUT IT THERE."

"*Long?* Well I should say so! Going on two *years*, by geeminy! Say, are you homesick?"

"No, I can't say that I am. Are you?"

"O, *hell* yes!" This with immense enthusiasm.

The Reverend shrunk a little, in his clothes, and we were aware, rather by instinct than otherwise, that he was throwing out signals of distress to us; but we did not interfere or try to succor him, for we were quite happy.

The young fellow hooked his arm into the Reverend's, now, with the confiding and grateful air of a waif who has been longing for a friend, and a sympathetic ear, and a chance to lisp once more the sweet accents of the mother tongue,— and then he limbered up the muscles of his mouth and turned himself loose,—and with such a relish! Some of his words were not Sunday school words, so I am obliged to put blanks where they occur.

"Yes indeedy! If *I* ain't an American there *ain't* any Americans, that's all. And when I heard you fellows gassing away in the good old American language, I'm———if it wasn't all I could do to keep from hugging you! My tongue's all warped with trying to curl it around these————— ———forsaken wind-galled nine-jointed German words here; now I *tell* you it's awful good to lay it over a Christian word once more and kind of let the old taste soak in. I'm from western New York. My name is Cholley Adams. I'm a student, you know. Been here going on two years. I'm learning to be a horse-doctor. I *like* that part of it, you know, but ————— these people, they won't learn a fellow in his own language, they make him learn in German; so before I could tackle the horse-doctoring I had to tackle this miserable language.

"First-off, I thought it would certainly give me the botts, but I don't mind it now. I've got it where the hair's short, I think; and dontchuknow, they made me learn Latin, too. Now between you and me, I wouldn't give a ——— for all the Latin that was ever jabbered; and the first thing *I* calculate to do when I get through, is to just sit down and forget it. 'Twont take me long, and I don't mind the time, anyway. And I tell you what! the difference between school-teaching over yonder and school-teaching over here,—sho! *We* don't know anything about it! Here you've got to peg and peg and peg and there just ain't any let-up,—and what you learn here, you've got to *know*, dontchuknow,—or else you'll have one of these ————— spavined, spectacled, ring-boned, knock-kneed old professors in your hair. I've been here long *enough*, and I'm getting blessed tired of it, mind I *tell* you. The old man wrote me that he was coming over in June, and said he'd take me home in August, whether I was done with my education or not, but durn him, he didn't come; never said why; just sent me a hamper of Sunday school books, and told me to be good, and hold on a while. I don't take to Sunday school books, dontchuknow, —I don't hanker after them when I can get pie,—but I *read* them, anyway, because whatever the old man tells me to do, that's the thing that I'm a-going to *do*, or tear something you know. I buckled in and read all of those books, because he wanted me to; but that kind of thing don't excite *me*, I like something *hearty*. But I'm awful homesick. I'm homesick from ear-socket to crupper, and from crupper to hock joint; but it ain't any use, I've got to stay here, till the old man drops the rag and gives the word,—yes, *sir*, right here in this ——————— country I've got to linger till the old man says *Come!*—and you bet your bottom dollar, Johnny, it *ain't* just as easy as it is for a cat to have twins!"

At the end of this profane and cordial explosion he

THE PARSON CAPTURED.

fetched a prodigious "*Whoosh!*" to relieve his lungs and make recognition of the heat, and then he straightway dived into his narrative again for "Johnny's" benefit, beginning, "Well,——————it ain't any use talking, some of those old American words *do* have a kind of a bully swing to them; a man can *express* himself with 'em,—a man can get at what he wants to *say*, dontchuknow."

When we reached our hotel and it seemed that he was about to lose the Reverend, he showed so much sorrow, and begged so hard and so earnestly that the Reverend's heart was not hard enough to hold out against the pleadings,—so he went away with the parent-honoring student, like a right Christian, and took supper with him in his lodgings and sat in the surf-beat of his slang and profanity till near midnight, and then left him,—left him pretty well talked out, but grateful " clear down to his frogs," as he expressed it.   The Reverend said it had transpired during the interview that " Cholley " Adams's father was an extensive dealer in horses in western New York; this accounted for Cholley's choice of a profession.   The Reverend brought away a pretty high opinion of Cholley as a manly young fellow, with stuff in him for a useful citizen; he considered him rather a rough gem, but a gem, nevertheless.

CHAPTER XXI.

BADEN-BADEN sits in the lap of the hills, and the natural and artificial beauties of the surroundings are combined effectively and charmingly. The level strip of ground which stretches through and beyond the town is laid out in handsome pleasure grounds, shaded by noble trees and adorned at intervals with lofty and sparkling fountain-jets. Thrice a day a fine band makes music in the public promenade before the Conversation-House, and in the afternoon and evenings that locality is populous with fashionably dressed people of both sexes, who march back and forth past the great music stand and look very much bored, though they make a show of feeling otherwise. It seems like a rather aimless and stupid existence. A good many of these people are there for a real purpose, however; they are racked with rheumatism, and they are there to stew it out in the hot baths. These invalids looked melancholy enough, limping about on their canes and crutches, and apparently brooding over all sorts of cheerless things. People say that Germany, with her damp stone houses, is the home of rheumatism. If that is so, Providence must have foreseen that it would be so, and therefore filled the land with these healing baths. Perhaps no other country is so generously supplied with medicinal springs as Germany. Some of these baths are good for one ailment, some for another; and again, peculiar ailments are conquered by combining the individual virtues of several different baths. For instance, for some forms of disease, the patient drinks the native hot water of Baden-Baden, with a spoonful of salt from the Carlsbad springs dissolved in it. That is not a dose to be forgotten right away.

They don't *sell* this hot water; no, you go into the great

Trinkhalle, and stand around, first on one foot and then on the other, while two or three young girls sit pottering at some sort of lady-like sewing work in your neighborhood and can't seem to see you,— polite as three-dollar clerks in government offices.

By and by one of these rises painfully, and " stretches ; " — stretches fists and body heavenward till she raises her heels from the floor, at the same

A COMPREHENSIVE YAWN.

time refreshing herself with a yawn of such comprehensiveness that the bulk of her face disappears behind her upper

lip and one is able to see how she is constructed inside,—
then she slowly closes her cavern, brings down her fists and
her heels, comes languidly forward, contemplates you contemptuously, draws you a glass of hot water and sets it down
where you can get it by reaching for it. You take it and
say,—

"How much?"—and she returns you, with elaborate indifference, a beggar's answer,—

"*Nach Beliebe*, (what you please.)

This thing of using the common beggar's trick and the
common beggar's shibboleth to put you on your liberality
when you were expecting a simple straight-forward commercial transaction, adds a little to your prospering sense of
irritation. You ignore her reply, and ask again,—

"How much?"

—and she calmly, indifferently, repeats,—

"*Nach Beliebe*."

You are getting angry, but you are trying not to show it;
you resolve to keep on asking your question till she changes
her answer, or at least her annoyingly indifferent manner.
Therefore, if your case be like mine, you two fools stand
there, and without perceptible emotion of any kind, or
any emphasis on any syllable, you look blandly into each

other's eyes, and hold
the following idiotic
conversation,—

"How much?"
"Nach Beliebe."
"How much?"
"Nach Beliebe."
"How much?"
"Nach Beliebe."
"How much?"
"Nach Beliebe."
"How much?"
"Nach Beliebe."
"How much?"

TESTING THE COIN.

" Nach Beliebe."

I do not know what another person would have done, but at this point I gave it up; that cast-iron indifference, that tranquil contemptuousness, conquered me, and I struck my colors. Now I knew she was used to receiving about a penny from manly people who care nothing about the opinions of scullery maids, and about tuppence from moral cowards; but I laid a silver twenty-five cent piece within her reach and tried to shrivel her up with this sarcastic speech,—

" If it isn't enough, will you stoop sufficiently from your official dignity to say so?"

She did not shrivel. Without deigning to look at me at all, she languidly lifted the coin and bit it!—to see if it was good. Then she turned her back and placidly waddled to her former roost again, tossing the money into an open till as she went along. She was victor to the last, you see.

I have enlarged upon the ways of this girl because they are typical; her manners are the manners of a goodly number of the Baden-Baden shop keepers. The shop keeper there swindles you if he can, and insults

BEAUTY AT THE BATH.

you whether he succeeds in swindling you or not. The keepers of baths also take great and patient pains to insult you. The frowsy woman who sat at the desk in the lobby of the great Friederichsbad and sold bath tickets, not only

insulted me twice every day, with rigid fidelity to her great
trust, but she took trouble enough to cheat me out of a shilling,
one day, to have fairly entitled her to ten. Baden-Baden's
splendid gamblers are gone, only her microscopic knaves
remain.

An English gentleman who had been living there several
years, said,—

"If you could disguise your nationality, you would not
find any insolence here. These shop-keepers detest the English and despise the Americans; they are rude to both, more
especially to ladies of your nationality and mine. If these
go shopping without a gentleman or a man servant, they are
tolerably sure to be subjected to petty insolences,—insolences of manner and tone, rather than word, though words
that are hard to bear are not always wanting. I know of
an instance where a shop-keeper tossed a coin back to an
American lady with the remark, snappishly uttered, 'We
don't take French money here.'—And I know of a case
where an English lady said to one of these shop-keepers,
'Don't you think you ask too much for this article?' and he
replied with the question, 'Do you think you are obliged to
buy it?' However, these people are not impolite to Russ-
ians or Germans. And as to rank, they worship that, for they
have long been used to generals and nobles. If you wish
to see to what abysses servility can descend, present yourself
before a Baden-Baden shop-keeper in the character of a
Russian prince."

It is an inane town, filled with sham, and petty fraud,
and snobbery, but the baths are good. I spoke with many
people, and they were all agreed in that. I had had twinges
of rheumatism unceasingly during three years, but the last
one departed after a fortnight's bathing there, and I have
never had one since. I fully believe I left my rheumatism
in Baden-Baden. Baden-Baden is welcome to it. It was
little, but it was all I had to give. I would have preferred
to leave something that was catching, but it was not in my
power.

There are several hot springs there, and during two thousand years they have poured forth a never diminishing abundance of the healing water. This water is conducted in pipes to the numerous bath houses, and is reduced to an endurable temperature by the addition of cold water. The new Friēderichsbad is a very large and beautiful building, and in it one may have any sort of bath that has ever been invented, and with all the additions of herbs and drugs that his ailment may need or that the physician of the establishment may consider a useful thing to put into the water. You go there, enter the great door, get a bow graduated to your style and clothes from the gorgeous portier, and a bath ticket and an insult from the frowsy woman for a quarter, she strikes a bell and a serving man conducts you down a long hall and shuts you into a commodious room which has a washstand, a mirror, a bootjack and a sofa in it, and there you undress at your leisure.

The room is divided by a great curtain; you draw this curtain aside, and find a large white marble bath-tub, with its rim sunk to the level of the floor, and with three white marble steps leading down into it. This tub is full of water which is as clear as crystal, and is tempered to 28° Reaumur, (about 95° Fahrenheit.) Sunk into the floor, by the tub, is

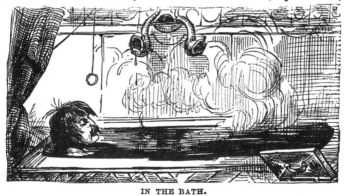

IN THE BATH.

a covered copper box which contains some warm towels and a sheet. You look fully as white as an angel when you are stretched out in that limpid bath. You remain in it ten minutes, the first time, and afterwards increase the duration from day to day, till you reach twenty-five or thirty minutes. There you stop. The appointments of the place are so luxurious, the benefit so marked, the price so moderate, and the insults so sure, that you very soon find yourself adoring the Friēderichsbad and infesting it.

We had a plain, simple, unpretending, good hotel, in Baden-Baden,—the Hotel de France,—and alongside my room I had a giggling, cackling, chattering family who always went to bed just two hours after me and always got up just two hours ahead of me. But that is common in German hotels; the people generally go to bed long after eleven and get up long before eight. The partitions convey sound like a drum-head, and everybody knows it; but no matter, a German family who are all kindness and consideration in the daytime make apparently no effort to moderate their noises for your benefit at night. They will sing, laugh and talk loudly, and bang furniture around in the most pitiless way. If you knock on your wall appealingly, they will quiet down and discuss the matter softly amongst themselves for a moment,—then, like the mice, they fall to persecuting you again, and as vigorously as before. They keep cruelly late and early hours, for such noisy folk.

Of course when one begins to find fault with foreign people's ways, he is very likely to get a reminder to look nearer home, before he gets far with it. I open my note book to see if I can find some more information of a valuable nature about Baden-Baden, and the first thing I fall upon is this:

Baden-Baden, (no date.) Lot of vociferous Americans at breakfast this morning. Talking *at* everybody, while pretending to talk among themselves. On their first travels, manifestly. Showing off. The usual signs,—airy, easy-going references to grand distances and foreign places. "Well, *good*-bye, old fellow,—if I don't run across you in Italy, you hunt me up in London before you sail."

The next item which I find in my note-book is this one :

" The fact that a band of 6,000 Indians are now murdering our frontiersmen at their impudent leisure, and that we are only able to send 1200 soldiers against them, is utilized here to discourage emigration to America. The common people think the Indians are in New Jersey."

This is a new and peculiar argument against keeping our army down to a ridiculous figure in the matter of numbers. It is rather a striking one, too. I have not distorted the truth in saying that the facts in the above item, about the army and the Indians, are made use of to discourage emigration to America. That the common people should be rather foggy in their geography, and foggy as to the location

JERSEY INDIANS.

of the Indians, is matter for amusement, maybe, but not of surprise.

There is an interesting old cemetery in Baden-Baden, and we spent several pleasant hours in wandering through it and spelling out the inscriptions on the aged tombstones. Apparently after a man has lain there a century or two, and has had a good many people buried on top of him, it is considered that his tombstone is not needed by him any longer. I judge so from the fact that hundreds of old gravestones have been removed from the graves and placed against the inner walls of the cemetery. What artists they had in the old times! They chiseled angels and cherubs and devils and skeletons on the tombstones in the most lavish and generous way,—as to supply,—but curiously grotesque and outlandish as to form. It is not always easy to tell which of the figures belong among the blest and which of them among the opposite party. But there was an inscription, in French, on one of those old stones, which was quaint and pretty, and was plainly not the work of any other than a poet. It was to this effect:

HERE

REPOSES IN GOD,

CAROLINE DE CLERY,

A RELIGIEUSE OF ST. DENIS,

AGED 83 YEARS,—AND BLIND.

THE LIGHT WAS RESTORED TO HER

IN BADEN THE 5TH OF JANUARY,

1839.

We made several excursions on foot to the neighboring villages, over winding and beautiful roads and through enchanting woodland scenery. The woods and roads were similar to those at Heidelberg, but not so bewitching. I suppose that roads and woods which are up to the Heidelberg mark are rare in the world.

Once we wandered clear away to La Favorita Palace, which is several miles from Baden-Baden. The grounds about the palace were fine; the palace was a curiosity. It was built by a Margravine in 1725, and remains as she left it at her death. We wandered through a great many of its rooms, and they all had striking peculiarities of decoration. For instance, the walls of one room were pretty completely covered with small pictures of the Margravine in all conceivable varieties of fanciful costumes, some of them male.

The walls of another room were covered with grotesquely and elaborately figured hand-wrought tapestry. The musty ancient beds remained in the chambers, and their quilts and curtains and canopies were decorated with curious hand-work,

and the walls and ceilings frescoed with historical and mytho-
logical scenes in glaring colors.   There was enough crazy and
rotten rubbish in the building to make the true brick-a-bracker
green with envy.   A painting in the dining hall verged upon
the indelicate,—but then the Margravine was herself a trifle
indelicate.

It is in every way a wildly and picturesquely decorated
house, and brimfull of interest as a reflection of the character
and tastes of that rude bygone time.

In the grounds, a few rods from the palace, stands the
Margravine's chapel, just as she left it,—a coarse wooden
structure, wholly barren of ornament.   It is said that the
Margravine would give herself up to debauchery and exceedingly fast living for several months at a time, and then retire
to this miserable wooden den and spend a few months in
repenting and getting ready for another good time.   She was
a devoted Catholic, and was perhaps quite a model sort of
a Christian as Christians went then, in high life.

Tradition says she spent the last two years of her life in
the strange den I have been speaking of, after having indulged
herself in one final, triumphant and satisfying spree.   She
shut herself up there, without company, and without even a
servant, and so abjured and forsook the world.   In her little
bit of a kitchen she did her own cooking; she wore a hair
shirt next the skin, and castigated herself with whips,—these
aids to grace are exhibited there yet.   She prayed and told
her beads, in another little room before a waxen Virgin niched
in a little box against the wall; she bedded herself like a
slave.

In another small room is an unpainted wooden table, and
behind it sit half-life-size waxen figures of the Holy Family,
made by the very worst artist that ever lived, perhaps, and
clothed in gaudy, flimsy drapery. *   The Margravine used

---

* The Savior was represented as a lad of about 15 years of age. This
figure had lost one eye.

to bring her meals to this table and *dine with the Holy Family.* What an idea that was! What a grisly spectacle it must have been! Imagine it: Those rigid, shock-headed figures, with corpsy complexions and fishy glass eyes, occupy-

NOT PARTICULARLY SOCIABLE.

ing one side of the table in the constrained attitudes and dead fixedness that distinguish all men that are born of wax, and this wrinkled, smouldering old fire-eater occupying the other side, mumbling her prayers and munching her sausages in the ghostly stillness and shadowy indistinctness of a winter twilight. It makes one feel crawly even to think of it.

In this sordid place, and clothed, bedded and fed like a pauper, this strange princess lived and worshiped during two years, and in it she died. Two or three hundred years ago, this would have made the poor den holy ground; and the church would have set up a miracle-factory there and made plenty of money out of it. The den could be moved into some portions of France and made a good property even now.

CHAPTER XXII.

FROM Baden-Baden we made the customary trip into the Black Forest. We were on foot most of the time. One cannot describe those noble woods, nor the feeling with which they inspire him. A feature of the feeling, however, is a deep sense of contentment; another feature of it is a buoyant, boyish gladness; and a third and very conspicuous feature of it is one's sense of the remoteness of the work-day world and his entire emancipation from it and its affairs.

Those woods stretch unbroken over a vast region; and everywhere they are such dense woods, and so still, and so piney and fragrant. The stems of the trees are trim and straight, and in many places all the ground is hidden for miles under a thick cushion of moss of a vivid green color, with not a decayed or ragged spot in its surface, and not a fallen leaf or twig to mar its immaculate tidiness. A rich cathedral gloom pervades the pillared aisles; so the stray flecks of sunlight that strike a trunk here and a bough yonder are strongly accented, and when they strike the moss they fairly seem to burn. But the wierdest effect, and the most enchanting, is that produced by the diffused light of the low afternoon sun; no single ray is able to pierce its way in, then, but the diffused light takes color from moss and foliage, and pervades the place like a faint, green-tinted mist, the theatrical fire of fairyland. The suggestion of mystery and the supernatural

13

which haunts the forest at all times, is intensified by this unearthly glow.

We found the Black Forest farm houses and villages all that the Black Forest stories have pictured them.   The first genuine specimen which we came upon was the mansion of a rich farmer and member of the Common Council of the parish or

BLACK FOREST GRANDEE.

district.   He was an important personage in the land and so was his wife also, of course.   His daughter was the " catch " of the region, and she may be already entering into immortality as the heroine of one of Auerbach's novels for all I know.   We shall see, for if he puts her in I shall recognize her by her Black Forest clothes, and her burned complexion, her plump figure, her fat hands, her dull expression, her gen-

GRANDEE'S DAUGHTER.

tle spirit, her generous feet, her bonnetless head, and the plait-
ed tails of hemp-colored hair hanging down her back.

The house was big enough for a hotel; it was a hundred
feet long and fifty wide, and ten feet high, from ground to

eaves; but from the eaves to the comb of the mighty roof was as much as forty feet, or maybe even more. This roof was of ancient mud-colored straw thatch a foot thick, and was covered all over, except in a few trifling spots, with a thriving and luxurious growth of green vegetation, mainly moss. The mossless spots were places where repairs had been made by the insertion of bright new masses of yellow straw. The eaves projected far down, like sheltering, hospitable wings. Across the gable that fronted the road, and about ten feet above the ground, ran a narrow porch, with a wooden railing; a row of small windows filled with very small panes looked upon the porch. Above were two or three other little windows, one clear up under the sharp apex of the roof. Before the ground-floor door was a huge pile of manure. The door of a second-story room on the side of the house was open, and occupied by the rear elevation of a cow. Was this probably the drawing-room? All of the front half of the house from the ground up seemed to be occupied by the people, the cows and the chickens, and all the rear half by draft animals and hay. But the chief feature, all around this house was the big heaps of manure.

We became very familiar with the fertilizer in the Forest. We fell unconsciously into the habit of judging of a man's station in life by this outward and eloquent sign. Sometimes we said "Here is a poor devil, this is manifest." When we saw a stately accumulation, we said, "Here is a banker" When we encountered a country seat surrounded by an Alpine pomp of manure, we said, "Doubtless a Duke lives here."

The importance of this feature has not been properly magnified in the Black Forest stories. Manure is evidently the Black Forester's main treasure,—his coin, his jewel, his pride, his Old Master, his keramics, his bric-a-brac, his darling, his title to public consideration, envy, veneration, and his first solicitude when he gets ready to make his will. The true Black Forest novel, if it is ever written, will be skeletoned somewhat in this way:

Skeleton for Black Forest Novel.

Rich old farmer, named Huss. Has inherited great wealth of manure, and by diligence has added to it. It is double-starred in Baedeker.* The Black Forest artist paints it—his masterpiece. The king comes to see it. Gretchen Huss, daughter and heiress. Paul Hoch, young neighbor, suitor for Gretchen's hand,—ostensibly; he really wants the manure. Hoch has a good many cart-loads of the Black Forest currency himself, and therefore is a good catch; but he is sordid, mean, and without sentiment, whereas Gretchen is all sentiment and poetry. Hans Schmidt,

RICH OLD HUSS.

young neighbor, full of sentiment, full of poetry, loves Gretchen, Gretchen loves him. But he has no manure. Old Huss forbids him the house. His heart breaks, he goes away to die in the woods, far from the cruel world,—for he says, bitterly, "What is man, without manure?"

[Interval of six months.]

Paul Hoch comes to old Huss and says, "I am at last as rich as you required,—come and view the pile." Old Huss views

GRETCHEN.

it and says, "It is sufficient—take her and be happy,"—meaning Gretchen.

[Interval of two weeks.]

---

* When Baedeker's guide books mention a thing and put two stars * * after it, it means "well worth visiting." M. T.

Wedding party assembled in old Huss's drawing room; Hoch placid and content, Gretchen weeping over her hard fate. Enter old Huss's head book-

keeper. Huss says fiercely, "I gave you three weeks to find out why your books don't balance, and to prove that you are not a default-er; the time is up,—find me the missing property or you go to prison as a thief." Book-keeper: "I have found it." "Where?" Book-keeper: sternly,—tragically: "In the bridegroom's pile!—behold the thief—see him blench and

PAUL HOCH.

tremble!" [Sensation.] Paul Hoch: "Lost, lost!"—falls over the cow in a swoon and is handcuffed. Gretchen: "Saved!" Falls over the calf in a swoon of joy, but is caught in the arms of Hans Schmidt, who springs in at

that moment. Old Huss: "What, you here, varlet? unhand the maid and quit the place." Hans: still supporting the insensible girl: "Nev-er! Cruel old man, know that I come with claims which even you can not despise."

Huss: "What, *you?* name them."

Hans: "Then listen. The world had forsaken me, I forsook the world I wandered in the solitude of the forest, longing for death but finding

HANS SCHMIDT.

none. I fed upon roots, and in my bitterness I dug for the bitterest, loathing the sweeter kind. Digging, three days agone, I struck a manure mine!—a Golconda, a limitless Bonanza, of solid manure! I can buy you *all*, and have mountain ranges of manure left! Ha-ha, *now* thou smilest a smile!" [Immense sensation.] Exhibition of specimens from the mine. Old Huss, enthusiastically: "Wake her up, shake her up,

noble young man, she is yours!" Wedding takes place on
the spot; book-keeper restored to his office and emoluments;
Paul Hoch led off to jail. The Bonanza king of the Black
Forest lives to a good old age, blessed with the love of his
wife and of his twenty-seven children, and the still sweeter
envy of everybody around.

ELECTING A NEW MEMBER.

We took our noon meal of fried trout one day at the Plow
Inn, in a very pretty village, (Ottenhöfen,) and then went
into the public room to rest and smoke. There we found
nine or ten Black Forest grandees assembled around a table.
They were the Common Council of the parish. They had gathered there at 8 o'clock that morning to elect a new member,
and they had now been drinking beer four hours at the new
member's expense. They were men of fifty or sixty years
of age, with grave good-natured faces, and were all dressed

in the costume made familiar to us by the Black Forest stories: broad, round-topped black felt hats with the brims curled up all around; long red waistcoats with large metal buttons, black alpaca coats with the waists up between the shoulders. There were no speeches, there was but little talk, there were no frivolities; the Council filled themselves gradually, steadily, but surely, with beer, and conducted themselves with sedate decorum, as became men of position, men of influence, men of manure.

We had a hot afternoon tramp up the valley, along the grassy bank of a rushing stream of clear water, past farm houses, water mills, and no end of wayside crucifixes and saints and Virgins. These crucifixes, etc., are set up in memory of departed friends by survivors, and are almost as frequent as telegraph poles are in other lands.

We followed the carriage road, and had our usual luck: we traveled under a beating sun, and always saw the shade leave the shady places before we could get to them. In all our wanderings we seldom managed to strike a piece of road at its time for being shady. We had a particularly hot time of it on that particular afternoon, and with no comfort but what we could get out of the fact that the peasants at work away up on the steep mountain sides above our heads were even worse off than we were. By and by it became impossible to endure the intolerable glare and heat any longer; so we struck across the ravine and entered the deep cool twilight of the forest, to hunt for what the guide book called the "old road."

We found an old road, and it proved eventually to be the right one, though we followed it at the time with the conviction that it was the wrong one. If it was the wrong one there could be no use in hurrying, therefore we did not hurry, but sat down frequently on the soft moss and enjoyed the restful quiet and shade of the forest solitudes. There had been distractions in the carriage road,—school children, peasants, wagons, troops of pedestrianizing students from all over Germany, —but we had the old road all to ourselves.

Now and then, while we rested, we watched the laborious ant at his work. I found nothing new in him,—certainly nothing to change my opinion of him. It seems to me that in the matter of intellect the ant must be a strangely overrated bird. During many summers, now, I have watched him, when I ought to have been in better business, and I have not yet come across a living ant that seemed to have any more sense than a dead one. I refer to the ordinary ant, of course; I have had no experience of those wonderful Swiss and African ones which vote, keep drilled armies, hold slaves, and dispute about religion. Those particular ants may be all that the naturalist paints them, but I am persuaded that the average ant is a sham. I admit his industry, of course; he is the hardest working creature in the world,—when anybody is looking,—but his leather-headedness is the point I make against him. He goes out foraging, he makes a capture, and then what does he do? Go home? No,—he goes anywhere but home. He doesn't know where home is. His home may be only three feet away,—no matter, he can't find it. He makes his capture, as I have said; it is generally something which can be of no sort of use to himself or anybody else; it is usually seven times bigger than it ought to be; he hunts out the awkwardest place to take hold of it; he lifts it bodily up in the air by main force, and starts: not toward home, but in the opposite direction; not calmly and wisely, but with a frantic haste which is wasteful of his strength; he fetches up against a pebble, and instead of going around it, he climbs

OVERCOMING OBSTACLES.

over it backwards dragging his booty after him, tumbles down on the other side, jumps up in a passion, kicks the dust off his clothes, moistens his hands, grabs his property viciously, yanks it this way then that, shoves it ahead of him a moment, turns tail and lugs it after him another moment, gets madder and madder, then presently hoists it into the air and goes tearing away in an entirely new direction; comes to a weed; it never occurs to him to go around it; no, he must climb it; and he does climb it, dragging his worthless property to the top—which is as bright a thing to do as it would be for me to carry a sack of flour from Heidelberg to Paris by way of Strasburg steeple; when he gets up there he finds that that is not the place; takes a cursory glance at the scenery and either climbs down again or tumbles down, and starts off once more—as usual, in a new direction. At the end of half an hour, he fetches up within six inches of the place he started from and lays his burden down; meantime he has been over all the ground for two yards around, and climbed all the weeds and pebbles he came across. Now he wipes the sweat from his brow, strokes his limbs, and then marches aimlessly off, in as violent a hurry as ever. He traverses a good deal of zig-zag country, and by and by stumbles on his same booty again. He does not remember to have ever seen it before; he looks around to see which is not the way home, grabs his bundle and starts; he goes through the same adventures he had before; finally stops to rest, and a friend comes along. Evidently the friend remarks that a last year's grasshopper leg is a very noble acquisition, and inquires where he got it.

FRIENDS.

Evidently the proprietor does not remember exactly where he did get it, but thinks he got it "around here somewhere." Evidently the friend contracts to help him freight it home.

Then, with a judgment peculiarly antic, (pun not intentional,) they take hold of opposite ends of that grasshopper leg and
begin to tug with all their might in opposite directions. Presently they take a rest and confer together. They decide that
something is wrong, they can't make out what. Then they
go at it again, just as before. Same result. Mutual recrimi-
nations follow. Evidently each accuses the other of being an
obstructionist. They warm up, and the dispute ends in a
fight. They lock themselves together and chew each other's
jaws for a while; then they roll and tumble on the ground
till one loses a horn or a leg and has to haul off for repairs.
They make up and go to work again in the same old insane
way, but the crippled ant is at a disadvantage; tug as he may,
the other one drags off the booty and him at the end of it.
Instead of giving up, he hangs on, and gets his shins bruised
against every obstruction that comes in the way. By and by,
when that grasshopper leg has been dragged all over the same
old ground once more, it is finally dumped at about the spot
where it originally lay, the two perspiring ants inspect it
thoughtfully and decide that dried grasshopper legs are a
poor sort of property after all, and then each starts off in a
different direction to see if he can't find an old nail or something else that is heavy enough to afford entertainment and
at the same time valueness enough to make an ant want to
own it.

There in the Black Forest, on the mountain side, I saw an
ant go through with such a performance as this with a dead
spider of fully ten times his own weight. The spider was
not quite dead, but too far gone to resist. He had a round
body the size of a pea. The little ant—observing that I was
noticing—turned him on his back, sunk his fangs into his
throat, lifted him into the air and started vigorously off with
him, stumbling over little pebbles, stepping on the spider's
legs and tripping himself up, dragging him backwards, shov-
ing him bodily ahead, dragging him up stones six inches high
instead of going around them, climbing weeds twenty times

his own height and jumping from their summits,—and finally leaving him in the middle of the road to be confiscated by any other fool of an ant that wanted him. I measured the ground which this ass traversed, and arrived at the conclusion that what he had accomplished inside of twenty minutes would constitute some such job as this,—relatively speaking, —for a man; to-wit: to strap two eight-hundred pound horses together, carry them eighteen hundred feet, mainly

PROSPECTING

over (not around) bowlders averaging six feet high, and in the course of the journey climb up and jump from the top of one precipice like Niagara, and three steeples, each a hundred and twenty feet high; and then put the horses down, in an exposed place, without anybody to watch them, and go off to indulge in some other idiotic miracle for vanity's sake.

Science has recently discovered that the ant does not lay up anything for winter use. This will knock him out of literature, to some extent. He does not work, except when people are looking, and only then when the observer has a green, naturalistic look, and seems to be taking notes. This amounts to deception, and will injure him for the Sunday schools. He has not judgment enough to know what is good to eat from what isn't. This amounts to ignorance, and will impair the world's respect for him. He cannot stroll around a stump and find his way home again. This amounts to

idiotcy, and once the damaging fact is established, thoughtful people will cease to look up to him, the sentimental will
cease to fondle him. His vaunted industry is but a vanity
and of no effect, since he never gets home with anything he
starts with. This disposes of the last remnant of his reputation and wholly destroys his main usefulness as a moral agent,
since it will make the sluggard hesitate to go to him any more.
It is strange beyond comprehension, that so manifest a humbug as the ant has been able to fool so many nations and
keep it up so many ages without being found out.

The ant is strong, but we saw another strong thing, where
we had not suspected the presence of much muscular power
before. A toadstool—that vegetable which springs to full
growth in a single night—had torn loose and lifted a matted
mass of pine needles and dirt of twice its own bulk into the
air, and supported it there, like a column supporting a shed.
Ten thousand toadstools, with the right purchase, could lift
a man, I suppose. But what good would it do?

All our afternoon's progress had been up hill. About five
or half past we reached the summit, and all of a sudden the
dense curtain of the forest parted and we looked down into
a deep and beautiful gorge and out over a wide panorama of
wooded mountains with their summits shining in the sun
and their glade-furrowed sides dimmed with purple shade.
The gorge under our feet—called Allerheiligen,—afforded
room in the grassy level at its head for a cosy and delightful
human nest, shut away from the world and its botherations,
and consequently the monks of the old times had not failed
to spy it out; and here were the brown and comely ruins of
their church and convent to prove that priests had as fine an
instinct seven hundred years ago in ferreting out the choicest
nooks and corners in a land as priests have to-day.

A big hotel crowds the ruins a little, now, and drives a
brisk trade with summer tourists. We descended into the
gorge and had a supper which would have been very satisfactory if the trout had not been boiled. The Germans are

pretty sure to boil a trout or anything else if left to their
own devices.   This is an argument of some value in support
of the theory that they were the original colonists of the
wild islands off the coast of Scotland.   A schooner laden
with oranges was wrecked upon one of those islands a few
years ago, and the gentle savages rendered the captain such
willing assistance that he gave them as many oranges as they
wanted.   Next day he asked them how they liked them.
They shook their heads and said,—

"Baked, they were tough; and even boiled, they warn't
things for a hungry man to hanker after."

We went down the glen after supper.   It is beautiful,—a
mixture of sylvan loveliness and craggy wildness.   A limpid
torrent goes whistling down the glen, and toward the foot of
it winds through a narrow cleft between lofty precipices and
hurls itself over a succession of falls.   After one passes the
last of these he has a backward glimpse at the falls which is
very pleasing,—they rise in a seven-stepped stairway of foamy
and glittering cascades, and make a picture which is as
charming as it is unusual.

CHAPTER XXIII.

WE were satisfied that we could walk to Oppenau in one day, now that we were in practice; so we set out next morning after breakfast determined to do it. It was all the way down hill, and we had the loveliest summer weather for it. So we set the pedometer and then stretched away on an easy, regular stride, down through the cloven forest, drawing in the fragrant breath of the morning in deep refreshing draughts, and wishing we might never have anything to do forever but walk to Oppenau and keep on doing it and then doing it over again.

Now the true charm of pedestrianism does not lie in the walking, or in the scenery, but in the talking. The walking is good to time the movement of the tongue by, and to keep the blood and the brain stirred up and active; the scenery and the woodsy smells are good to bear in upon a man an unconscious and unobtrusive charm and solace to eye and soul and sense; but the supreme pleasure comes from the talk. It is no matter whether one talks wisdom or nonsense, the case is the same, the bulk of the enjoyment lies in the wagging of the gladsome jaw and the flapping of the sympathetic ear.

And what a motley variety of subjects a couple of people will casually rake over in the course of a day's tramp! There being no constraint, a change of subject is always in order, and so a body is not likely to keep pegging at a single topic until it grows tiresome. We discussed everything we knew, during the first fifteen or twenty minutes, that morning, and then branched out into the glad, free, boundless realm of the things we were not certain about.

Harris said that if the best writer in the world once got the slovenly habit of doubling up his " have's " he could never get rid of it while he lived. That is to say, if a man gets the habit of saying " I should have liked to have known more about it" instead of saying simply and sensibly, " I should have liked to know more about it," that man's disease is incurable. Harris said that this sort of lapse is to be found in every copy of every newspaper that has ever been printed in English, and in almost all of our books. He said he had observed it in Kirkham's grammar and in Macaulay. Harris believed that milk-teeth are commoner in men's mouths than those " doubled-up have's."*

That changed the subject to dentistry. I said I believed the average man dreaded tooth-pulling more than amputation, and that he would yell quicker under the former operation than he would under the latter. The philosopher Harris said that the average man would not yell in either case if he had an audience. Then he continued:

" When our brigade first went into camp on the Potomac, we used to be brought up standing, occasionally, by an ear-splitting howl of anguish. That meant that a soldier was getting a tooth pulled in a tent. But the surgeons soon changed that; they instituted open-air dentistry. There never was a howl afterwards,—that is, from the man who was having the tooth pulled. At the daily dental hour there would always be about five hundred soldiers gathered together in the neigh-

---

* I do not know that there have not been moments in the course of the present session when I should have been very glad to have accepted the proposal of my noble friend, and to have exchanged parts in some of our evenings of work.—[From a Speech of the English Chancellor of the Exchequer, August, 1879.

borhood of that dental chair waiting to see the performance,
—and help ; and the moment the surgeon took a grip on the
candidate's tooth and began to lift, every one of those five
hundred rascals would clap his hand to his jaw and begin to
hop around on one leg and howl with all the lungs he had !

GENERAL HOWL.

It was enough to raise your hair to hear that variegated and
enormous unanimous caterwaul burst out ! With so big and
so derisive an audience as that, a sufferer wouldn't emit a
sound though you pulled his head off. The surgeons said
that pretty often a patient was compelled to laugh, in the
midst of his pangs, but that they had never caught one crying out, after the open-air exhibition was instituted."

Dental surgeons suggested doctors, doctors suggested death,
death suggested skeletons,—and so, by a logical process the
conversation melted out of one of these subjects and into the
next, until the topic of skeletons raised up Nicodemus Dodge

14

out of the deep grave in my memory where he had lain buried and forgotten for twenty-five years.   When I was a boy in a printing office in Missouri, a loose-jointed, long-legged, tow-headed, jeans-clad, countrified cub of about sixteen lounged in one day, and without removing his hands from the depths of his trowsers pockets or taking off his faded ruin of a slouch hat, whose broken brim hung limp and ragged about

SEEKING A SITUATION.

his eyes and ears like a bug-eaten cabbage leaf, stared indifferently around, then leaned his hip against the editor's table, crossed his mighty brogans, aimed at a distant fly from a crevice in his upper teeth, laid him low, and said with composure,

"Whar's the boss?"

"I am the boss," said the editor, following this curious bit of architecture wonderingly along up to its clock-face with his eye.

"Don't want anybody fur to learn the business, 't ain't likely?"

"Well, I don't know. Would you like to learn it?"

" Pap's so po' he cain't run me no mo,' so I want to git a show somers if I kin, ' tain't no diffunce what,—I' m strong and hearty, and I don't turn my back on no kind of work, hard nur soft."

" Do you think you would like to learn the printing business ? "

" Well, I don't re'ly k'yer a durn what I *do* learn, so's I git a chance fur to make my way. I'd jist as soon learn print'n 's anything."

" Can you read ? "

" Yes,—middlin'."

" Write ? "

" Well, I've seed people could lay over me thar."

" Cipher ? "

" Not good enough to keep store, I don't reckon, but up as fur as twelve-times-twelve I ain't no slouch. ' Tother side of that is what gits me."

" Where is your home ? "

" I'm f'm old Shelby."

" What's your father's religious denomination ? "

" Him ? O, he's a blacksmith."

" No, no,—I don't mean his trade. What's his *religious* denomination ? "

" *O*,—I didn't understand you befo'. He's a Freemason."

" No-no, you don't get my meaning yet. What I mean is, does he belong to any *church* ? "

" *Now* you're talkin' ! Couldn't make out what you was a tryin' to git through yo' head no way. B'long to a *church!* Why boss he's ben the pizenest kind of a Free-will Babtis' for forty year. They ain't no pizener ones 'n' what *he* is. Mighty good man, pap is. Everybody says that. If they said any diffrunt they wouldn't say it whar *I* wuz,—not *much* they wouldn't."

" What is your own religion ? "

" Well, boss, you've kind o' got me, thar,—and yit you hain't got me so mighty much, nuther. I think 't if a feller he'ps another feller when he's in trouble, and don't cuss, and don't do no mean things, nur noth'n' he ain' no business to do, and don't spell the Savior's name with a little g, he ain't runnin' no resks,—he's about as saift as if he b'longed to a church."

" But suppose he did spell it with a little g,—what then?"

" Well, if he done it a-purpose, I reckon he wouldn't stand no chance,—he *oughtn't* to have no chance, anyway, I'm most rotten certain 'bout that."

" What is your name?"

" Nicodemus Dodge."

" I think maybe you'll do, Nicodemus. We'll give you a trial, anyway."

" All right."

" When would you like to begin?"

" Now."

So, within ten minutes after we had first glimpsed this nondescript he was one of us, and with his coat off and hard at it.

Beyond that end of our establishment which was furthest from the street, was a deserted garden, pathless, and thickly grown with the bloomy and villainous " jimpson " weed and its common friend the stately sunflower. In the midst of this mournful spot was a decayed and aged little "frame" house with but one room, one window, and no ceiling,—it had been a smoke-house a generation before. Nicodemus was given this lonely and ghostly den as a bed chamber.

The village smarties recognized a treasure in Nicodemus, right away,—a butt to play jokes on. It was easy to see that he was inconceivably green and confiding. George Jones had the glory of perpetrating the first joke on him; he gave him a cigar with a fire-cracker in it and winked to the crowd to come; the thing exploded presently and swept away the bulk of Nicodemus's eyebrows and eyelashes. He simply said,—

" I consider them kind of seeg'yars dangersome,"—and

seemed to suspect nothing. The next evening Nicodemus
waylaid George and poured a bucket of ice-water over him.

One day, while Nicodemus was in swimming, Tom McEl-
roy "tied" his clothes. Nicodemus made a bonfire of Tom's,
by way of retaliation.

A third joke was played upon Nicodemus, a day or two
later,—he walked up the middle aisle of the village church,
Sunday night, with a staring hand-bill pinned between his
shoulders. The joker spent the remainder of the night, after

STANDING GUARD.

church, in the cellar of a deserted house, and Nicodemus sat
on the cellar door till toward breakfast time to make sure
that the prisoner remembered that if any noise was made,
some rough treatment would be the consequence. The cellar

had two feet of stagnant water in it, and was bottomed with six inches of soft mud.

But I wander from the point. It was the subject of skeletons that brought this boy back to my recollection. Before a very long time had elapsed, the village smarties began to feel an uncomfortable consciousness of not having made a very shining success out of their attempts on the simpleton from "old Shelby." Experimenters grew scarce and chary. Now the young doctor came to the rescue. There was delight and applause when he proposed to scare Nicodemus to death, and explained how he was going to do it. He had a noble new skeleton,—the skeleton of the late and only local celebrity, Jimmy Finn, the village drunkard,—a grisly piece of property which he had bought of Jimmy Finn himself, at auction, for fifty dollars, under great competition, when Jimmy lay very sick in the tan-yard a fortnight before his death. The fifty dollars had gone promptly for whisky and had considerably hurried up the change of ownership in the skeleton. The doctor would put Jimmy Finn's skeleton in Nicodemus's bed!

This was done,—about half past ten in the evening. About Nicodemus's usual bedtime,—midnight,—the village jokers came creeping stealthily through the jimpson weeds and sunflowers toward the lonely frame den. They reached the window and peeped in. There sat the long-legged pauper, on his bed, in a very short shirt, and nothing more; he was

RESULT OF A JOKE.   dangling his legs contentedly back and forth, and wheezing the music of " Camptown

Races" out of a paper-overlaid comb which he was pressing against his mouth; by him lay a new jewsharp, a new top, a solid india-rubber ball, a handful of painted marbles, five pounds of "store" candy, and a well-gnawed slab of gingerbread as big and as thick as a volume of sheet music. He had sold the skeleton to a traveling quack for three dollars and was enjoying the result!

Just as we had finished talking about skeletons and were drifting into the subject of fossils, Harris and I heard a shout, and glanced up the steep hillside. We saw men and women standing away up there looking frightened, and there was a bulky object tumbling and floundering down the steep slope toward us. We  got out of the way, and when the object landed in the road it proved to be a boy. He had tripped and fallen, and there was nothing for him to do but trust to luck and take what might come.

When one starts to roll down a place like that, there is no stopping till the bottom is reached. Think of people *farming* on a slant which

DESCENDING A FARM.

is so steep that the best you can say of it,—if you want to be fastidiously accurate,—is, that it is a little steeper than a ladder and not quite so steep as a mansard roof. But that is what they do. Some of the little farms on the hillside opposite Heidelberg were stood up "edgeways." The boy was wonderfully jolted up, and his head was bleeding, from cuts which it had got from small stones on the way.

Harris and I gathered him up and set him on a stone, and by that time the men and women had scampered down and brought his cap.

Men, women and children flocked out from neighboring

cottages and joined the crowd; the pale boy was petted, and stared at, and commiserated, and water was brought for him to drink, and bathe his bruizes in. And such another clatter of tongues! All who had seen the catastrophe were describing it at once, and each trying to talk louder than his neighbor; and one youth of a superior genius ran a little way up the hill, called attention, tripped, fell, rolled down among us, and thus triumphantly showed exactly how the thing had been done.

Harris and I were included in all the descriptions: how we were coming along; how Hans Gross shouted; how we looked up startled; how we saw Peter coming like a cannon-shot; how judiciously we got out of the way, and let him come; and with what presence of mind we picked him up and brushed him off and set him on a rock when the performance was over. We were as much heroes as anybody else, except Peter, and were so recognized; we were taken with Peter and the populace to Peter's mother's cottage, and there we ate bread and cheese, and drank milk and beer with everybody, and had a most sociable good time; and when we left we had a hand-shake all around, and were receiving and shouting back *Leb' wohl's* until a turn in the road separated us from our cordial and kindly new friends forever.

We accomplished our undertaking. At half past 8 in the evening we stepped into Oppenau, just eleven hours and a half out from Allerheiligen,—146 miles. This is the distance by pedometer; the guide-book and the Imperial Ordnance maps make it only ten and a quarter,—a surprising blunder, for these two authorities are usually singularly accurate in the matter of distances.

CHAPTER XXIV.

THAT was a thoroughly satisfactory walk,—and the only one we were ever to have which was all the way down hill. We took the train next morning and returned to Baden-Baden through fearful fogs of dust. Every seat was crowded, too; for it was Sunday, and consequently everybody was taking a "pleasure" excursion. Hot! the sky was an oven,—and a sound one, too, with no cracks in it to let in any air. An odd time for a pleasure excursion, certainly.

Sunday is the great day, on the continent,—the free day, the happy day. One can break the Sabbath in a hundred ways without committing any sin.

We do not work on Sunday, because the commandment forbids it; the Germans do not work on Sunday, because the commandment forbids it. We rest on Sunday, because the commandment requires it; the Germans rest on Sunday, because the commandment requires it. But in the definition of the word " rest " lies all the difference. With us, its Sunday meaning is, stay in the house and keep still; with the Germans its Sunday and week-day meanings seems to be the same,—rest the *tired part*, and never mind the other parts of the frame; rest the tired part, and use the means best calculated to rest that particular part. Thus: If one's duties have kept him in the house all the week, it will rest him to be out on Sunday; if his duties have required him to read weighty

231

and serious matter all the week, it will rest him to read light matter on Sunday ; if his occupation has busied him with

KEEPING SUNDAY.

death and funerals all the week, it will rest him to go to the theatre Sunday night and put in two or three hours laughing at a comedy ; if he is tired with digging ditches or felling trees all the week, it will rest him to lie quiet in the house on Sunday ; if the hand, the arm, the brain, the tongue, or any other member, is fatigued with in-anition, it is not to be rested by adding a day's inanition ; but if a member is fatigued with exertion, inanition is the right rest for it. Such is the way in which the Germans seem to define the word "rest;" that is to say, they rest a member by recreating, recuperating. restoring its forces. But our definition is less broad. We all rest alike on Sunday,—by secluding ourselves and keeping still, whether that is the surest way to rest the most of us or not. The Germans make the actors, the preachers, etc., work on Sunday. We encourage the preachers, the editors, the printers, etc., to work on Sunday, and imagine that none of the sin of it falls upon us ; but I do not know how we are going to get around the fact that if it is wrong for the printer to work at his trade on Sunday it must be equally wrong for the preacher to work at his, since the commandment has made no exception in his favor. We buy Monday morning's paper and read it, and thus encourage Sunday-printing. But I shall never do it again.

The Germans remember the Sabbath day to keep it holy, by abstaining from work, as commanded ; we keep it holy by

abstaining from work, as commanded, and by also abstaining
from play, which is not commanded. Perhaps we construct-
ively *break* the command to rest, because the resting we do
is in most cases only a name, and not a fact.

These reasonings have sufficed, in a measure, to mend the
rent in my conscience which I made by traveling to Baden-
Baden that Sunday. We arrived in time to furbish up and
get to the English church before services began. We arrived
in considerable style, too, for the landlord had ordered the
first carriage that could be found, since there was no time to
lose, and our coachman was so splendidly liveried that we
were probably mistaken for a brace of stray dukes ; else why
were we honored with a pew all to ourselves, away up among
the very elect at the left of the chancel ? That was my first
thought. In the pew directly in front of us sat an elderly
lady, plainly and cheaply dressed ; at her side sat a young
lady with a very sweet face, and she also was quite simply
dressed ; but around us and about us were clothes and jewels
which it would do anybody's heart good to worship in.

I thought it was pretty manifest that the elderly lady was
embarrassed at finding herself in such a conspicuous place arrayed in such cheap apparel ; I began to feel sorry for her
and troubled about her. She tried to seem very busy with
her prayer book and her responses, and unconscious that she
was out of place, but I said to myself, " She is not succeeding,
—there is a distressed tremulousness in her voice which be-
trays increasing embarrassment." Presently the Savior's
name was mentioned, and in her flurry she lost her head completely, and rose and curtsied, instead of making a slight nod
as everybody else did. The sympathetic blood surged to my
temples and I turned and gave those fine birds what I intended to be a beseeching look, but my feelings got the better of
me and changed it into a look which said, " If any of you
pets of fortune laugh at this poor soul, you will deserve to be
flayed for it." Things went from bad to worse, and I shortly
found myself mentally taking the unfriended lady under my

protection. My mind was wholly upon her, I forgot all about
the sermon. Her embarrassment took stronger and stronger

AN OBJECT OF SYMPATHY.

hold upon her; she got to snapping the lid of her smelling
bottle,—it made a loud sharp sound, but in her trouble she
snapped and snapped away, unconscious of what she was doing. The last extremity was reached when the collection-
plate began its rounds; the moderate people threw in pennies,
the nobles and the rich contributed silver, but she laid a
twenty-mark gold piece upon the book-rest before her with a
sounding slap! I said to myself, "She has parted with all
her little hoard to buy the consideration of these unpitying
people,—it is a sorrowful spectacle." I did not venture to
look around this time; but as the service closed, I said to myself, "Let them laugh, it is their opportunity; but at the door
of this church they shall see her step into our fine carriage
with us, and our gaudy coachman shall drive her home."
    Then she rose,—and all the congregation stood while she

walked down the aisle. She was the Empress of Germany !

No,—she had not been so much embarrassed as I had supposed. My imagination had got started on the wrong scent,
and that is always hopeless; one is sure, then, to go straight
on misinterpreting everything, clear through to the end. The
young lady with her imperial Majesty was a maid of honor,
—and I had been taking her for one of her boarders, all the
time.

This is the only time I have ever had an Empress under
my personal protection ; and considering my inexperience, I
wonder I got through with it so well. I should have been a
little embarrassed myself if I had known earlier what sort of
a contract I had on my hands.

We found that the Empress had been in Baden-Baden several days. It is said that she never attends any but the English form of church service.

I lay abed and read and rested from my journey's fatigues
the remainder of that Sunday, but I sent my agent to repre-
sent me at the afternoon service, for I never allow anything
to interfere with my habit of attending church twice every
Sunday.

There was a vast crowd in the public grounds that night
to hear the band play the " Fremersberg." This piece tells
one of the old legends of the region : how a great noble of
the Middle Ages got lost in the mountains, and wandered
about with his dogs in a violent storm, until at last the faint
tones of a monastery bell, calling the monks to a midnight
service, caught his ear, and he followed the direction the
sounds came from and was saved. A beautiful air ran through
the music, without ceasing ; sometimes loud and strong, sometimes so soft that it could hardly be distinguished,—but it
was always there; it swung grandly along through the shrill
whistling of the storm-wind, the rattling patter of the rain,
and the boom and crash of the thunder ; it wound soft and
low through the lesser sounds, the distant ones, such as the
throbbing of the convent bell, the melodious winding of the

hunter's horn, the distressed bayings of his dogs, and the solemn chanting of the monks; it rose again, with a jubilant ring, and mingled itself with the country songs and dances of the peasants assembled in the convent hall to cheer up the rescued huntsman while he ate his supper. The instruments imitated all these sounds with a marvelous exactness. More than one man started to raise his umbrella when the storm burst forth and the sheets of mimic rain came driving by; it was hardly possible to keep from putting your hand to your hat when the fierce wind began to rage and shriek; and it

A NON-CLASSICAL STYLE.

was *not* possible to refrain from starting when those sudden and charmingly real thundercrashes were let loose.

I suppose the Fremersberg is very low-grade music; I

know, indeed, that it *must* be low-grade music, because it so
delighted me, warmed me, moved me, stirred me, uplifted me,
enraptured me, that I was full of cry all the time, and mad
with enthusiasm. My soul had never had such a scouring out
since I was born. The solemn and majestic chanting of the
monks was not done by instruments, but by men's voices; and
it rose and fell, and rose again in that rich confusion of war-
ring sounds, and pulsing bells, and the stately swing of that
ever-present enchanting air, and it seemed to me that nothing
but the very lowest of low-grade music *could* be so divinely
beautiful. The great crowd which the Fremersberg had called out was another evidence that it was low-grade music; for
only the few are educated up to a point where high-grade
music gives pleasure. I have never heard enough classic
music to be able to enjoy it. I dislike the opera because I
want to love it and can't.

I suppose there are two kinds of music,—one kind which
one feels, just as an oyster might, and another sort which
requires a higher faculty, a faculty which must be assisted
and developed by teaching. Yet if base music gives certain
of us wings, why should we want any other? But we do.
We want it because the higher and better like it. But we
want it without giving it the necessary time and trouble; so
we climb into that upper tier, that dress circle, by a lie: we
pretend we like it. I know several of that sort of people,—
and I propose to be one of them myself when I get home
with my fine European education.

And then there is painting. What a red rag is to a bull,
Turner's "Slave Ship" was to me, before I studied Art. Mr.
Ruskin is educated in art up to a point where that picture
throws him into as mad an ecstacy of pleasure as it used to
throw me into one of rage, last year, when I was ignorant.
His cultivation enables him,—and me, now,—to see water in
that glaring yellow mud, and natural effects in those lurid explosions of mixed smoke and flame, and crimson sunset glo-
ries; it reconciles him,—and me, now,—to the floating of

iron cable-chains and other unfloatable things; it reconciles us to fishes swimming around on top of the mud,—I mean the water. The most of the picture is a manifest impossibility,—that is to say, a lie; and only rigid cultivation can enable a man to find truth in a lie. But it enabled Mr. Ruskin to do it, and it has enabled me to do it, and I am thankful for it. A Boston newspaper reporter went and took a look at the Slave Ship floundering about in that fierce conflagration of reds and yellows, and said it reminded him of a tortoise-shell cat having a fit in a platter of tomatoes. In my then uneducated state, that went home to my non-cultivation, and I thought here is a man with an unobstructed eye. Mr. Ruskin would have said : This person is an ass. That is what I would say, now.*

However, our business in Baden-Baden this time, was to join our courier. I had thought it best to hire one, as we should be in Italy, by and by, and we did not know that language. Neither did he. We found him at the hotel, ready to take charge of us. I asked him if he was " all fixed." He said he was. That was very true. He had a trunk, two small satchels, and an umbrella. I was to pay him $55 a month and railway fares. On the continent the railway fare on a trunk is about the same it is on a man. Couriers do not have to pay any board and lodging. This seems a great saving to the tourist,—at first. It does not occur to the tourist that *somebody* pays that man's board and lodging. It occurs to him by and by, however, in one of his lucid moments.

---

*Months after this was written, I happened into the National Gallery in London, and soon became so fascinated with the Turner pictures that I could hardly get away from the place. I went there often, afterward, meaning to see the rest of the gallery, but the Turner spell was too strong; it could not be shaken off. However, the Turners which attracted me most did not remind me of the Slave Ship.

TRADITIONAL CHAMOIS.

CHAPTER XXV.

NEXT morning we left in the train for Switzerland, and reached Lucerne about ten o'clock at night. The first discovery I made was that the beauty of the lake had not been exaggerated. Within a day or two I made another discovery. This was, that the lauded chamois is not a wild goat; that it is not a horned animal; that it is not shy; that it does not avoid human society; and that there is no peril in hunting it. The chamois is a black or brown creature no bigger than a mustard seed; you do not have to go after it, it comes after you; it arrives in vast herds and skips and scampers all over your body, inside your clothes; thus it is not shy, but extremely sociable; it is not afraid of man, on the contrary it will attack him; its bite is not dangerous, but neither is it pleasant; its activity has not been overstated,—if you try to put your finger on it, it will skip a thousand times its own length at one jump, and no eye is sharp enough to see where it lights. A great deal of romantic nonsense has been written about the Swiss chamois and the perils of hunting it, whereas the truth is that even women and children hunt it, and fearlessly; indeed, everybody hunts it; the hunting is going on all the time, day and night, in bed and out of it. It is poetic foolishness to hunt it with a gun; very few people do that; there is not one man in a million who can hit it with a gun. It is much easier to catch it than it is to shoot it, and

only the experienced chamois hunter can do either. Another
common piece of exaggeration is that about the "scarcity" of
the chamois. It is the reverse of scarce. Droves of 100,-
000,000 chamois are not unusual in the Swiss hotels. Indeed
they are so numerous as to be a great pest. The romancers
always dress up the chamois hunter, in a fanciful and picturesque costume, whereas the best way to hunt this game is
to do it without any costume at all. The article of commerce

HUNTING CHAMOIS—THE TRUE WAY.

called chamois-skin is another fraud; nobody could skin a
chamois, it is too small. The creature is a humbug in every
way, and everything which has been written about it is sentimental exaggeration. It was no pleasure to me to find
the chamois out, for he had been one of my pet illusions; all
my life it had been my dream to see him in his native wilds
some day, and engage in the adventurous sport of chasing
him from cliff to cliff. It is no pleasure to me to expose
him, now, and destroy the reader's delight in him and respect
for him, but still it must be done, for when an honest writer
discovers an imposition it is his simple duty to strip it bare
and hurl it down from its place of honor, no matter who suf-
fers by it; any other course would render him unworthy of
the public confidence.

HUNTING CHAMOIS (AS REPORTED).

Lucerne is a charming place. It begins at the water's edge, with a fringe of hotels, and scrambles up and spreads itself over two or three sharp hills in a crowded, disorderly, but picturesque way, offering to the eye a heaped-up confusion of red roofs, quaint gables, dormer windows, toothpick steeples, with here and there a bit of ancient embattled wall bending itself over the ridges, worm-fashion, and here and there an old square tower of heavy masonry. And also here and there a town clock with only one hand,—a hand which stretches straight across the dial and has no joint in it ; such a clock helps out the picture, but you cannot tell the time of day by it. Between the curving line of hotels and the lake is a broad avenue with lamps and a double rank of low shade trees. The lake front is walled with masonry like a pier, and has a railing, to keep people from walking overboard. All day long the vehicles dash along the avenue, and nurses, children and tourists sit in the shade of the trees, or lean on the railing and watch the schools of fishes darting about in the clear water or gaze out over the lake at the stately border of snow-hooded mountain peaks. Little pleasure-steamers, black with people, are coming and going all the time ; and everywhere one sees young girls and young men paddling about in fanciful row-boats, or skimming along by the help of sails when there is any wind. The front rooms of the hotels have little railed balconies, where one may take his private luncheon in calm cool comfort and look down upon this busy and pretty scene and enjoy it without having to do any of the work connected with it.

Most of the people, both male and female, are in walking costume, and carry alpenstocks. Evidently it is not considered safe to go about in Switzerland, even in town, without an alpenstock. If the tourist forgets, and comes down to breakfast without his alpenstock, he goes back and gets it, and stands it up in the corner. When his touring in Switzerland is finished, he does not throw that broomstick away, but lugs it home with him, to the far corners of the earth,

although this costs him more trouble and bother than a baby
or a courier could.   You see, the alpenstock is his trophy ;
his name is burned upon it ; and if he has climbed a hill, or
jumped a brook, or traversed a brickyard with it, he has the
names of those places burned upon it, too.   Thus it is his
regimental flag, so to speak, and bears the record of his achieve-
ments.   It is worth three francs when he buys it, but a bonanza could not purchase it after his great deeds have been
inscribed upon it.   There are artisans all about Switzerland

MARKING ALPENSTOCKS.

whose trade it is to burn these things upon the alpenstock of
the tourist.   And observe, a man is respected in Switzerland
according to his alpenstock.   I found I could get no attention
there, while I carried an unbranded one.   However, brand-
ing is not expensive, so I soon remedied that.   The effect
upon the next detachment of tourists was very marked.   I
felt repaid for my trouble.

Half of the summer horde in Switzerland is made up of
English people ; the other half is made up of many nationalities, the Germans leading and the Americans coming next.
The Americans were not as numerous as I had expected they
would be.

The 7.30 table d'hote at the great Schweitzerhof furnished
a mighty array and variety of nationalities, but it offered a
better opportunity to observe costumes than people, for the
multitude sat at immensely long tables, and therefore the
faces were mainly seen in perspective ; but the breakfasts
were served at small round tables, and then if one had the
fortune to get a table in the midst of the assemblage he could
have as many faces to study as he could desire. We used to
try to guess out the nationalities, and generally succeeded
tolerably well. Sometimes we tried to guess people's names ;
but that was a failure ; that is a thing which probably requires
a good deal of practice. We
presently dropped it and gave
our efforts to less difficult particulars. One morning I said,—

" There is an American party."

Harris said,—

" Yes,—but name the State."

I named one State, Harris
named another. We agreed upon one thing, however,—that the
young girl with the party was
very beautiful, and very tastefully dressed. But we disagreed as
to her age. I said she was eight-

IS SHE EIGHTEEN OR TWENTY ?

een, Harris said she was twenty. The dispute between us
waxed warm and I finally said, with a pretense of being in
earnest,—

" Well, there is one way to settle the matter,—I will go
and ask her."

Harris said, sarcastically, " Certainly, that is the thing to

do. All you need to do is to use the common formula over
here : go and say, ' I'm an American ! ' Of course she will
be glad to see you."

Then he hinted that perhaps there was no great danger of
my venturing to speak to her.

I said, " I was only talking,—I didn't intend to approach
her, but I see that you do not know what an intrepid person
I am. I am not afraid of any woman that walks. I will go
and speak to this young girl."

The thing I had in my mind was not difficult. I meant to
address her in the most respectful way and ask her to pardon
me if her strong resemblance to a former acquaintance of
mine was deceiving me; and when she should reply that the
name I mentioned was not the name she bore, I meant to beg
pardon again, most respectfully, and retire. There would be
no harm done. I walked to her table, bowed to the gentleman, then turned to her and was about to begin my little
speech when she exclaimed,—

" I *knew* I wasn't mistaken,—I told John it was you ! John
said it probably wasn't, but I knew I was right. I said you
would recognize me presently and come over ; and I'm glad
you did, for I shouldn't have felt much flattered if you had
gone out of this room without recognizing me. Sit down, sit
down,—how odd it is,—you are the last person I was ever
expecting to see again."

This was a stupefying surprise. It took my wits clear
away, for an instant. However, we shook hands cordially all
around, and I sat down. But truly this was the tightest place
I ever was in. I seemed to vaguely remember the girl's face,
now, but I had no idea where I had seen it before, or what
name belonged with it. I immediately tried to get up a di-
version about Swiss scenery, to keep her from launching into
topics that might betray that I did not know her, but it was
of no use, she went right along upon matters which interested
her more :

" O dear, what a night that was, when the sea washed the
forward boats away,—do you remember it ?"

"O, *don't* I!" said I,—but I didn't. I wished the sea had washed the rudder and the smoke-stack and the captain away, —then I could have located this questioner.

"And don't you remember how frightened poor Mary was, and how she cried?"

"Indeed I do!" said I. "Dear me, how it all comes back!"

I fervently wished it *would* come back,—but my memory

"I KNEW I WASN'T MISTAKEN."

was a blank. The wise way would have been to frankly own up; but I could not bring myself to do that, after the young girl had praised me so for recognizing her; so I went on, deeper and deeper into the mire, hoping for a chance clue but never getting one. The Unrecognizable continued, with vivacity,—

"Do you know, George married Mary, after all?"

"Why, no! Did he?"

"Indeed he did. He said he did not believe she was half

as much to blame as her father was, and I thought he was
right. Didn't you?"

"Of course he was. It was a perfectly plain case. I
always said so."

"Why no you didn't!—at least that summer."

"Oh, no, not that summer. No, you are perfectly right
about that. It was the following winter that I said it."

"Well, as it turned out, Mary was not in the least to blame,
—it was all her father's fault,—at least his and old Darley's."

It was necessary to say something,—so I said,—

"I always regarded Darley as a troublesome old thing."

"So he was, but then they always had a great affection for
him, although he had so many eccentricities. You remember that when the weather was the least cold, he would try
to come into the house."

I was rather afraid to proceed. Evidently Darley was not
a man,—he must be some other kind of animal,—possibly a
dog, maybe an elephant. However, tails are common to all
animals, so I ventured to say,—

"And what a tail he had!"

"*One!* He had a thousand!"

This was bewildering. I did not quite know what to say,
so I only said,—

"Yes, he *was* rather well fixed in the matter of tails."

"For a negro, and a crazy one at that, I should say he
was," said she.

It was getting pretty sultry for me. I said to myself, "Is
it possible she is going to stop there, and wait for me to
speak? If she does, the conversation is blocked. A negro
with a thousand tails is a topic which a person cannot talk
upon fluently and instructively without more or less preparation. As to diving rashly into such a vast subject,—"

But here, to my gratitude, she interrupted my thought by
saying,—

"Yes, when it came to tales of his crazy woes, there was
simply no end to them if anybody would listen. His own

quarters were comfortable enough, but when the weather was cold, the family were sure to have his company,—nothing could keep him out of the house. But they always bore it kindly because he had saved Tom's life, years before. You remember Tom?"

"O, perfectly. Fine fellow he was, too."

"Yes he was. And what a pretty little thing his child was!"

"You may well say that. I never saw a prettier child."

"I used to delight to pet it and dandle it and play with it."

"So did I."

"You named it. What *was* that name? I can't call it to mind."

It appeared to me that the ice was getting pretty thin, here. I would have given something to know what the child's sex was. However, I had the good luck to think of a name that would fit either sex,—so I brought it out,—

"I named it Frances."

"From a relative, I suppose? But you named the one that died, too,—one that I never saw. What did you call that one?"

I was out of neutral names, but as the child was dead and she had never seen it, I thought I might risk a name for it and trust to luck. Therefore I said,—

"I called that one Thomas Henry."

She said, musingly,—

"That is very singular......very singular."

I sat still and let the cold sweat run down. I was in a good deal of trouble, but I believed I could worry through if she wouldn't ask me to name any more children. I wondered where the lightning was going to strike next. She was still ruminating over that last child's title, but presently she said,—

"I have always been sorry you were away at the time,— I would have had you name my child."

" *Your* child !   Are you married ? "

" I have been married thirteen years."

" Christened, you mean."

" No, married.   The youth by your side is my son."

" It seems incredible,—even impossible.   I do not mean any harm by it, but would you mind telling me if you are any over eighteen ?—that is to say, will you tell me how old you are ? "

" I was just nineteen the day of the storm we were talking about.   That was my birth-day."

That did not help matters much, as I did not know the date of the storm.   I tried to think of some non-committal thing to say, to keep up my end of the talk and render my poverty in the matter of reminiscences as little noticeable as possible, but I seemed to be about out of non-committal things.   I was about to say, " You haven't changed a bit since then,"— but that was risky.   I thought of saying " You have improved ever so much since then,"—but that wouldn't answer, of course.   I was about to try a shy at the weather, for a saving change, when the girl slipped in ahead of me and said,—

" How I have enjoyed this talk over those happy old times, —haven't you ? "

" I never have spent such a half hour in all my life before ! " said I, with emotion ; and I could have added, with a near approach to truth, " and I would rather be scalped than spend another one like it."   I was holily grateful to be through with the ordeal, and was about to make my good-byes and get out, when the girl said,—

" But there is one thing that is ever so puzzling to me."

" Why what is that ? "

" That dead child's name.   What did you say it was ? "

Here was another balmy place to be in : I had forgotten the child's name ; I hadn't imagined it would be needed again. However, I had to pretend to know, anyway, so I said,—

" Joseph William."

The youth at my side corrected me, and said,—

" No,—Thomas Henry."

I thanked him,—in words,—and said, with trepidation,—

" O yes,—I was thinking of another child that I named,—
I have named a great many, and I get them confused,—this
one *was* named Henry Thompson,—"

"Thomas Henry," calmly interposed the boy.

I thanked him again,—strictly in words,—and stammered
out,—

" Thomas Henry,—yes, Thomas Henry was the poor child's
name. I named him for Thomas,—er,—Thomas Carlyle, the
great author, you know,—and Henry—er,—er,—Henry the
Eighth. The parents were very grateful to have a child
named Thomas Henry."

" That makes it more singular than ever," murmured my
beautiful friend.

" Does it ? Why ?"

" Because when the parents speak of that child now, they
always call it Susan Amelia."

That spiked my gun. I could not say anything. I was
entirely out of verbal obliquities ; to go further would be to
lie, and that I would not do ; so I simply sat still and suffered,—sat mutely and resignedly there, and sizzled,—for I
was being slowly fried to death in my own blushes. Presently the enemy laughed a happy laugh and said,—

" I *have* enjoyed this talk over old times, but you have not.
I saw very soon that you were only pretending to know me,
and so as I had wasted a compliment on you in the beginning,
I made up my mind to punish you. And I have succeeded
pretty well. I was glad to see that you knew George and
Tom and Darley, for I had never heard of them before and
therefore could not be sure that you had ; and I was glad to
learn the names of those imaginary children, too. One can
get quite a fund of information out of you if one goes at it
cleverly. Mary and the storm, and the sweeping away of the
forward boats, were facts—all the rest was fiction. Mary was
my sister ; her full name was Mary ——. *Now* do you remember me ?"

" Yes," I said, "I do remember you now; and you are as hard-hearted as you were thirteen years ago in that ship, else you wouldn't have punished me so. You haven't changed your nature nor your person, in any way at all; you look just as young as you did then, you are just as beautiful as you were then, and you have transmitted a deal of your comeliness to this fine boy. There,—if that speech moves you any, let's fly the flag of truce, with the understanding that I am conquered and confess it."

All of which was agreed to and accomplished, on the spot. When I went back to Harris, I said,—

" Now you see what a person with talent and address can do."

"Excuse me, I see what a person of colossal ignorance and simplicity can do. The idea of your going and intruding on a party of strangers, that way, and talking for half an hour; why I never heard of a man in his right mind doing such a thing before. What did you say to them?"

"I never said any harm. I merely asked the girl what her name was."

"I don't doubt it. Upon my word I don't. I think you were capable of it. It was stupid in me to let you go over there and make such an exhibition of yourself. But you know I couldn't really believe you would do such an inexcusable thing. What will those people think of us? But how did you say it?—I mean the manner of it. I hope you were not abrupt."

"No, I was careful about that. I said 'My friend and I would like to know what your name is, if you don't mind.'"

"No, that was not abrupt. There is a polish about it that does you infinite credit. And I am glad you put me in; that was a delicate attention which I appreciate at its full value. What did she do?"

"She didn't do anything in particular. She told me her name."

"Simply told you her name. Do you mean to say she did not show any surprise?"

" Well, now I come to think, she did show something; may be it was surprise; I hadn't thought of that,—I took it for gratification."

" O, undoubtedly you were right; it must have been gratification; it could not be otherwise than gratifying to be assaulted by a stranger with such a question as that. Then what did you do?"

" I offered my hand and the party gave me a shake."

"I saw it! I did not believe my own eyes, at the time. Did the gentleman say anything about cutting your throat?"

" No, they all seemed glad to see me, as far as I could judge."

"And do you know, I believe they were. I think they said to themselves, 'Doubtless this curiosity has got away from his keeper—let us amuse ourselves with him.' There is no other way of accounting for their facile docility. You sat down. Did they *ask* you to sit down?"

"No, they did not ask me, but I supposed they did not think of it."

" You have an un-

HARRIS ASTONISHED.

erring instinct. What else did you do? What did you talk about?"

" Well, I asked the girl how old she was?"

" *Un*doubtedly. Your delicacy is beyond praise. Go on, go on,—don't mind my apparent misery,—I always look so when I am steeped in a profound and reverent joy. Go on, —she told you her age?"

" Yes, she told me her age, and all about her mother, and her grandmother, and her other relations, and all about herself."

" Did she volunteer these statistics?"

"No, not exactly that. I asked the questions and she answered them."

"This is divine. Go on,—it is not possible that you forgot to inquire into her politics?"

"No, I thought of that. She is a democrat, her husband is a republican, and both of them are Baptists."

"Her husband? Is that child married?"

"She is not a child. She is married, and that is her husband who is there with her."

"Has she any children?"

"Yes,—seven and a half."

"That is impossible."

"No, she has them. She told me herself."

"Well, but seven and a *half*? How do you make out the half? Where does the half come in?"

"That is a child which she had by another husband,—not this one but another one,—so it is a step-child, and they do not count it full measure."

"Another husband? Has she had another husband?"

"Yes, four. This one is number four."

"I do not believe a word of it. It is impossible, upon its face. Is that boy there her brother?"

"No, that is her son. He is her youngest. He is not as old as he looks; he is only eleven and a half."

"These things are all manifestly impossible. This is a wretched business. It is a plain case: they simply took your measure, and concluded to fill you up. They seem to have succeeded. I am glad I am not in the mess; they may at least be charitable enough to think there ain't a pair of us. Are they going to stay here long?"

"No, they leave before noon."

"There is one man who is deeply grateful for that. How did you find out? You asked, I suppose?"

"No, along at first I inquired into their plans, in a general way, and they said they were going to be here a week, and make trips round about; but toward the end of the interview, when I said you and I would tour around with them with pleasure, and offered to bring you over and introduce you, they hesitated a little, and asked if you were from the same establishment that I was. I said you were, and then they said they had changed their mind and considered it necessary to start at once and visit a sick relative in Siberia."

"Ah me, you struck the summit! You struck the loftiest altitude of stupidity that human effort has ever reached. You shall have a monument of jackass's skulls as high as the Strasburg spire if you die before I do. They wanted to know if I was from the same 'establishment' that you hail from, did they? What did they mean by 'establishment?'"

"I don't know; it never occurred to me to ask."

"Well *I* know. They meant an asylum—an *idiot* asylum, do you understand? So they *do* think there's a pair of us, after all. Now what do you think of yourself?"

"Well I don't know. I didn't know I was doing any harm; I didn't *mean* to do any harm. They were very nice people, and they seemed to like me."

Harris made some rude remarks and left for his bedroom, —to break some furniture, he said. He was a singularly irascible man; any little thing would disturb his temper.

I had been well scorched by the young woman, but no matter, I took it out of Harris. One should always "get even" in some way, else the sore place will go on hurting.

CHAPTER XXVI.

THE Hofkirsche is celebrated for its organ concerts. All summer long the tourists flock to that church about six o'clock in the evening, and pay their franc, and listen to the noise. They don't stay to hear all of it, but get up and tramp out over the sounding stone floor, meeting late comers who tramp in in a sounding and vigorous way. This tramping back and forth is kept up nearly all the time, and is accented by the continuous slamming of the door, and the coughing and barking and sneezing of the crowd. Meantime the big organ is booming and crashing and thundering away, doing its best to prove that it is the biggest and loudest organ in Europe, and that a tight little box of a church is the most favorable place to average and appreciate its powers in. It is true, there were some soft and merciful passages occasionally, but the tramp-tramp of the tourists only allowed one to get fitful glimpses of them, so to speak. Then right away the organist would let go another avalanche.

The commerce of Lucerne consists mainly in gimcrackery of the souvenir sort; the shops are packed with Alpine crystals, photographs of scenery, and wooden and ivory carvings. I will not conceal the fact that miniature figures of the Lion of Lucerne are to be had in them. Millions of them. But they are libels upon him, every one of them. There is a subtle something about the majestic pathos of the original which

258

the copyist cannot get. Even the sun fails to get it; both the photographer and the carver give you a dying lion, and that is all. The shape is right, the attitude is right, the proportions are right, but that indescribable something which makes the Lion of Lucerne the most mournful and moving piece of stone in the world, is wanting.

The Lion lies in his lair in the perpendicular face of a low cliff,—for he is carved from the living rock of the cliff. His

LION OF LUCERNE.

size is colossal, his attitude is noble. His head is bowed, the broken spear is sticking in his shoulder, his protecting paw rests upon the lilies of France. Vines hang down the cliff and wave in the wind, and a clear stream trickles from above and empties into a pond at the base, and in the smooth surface of the pond the lion is mirrored, among the water lilies.

Around about are green trees and grass. The place is a sheltered, reposeful, woodland nook, remote from noise and stir and confusion,—and all this is fitting, for lions do die in

16

such places, and not on granite pedestals in public squares fenced with fancy iron railings. The Lion of Lucerne would be impressive anywhere, but nowhere so impressive as where he is.

Martyrdom is the luckiest fate that can befall some people. Louis XVI did not die in his bed, consequently history is very gentle with him; she is charitable toward his failings, and she finds in him high virtues which are not usually considered to be virtues when they are lodged in kings. She makes him out to be a person with a meek and modest spirit the heart of a female saint, and a wrong head. None of these qualities are kingly but the last. Taken together they make a character which would have fared harshly at the hands of history if its owner had had the ill luck to miss martyrdom. With the best intentions to do the right thing, he always managed to do the wrong one. Moreover, nothing could get the female saint out of him. He knew, well enough, that in national emergencies he must not consider how he ought to act, as a man, but how he ought to act as a king; so he honestly tried to sink the man and be the king,—but it was a failure, he only succeeded in being the female saint. He was not instant in season, but out of season. He could not be persuaded to do a thing while it could do any good,—he was iron, he was adamant in his stubbornness then,—but as soon as the thing had reached a point where it would be positively harmful to do it, do it he would, and nothing could stop him. He did not do it because it would be harmful, but because he hoped it was not yet too late to achieve by it the good which it would have done if applied earlier. His comprehension was always a train or two behind-hand. If a national toe required amputating, he could not see that it needed anything more than poulticing; when others saw that the mortification had reached the knee, he first perceived that the toe needed cutting off,—so he cut it off; and he severed the leg at the knee when others saw that the disease had reached the thigh. He was good, and honest, and well meaning, in the

matter of chasing national diseases, but he never could overtake one. As a private man, he would have been lovable;
but viewed as a king, he was strictly contemptible.

His was a most unroyal career, but the most pitiable spectacle in it, was his sentimental treachery to his Swiss guard
on that memorable 10th of August, when, he allowed those
heroes to be massacred in his cause, and forbade them to shed
the " sacred French blood " purporting to be flowing in the
veins of the red-capped mob of miscreants that was raging
around the palace. He meant to be kingly, but he was only
the female saint once more. Some of his biographers think
that upon this occasion the spirit of Saint Louis had descended upon him. It must have found pretty cramped quarters.
It Napoleon the First had stood in the shoes of Louis XVI
that day, instead of being merely a casual and unknown
looker-on, there would be no Lion of Lucerne, now, but
there would be a well stocked Communist graveyard in Paris
which would answer just as well to remember the 10th of
August by.

Martyrdom made a saint of Marie Queen of Scots three
hundred years ago, and she has hardly lost all of her saint-
ship yet. Martyrdom made a saint of the trivial and foolish
Marie Antoinette, and her biographers still keep her fragrant
with the odor of sanctity to this day, while unconsciously
proving upon almost every page they write that the only
calamitous instinct which her husband lacked, she supplied,
—the instinct to root out and get rid of an honest, able, and
loyal official, wherever she found him. The hideous but beneficent French Revolution would have been deferred, or
would have fallen short of completeness, or even might not
have happened at all, if Marie Antoinette had made the un-
wise mistake of not being born. The world owes a great deal
to the French Revolution, and consequently to its two chief
promoters, Louis the Poor in Spirit and his queen.

We did not buy any wooden images of the Lion, nor any
ivory or ebony or marble or chalk or sugar or chocolate ones,

or even any photographic slanders of him.   The truth is, these
copies were so common, so universal, in the shops and everywhere, that they presently became as intolerable to the wearied eye as the latest popular melody usually becomes to the
harassed ear.   In Lucerne, too, the wood carvings of other
sorts, which had been so pleasant to look upon when one saw
them occasionally at home, soon began to fatigue us.   We
grew very tired of seeing wooden quails and chickens picking and strutting around clock-faces, and still more tired of
seeing wooden images of the alleged chamois skipping about
wooden rocks, or lying upon them in family groups, or peer-
ing alertly up from behind them.   The first day, I would
have bought a hundred and fifty of these clocks if I had had

HE LIKED CLOCKS.

the money,—and I did buy three,—but on the third day the
disease had run its course, I had convalesced, and was in the
market once more,—trying to sell.   However, I had no luck;
which was just as well, for the things will be pretty enough,
no doubt, when I get them home.

For years my pet aversion had been the cuckoo clock; now
here I was, at last, right in the creature's home; so wherever
I went, that distressing " *hoo*'hoo! *hoo*'hoo! *hoo*'hoo!" was
always in my ears.   For a nervous man, this was a fine state of

things. Some sounds are hatefuller than others, but no sound is quite so inane, and silly, and aggravating as the "*hoo'*hoo" of a cuckoo clock, I think. I bought one, and am carrying it home to a certain person; for I have always said that if the opportunity ever happened, I would do that man an ill turn. What I meant, was, that I would break one of his legs, or something of that sort; but in Lucerne I instantly saw that I could impair his mind. That would be more lasting, and more satisfactory every way. So I bought the cuckoo clock; and if I ever get home with it, he is "my meat," as as they say in the mines. I thought of another candidate,— a book reviewer whom I could name if I wanted to,—but after thinking it over, I didn't buy him a clock. I couldn't injure his mind.

We visited the two long, covered wooden bridges which span the green and brilliant Reuss just below where it goes plunging and hurrahing out of the lake. These rambling, swaybacked tunnels are very attractive things, with their alcoved outlooks upon the lovely and inspiriting water. They contain two or three hundred queer old pictures, by old Swiss masters,—old boss sign painters, who flourished before the decadence of art.

The lake is alive with fishes, plainly visible to the eye, for the water is very clear. The parapets in front of the hotels were usually fringed with fishers of all ages. One day I thought I would stop and see a fish caught. The result brought back to my mind, very forcibly, a circumstance which I had not thought of before for twelve years. This one:

THE MAN WHO PUT UP AT GADSBY'S.

When my odd friend Riley and I were newspaper correspondents in Washington, in the winter of '67, we were coming down Pennsylvania Avenue one night, near midnight, in a driving storm of snow, when the flash of a street lamp fell upon a man who was eagerly tearing along in the opposite direction. This man instantly stopped, and exclaimed,

"This is lucky! You are Mr. Riley, ain't you?"

Riley was the most self-possessed and solemnly deliberate person in the republic. He stopped, looked his man over from head to foot, and finally said,—

"I am Mr. Riley. Did you happen to be looking for me?"

"That's just what I was doing," said the man, joyously, "and it's the biggest luck in the world that I've found you. My name is Lykins. I'm one of the teachers of the high school—San Francisco. As soon as I heard the San Francisco post-mastership was vacant, I made up my mind to get it,—and here I am."

"Yes," said Riley, slowly, "as you have remarked,....... Mr. Lykins.........here you are. And have you got it?"

"Well, not exactly *got* it, but the next thing to it. I've brought a petition, signed by the Superintendent of Public Instruction, and all the teachers, and by more than two hundred other people. Now I want you, if you'll be so good, to go around with me to the Pacific delegation, for I want to rush this thing through and get along home."

"If the matter is so pressing, you will prefer that we visit the delegation to-night," said Riley, in a voice which had nothing mocking in it,—to an unaccustomed ear.

"O, to-night, by all means! I haven't got any time to fool around. I want their promise before I go to bed,—I ain't the talking kind, I'm the *doing* kind!"

"Yes......you've come to the right place for that. When did you arrive?"

"Just an hour ago."

"When are you intending to leave?"

"For New York to-morrow evening,—for San Francisco next morning."

"Just so......What are you going to do to-morrow?"

"*Do!* Why I've got to go to the President with the petition and the delegation, and get the appointment, haven't I?"

"Yes........very true.........that is correct. And then what?"

"Executive session of the Senate at 2 p. m.,—got to get the appointment confirmed,—I reckon you'll grant that?"

"Yes......yes," said Riley, meditatively, "you are right again. Then you take the train for New York in the evening, and the steamer for San Francisco next morning?"

"That's it,—that's the way I map it out?"

Riley considered a while, and then said,—

"You couldn't stay.......a day......well, say two days longer?"

"Bless your soul, no! It's not my style. I ain't a man to go fooling around,—I'm a man that *does* things, I tell you.'

The storm was raging, the thick snow blowing in gusts. Riley stood silent, apparently deep in a reverie, during a minute or more, then he looked up and said,—

"Have you ever heard about that man who put up at Gadsby's, once?.....But I see you haven't."

He backed Mr. Lykins against an iron fence, buttonholed him, fastened him with his eye, like the ancient mariner, and proceeded to unfold his narrative as placidly and peacefully as if we were all stretched comfortably in a blossomy summer meadow instead of being persecuted by a wintry midnight tempest:

"I will tell you about that man. It was in Jackson's time. Gadsby's was the principal hotel, then.

"I WILL TELL YOU."

Well, this man arrived from Tennessee about nine o'clock, one morning, with a black coachman and a splendid four-

horse carriage and an elegant dog, which he was evidently
fond and proud of; he drove up before Gadsby's and the clerk
and the landlord and everybody rushed out to take charge of
him, but he said, 'Never mind' and jumped out and told the
coachman to wait,—said he hadn't time to take anything to
eat, he only had a little claim against the government to collect, would run across the way, to the Treasury, and fetch

COULDN'T WAIT.

the money, and then get right along back to Tennessee, for
he was in considerable of a hurry.

"Well, about eleven o'clock that night he came back and
ordered a bed and told them to put the horses up,—said he
would collect the claim in the morning.   This was in January, you understand,—January 1834,—the 3d of January,—
Wednesday.

"Well, on the 5th of February, he sold the fine carriage,

DIDN'T CARE FOR STYLE.

and bought a cheap second-hand one,—said it would answer
just as well to take the money home in, and he didn't care
for style.

" On the 11th of August he sold a pair of the fine horses,

—said he'd often thought a pair was better than four, to go over the rough mountain roads with where a body had to be careful about his driving,—and there wasn't so much of his

A PAIR BETTER THAN FOUR.

claim but he could lug the money home with a pair easy enough.

"On the 13th of December he sold another horse,—said two warn't necessary to drag that old light vehicle with,—in fact one could snatch it along faster than was absolutely necessary,

TWO WASN'T NECESSARY.

now that it was good solid winter weather and the roads in splendid condition.

"On the seventeenth of February, 1835, he sold the old carriage and bought a cheap second-hand buggy,—said a buggy was just the trick to skim along mushy, slushy early

JUST THE TRICK.

spring roads with, and he had always wanted to try a buggy on those mountain roads, anyway.

"On the 1st of August he sold the buggy and bought the

remains of an old sulky,—said he just wanted to see those green Tennesseans stare and gawk when they saw him come

GOING TO MAKE THEM STARE.

a-ripping along in a sulky,—didn't believe they'd ever heard of a sulky in their lives.

"Well, on the 29th of August he sold his colored coachman,—said he didn't need a coachman for a sulky,—wouldn't be room enough for two in it anyway,—and besides it wasn't

NOT THROWN AWAY.

every day that Providence sent a man a fool who was willing to pay nine hundred dollars for such a third-rate negro as that,—been wanting to get rid of the creature for years, but didn't like to *throw* him away.

"Eighteen months later,—that is to say, on the 15th of February, 1837,—he sold the sulky and bought a saddle,—

WHAT THE DOCTOR RECOMMENDED.

said horse-back riding was what the doctor had always recommended *him* to take, and dog'd if he wanted to risk *his* neck going over those mountain roads on wheels in the dead of winter, not if he knew himself.

"On the 9th of April he sold the saddle,—said he wasn't going to risk *his* life with any perishable saddle-girth that ever

WANTED TO FEEL SAFE.

was made, over a rainy, miry April road, while he could ride bareback and know and feel he was safe,—always *had* despised to ride on a saddle, anyway.

"On the 24th of April he sold his horse,—said 'I'm just 57 to-day, hale and hearty,—it would be a *pretty* howdy-do for me to be wasting such a trip as that and such weather as

PREFERRED TO TRAMP ON FOOT.

this, on a horse, when there ain't anything in the world so splendid as a tramp on foot through the fresh spring woods and over the cheery mountains, to a man that *is* a man,— and I can make my dog carry my claim in a little bundle anyway, when it's collected. So to-morrow I'll be up bright and early, make my little old collection, and mosey off to Tennessee, on my own hind legs, with a rousing Good-bye, to Gadsby's.'

"On the 22d of June he sold his dog,—said 'Dern a dog, anyway, where you're just starting off on a rattling bully pleasure-tramp through the summer woods and hills,—perfeet nuisance,—chases the squirrels, barks at everything, goes a-capering and splattering around in the fords,—man can't get any chance to reflect and enjoy nature,—and I'd a blamed sight ruther carry the claim myself, it's a mighty sight safer;

DERN A DOG, ANYWAY.

a dog's mighty uncertain in a financial way,—always noticed it,—well, *good*-bye, boys,—last call,—I'm off for Tennessee with a good leg and a gay heart, early in the morning!'"

There was a pause and a silence,—except the noise of the wind and the pelting snow. Mr. Lykins said, impatiently,—

"Well?"

Riley said,—

"Well,—that was thirty years ago."

"Very well, very well,—what of it?"

"I'm great friends with that old patriarch. He comes every evening to tell me good-bye. I saw him an hour ago, —he's off for Tennessee early to-morrow morning,—as usual; said he calculated to get his claim through and be off before night-owls like me have turned out of bed. The tears were in his eyes, he was so glad he was going to see his old Tennessee and his friends once more."

Another silent pause. The stranger broke it,—

"Is that all?"

"That is all."

"Well, for the *time* of night, and the *kind* of night, it seems to me the story was full long enough. But what's it all *for*?"

"O, nothing in particular."

"Well, where's the point of it?"

"O, there isn't any particular point to it. Only, if you are not in *too* much of a hurry to rush off to San Francisco with that post-office appointment, Mr. Lykins, I'd advise you to '*put up at Gadsby's*' for a spell, and take it easy. Good-bye. *God* bless you!"

So saying, Riley blandly turned on his heel and left the astonished school teacher standing there, a musing and motionless snow image shining in the broad glow of the street lamp.

He never got that post-office.

To go back to Lucerne and its fishers, I concluded, after about nine hours' waiting, that the man who proposes to tarry till he sees somebody hook one of those well-fed and experienced fishes will find it wisdom to "put up at Gadsby's" and take it easy. It is likely that a fish has not been caught on that lake pier for forty years; but no matter, the patient fisher watches his cork there all the day long, just the same, and seems to enjoy it. One may see the fisher-loafers just as thick and contented and happy and patient all along the Seine at Paris, but tradition says that the only thing ever caught there in modern times is a thing they don't fish for at all,—the recent dog and the translated cat.

CHAPTER XXVII.

CLOSE by the Lion of Lucerne is what they call the " Glacier Garden,"—and it is the only one in the world. It is on high ground. Four or five years ago, some workmen who were digging foundations for a house came upon this interesting relic of a long departed age. Scientific men perceived in it a confirmation of their theories concerning the glacial period; so through their persuasions the little tract of ground was bought and permanently protected against being built upon. The soil was removed, and there lay the rasped and guttered track which the ancient glacier had made as it moved along upon its slow and tedious journey. This track was perforated by huge pot-shaped holes in the bed-rock, formed by the furious washing-around in them of boulders by the turbulent torrent which flows beneath all glaciers. These huge round boulders still remain in the holes; they and the walls of the holes are worn smooth by the long continued chafing which they gave each other in those old days. It took a mighty force to churn these big lumps of stone around in that vigorous way. The neighboring country had a very different shape, at that time,—the valleys have risen up and become hills, since, and the hills have become valleys. The boulders discovered in the pots had traveled a great distance, for there is no rock like them nearer than the distant Rhone Glacier.

GLACIER GARDEN.

For some days we were content to enjoy looking at the blue lake Lucerne and at the piled-up masses of snow mountains that border it all around,—an enticing spectacle, this last, for there is a strange and fascinating beauty and charm about a majestic snow-peak with the sun blazing upon it or the moonlight softly enriching it,—but finally we concluded to try a bit of excursioning around on a steamboat, and a dash on foot at the Rigi. Very well, we had a delightful trip to Fluelen, on a breezy, sunny day. Everybody sat on the upper deck, on benches, under an awning; everybody talked, laughed, and exclaimed at the wonderful scenery; in truth, a trip on that lake is almost the perfection of pleasuring. The mountains were a never ceasing marvel. Sometimes they rose

THE LAKE AND MOUNTAINS. (MONT PILATUS).

straight up out of the lake, and towered aloft and overshadowed our pigmy steamer with their prodigious bulk in the most impressive way. Not snow-clad mountains, these, yet they climbed high enough toward the sky to meet the clouds and veil their foreheads in them.   They were not barren **and** repulsive, but clothed in green, and restful and pleasant **to** the eye.   And they were so almost straight-up-and-down, sometimes, that one could not imagine a man being able **to**

keep his footing upon such a surface, yet there are paths, and the Swiss people go up and down them eve- ry day.

Some- times one

of these monster precipices had the slight inclination of the huge ship-houses in dock yards,—then high a- loft, toward the sky, it took a little stronger inclination, like that of a mansard roof,—and perched on this dizzy mansard one's eye detected little things like martin boxes, and presently perceived that these were the dwellings of peasants,—an airy place for a home, truly. And suppose a peasant should walk in his sleep, or his child should fall out of the

MOUNTAIN PATHS.

front yard ?—the friends would have a tedious long journey down out of those cloud-heights before they found the re- mains.   And yet those far-away homes looked ever so seduc- **tive,** they were so remote from the troubled world, they dozed **in** such an atmosphere of peace and dreams,—surely no one who had learned to live up there would ever want to live on a meaner level.

We swept through the prettiest little curving arms of the lake, among these colossal green walls, enjoying new delights, always, as the stately panorama unfolded itself before us and re-rolled and hid itself behind us; and now and then we had the thrilling surprise of bursting suddenly upon a tremendous white mass like the distant and dominating Jungfrau, or some kindred giant, looming head and shoulders above a tumbled waste of lesser Alps.

Once, while I was hungrily taking in one of these surprises, and doing my best to get all I possibly could of it while it should last, I was interrupted by a young and care-free voice,

"You're an American, I think,—so'm I."

He was about eighteen, or possibly nineteen; slender and of medium height; open, frank, happy face; a restless but independent eye; a snub nose, which had the air of drawing back with a decent reserve from the silky new-born moustache below it until it should be introduced; a loosely hung jaw, calculated to work easily in the sockets. He wore a low-crowned, narrow-brimmed straw hat, with a broad blue ribbon around it which had a white anchor embroidered on it in front; nobby short-tailed coat, pantaloons, vest, all trim and neat and up with the fashion; red-striped stockings, very low-quarter patent leather shoes, tied with black ribbon; blue ribbon around his neck, wide-open collar; tiny diamond studs; wrinkleless kids; projecting cuffs, fastened with large oxydized silver sleeve-buttons, bearing the device of a dog's face,—English pug. He carried a slim cane, surmounted with an English pug's head with red glass eyes. Under his arm he carried a German Grammar,—Otto's. His hair was short, straight and smooth, and presently when he turned his head a moment, I saw that it was nicely parted behind. He took a cigarette out of a dainty box, stuck it into a meerschaum holder which he carried in a morocco case, and reached for my cigar. While he was lighting, I said,—

17

"Yes,—I am an American."

"I knew it,—I can always tell them.   What ship did you come over in?"

"Holsatia."

"We came in the Batavia,—Cunard, you know.   What kind of a passage did you have?"

"Tolerably rough."

"So did we.   Captain said he'd hardly ever seen it rougher. Where are you from?"

"New England."

"So'm I.   I'm from New Bloomfield.   Anybody with you?"

"Yes,—a friend."

"Our whole family's along. It's awful slow, going around alone,—don't you think so?"

"Rather slow."

"Ever been over here before?"

"Yes."

"I haven't.   My first trip. But we've been all around,— Paris and everywhere.   I'm to enter Harvard next year.

"YOU'RE AN AMERICAN—SO AM I." Studying German all the time, now.   Can't enter till I know German.   I know considerable French,—I get along pretty well in Paris, or anywhere where they speak French.   What hotel are you stopping at?"

"Schweitzerhof."

"No! is that so?   I never see you in the reception room. I go to the reception room a good deal of the time, because there's so many Americans there.   I make lots of acquaintances.   I know an American as soon as I see him,—and so I speak to him and make his acquaintance.   I like to be always making acquaintances,—don't you?"

"Lord, yes!"

"You see it breaks up a trip like this, first rate. I never get bored on a trip like this, if I can make acquaintances and have somebody to talk to. But I think a trip like this would be an awful bore, if a body couldn't find anybody to get acquainted with and talk to on a trip like this. I'm fond of talking, ain't you?"

"Passionately."

"Have you felt bored, on this trip?"

"Not all the time, part of it."

"That's it!—you see you ought to go around and get acquainted, and talk. That's my way. That's the way I always do,—I just go 'round, 'round, 'round, and talk, talk, talk,—I never get bored. You been up the Rigi yet?"

"No"

"Going?"

"I think so."

"What hotel you going to stop at?"

"I don't know. Is there more than one?"

"Three. You stop at the Schreiber—you'll find it full of Americans. What ship did you say you came over in?"

"City of Antwerp."

"German, I guess. You going to Geneva?"

"Yes."

"What hotel you going to stop at?"

"Hotel de l' Ecu de Genève."

"Don't you do it! No Americans there? You stop at one of those big hotels over the bridge,—they're packed full of Americans."

"But I want to practice my Arabic."

"Good gracious, do you speak Arabic?"

"Yes,—well enough to get along."

"Why, hang it, you won't get along in Geneva,—*they* don't speak Arabic, they speak French. What hotel are you stopping at here?"

"Hotel Pension-Beaurivage."

"Sho, you ought to stop at the Schweitzerhof. Didn't you know the Schweitzerhof was the best hotel in Switzerland?—look at your Baedecker."

"Yes, I know,—but I had an idea there warn't any Americans there."

"No Americans! Why bless your soul it's just alive with them! I'm in the great reception room most all the time. I make lots of acquaintances there. Not as many as I did at first, because now only the new ones stop in there,—the others go right along through. Where are you from?"

"Arkansaw."

"Is that so? I'm from New England,—New Bloomfield's my town when I'm at home. I'm having a mighty good time to-day, ain't you?"

"Divine."

"That's what I call it. I like this knocking around, loose and easy, and making acquaintances and talking. I know an American, soon as I see him; so I go and speak to him and make his acquaintance. I ain't ever bored, on a trip like this, if I can make new acquaintances and talk. I'm awful fond of talking when I can get hold of the right kind of a person, ain't you?"

"I prefer it to any other dissipation."

"That's my notion, too. Now some people like to take a book and sit down and read, and read, and read, or moon around yawping at the lake or these mountains and things, but that ain't my way; no, sir, if they like it, let 'em do it, I don't object; but as for me, talking's what *I* like. You been up the Rigi?"

"Yes."

"What hotel did you stop at?"

"Schreiber."

"That's the place!—I stopped there too. *Full* of Americans, *wasn't* it? It always is,—always is. That's what they say. Everybody says that. What ship did you come over in?"

" Ville de Paris."

" French, I reckon. What kind of a passage did . . . . excuse me a minute, there's some Americans I haven't seen before."

And away he went. He went uninjured, too,—I had the murderous impulse to harpoon him in the back with my alpenstock, but as I raised the weapon the disposition left me; I found I hadn't the heart to kill him, he was such a joyous, innocent, good-natured numscull.

Half an hour later I was sitting on a bench inspecting, with strong interest, a noble monolith which we were skimming by,—a monolith not shaped by man, but by Nature's free great hand,—a massy pyramidal rock eighty feet high, devised by Nature ten million years ago against the day when a man worthy of it should need it for his monument. The time came at last, and now this grand remembrancer bears Schiller's name in huge letters upon its face. Curiously enough, this rock was not degraded or defiled in any way. It is said that two years ago a stranger let himself down from the top of it with ropes and pulleys, and painted all over it, in blue letters bigger than those in Schiller's name, these words:

" Try Sozodont;"
" Buy Sun Stove Polish ; "
" Helmbold's Buchu ; "
" Try Benzaline for the Blood."

He was captured, and it turned out that he was an American. Upon his trial the judge said to him,—

" You are from a land where any insolent that wants to, is privileged to profane and insult Nature, and through her, Nature's God, if by so doing he can put a sordid penny in his pocket. But here the case is different. Because you are a foreigner and ignorant, I will make your sentence light; if you were a native I would deal strenuously with you.— Hear and obey· You will immediately remove every trace of your offensive work from the Schiller monument; you

you pay a fine of ten thousand francs; you will suffer two years' imprisonment at hard labor; you will then be horse-whipped, tarred and feathered, deprived of your ears, ridden on a rail to the confines of the canton, and banished forever. The severer penalties are omitted in your case,—not as a grace to you, but to that great republic which had the misfortune to give you birth."

The steamers's benches were ranged back to back across the deck. My back hair was mingling innocently with the back hair of a couple of ladies. Presently they were addressed by some one and I overheard this conversation:

"You are Americans, I think? So'm I."

"Yes,—we are Americans."

"I knew it,—I can always tell them. What ship did you come over in?"

"City of Chester."

"O yes,—Inman line. We came in the Batavia,—Cunard, you know. What kind of a passage did you have?"

"Pretty fair."

ENTERPRISE.

"That was luck. We had it awful rough. Captain said he'd hardly ever seen it rougher. Where are you from?"

"New Jersey."

"So'm I. No—I didn't mean that; I'm from New England. New Bloomfield's my place. These your children? —belong to both of you?"

"Only to one of us; they are mine; my friend is not married."

"Single, I reckon? So'm I. Are you two ladies traveling alone?"

"No,—my husband is with us."

"Our whole family's along. It's awful slow, going around alone,—don't you think so?"

"I suppose it must be."

"Hi, there's Mount Pilatus coming in sight again. Named after Pontius Pilate, you know, that shot the apple off of William Tell's head. Guide-book tells all about it, they say. I didn't read it—an American told me. I don't read when I'm knocking around like this, having a good time. Did you ever see the chapel where William Tell used to preach?"

"I did not know he ever preached there."

"O, yes he did. That American told me so. He don't ever shut up his guide-book. He knows more about this lake than the fishes in it Besides, they *call* it 'Tell's Chapel'—you know that yourself. You ever been over here before?"

"Yes."

"I haven't. It's my first trip. But we've been all around,—Paris and everywhere. I'm to enter Harvard next year.—Studying German all the time now. Can't enter till I know German. This book's Otto's Grammar. It's a mighty good book to get the *ich habe gehabt haben's* out of.

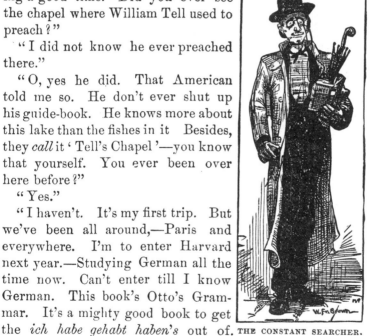

THE CONSTANT SEARCHER.

But I don't really study when I'm knocking around this way. If the notion takes me, I just run over my little old *ich habe gehabt, du hast gehabt, er hat gehabt, wir haben gehabt, ihr habet gehabt, sie haben gehabt,*—kind of 'Now-I-lay-me-down-to-sleep' fashion, you know, and after that, maybe I don't buckle to it again for three days. It's awful undermining to the intellect, German is; you want to take it in small doses,or first you know your brains all run together, and you feel them sloshing around in your head same as so much drawn butter. But French is different; *French* aint' anything. I ain't any more afraid of French than a tramp's afraid of pie; I can rattle off my little *j'ai*, *tu as*, *il a*, and the rest of it, just as easy as a-b-c. I get along pretty well in Paris, or anywhere where they speak French. What hotel you stopping at?"

"The Schweitzerhof."

"No! is that so? I never see you in the big reception room. I go in there a good deal of the time, because there's so many Americans there. I make lots of acquaintances. You been up the Rigi yet?"

"No."

"Going?"

"We think of it."

"What hotel you going to stop at?"

"I don't know."

"Well, then, you stop at the Schreiber,—it's full of Americans. What ship did you come over in?"

"City of Chester."

"O, yes, I remember I asked you that before. But I always ask everybody what ship they came over in, and so sometimes I forget and ask again. You going to Geneva?"

"Yes."

"What hotel you going to stop at?"

"We expect to stop in a pension."

"I don't hardly believe you'll like that: there's very few Americans in the pensions. What hotel are you stopping at here?"

"The Schweitzerhof."

"O, yes, I asked you that before, too. But I always ask everybody what hotel they're stopping at, and so I've got my head all mixed up with hotels. But it makes talk, and I love to talk. It refreshes me up so,—don't it you—on a trip like this?"

"Yes,—sometimes."

"Well, it does me, too. As long as I'm talking I never feel bored,—ain't that the way with you?"

"Yes—generally. But there are exceptions to the rule."

"O, of course. *I* don't care to talk to everybody, *myself*. If a person starts in to jabber-jabber-jabber about scenery, and history, and pictures, and all sorts of tiresome things, I get the fan-tods mighty soon. I say 'Well, I must be going now,—hope I'll see you again'—and then I take a walk. Where you from?"

"New Jersey."

"Why, bother it all, I asked you *that* before, too. Have you seen the Lion of Lucerne?"

"Not yet."

"Nor I, either. But the man who told me about Mount Pilatus says it's one of the things to see. It's twenty-eight feet long. It don't seem reasonable, but he said so, anyway. He saw it yesterday ; said it was dying, then, so I reckon it's dead by this time. But that ain't any matter, of course they'll stuff it. Did you say the children are yours,—or *hers?*"

"Mine."

"O, so you did. Are you going up the......no, I asked you that. What ship.......no, I asked you that, too. What hotel are you.......no, you told me that. Let me see......um......O, what kind of a voy........no, we've been over that ground, too. Um......um......well, I believe that is all. *Bonjour*—I am very glad to have made your acquaintance, ladies. *Guten Tag.*"

CHAPTER XXVIII.

THE Rigi-Kulm is an imposing Alpine mass, 6,000 feet high, which stands by itself, and commands a mighty prospect of blue lakes, green valleys, and snowy mountains —a compact and magnificent picture three hundred miles in circumference. The ascent is made by rail, or horseback, or on foot, as one may prefer. I and my agent panoplied ourselves in walking costume, one bright morning, and started down the lake on the steamboat; we got ashore at the village of Wäggis, three quarters of an hour distant from Lucerne. This village is at the foot of the mountain.

We were soon tramping leisurely up the leafy mule-path, and then the talk began to flow, as usual. It was twelve o'clock noon, and a breezy, cloudless day; the ascent was gradual, and the glimpses, from under the curtaining boughs, of blue water, and tiny sail boats, and beetling cliffs, were as charming as glimpses of dreamland. All the circumstances were perfect—and the anticipations, too, for we should soon be enjoying, for the first time, that wonderful spectacle, an Alpine sunrise—the object of our journey. There was (apparently) no real need to hurry, for the guide-book made the walking distance from Wäggis to the summit only three hours and a quarter. I say "apparently," because the guide-book had already fooled us once,—about the distance from Allerheiligen to Oppenau,—and for aught I knew it might

be getting ready to fool us again. We were only certain as
to the altitudes,—we calculated to find out for ourselves how
many hours it is from the bottom to the top. The summit is
6,000 feet above the sea, but only 4,500 feet above the lake.
When we had walked half an hour, we were fairly into the
swing and humor of the undertak-
ing, so we cleared for action ; that is
to say, we got a boy whom we met to
carry our alpenstocks and satchels
and overcoats and things for us; that
left us free for business.

I suppose we must have stopped
oftener to stretch out on the grass in
the shade and take a bit of a smoke
than this boy was used to, for presently he asked if it had been our idea to
hire him by the job, or by the year ?
We told him he could move along if
he was in a hurry. He said he wasn't
in such a very particular hurry, but he
wanted to get to the top while he was
young. We told him to clear out,
then, and leave the things at the uppermost hotel and say we should be along
presently. He said he would secure
us a hotel if he could, but if they
were all full he would ask them to
build another one and hurry up and
get the paint and plaster dry against
we arrived. Still gently chaffing us
he pushed ahead, up the trail, and soon
disappeared. By six o'clock we were pretty high up in the
air, and the view of lake and mountains had greatly grown in
breadth and interest. We halted a while at a little public
house, where we had bread and cheese and a quart or two of
fresh milk, out on the porch, with the big panorama all before
us,—and then moved on again.

Ten minutes afterward we met a hot, red-faced man plunging down the mountain, with mighty strides, swinging his alpenstock ahead of him and taking a grip on the ground with its iron point to support these big strides. He stopped, fanned himself with his hat, swabbed the perspiration from his face and neck with a red handkerchief, panted a moment or two, and asked how far it was to Wäggis. I said three hours. He looked surprised, and said,—

THE ENGLISHMAN.

"Why, it seems as if I could toss a biscuit into the lake from here, it's so close by. Is that an inn, there?"

I said it was.

"Well," said he, "I can't stand another three hours, I've had enough for to-day; I'll take a bed there."

I asked,—

"Are we nearly to the top?"

"Nearly to the *top!* Why, bless your soul, you haven't really started, yet."

I said we would put up at the inn, too. So we turned back and ordered a hot supper, and had quite a jolly evening of it with this Englishman.

The German landlady gave us neat rooms and nice beds, and when I and my agent turned in, it was with the resolution to be up early and make the utmost of our first Alpine sunrise. But of course we were dead tired, and slept like policemen; so when we awoke in the morning and ran to the window it was already too late, because it was half past eleven.

It was a sharp disappointment. However, we ordered breakfast and told the landlady to call the Englishman, but she said
he was already up and off at daybreak,—and swearing mad
about something or other. We could not find out what the
matter was. He had asked the landlady the altitude of her
place above the level of the lake, and she had told him fourteen hundred and ninety-five feet. That was all that was
said; then he lost his temper. He said that between ——
fools and guide-books, a man could acquire ignorance enough
in twenty-four hours in a country like this to last him a year.
Harris believed our boy had been loading him up with misinformation; and this was probably the case, for his epithet
described that boy to a dot.

We got under way about the turn of noon, and pulled out
for the summit again, with a fresh and vigorous step. When
we had gone about two hundred yards, and stopped to rest,
I glanced to the left while I was lighting my pipe, and in the
distance detected a long worm of black smoke crawling lazily
up the steep mountain. Of course that was the locomotive.
We propped ourselves on our elbows at once, to gaze, for we
had never seen a mountain railway yet. Presently we could
make out the train. It seemed incredible that that thing
should creep straight up a sharp slant like the roof of a house,
—but there it was, and it was doing that very miracle.

In the course of a couple of hours we reached a fine breezy
altitude where the little shepherd-huts had big stones all over
their roofs to hold them down to the earth when the great
storms rage. The country was wild and rocky about here,
but there were plenty of trees, plenty of moss, and grass.

Away off on the opposite shore of the lake we could see
some villages, and now for the first time we could observe
the real difference between their proportions and those of the
giant mountains at whose feet they slept. When one is in
one of those villages it seems spacious, and its houses seem
high and not out of proportion to the mountain that over-
hangs them—but from our altitude, what a change! The

mountains were bigger and grander than ever, as they stood
there thinking their solemn thoughts with their heads in the
drifting clouds, but the villages at their feet,—when the pains-
taking eye could trace them up and find them,—were so reduced, so almost invisible, and lay so flat against the ground,

THE "JODLER."

that the exactest simile I
can devise is to compare
them to ant-deposits of
granulated dirt over-shad-
owed by the huge bulk of
a cathedral. The steam-
boats skimming along un-
der the stupendous preci-
pices were diminished by
distance to the daintiest
little toys, the sail-boats and row-boats to shallops proper
for fairies that keep house in the cups of lilies and ride to
court on the backs of bumble-bees.

Presently we came upon half a dozen sheep nibbling grass
in the spray of a stream of clear water that sprang from a

rock wall a hundred feet high, and all at once our ears were startled with a melodious "Lul...l....l.... lul-lul-*lahee*-o-

o-o!" pealing joy- ously from a near but invisible source, and recognized that we were hearing for the first time the famous Alpine *jodel* in its own native wilds. And we recognized, also, that it was that sort of quaint comming- ling of baritone and falsetto which at home we call "Tyrolese warb- ling."

The jodling (pro- nounced yodling, —emphasis on the o,) continued, and was very pleasant and inspiriting to hear. Now the jod-

ANOTHER VOCALIST.

ler appeared,—a shepherd boy of sixteen,—and in our glad- ness and gratitude we gave him a franc to jodel some more. So he jodeled, and we listened. We moved on, presently, and he generously jodeled us out of sight. After about fifteen minutes we came across another shepherd boy who was jodling, and gave him half a franc to keep it up. He also jodled us out of sight. After that, we found a jodler every ten minutes; we gave the first one eight cents, the sec- ond one six cents, the third one four, the fourth one a penny, contributed nothing to Nos. 5, 6, and 7, and during the remainder of the day hired the rest of the jodlers, at a franc apiece, not to jodel any more.   There is somewhat too much of this jodling in the Alps.

About the middle of the afternoon we passed through a

prodigious natural gateway called the Felsenthor, formed by two enormous upright rocks, with a third lying across the top.   There was a very attractive little hotel close by, but our energies were not conquered yet, so we went on.

Three hours afterward we came to the railway track. It was planted straight up the mountain with the slant of a ladder that leans against a house, and it seemed to us that a man would need good nerves who proposed to travel up it or down it either.

THE FELSENTHOR.   During the latter part of the afternoon we cooled our roasting interiors with ice-cold water from clear streams, the only really satisfying water we had tasted since we left home, for at the hotels on the continent they merely give you a tumbler of ice to soak your water in, and that only modifies its hotness, doesn't make it cold. Water can only be made cold enough for summer comfort by being prepared in a refrigerator or a closed ice-pitcher. Europeans say ice water impairs digestion.   How do they know?—they never drink any.

At ten minutes past six we reached the Kaltbad station, where there is a spacious hotel with great verandahs which command a majestic expanse of lake and mountain scenery. We were pretty well fagged out, now, but as we did not wish to miss the Alpine sunrise, we got through with our dinner as quickly as possible and hurried off to bed.   It was unspeaka-

A VIEW FROM THE STATION.

bly comfortable to stretch our weary limbs between the cool damp sheets.   And how we did sleep !—for there is no opiate like Alpine pedestrianism.

In the morning we both awoke and leaped out of bed at the same instant and ran and stripped aside the window curtains ; but we suffered a bitter disappointment again : it was already half past three in the afternoon.

We dressed sullenly and in ill spirits, each accusing the other of over-sleeping.   Harris said if we had brought the courier along, as we ought to have done, we should not have missed these sunrises.   I said he knew very well that one of us would have had to sit up and wake the courier; and I added that we were having trouble enough to take care of ourselves, on this climb, without having to take care of a courier besides.

During breakfast our spirits came up a little, since we found
18

by the guide-book that in the hotels on the summit the tourist is not left to trust to luck for his sunrise, but is roused betimes by a man who goes through the halls with a great Alpine horn, blowing blasts that would raise the dead. And there was another consoling thing: the guide-book said that up there on the summit the guests did not wait to dress much, but seized a red bed-blanket and sailed out arrayed like an Indian. This was good; this would be romantic; two hundred and fifty people grouped on the windy summit, with their hair flying and their red blankets flapping, in the solemn presence of the snowy ranges and the messenger splendors of the coming sun, would be a striking and memorable spectacle. So it was good luck, not ill luck, that we had missed those other sunrises.

We were informed by the guide-book that we were now 3,228 feet above the level of the lake,—therefore full two-thirds of our journey had been accomplished. We got away at a quarter past four, p. m.; a hundred yards above the hotel the railway divided; one track went straight up the steep hill, the other one turned square off to the right, with a very slight grade. We took the latter, and followed it more than a mile, turned a rocky corner and came in sight of a handsome new hotel. If we had gone on, we should have arrived at the summit, but Harris preferred to ask a lot of questions,—as usual, of a man who didn't know anything,—and he told us to go back and follow the other route. We did so. We could ill afford this loss of time.

We climbed, and climbed; and we kept on climbing; we reached about forty summit's but there was always another one just ahead. It came on to rain, and it rained in dead earnest. We were soaked through, and it was bitter cold. Next a smoky fog of clouds covered the whole region densely, and we took to the railway ties to keep from getting lost. Sometimes we slopped along in a narrow path on the left hand side of the track, but by and by when the fog blew aside a little and we saw that we were treading the rampart of a precipice and that our left elbows were projecting over a perfectly boundless and bottomless vacancy, we gasped, and jumped for the ties again.

The night shut down, dark and drizzly and cold. About eight in the evening the fog lifted and showed us a well worn path which led up a very steep rise to the left. We took it and as soon as we had got far enough from the railway to render the finding it again an impossibility, the fog shut down on us once more.

We were in a bleak unsheltered place, now, and had to trudge right along, in order to keep warm, though we rather expected to go over a precipice sooner or later. About nine o'clock we made an important discovery,—that we were not in any path. We groped around a while on our hands and knees, but could not find it; so we sat down in the mud and the wet scant grass to wait. We were terrified into this by

LOST IN THE MIST.

being suddenly confronted with a vast body which showed itself vaguely for an instant and in the next instant was smothered in the fog again. It was really the hotel we were after, monstrously magnified by the fog, but we took it for the face of a precipice and decided not to try to claw up it.

We sat there an hour, with chattering teeth and quivering bodies, and quarreled over all sorts of trifles, but gave most of our attention to abusing each other for the stupidity of deserting the railway track. We sat with our backs to that precipice, because what little wind there was came from that quarter. At some time or other the fog thinned a little; we did not know when, for we were facing the empty universe and the thinness could not show ; but at last Harris happened to look around, and there stood a huge, dim, spectral hotel

THE RIGI-KULM HOTEL.

where the precipice had been. One could faintly discern the windows and chimneys, and a dull blur of lights. Our first emotion was deep, unutterable gratitude, our next was a foolish rage, born of the suspicion that possibly the hotel had been visible three-quarters of an hour while we sat there in those cold puddles quarreling.

Yes, it was the Rigi-Kulm hotel—the one that occupies

the extreme summit, and whose remote little sparkle of lights
we had often seen glinting high aloft among the stars from
our balcony away down yonder in Lucerne. The crusty
portier and the crusty clerks gave us the surly reception which
their kind deal in in prosperous times, but by mollifying them
with an extra display of obsequiousness and servility we finally got them to show us to the room which our boy had engaged for us.

We got into some dry clothing, and while our supper was
preparing we loafed forsakenly through a couple of vast cavernous drawing rooms, one of which had a stove in it. This
stove was in a corner, and densely walled around with people. We could not get near the fire, so we moved at large
in the arctic spaces, among a multitude of people who sat
silent, smileless, forlorn and shivering,—thinking what fools
they were to come, perhaps. There were some Americans,
and some Germans, but one could see that the great majority
were English.

We lounged into an apartment where there was a great
crowd, to see what was going on. It was a memento-maga-
zine. The tourists were eagerly buying all sorts and styles
of paper-cutters, marked "Souvenir of the Rigi," with handles
made of the little curved horn of the ostensible chamois;
there were all manner of wooden goblets and such things,
similarly marked. I was going to buy a paper-cutter, but I
believed I could remember the cold comfort of the Rigi-Kulm
without it, so I smothered the impulse.

Supper warmed us, and we went immediately to bed,—
but first, as Mr. Baedeker requests all tourists to call his attention to any errors which they may find in his guide-books,
I dropped him a line to inform him that when he said the
foot-journey from Wäggis to the summit was only three
hours and a quarter, he missed it by just about three days.
I had previously informed him of his mistake about the distance from Allerheiligen to Oppenau, and had also informed
the Ordnance Department of the German government of

the same error in the imperial maps. I will add, here, that
I never got any answer to these letters, or any thanks from
either of those sources; and what is still more discourteous,
these corrections have not been made, either in the maps or
the guide-books. But I will write again when I get time,
for my letters may have miscarried.

We curled up in the clammy beds, and went to sleep without rocking. We were so sodden with fatigue that we never
stirred nor turned over till the booming blasts of the Alpine

WHAT AWAKENED US.

horn aroused us. It may well be imagined that we did not
lose any time. We snatched on a few odds and ends of clothing, cocooned ourselves in the proper red blankets, and plunged along the halls and out into the whistling wind bare-headed.
We saw a tall wooden scaffolding on the very peak of the summit, a hundred yards away, and made for it. We rushed up
the stairs to the top of this scaffolding, and stood there, above
the vast outlying world, with hair flying and ruddy blankets
waving and cracking in the fierce breeze.

"Fifteen minutes too late, at last!" said Harris, in a vexed
voice. "The sun is clear above the horizon."

"No matter," I said, "it is a most magnificent spectacle,
and we will see it do the rest of its rising, anyway."

A SUMMIT SUNRISE

In a moment we were deeply absorbed in the marvel before us, and dead to everything else. The great cloud-barred disk of the sun stood just above a limitless expanse of tossing white-caps,—so to speak,—a billowy chaos of massy mountain domes and peaks draped in imperishable snow, and flooded with an opaline glory of changing and dissolving splendors, whilst through rifts in a black cloud-bank above the sun, radiating lances of diamond dust shot to the zenith. The cloven valleys of the lower world swam in a tinted mist which veiled the ruggedness of their crags and ribs and ragged forests, and turned all the forbidding region into a soft and rich and sensuous paradise.

We could not speak. We could hardly breathe. We could only gaze in drunken ecstasy and drink it in. Presently Harris exclaimed,—

"Why——nation, its going *down!*"

Perfectly true. We had missed the *morning* horn-blow, and slept all day. This was stupefying. Harris said,—

"Look here, the sun isn't the spectacle,—its *us*,—stacked up here on top of this gallows, in these idiotic blankets, and two hundred and fifty well dressed men and women down here gawking up at us and not caring a straw whether the sun rises or sets, as long as they've got such a ridiculo s spectacle as this to set down in their memorandum-books. They seem to be laughing their ribs loose, and there's one girl there that appears to be going all to pieces. I never saw such a man as you before. I think you are the very last possibility in the way of an ass."

"What have *I* done?" I answered with heat.

"What have you done? You've got up at half past seven o'clock in the evening to see the sun rise, that's what you've done."

"And have you done any better, I'd like to know? I always used to get up with the lark, till I came under the petrifying influence of your turgid intellect."

"*You* used to get up with the lark,—O, no doubt,—you'll

get up with the hangman one of these days. But you ought
to be ashamed to be jawing here like this, in a red blanket,
on a forty-foot scaffold on top of the Alps. And no end of
people down here to boot; this isn't any place for an exhibition of temper."

And so the customary quarrel went on. When the sun
was fairly down, we slipped back to the hotel in the charitable gloaming, and went to bed again. We had encountered
the horn-blower on the way, and he had tried to collect compensation, not only for announcing the sunset, which we did
see, but for the sunrise, which we had totally missed; but we
said no, we only took our solar rations on the "European
plan"—pay for what you get. He promised to make us
hear his horn in the morning, if we were alive.

CHAPTER XXIX.

HE kept his word. We heard his horn and instantly got up. It was dark and cold and wretched. As I fumbled around for the matches, knocking things down with my quaking hands, I wished the sun would rise in the middle of the day, when it was warm and bright and cheerful, and one wasn't sleepy. We proceeded to dress by the gloom of a couple of sickly candles, but we could hardly button anything, our hands shook so. I thought of how many happy people there were in Europe, Asia and America, and everywhere, who were sleeping peacefully in their beds and did not have to get up and see the Rigi sunrise,—people who did not appreciate their advantage, as like as not, but would get up in the morning wanting more boons of Providence. While thinking these thoughts I yawned, in a rather ample way, and my upper teeth got hitched on a nail over the door, and whilst I was mounting a chair to free myself, Harris drew the window curtain and said,—

"O, this is luck! We shan't have to go out at all,—yonder are the mountains, in full view."

That was glad news, indeed. It made us cheerful right away. One could see the grand Alpine masses dimly outlined against the black firmament, and one or two faint stars blinking through rifts in the night. Fully clothed, and wrapped in blankets, we huddled ourselves up, by the window,

301

with lighted pipes, and fell into chat, while we waited in exceeding comfort to see how an Alpine sunrise was going to look by candle light. By and by a delicate, spiritual

sort of effulgence spread itself by imperceptible degrees over the loftiest altitudes of the snowy wastes, —but there the effort seemed to stop. I said, presently,—

"There is a hitch about this sunrise somewhere. It doesn't seem to go. What do you reckon is the matter with it?"

"I don't know. It appears to hang fire somewhere. I never saw a sunrise act like that before. Can it be that the hotel is playing anything on us?"

"Of course not. The hotel merely has a property interest in the sun, it has nothing to do with the management of it. It is a precarious kind of

EXCEEDINGLY COMFORTABLE.

property, too; a succession of total eclipses would probably ruin this tavern. Now what can be the matter with this sunrise?"

Harris jumped up and said,—

"I've got it! I know what's the matter with it! We've been looking at the place where the sun *set* last night!"

"It is perfectly true! Why couldn't you have thought of that sooner? Now we've lost another one! And all through your blundering. It was exactly like you to light a pipe and sit down to wait for the sun to rise in the west."

"It was exactly like me to find out the mistake, too. You never would have found it out. I find out all the mistakes."

You make them all, too, else your most valuable faculty

THE SUNRISE.

would be wasted on you. But don't stop to quarrel, now,—maybe we are not too late yet."

But we were. The sun was well up when we got to the exhibition ground.

On our way up we met the crowd returning—men and women dressed in all sorts of queer costumes, and exhibiting all degrees of cold and wretchedness in their gaits and countenances. A dozen still remained on the ground when we reached there, huddled together about the scaffold with their backs to the bitter wind. They had their red guide-books open at the diagram of the view, and were painfully picking out the several mountains and trying to impress their names and positions on their memories. It was one of the saddest sights I ever saw.

Two sides of this place were guarded by railings, to keep people from being blown over the precipices. The view, looking sheer down into the broad valley, eastward, from this great elevation,—almost a perpendicular mile,—was very quaint and curious. Counties, towns, hilly ribs and ridges, wide stretches of green meadow, great forest tracts, winding streams, a dozen blue lakes, a flock of busy steamboats —we saw all this little world in unique circumstantiality of detail — saw it just as the birds see it — and all reduced to the smallest of scales and as sharply worked out and finished as a steel engraving. The numerous toy villages, with tiny spires projecting out of them, were just as the children might have left them when done with play the day before; the forest tracts were diminished to cushions of moss; one or two big lakes were dwarfed to ponds, the smaller ones to puddles,—though they did not look like puddles, but like blue ear-drops which had fallen and lodged in slight depressions, conformable to their shapes, among the moss-beds and the smooth levels of dainty green farm-land; the microscopic steamboats glided along, as in a city reservoir, taking a mighty time to cover the distance between ports which seemed only a yard apart; and the isthmus which separated two lakes looked as if one might stretch out on it and lie with both elbows in the water, yet we knew invisible wagons were toiling across it and finding the distance a tedious one. This beautiful miniature world had exactly the appearance of those "relief maps" which reproduce nature precisely, with the heights and depressions and other details graduated to a reduced scale, and with the rocks, trees, lakes, etc., colored after nature.

I believed we could walk down to Wäggis or Vitznau in a day, but I knew we could go down by rail in about an hour, so I chose the latter method. I wanted to see what it was like, anyway. The train came along about the middle of the forenoon, and an odd thing it was. The locomotive boiler stood on end, and it and the whole locomotive were tilted

THE RIGI-KULM.

sharply backward. There were two passenger cars, roofed,

but wide open all around. These cars were not tilted back, but the seats were; this enables the passenger to sit level while going down a steep incline.

There are three railway tracks; the central one is cogged; the "lantern wheel" of the engine grips its way along these cogs, and pulls the train up the hill or retards its motion on the down trip. About the same speed,—three miles an hour, —is maintained both ways. Whether going up or down, the locomotive is always at the lower end of the train. It pushes, in the one case, braces back in the other. The passenger rides backward, going up, and faces forward going down.

We got front seats, and while the train moved along about fifty yards on level ground, I was not the least frightened; but now it started abruptly down stairs, and I caught my breath. And I, like my neighbors, unconsciously held back all I could, and threw my weight to the rear, but of course that did no particular good. I had slidden down the balusters when I was a boy, and thought nothing of it, but to slide down the balusters in a railway train is a thing to make one's flesh creep. Sometimes we had as much as ten yards of almost level ground, and this gave us a few full breaths in comfort; but straightway we would turn a corner and see a long steep line of rails stretching down below us, and the comfort was at an end. One expected to see the locomotive pause, or slack up a little, and approach this plunge cautiously, but it did nothing of the kind; it went calmly on, and when it reached the jumping-off place it made a sudden bow, and went gliding smoothly down stairs, untroubled by the circumstances.

It was wildly exhilarating to slide along the edge of the precipices, after this grisly fashion, and look straight down upon that far-off valley which I was describing a while ago.

There was no level ground at the Kaltbad station; the railbed was as steep as a roof; I was curious to see how the stop was going to be managed. But it was very simple: the train came sliding down, and when it reached the right spot it just stopped—that was all there was "to it"—stopped on the steep incline, and when the exchange of passengers and baggage had been made, it moved off and went sliding down again. The train can be stopped anywhere, at a moment's notice.

There was one curious effect, which I need not take the trouble to describe,—because I can scissor a description of it out of the railway company's advertising pamphlet, and save my ink :

"On the whole tour, particularly at the Descent, we undergo an optical illusion which often seems to be incredible. All the shrubs, fir-trees, stables, houses, etc., seem to be bent in a slanting direction, as by an immense pressure of air. They are all standing awry, so much awry that the chalets and cottages of the peasants seem to be tumbling down. It is the consequence of the steep inclination of the line. Those who are seated in the carriage do not observe that they are going down a declivity of 20 to 25° (their seats being adapted to this course of proceeding and being bent down at

AN OPTICAL ILLUSION.

their backs.) They mistake their carriage and its horizontal lines for a proper measure of the normal plain, and therefore all the objects outside which really are in a horizontal position, must show a disproportion of 20 to 25° declivity, in regard to the mountain."

By the time one reaches Kaltbad, he has acquired confidence in the railway, and he now ceases to try to ease the locomotive by holding back. Thenceforward he smokes his pipe in serenity, and gazes out upon the magnificent picture below and about him with unfettered enjoyment. There is nothing to interrupt the view or the breeze; it is like inspecting the world on the wing. However,—to be exact,—there is one place where the serenity lapses for a while: this is while one is crossing the Schnurrtobel Bridge, a frail structure which swings its gossamer frame down through the dizzy air, over a gorge, like a vagrant spider-strand.

One has no difficulty in remembering his sins while the train is creeping down this bridge; and he repents of them, too; though he sees, when he gets to Vitznau, that he need not have done it, the bridge was perfectly safe.

So ends the eventful trip which we made to the Rigi-Kulm to see an Alpine sunrise.

RAILWAY DOWN THE MOUNTAIN.

CHAPTER XXX.

AN hour's sail brought us to Lucerne again. I judged it best to go to bed and rest several days, for I knew that the man who undertakes to make the tour of Europe on foot must take care of himself.

Thinking over my plans, as mapped out, I perceived that they did not take in the Furka Pass, the Rhone Glacier, the Finsteraarhorn, the Wetterhorn, etc. I immediately examined the guide-book to see if these were important, and found they were; in fact, a pedestrian tour of Europe could not be complete without them. Of course that decided me at once to see them, for I never allow myself to do things by halves, or in a slurring, slip-shod way.

I called in my agent and instructed him to go without delay and make a careful examination of these noted places, on foot, and bring me back a written report of the result, for insertion in my book. I instructed him to go to Hospenthal as quickly as possible, and make his grand start from there; to extend his foot expedition as far as the Giesbach fall, and return to me from thence by diligence or mule. I told him to take the courier with him.

He objected to the courier, and with some show of reason, since he was about to venture upon new and untried ground; but I thought he might as well learn how to take care of the courier now as later, therefore I enforced my point. I said

that the trouble, delay and inconvenience of traveling with
a courier were balanced by the deep respect which a courier's
presence commands, and I must insist that as much style be
thrown into my journeys as possible.

So the two assumed complete mountaineering costumes
and departed. A week later they returned, pretty well used
up, and my agent handed me the following

Official Report

Of a Visit to the Furka Region. By H. Harris, Agent.

About 7 o'clock in the morning, with perfectly fine
weather, we started from Hospenthal, and arrived at the
maison on the Furka in a little under *quatre* hours. The
want of variety in the scenery from Hospenthal made the
kahkahponeeka wearisome; but let none be discouraged: no
one can fail to be completely *recompensée* for his fatigue,
when he sees, for the first time, the monarch of the Oberland,
the tremendous Finsteraarhorn. A moment before all was
dulness, but a *pas* further has placed us on the summit of
the Furka; and exactly in front of us, at a *hopow* of only
fifteen miles, this magnificent mountain lifts its snow-wreath-
ed precipices into the deep blue sky. The inferior mountains on each side of the pass form a sort of frame for the
picture of their dread lord, and close in the view so completely that no other prominent feature in the Oberland is
visible from this *bong-a-bong*; nothing withdraws the attention from the solitary grandeur of the Finsteraarhorn and
the dependent spurs which form the abutments of the
central peak.

With the addition of some others, who were also bound
for the Grimsel, we formed a large *xhvloj* as we descended
the *steg* which winds round the shoulder of a mountain
toward the Rhone glacier. We soon left the path and took
to the ice; and after wandering amongst the crevasses *un
peu*, to admire the wonders of these deep blue caverns, and
hear the rushing of waters through their subglacial channels, we struck out a course towards *l'autre coté* and crossed

the glacier successfully, a little above the cave from which the infant Rhone takes its first bound from under the grand

SOURCE OF THE RHONE.

precipice of ice. Half a mile below this we began to climb the flowery side of the Meienwand. One of our party started before the rest, but the *Hitze* was so great, that we found *ihm* quite exhausted, and lying at full length in the shade of a large *Gestein*. We sat down with him for a time, for all felt the heat exceedingly in the climb up this very steep *bolwoggoly*, and then we set out again together, and arrived at last near the Dead Man's Lake, at the foot of the Sidelhorn. This lonely spot, once used for an extempore burying place, after a sanguinary *battue* between the French and Austrians, is the perfection of desolation : there is nothing in sight to mark the hand of man, except the line of weatherbeaten whitened posts, set up to indicate the direction of the pass in the *owdawakk* of winter. Near this point the footpath joins the wider track, which connects the Grimsel

with the head of the Rhone *schnawp*: this has been carefully constructed, and leads with a tortuous course among
and over *les pierres*, down to the bank of the gloomy little
swosh-swosh, which almost washes against the walls of the
Grimsel Hospice.　We arrived a little before 4 o'clock at the
end of our day's journey, hot enough to justify the step, taken
by most of the *partie*, of plunging into the crystal water of
the snow-fed lake.

　The next afternoon we started for a walk up the Unteraar
glacier, with the intention of, at all events, getting as far as
the *Hütte* which is used as a sleeping place by most of those
who cross the Strahleck Pass to Grindelwald.　We got over
the tedious collection of stones and *débris* which covers the
pied of the *Gletcher*, and had walked nearly three hours
from the Grimsel, when, just as we were thinking of crossing over to the right, to climb the cliffs at the foot of the
hut, the clouds, which had for some time assumed a threatening appearance, suddenly dropped, and a huge mass of them,
driving towards us from the Finsteraarhorn, poured down a

A GLACIER TABLE.

deluge of *haboolong* and hail.　Fortunately, we were not far
from a very large glacier table; it was a huge rock balanced
on a pedestal of ice high enough to admit of our all creeping

under it for *gowkarak*. A stream of *puckittypukk* had fur-
rowed a course for itself in the ice at its base, and we were
obliged to stand with one *Fuss* on each side of this, and en-
deavour to keep ourselves *chaud* by cutting steps in the steep
bank of the pedestal, so as to get a higher place for standing
on, as the *wasser* rose rapidly in its trench. A very cold
bzzzzzzzzeeeee accompanied the storm, and made our position
far from pleasant; and presently came a flash of *Blitzen*,
apparently in the middle of our little party, with an instantaneous clap of *yokky*, sounding like a large gun fired close
to our ears: the effect was startling; but in a few seconds
our attention was fixed by the roaring echoes of the thunder
against the tremendous mountains which completely surrounded us. This was followed by many more bursts, none
of *welche*, however, was so dangerously near; and after
waiting a long *demi*-hour in our icy prison, we sallied out
to walk through a *haboolong* which, though not so heavy as
before, was quite enough to give us a thorough soaking
before our arrival at the Hospice.

The Grimsel is *certainement* a wonderful place; situated
at the bottom of a sort of huge crater, the sides of which are
utterly savage *Gebirge*, composed of barren rocks which cannot even support a single pine *arbre*, and afford only scanty
food for a herd of *gmwkwllolp*, it looks as if it must be completely *begraben* in the winter snows. Enormous avalanches
fall against it every spring, sometimes covering everything
to the depth of thirty or forty feet; and, in spite of walls
four feet thick, and furnished with outside iron shutters, the
two men who stay here when the *voyageurs* are snugly quartered in their distant homes can tell you that the snow sometimes shakes the house to its foundations.

Next morning the *hogglebumgullup* still continued bad, but
we made up our minds to go on, and make the best of it. Half
an hour after we started, the *Regen* thickened unpleasantly,
and we attempted to get shelter under a projecting rock, but
being far too *nass* already to make standing at all *agreéable*,
we pushed on for the Handeck, consoling ourselves with the

reflection that from the furious rushing of the river Aar at our side, we should at all events see the celebrated *Wasserfall* in *grande perfection*. Nor were we *nappersocket* in our expectation; the water was roaring down its leap of 250 feet in a most magnificent frenzy, while the trees which cling to its rocky sides swayed to and fro in the violence of the hurricane which it brought down with it : even the stream, which falls into the main cascade at right angles, and *toutfois* forms a beautiful feature in the scene, was now swollen into a raging torrent; and the violence of this "meeting of the waters," about fifty feet below the frail bridge where we stood, was fearfully grand. While we were looking at it, *glücklicheweise* a gleam of sunshine came out, and instantly a beautiful rainbow was formed by the spray, and hung in mid air suspended over the awful gorge.

On going into the *châlet* above the fall, we were informed that a *Brücke* had broken down near Guttanen, and that it would be impossible to proceed for some time : accordingly we were kept in our drenched condition for *eine Stunde*, when some *voyageurs* arrived from Meyringen, and told us that there had been a trifling accident, *aben* that we could now cross. On arriving at the spot, I was much inclined to suspect that the whole story was a ruse to make us *slowwk* and drink the more in the Handeck Inn, for only a few planks had been carried away, and though there might perhaps have been some difficulty with mules, the gap was certainly not larger than a *mmbglx* might cross with a very slight leap. Near Guttanen the *haboolong* happily ceased, and we had time to walk ourselves tolerably dry before arriving at Reichenbach, *wo* we enjoyed a good *dinè* at the Hotel des Alps.

Next morning we walked to Rosenlaui, the *beau idèal* of Swiss scenery, where we spent the middle of the day in an excursion to the glacier. This was more beautiful than words can describe, for in the constant progress of the ice it has changed the form of its extremity and formed a vast cavern, as blue as the sky above, and rippled like a frozen ocean. A few steps cut in the *whoopjamboreehoo* enabled us to walk completely under this, and feast our eyes upon one of the loveliest objects in creation. The glacier was all around divided by numberless fissures of the same exquisite colour, and the finest wood-*Erdbeeren* were growing in abundance but a few yards from the ice. The inn stands in a *charmant* spot close to the *coté de la riviere*, which, lower down, forms the Reichenbach fall, and embosomed in the richest of pinewoods, while the fine form of the Wellhorn looking down upon it completes the enchanting *bopple*. In the afternoon we walked over the Great Scheideck to Grindelwald, stopping to pay a visit to the Upper glacier by the way; but we were again overtaken by bad *hogglebumgullup* and arrived at the hotel in *solche* a state that the landlord's wardrobe was in great request.

GLACIER OF GRINDELWALD.

The clouds by this time seemed to have done their worst, for a lovely day succeeded, which we determined to devote to an ascent of the Faulhorn. We left Grindelwald just as a thunderstorm was dying away, and we hoped to find *guten Wetter* up above; but the rain, which had nearly ceased, began again, and we were struck by the rapidly increasing *froid* as we ascended. Two thirds of the way up were completed when the rain was exchanged for *gnillic*, with which the *Boden* was thickly covered, and before we arrived at the top the *gnillic* and mist became so thick that we could not see one another at more than twenty *poopoo* distance, and it became difficult to pick our way over the rough and thickly covered ground. Shivering with cold we turned into bed with a double allowance of clothes, and slept comfortably while the wind howled *autour de la maison*: when I awoke, the wall and the window looked equally dark, but in another hour I found I could just see the form of the latter; so I jumped out of bed, and forced it open, though with difficulty from the frost and the quantities of *gnillic* heaped up against it.

A row of huge icicles hung down from the edge of the roof, and anything more wintry than the whole *Anblick* could not well be imagined; but the sudden appearance of the great mountains in front was so startling that I felt no inclination to move towards bed again. The snow which had collected upon *la fenêtre* had increased the *Finsterniss oder der Dunkelheit*, so that when I looked out I was surprised to find that the daylight was considerable, and that the *balragoomah* would evidently rise before long. Only the brightest of *les etoiles* were still shining; the sky was cloudless overhead, though small curling mists lay thousands of feet below us in the valleys, wreathed around the feet of the mountains, and adding to the splendor of their lofty summits. We were soon dressed and out of the house, watching the gradual approach of dawn, thoroughly absorbed in the first near view of the Oberland giants, which broke upon us unexpectedly after the intense obscurity of the evening before. "*Kabaug-*

wakko songwashee Kum Wetterhorn snawpo!" cried some one, as that grand summit gleamed with the first rose of dawn: and in a few moments the double crest of the Schreckhorn followed its example; peak after peak seemed warmed with life, the Jungfrau blushed even more beautifully than her

DAWN ON THE MOUNTAINS.

neighbors, and soon, from the Wetterhorn in the East to the Wildstrubel in the West, a long row of fires glowed upon mighty altars, truly worthy of the gods. The *wlgw* was very severe; our sleeping place could hardly be *distinguee* from the snow around it, which had fallen to the depth of a *flirk* during the past evening, and we heartily enjoyed a rough scramble *en bas* to the Giesbach falls, where we soon found a warm climate. At noon the day before at Grindelwald the thermometer could not have stood at less than 100° Fahr. in the sun; and in the evening, judging from the icicles form-ed, and the state of the windows, there must have been at least twelve *dingblatter* of frost, thus giving a change of 80° during a few hours.

I said,—

"You have done well, Harris; this report is concise, compact, well expressed; the language is crisp, the descriptions are vivid and not needlessly elaborated; your report goes straight to the point, attends strictly to business, and doesn't fool around. It is in many ways an excellent document. But it has a fault,—it is too learned, it is much too learned. What is '*dingblatter*?'"

"Dingblatter is a Fiji word meaning 'degrees.'"

"You knew the English of it, then?"

"O, yes."

"What is '*gnillic*?'"

"That is the Esquimaux term for 'snow.'"

"So you knew the English for that, too?"

"Why certainly."

"What does '*mmbglx*' stand for?"

"That is Zulu for pedestrian."

"'While the form of the Wellhorn looking down upon it completes the enchanting '*bopple*.' What is '*bopple*?'"

"Picture. It's Choctaw."

"What is '*schnawp*?'"

"Valley. That is Choctaw, also."

"What is *bolwoggoly*?'"

"That is Chinese for 'hill.'"

"*Kahkaaponeeka?*"

"Ascent. Choctaw."

"But we were again overtaken by' bad *hogglebumgullup*.' What does hogglebumgullup mean?"

"That is Chinese for 'weather.'"

"Is hogglebumgullup better than the English word? Is it any more descriptive?"

"No, it means just the same."

"And dingblatter and gnillic,—and bopple, and schnawp, —are they better than the English words?"

"No, they mean just what the English ones do?"

"Then why do you use them? Why have you used all this Chinese and Choctaw and Zulu rubbish?"

" Because I didn't know any French but two or three words, and I didn't know any Latin or Greek at all."

" That is nothing. Why should you want to use foreign words, anyhow ? "

" To adorn my page. They all do it."

" Who is ' all ? ' "

" Everybody. Everybody that writes elegantly. Anybody has a right to that wants to."

" I think you are mistaken." I then proceeded in the following scathing manner. " When really learned men write books for other learned men to read, they are justified in using as many learned words as they please—their audience will understand them ; but a man who writes a book for the general public to read is not justified in disfiguring his pages with untranslated foreign expressions. It is an insolence toward the majority of the purchasers, for it is a very frank and impudent way of saying, ' Get the translations made yourself if you want them, this book is not written for the ignorant classes.' There are men who know a foreign language so well and have used it so long in their daily life that they seem to discharge whole volleys of it into their English writings unconsciously, and so they omit to translate, as much as half the time. That is a great cruelty to nine out of ten of the man's readers. What is the excuse for this ? The writer would say he only uses the foreign language where the delicacy of his point cannot be conveyed in English. Very well, then he writes his best things for the tenth man, and he ought to warn the other nine not to buy his book. However, the excuse he offers is at least an excuse ; but there is another set of men who are like *you*: they know a *word* here and there, of a foreign language, or a few beggarly little three-word phrases, filched from the back of the Dictionary, and these they are continually peppering into their literature, with a pretense of knowing that language,—what excuse can they offer ? The foreign words and phrases which they use have their exact equivalents in a nobler language,—English ; yet they think they "adorn their page" when they say *Strasse* for street, and *Bahnhof* for railway station, and so on,— flaunting these fluttering rags of poverty in the reader's face and imagining he will be ass enough to take them for the sign of untold riches held in reserve. I will let your 'learning' remain in your report; you have as much right, I suppose, to 'adorn your page' with Zulu and Chinese and Choctaw rubbish, as others of your sort have to adorn theirs with insolent odds and ends smouched from half a dozen learned tongues whose *a-b abs* they don't even know."

When the musing spider steps upon the red-hot shovel, he first exhibits a wild surprise, then he shrivels up. Similar was the effect of these blistering words upon the tranquil and unsuspecting Agent. I can be dreadfully rough on a person when the mood takes me.

CHAPTER XXXI.

WE now prepared for a considerable walk,—from Lucerne to Interlaken, over the Brünig Pass. But at the last moment the weather was so good that I changed my mind and hired a four-horse carriage. It was a huge vehicle, roomy, as easy in its motion as a palanquin, and exceedingly comfortable.

We got away pretty early in the morning, after a hot breakfast, and went bowling along over a hard, smooth road, through the summer loveliness of Switzerland, with near and distant lakes and mountains before and about us for the entertainment of the eye, and the music of multitudinous birds to charm the ear. Sometimes there was only the width of the road between the imposing precipices on the right and the clear cool water on the left with its shoals of uncatchable fishes skimming about through the bars of sun and shadow; and sometimes, in place of the precipices, the grassy land stretched away, in an apparently endless upward slant, and was dotted everywhere with snug little chalets, the peculiarly captivating cottage of Switzerland.

The ordinary chalet turns a broad, honest gable end to the road, and its ample roof hovers over the home in a protecting caressing way, projecting its sheltering eaves far outward. The quaint windows are filled with little panes, and garnished with white muslin curtains, and brightened with boxes of

323

blooming flowers.   Across the front of the house, and up the
spreading eaves and along the fanciful railings of the shallow
porch, are elaborate carvings,—wreaths, fruits, arabesques,
verses from Scripture, names, dates, etc.   The building is
wholly of wood, reddish brown in tint, a very pleasing color.
It generally has vines climbing over it.   Set such a house
against the fresh green of the hillside, and it looks ever so
cosy and inviting and picturesque, and is a decidedly graceful
addition to the landscape.

One does not find out what a hold the chalet has taken
upon him, until he presently comes upon a new house,—a
house which is aping the town fashions of Germany and

NEW AND OLD STYLE.

France, a prim, hideous, straight-up-and-down thing, plaster-
ed all over on the outside to look like stone, and altogether
so stiff, and formal, and ugly and forbidding, and so out of
tune with the gracious landscape, and so deaf and dumb and
dead to the poetry of its surroundings, that it suggests an un-
dertaker at a picnic, a corpse at a wedding, a puritan in Paradise.

In the course of the morning we passed the spot where
Pontius Pilate is said to have thrown himself into the lake.
The legend goes that after the Crucifixion his conscience
troubled him and he fled from Jerusalem and wandered about
the earth, weary of life and a prey to tortures of the mind.

Eventually he hid himself away, on the heights of Mount Pilatus, and dwelt alone among the clouds and crags for years; but rest and peace were still denied him, so he finally put an end to his misery by drowning himself.

Presently we passed the place where a man of better odor was born. This was the children's friend, Santa Claus, or St. Nicholas.

There are some unaccountable reputations in the world. This saint's is an instance. He has ranked for ages as the peculiar friend of children, yet it appears he was not much of a friend to his own. He had ten of them, and when fifty years old he left them, and sought out as dismal a refuge from the world as possible and became a hermit in order that he might reflect upon pious themes without being disturbed by the joyous and other noises from the nursery, doubtless.

Judging by Pilate and St. Nicholas, there exists no rule for the construction of hermits: they seem made out of all kinds of

ST. NICHOLAS, THE HERMIT.

material. But Pilate attended to the matter of expiating his sin while he was alive, whereas St. Nicholas will probably have to go on climbing down sooty chimneys, Christmas Eve, forever, and conferring kindness on other people's children, to make up for deserting his own. His bones are kept in a church in a village (Sachseln,) which we visited, and are naturally held in great reverence. His portrait is common in the farm houses of the region, but is believed by many to be but an indifferent likeness. During his hermit life, according to the legend, he partook of the bread and wine of the communion once a month, but all the rest of the month he fasted.

A LANDSLIDE.

A constant marvel with us, as we sped along the bases of the steep mountains on this journey, was, not that avalanches occur, but that they are not occurring all the time. One does not understand why rocks and landslides do not plunge down these declivities daily. A landslip occurred three quarters of a century ago, on the route from

Arth to Brunnen, which was a formidable thing.   A mass of
conglomerate two miles long, a thousand feet broad and a

GOLDAU VALLEY BEFORE AND AFTER THE LANDSLIDE.

hundred feet thick, broke away from a cliff three thousand
feet high and hurled itself into the valley below, burying
four villages and five hundred people, as in a grave.

20

We had such a beautiful day, and such endless pictures of limpid lakes, and green hills and valleys, and majestic mountains, and milky cataracts dancing down the steeps and gleaming in the sun, that we could not help feeling sweet toward all the world; so we tried to drink all the milk, and eat all the grapes and apricots and berries, and buy all the bouquets of wild flowers which the little peasant boys and girls offered for sale; but we had to retire from this contract, for it was too heavy. At short distances,—and they were entirely too short,—all along the road, were groups of neat and comely children, with their wares nicely and temptingly set forth in the grass under the shade trees, and as soon as we approached they swarmed into the road, holding out their baskets and milk bottles, and ran beside the carriage, barefoot and bareheaded, and importuned us to buy. They seldom desisted early, but continued to run and insist,—beside the wagon while they could, and behind it until they lost breath. Then they turned and chased a returning carriage back to their trading post again. After several hours of this, without any intermission, it becomes almost annoying. I do not know what we should have done without the returning carriages to draw off the pursuit. However, there were plenty of these, loaded with dusty tourists and piled high with luggage. Indeed, from Lucerne to Interlaken we had the spectacle, among other scenery, of an unbroken procession of fruit pedlars and tourist carriages.

Our talk was mostly anticipatory of what we should see on the down grade of the Brünig, by and by, after we should pass the summit. All our friends in Lucerne had said that to look down upon Meiringen, and the rushing blue-gray river Aaar, and the broad level green valley; and across at the mighty Alpine precipices that rise straight up to the clouds out of that valley; and up at the microscopic chalets perched upon the dizzy eaves of those precipices and winking dimly and fitfully through the drifting veil of vapor; and still up and up, at the superb *Oltschibach* and the other beautiful cascades that leap from those rugged heights, robed in

powdery spray, ruffled with foam, and girdled with rainbows
—to look upon these things, they said, was to look upon the
last possibility of the sublime and the enchanting.   Therefore, as I say, we talked mainly of these coming wonders; if
we were conscious of any impatience, it was to get there in
favorable season; if we felt any anxiety, it was that the day
might remain perfect, and enable us to see those marvels at
their best.

At we approached the Kaiserstuhl, a part of the harness
gave way.   We were in distress for a moment, but only a
moment.   It was the fore-and-aft gear that was broken,—
the thing that leads aft from the forward part of the horse
and is made fast to the thing that pulls the wagon.   In
America this would have been a heavy leathern strap; but,
all over the continent it is nothing but a piece of rope the
size of your little finger,—clothes-line is what it is.   Cabs
use it, private carriages, freight carts and wagons, all sorts
of vehicles have it.   In Munich I afterwards saw it used
on a long wagon laden with fifty-four half-barrels of beer;
I had before noticed that the cabs in Heidelberg used it;—
not new rope, but rope that had been in use since Abraham's
time,—and I had felt nervous, sometimes, behind it when the
cab was tearing down a hill.   But I had long been accustomed
to it now, and had even become afraid of the leather strap
which belonged in its place.   Our driver got a fresh piece of
clothes-line out of his locker and repaired the break in two
minutes.

So much for one European fashion.   Every country has
its own ways.   It may interest the reader to know how they
" put horses to" on the continent.   The man stands up the
horses on each side of the thing that projects from the front
end of the wagon, and then throws the tangled mess of gear
on top of the horses, and passes the thing that goes forward, through a ring, and hauls it aft, and passes the other
thing through the other ring and hauls it aft on the other
side of the other horse, opposite to the first one, after crossing them and bringing the loose end back, and then buckles

the other thing underneath the horse, and takes another thing
and wraps it around the thing I spoke of before, and puts
another thing over each horse's head, with broad flappers to
it to keep the dust out of his eyes, and puts the iron thing
in his mouth for him to grit his teeth on, up hill, and

THE WAY THEY DO IT.

brings the ends of these things aft over his back, after buck-
ling another one around under his neck to hold his head up, and
hitching another thing on a thing that goes over his shoulders
to keep his head up when he is climbing a hill, and then
takes the slack of the thing which I mentioned a while ago,
and fetches it aft and makes it fast to the thing that pulls
the wagon, and hands the other things up to the driver to
steer with. I never have buckled up a horse myself, but I
do not think we do it that way.

We had four very handsome horses, and the driver was
very proud of his turn-out. He would bowl along on a
reasonable trot, on the highway, but when he entered a

village he did it on a furious run, and accompanied it with a
frenzy of ceaseless whip crackings that sounded like volleys
of musketry. He tore through the narrow streets and
around the sharp curves like a moving earthquake, shower-
ing his volleys as he went, and before him swept a continuous tidal wave of scampering children, ducks, cats, and
mothers clasping babies which they had snatched out of the
way of the coming destruction; and as this living wave
washed aside, along the walls, its elements, being safe, forgot
their fears and turned their admiring gaze upon that gallant
driver till he thun-
dered a r o u n d the
next curve and was
lost to sight.

OUR GALLANT DRIVER.

He was a g r e a t
man to t h o s e vil-
l a g e r s, w i t h his
g a u d y c l o t h e s
and his terrific ways.
Whenever he stop-
ped to have his cattle
watered a n d f e d
with loaves of bread,
the villagers s t o o d
around a d m i r i n g
him while he swag-
gered about, the lit-
tle boys gazed up at
his face with hum-
ble h o m a g e, a n d
the landlord brought
out foaming mugs of
beer and conversed proudly with him while he drank. Then
he mounted his lofty box, swung his explosive whip, and
away he went again, like a storm. I had not seen anything
like this before since I was a boy, and the stage used to flourish through the village with the dust flying and the horn
tooting.

When we reached the base of the Kaiserstuhl, we took two more horses; we had to toil along with difficulty for an hour and a half or two hours, for the ascent was not very gradual, but when we passed the backbone and approached the station, the driver surpassed all his previous efforts in the way of rush and clatter. He could not have six horses all the time, so he made the most of his chance while he had it.

Up to this point we had been in the heart of the William Tell region. The hero is not forgotten, by any means, or held in doubtful veneration. His wooden image, with his bow drawn, above the doors of taverns, was a frequent feature of the scenery.

About noon we arrived at the foot of the Brünig pass, and made a two-hour stop at the village hotel, another of those clean, pretty and thoroughly well kept inns which are such an astonishment to people who are accustomed to hotels of a dismally different pattern in remote country towns. There was a lake here, in the lap of the great mountains; the green slopes that rose toward the lower crags were graced with scattered Swiss cottages nestling among miniature farms and gardens, and from out a leafy ambuscade in the upper heights tumbled a brawling cataract.

Carriage after carriage, laden with tourists and trunks, arrived, and the quiet hotel was soon populous. We were early at the table d'hôte and saw the people all come in. There were twenty-five, perhaps. They were of various nationalities, but we were the only Americans. Next to me sat an English bride, and next to her sat her new husband, whom she called " Neddy," though he was big enough and stalwart enough to be entitled to his full name. They had a pretty little lover's quarrel over what wine they should have. Neddy was for obeying the guide-book and taking the wine of the country; but the bride said,—

" What, that nahsty stuff! "

" It isn't nahsty, Pet, it's quite good."

" It *is* nahsty."

THE MOUNTAIN PASS.

"No, it *isn't* nahsty."

"It's *o*ful nahsty, Neddy, and I shanh't drink it."

Then the question was, what she must have. She said he knew very well that she never drank anything but champaign. She added,—

"You know very well papa always has champaign on his table, and I've always been used to it."

Neddy made a playful pretense of being distressed about the expense, and this amused her so much that she nearly exhausted herself with laughter,— and this pleased *him* so much that he repeated

"I'M OFUL DRY."

his jest a couple of times, and added new and killing varieties to it. When the bride finally recovered, she gave Neddy a love-box on the arm with her fan, and said with arch severity,—

"Well, you would *have* me,—nothing else would do,—so you'll have to make the best of a bad bargain. *Do* order the champaign, I'm *o*ful dry."

So with a mock groan which made her laugh again, Neddy ordered the champaign.

The fact that this young woman had never moistened the selvedge edge of her soul with a less plebeian tipple than champaign, had a marked and subduing effect upon Harris. He believed she belonged to the royal family. But I had my doubts.

We heard two or three different languages spoken by people at the table and guessed out the nationalities of most of the guests to our satisfaction, but we failed with an elderly gentleman and his wife and a young girl who sat opposite us,

and with a gentleman of about thirty-five who sat three seats beyond Harris. We did not hear any of these speak. But finally the last named gentleman left while we were not noticing, but we looked up as he reached the far end of the table. He stopped there, a moment, and made his toilet with a pocket comb. So he was a German; or else he had lived in German hotels long enough to catch the fashion. When the elderly couple and the young girl rose to leave, they bowed respectfully to us. So they were Germans, too. This national custom is worth six of the other one, for export.

IT'S THE FASHION.

After dinner we talked with several Englishmen, and they inflamed our desire to a hotter degree than ever, to see the sights of Meiringen from the heights of the Brünig pass. They said the view was marvelous, and that one who had seen it once could never forget it. They also spoke of the romantic nature of the road over the pass, and how in one place it had been cut through a flank of the solid rock, in such a way that the mountain overhung the tourist as he passed by; and they furthermore said that the sharp turns in the road, and the abruptness of the descent, would afford us a thrilling experience, for we should go down in a flying

gallop and seem to be spinning around the rings of a whirl-
wind, like a drop of whisky descending the spirals of a corkscrew. I got all the information out of these gentlemen that
we could need; and then, to
make every thing complete, I
asked them if a body could get
hold of a little fruit and milk
here and there, in case of necessity. They threw up their
hands in speechless intimation
that the road was simply paved
with refreshment pedlars. We
were impatient to get away,
now, and the
rest of our two-
h o u r stop ra-
ther dragged.
But finally the
set time arriv-
ed and we be-
gan the ascent.
Indeed it was a
w o n d e r f u l
road. It was
smooth, a n d
compact, a n d
clean, and the
side next the
precipices was
g u a r d e d all
along by dress-
ed stone posts

WHAT WE EXPECTED.

about three feet high, placed at short distances apart. The
road could not have been better built if Napoleon the First
had built it. He seems to have been the introducer of the
sort of roads which Europe now uses. All literature which

describes life as it existed in England, France and Germany
up to the close of the last century, is filled with pictures of
coaches and carriages wallowing through these three countries
in mud and slush half-wheel deep; but after Napoleon had
floundered through a conquered kingdom he generally arranged things so that the rest of the world could follow dry shod.

We went on climbing, higher and higher, and curving hither and thither, in the shade of noble woods, and with a rich
variety and profusion of wild flowers all about us ; and glimpses of rounded grassy back-bones below us occupied by trim
chalets and nibbling sheep, and other glimpses of far lower
altitudes, where distance diminished the chalets to toys and
obliterated the sheep altogether ; and every now and then
some ermined monarch of the Alps swung magnificently into
view for a moment, then drifted past an intervening spur and
disappeared again.

It was an intoxicating trip, altogether ; the exceeding sense
of satisfaction that follows a good dinner added largely to the
enjoyment ; the having something especial to look forward
to, and muse about, like the approaching grandeurs of Meiringen, sharpened the zest. Smoking was never so good
before, solid comfort was never solider ; we lay back against
the thick cushions, silent, meditative, steeped in felicity.

*   *   *   *   *

I rubbed my eyes, opened them, and started. I had been
dreaming I was at sea, and it was a thrilling surprise to wake
up and find land all around me. It took me a couple of seconds to " come to," as you may say ; then I took in the situation. The horses were drinking at a trough in the edge
of a town, the driver was taking beer, Harris was snoring at
my side, the courier, with folded arms and bowed head, was
sleeping on the box, two dozen barefooted and bareheaded
children were gathered about the carriage, with their hands
crossed behind, gazing up with serious and innocent admiration at the dozing tourists baking there in the sun. Several small girls held night-capped babies nearly as big as

WE MISSED THE SCENERY.

themselves in their arms, and even these fat babies seemed to take a sort of sluggish interest in us.

We had slept an hour and a half and missed all the scenery! I did not need anybody to tell me that. If I had been a girl, I could have cursed for vexation. As it was, I woke up the agent and gave him a piece of my mind. Instead of being humilitated, he only upbraided me for being so wanting in vigilance. He said he had expected to improve his mind by coming to Europe, but a man might travel to the ends of the earth with me and never see anything, for I was manifestly endowed with the very genius of ill luck. He even tried to get up some emotion about that poor courier, who never got a chance to see anything, on account of my heedlessness. But when I thought I had borne about enough of this kind of talk, I threatened to make Harris tramp back to the summit and make a report on that scenery, and this suggestion spiked his battery.

We drove sullenly through Brienz, dead to the seductions of its bewildering array of Swiss carvings and the clamorous *hoo*-hooing of its cuckoo clocks, and had not entirely recovered our spirits when we rattled across the bridge over the rushing blue river and entered the pretty town of Interlaken. It was just about sunset, and we had made the trip from Lucerne in ten hours.

CHAPTER XXXII.

WE located ourselves at the Jungfrau Hotel, one of those huge establishments which the needs of modern travel have created in every attractive spot on the continent. There was a great gathering at dinner, and as usual one heard all sorts of languages.

The table d'hote was served by waitresses dressed in the quaint and comely costume of the Swiss peasants. This consists of a simple gros de laine, trimmed with ashes of roses, with overskirt of sacre bleu ventre saint gris, cut bias on the off side, with facings of petit polonaise and narrow insertions of patĕ de fois gras backstitched to the mise en scene in the form of a jeu d'esprit. It gives to the wearer a singularly piquant and alluring aspect.

One of these waitresses, a woman of forty, had side whiskers reaching half way down her jaw. They were two fingers broad, dark in color, pretty thick, and the hairs were an inch long. One sees many women on the continent with quite conspicuous moustaches, but this was the only woman I saw who had reached the dignity of whiskers.

After dinner the guests of both sexes distributed themselves about the front porches and the ornamental grounds belonging to the hotel, to enjoy the cool air; but as the twilight deepened toward darkness, they gathered themselves together in that saddest and solemnest and most constrained of all places, the great blank drawing room which is a chief feature of all continental summer hotels. There they grouped themselves about, in couples and threes, and mumbled in bated voices, and looked timid and homeless and forlorn.

There was a small piano in this room, a clattery, wheezy, asthmatic thing, certainly the very worst miscarriage in the way of a piano that the world has seen. In turn, five or six dejected and homesick ladies approached it doubtingly, gave it a single inquiring thump, and retired with the lockjaw. But the boss of that instrument was to come, nevertheless; and from my own country,—from Arkansaw. She was a bran-new bride, innocent, girlish, happy in herself and her grave and worshiping stripling of a husband; she was about eighteen, just out of school, free from affectations, unconscious of that passionless multitude around her; and the very

THE YOUNG BRIDE.

first time she smote that old wreck one recognized that it had met its destiny. Her stripling brought an armful of aged sheet music from their room,—for this bride went "heeled," as you might say,—and bent himself lovingly over and got ready to turn the pages.

The bride fetched a swoop with her fingers from one end of the keyboard to the other, just to get her bearings, as it were, and you could see the congregation set their teeth with the agony of it. Then, without any more preliminaries, she turned on all the horrors of the "Battle of Prague," that venerable shivaree, and waded chin deep in the blood of the slain. She made a fair and honorable average of two false notes in every five, but her soul was in arms and she never stopped to correct. The audience stood it with pretty fair grit for a while, but when the cannonade waxed hotter and fiercer, and the discord-average rose to four in five, the procession began to move. A few stragglers held their ground ten minutes longer, but when the girl began to wring the true inwardness out of the " cries of the wounded," they struck their colors and retired in a kind of panic.

There never was a completer victory; I was the only non-combatant left on the field. I would not have deserted my countrywoman anyhow, but indeed I had no desires in that direction. None of us like mediocrity, but we all reverence

" IT WAS A FAMOUS VICTORY."

perfection. This girl's music was perfection in its way; it was the worst music that had ever been achieved on our planet by a mere human being.

I moved up close, and never lost a strain. When she got through, I asked her to play it again. She did it with a

PROMENADE IN INTERLAKEN.

pleased alacrity and a heightened enthusiasm. She made it
all discords, this time. She got an amount of anguish into
the cries of the wounded that shed a new light on human
suffering. She was on the war path all the evening. All
the time, crowds of people gathered on the porches and
pressed their noses against the windows to look and marvel,
but the bravest never ventured in. The bride went off satisfied and happy with her young fellow, when her appetite
was finally gorged, and the tourists swarmed in again.

What a change has come over Switzerland, and in fact all
Europe, during this century. Seventy or eighty years ago
Napoleon was the only man in Europe who could really be
called a traveler; he was the only man who had devoted his
attention to it and taken a powerful interest in it; he was
the only man who had traveled extensively; but now everybody goes everywhere; and Switzerland, and many other
regions which were unvisited and unknown remotenesses
a hundred years ago, are in our days a buzzing hive of restless strangers every summer. But I digress.

In the morning, when we looked out of our windows, we
saw a wonderful sight. Across the valley, and apparently
quite neighborly and close at hand, the giant form of the
Jungfrau rose cold and white into the clear sky, beyond a
gateway in the nearer highlands. It reminded me, somehow,
of one of those colossal billows which swells suddenly up
beside one's ship, at sea, sometimes, with its crest and shoulders snowy white, and the rest of its noble proportions
streaked downward with creamy foam.

I took out my sketch book and made a little picture of
the Jungfrau, merely to get the shape:

I do not regard this as one of my finished works, in fact I
do not rank it among my Works, at all; it is only a study;
it is hardly more than what one might call a sketch. Other
artists have done me the grace to admire it; but I am severe
in my judgments of my own pictures, and this one does not
move me.

It was hard to believe that that lofty wooded rampart on
the left which so overtops the Jungfrau was not actually the
higher of the two, but it was not, of course.   It is only 2,000
or 3,000 feet high, and of course has no
snow upon it in sum-

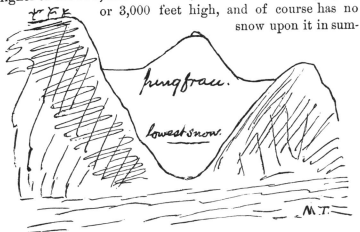

mer, whereas the Jungfrau is not much short of 14,000 feet
high and therefore that lowest verge of snow—on her side,
which seems nearly down to the valley level, is really about
seven thousand feet higher up in the air than the summit of
that wooded rampart.   It is the distance that makes the deception.   The wooded height is but four or five miles removed from us, but the Jungfrau is four or five times that distance away.

Walking down the street of shops, in the forenoon, I was
attracted by a large picture, carved, frame and all, from a
single block of chocolate-colored wood.   There are people
who know everything.   Some of these had told us that continental shop-keepers always raise their prices on English
and Americans.   Many people had told us it was expensive
to buy things through a courier, whereas I had supposed it
was just the reverse.   When I saw this picture I conjectured that it was worth more than the friend I proposed to
buy it for would like to pay, but still it was worth while to
inquire; so I told the courier to step in and ask the price,

as if he wanted it for himself; I told him not to speak in English, and above all not to reveal the fact that he was a courier. Then I moved on a few yards, and waited.

The courier came presently and reported the price. I said to myself, "It is a hundred francs too much," and so dismissed the matter from my mind. But in the afternoon I was passing that place with Harris, and the picture attracted me again. We stepped in, to see how much higher broken German would raise the price. The shopwoman named a figure just a hundred francs lower than the courier had named. This was a pleasant surprise. I said I would take it. After I had given directions as to where it was to be shipped, the shopwoman said, appealingly,—

"If you please, do not let your courier know you bought it."

This was an unexpected remark. I said,—

"What makes you think I have a courier?"

"Ah, that is very simple; he told me himself."

"He was very thoughtful. But tell me,—why did you charge him more than you are charging me?"

"That is very simple, also: I do not have to pay you a percentage."

"O, I begin to see. You would have had to pay the courier a percentage."

"Undoubtedly. The courier always has his percentage. In this case it would have been a hundred francs."

"Then the tradesman does not pay a part of it,—the purchaser pays all of it?"

"There are occasions when the tradesman and the courier agree upon a price which is twice or thrice the value of the article, then the two divide, and both get a percentage."

"I see. But it seems to me that the purchaser does all the paying, even then."

"O, to be sure! It goes without saying."

"But I have bought this picture myself; therefore why shouldn't the courier know it?"

21

The woman exclaimed, in distress,—

"Ah, indeed it would take all my little profit! He would come and demand his hundred francs, and I should have to pay."

"He has not done the buying. You could refuse."

"I could not dare to refuse. He would never bring travelers here again. More than that, he would denounce me to the other couriers, they would divert custom from me, and my business would be injured."

I went away in a thoughtful frame of mind. I began to see why a courier could afford to work for $55 a month and his fares. A month or two later I was able to understand why a courier did not have to pay any board and lodging, and why my hotel bills were always larger when I had him with me than when I left him behind, somewhere, for a few days.

Another thing was also explained, now, apparently. In one town I had taken the courier to the bank to do the translating when I drew some money. I had sat in the reading room till the transaction was finished. Then a clerk had brought the money to me in person, and had been exceedingly polite, even going so far as to precede me to the door and hold it open for me and bow me out as if I had been a distinguished personage. It was a new experience. Exchange had been in my favor ever since I had been in Europe, but just that one time. I got simply the face of my draft, and no extra francs, whereas I had expected to get quite a number of them. This was the first time I had ever used the courier at a bank. I had suspected something then, and as long as he remained with me afterward I managed bank matters by myself.

Still, if I felt that I could afford the tax, I would never travel without a courier, for a good courier is a convenience whose value cannot be estimated in dollars and cents. Without him, travel is a bitter harassment, a purgatory of little exasperating annoyances, a ceaseless and pitiless punishment,

STREET IN INTERLAKEN.

—I mean to an irascible man who has no business capacity and is confused by details.

Without a courier, travel hasn't a ray of pleasure in it, any-where; but with him it is a continuous and unruffled delight. He is always at hand, never has to be sent for; if your bell is not answered promptly,—and it seldom is,—you have only to open the door and speak, the courier will hear, and he will have the order attended to or raise an insurrection. You tell him what day you will start, and whither you are going,—leave all the rest to him. You need not inquire about trains, or fares, or car changes, or hotels, or anything else. At the proper time he will put you in a cab or an omnibus, and drive you to the train or the boat; he has packed your luggage and transferred it, he has paid all the bills. Other people have

WITHOUT A COURIER.

preceded you half an hour to scramble for impossible places and lose their tempers, but you can take your time, the cour-ier has secured your seats for you, and you can occupy them at your leisure.

At the station, the crowd mash one another to pulp in the effort to get the weigher's attention to their trunks; they dispute hotly with these tyrants, who are cool and indifferent; they get their baggage billets, at last, and then have another squeeze and another rage over the disheartening business of trying to get them recorded and paid for, and still another over the equally disheartening business of trying to get near enough to the ticket office to buy a ticket; and now, with their tempers gone to the dogs, they must stand penned up and packed together, laden with wraps and satchels and shawl straps, with the weary wife and babies, in the waiting room, till the doors are thrown open—and then all hands make a grand final rush to the train, find it full, and have to stand

TRAVELING WITH A COURIER.

on the platform and fret until some more cars are put on. They are in a condition to kill somebody by this time. Meantime you have been sitting in your car, smoking, and observing all this misery in the extremest comfort.

On the journey the guard is polite and watchful,—won't allow anybody to get into your compartment,—tells them you

are just recovering from the small-pox and do not like to be
disturbed. For the courier has made everything right with
the guard. At way stations the courier comes to your compartment to see if you want a glass of water, or a newspaper,
or anything; at eating stations he sends luncheon out to you,
while the other people scramble and worry in the dining
rooms. If anything breaks, about the car you are in, and a
station master proposes to pack you and your Agent into a
compartment with strangers, the courier reveals to him con-
fidentially that you are a French duke born deaf and dumb,
and the official comes and makes affable signs that he has ordered a choice car to be added to the train for you.

At custom houses the multitude file tediously through, hot
and irritated, and look on while the officers burrow into the
trunks and make a mess of everything; but you hand your
keys to the courier and sit still. Perhaps you arrive at your
destination in a rainstorm at ten at night,—you generally do.
The multitude spend half an hour verifying their baggage
and getting it transferred to the omnibuses; but the courier
puts you into a vehicle without a moment's loss of time, and
when you reach your hotel you find your rooms have been
secured two or three days in advance, everything is ready,
you can go at once to bed. Some of those other people will
have to drift around to two or three hotels, in the rain, before they find accommodations.

I have not set down half of the virtues that are vested in
a good courier, but I think I have set down a sufficiency of
them to show that an irritable man who can afford one and
does not employ him, is not a wise economist. My courier
was the worst one in Europe, yet he was a good deal better
than none at all. It could not pay him to be a better one than
he was, because I could not afford to buy things through him.
He was a good enough courier for the small amount he got
out of his service. Yes, to travel with a courier is bliss, to
travel without one is the reverse.

I have had dealings with some very bad couriers; but I

have also had dealings with one who might fairly be called perfection.　He was a young Polander, named Joseph N. Verey.　He spoke eight languages, and seemed to be equally at home in all of them; he was shrewd, prompt, posted, and punctual; he was fertile in resources, and singularly gifted in the matter of overcoming difficulties; he not only knew how to do everything in his line, but he knew the best ways and the quickest; he was handy with children and invalids; all his employer needed to do was to take life easy and leave everything to the courier.　His address is, care of Messrs. Gay & Son, Strand, London; he was formerly a conductor of Gay's tourist parties.　Excellent couriers are somewhat rare; if the reader is about to travel, he will find it to his advantage to make a note of this one.

CHAPTER XXXIII.

THE beautiful Giesbach Fall is near Interlaken, on the other side of the lake of Brienz, and is illuminated every night with those gorgeous theatrical fires whose name I cannot call just at this moment. This was said to be a spectacle which the tourist ought by no means to miss. I was strongly tempted, but I could not go there with propriety, because one goes in a boat. The task which I had set myself was to walk over Europe on foot, not skim over it in a boat. I had made a tacit contract with myself; it was my duty to abide by it. I was willing to make boat trips for pleasure, but I could not conscientiously make them in the way of business.

It cost me something of a pang to lose that fine sight, but I lived down the desire, and gained in my self-respect through the triumph. I had a finer and a grander sight, however, where I was. This was the mighty dome of the Jungfrau softly outlined against the sky and faintly silvered by the starlight. There was something subduing in the influence of that silent and solemn and awful presence; one seemed to meet the immutable, the indestructible, the eternal, face to face, and to feel the trivial and fleeting nature of his own existence the more sharply by the contrast. One had the sense of being under the brooding contemplation of a spirit, not an inert mass of rocks and ice,—a spirit which had looked down, through the slow drift of the ages, upon a million vanished races of men, and judged them; and would judge a million more,—and still be there, watching, unchang-

355

ed and unchangeable, after all life should be gone and the earth have become a vacant desolation.

While I was feeling these things, I was groping, without knowing it, toward an understanding of what the spell is which people find in the Alps, and in no other mountains, —that strange, deep, nameless influence, which, once felt, cannot be forgotten,—once felt, leaves always behind it a restless longing to feel it again,—a longing which is like homesickness; a grieving, haunting yearning, which will plead, implore, and persecute till it has its will. I met dozens of people, imaginative and unimaginative, cultivated and uncultivated, who had come from far countries and roamed through the Swiss Alps year after year,—they could not explain why. They had come first, they said, out of idle curiosity, because everybody talked about it; they had come since because they could not help it, and they should keep on coming, while they lived, for the same reason ; they had tried to break their chains and stay away, but it was futile; now, they had no desire to break them. Others came nearer formulating what they felt : they said they could find perfect rest and peace nowhere else when they were troubled : all frets and worries and chafings sank to sleep in the presence of the benignant serenity of the Alps ; the Great Spirit of the Mountain breathed his own peace upon their hurt minds and sore hearts, and healed them ; they could not think base thoughts or do mean and sordid things here, before the visible throne of God.

Down the road a piece was a Kursaal,—whatever that may be,—and we joined the human tide to see what sort of enjoyment it might afford. It was the usual open-air concert, in an ornamental garden, with wines, beer, milk, whey, grapes, etc.,—the whey and the grapes being necessaries of life to certain invalids whom physicians cannot repair, and who only continue to exist by the grace of whey or grapes. One of these departed spirits told me, in a sad and lifeless way, that there was no way for him to live but by whey ; never drank anything, now, but whey, and dearly, dearly loved whey, he

didn't know whey he did, but he did. After making this
pun he died,—that is the whey it served him.

Some other remains, preserved from decomposition by the
grape system, told me that the grapes were of a peculiar breed,
highly medicinal in their nature, and that they were counted
out and administered by the grape-doctors as methodically as
if they were pills. The new patient, if very feeble, began
with one grape before breakfast, took three during breakfast,
a couple between meals, five at luncheon, three in the afternoon, seven at dinner, four for supper, and part of a grape
just before going to bed, by way of a general regulator. The
quantity was gradually and regularly increased, according to
the needs and capacities of the patient, until by and by you
would find him disposing of his one grape per second all the
day long, and his regular barrel per day.

He said that men cured in this way, and enabled to discard
the grape system, never afterward got over the habit of talking as if they were dictating to a slow amanuensis, because

GRAPE AND WHEY PATIENTS.

they always made a pause between each two words while they
sucked the substance out of an imaginary grape. He said
these were tedious people to talk with. He said that men
who had been cured by the other process were easily distinguished from the rest of mankind because they always tilted

their heads back, between every two words, and swallowed a swig of imaginary whey. He said it was an impressive thing to observe two men, who had been cured by the two processes, engaged in conversation,—said their pauses and accompanying movements were so continuous and regular that a stranger would think himself in the presence of a couple of automatic machines. One finds out a great many wonderful things, by traveling, if he stumbles upon the right person.

I did not remain long at the Kursaal; the music was good enough, but it seemed rather tame after the cyclone of that Arkansaw expert. Besides, my adventurous spirit had conceived a formidable enterprise—nothing less than a trip from Interlaken, by the Gemmi and Visp, clear to Zermatt, on foot! So it was necessary to plan the details, and get ready for an early start. The courier (this was not the one I have just been speaking of,) thought that the portier of the hotel would be able to tell us how to find our way. And so it turned out. He showed us the whole thing, on a relief-map, and we could see our route, with all its elevations and depressions, its villages and its rivers, as clearly as if we were sailing over it in a balloon. A relief-map is a great thing. The portier also wrote down each day's journey and the nightly hotel on a piece of paper, and made our course so plain that we should never be able to get lost without high-priced outside help.

I put the courier in the care of a gentleman who was going to Lausanne, and then we went to bed, after laying out the walking costumes and putting them into condition for instant occupation in the morning.

However, when we came down to breakfast at 8 a. m., it looked so much like rain that I hired a two-horse top-buggy for the first third of the journey. For two or three hours we jogged along the level road which skirts the beautiful lake of Thun, with a dim and dreamlike picture of watery expanses and spectral Alpine forms always before us, veiled in a mellowing mist. Then a steady down-pour set in, and hid everything but the nearest objects. We kept the rain out of our faces with umbrellas, and away from our bodies with the leather apron of the buggy; but the driver sat unsheltered and placidly soaked the weather in and seemed to like it. We had the road all to ourselves, and I never had a pleasanter excursion.

The weather began to clear while we were driving up a valley called the Kienthal, and presently a vast black cloud-bank in front of us dissolved away and uncurtained the grand proportions and the soaring loftinesses of the Blumis Alp. It was a sort of breath-taking surprise; for we had not supposed there was anything behind that low-hung blanket of sable cloud but level valley.. What we had been mistaking for fleeting glimpses of sky away aloft there, were really patches of the Blumis's snowy crest caught through shredded rents in the drifting pall of vapor.

We dined in the inn at Frutigen, and our driver ought to have dined there, too, but he would not have had time to dine and get drunk both, so he gave his mind to making a master-piece of the latter, and succeeded. A German gentleman and his two young lady daughters had been taking their noon-ing at the inn, and when they left, just ahead of us, it was plain that their driver was as drunk as ours, and as happy and good natured, too, which was saying a good deal. These rascals overflowed with attentions and information for their guests, and with brotherly love for each other. They tied their reins, and took off their coats and hats, so that they might be able to give unencumbered attention to conversa-tion and to the gestures necessary for its illustration.

The road was smooth; it led up and over and down a con-tinual succession of hills; but it was narrow, the horses were used to it, and could not well get out of it anyhow; so why shouldn't the drivers entertain themselves and us? The noses of our horses projected sociably into the rear of the forward carriage, and as we toiled up the long hills our driver stood up and talked to his friend, and his friend stood up and talked back to him, with his rear to the scenery. When the top

was reached and we went flying down the other side, there
was no change in the program. I carry in my memory yet,
the picture of that forward driver, on his knees on his high
seat, resting his elbows on its back, and beaming down on his

SOCIABLE DRIVERS.

passengers, with happy eye, and flying hair, and jolly red
face, and offering his card to the old German gentleman while
he praised his hack and horses and both teams were whizzing
down a long hill with nobody in a position to tell whether
we were bound to destruction or an undeserved safety.

Toward sunset we entered a beautiful green valley dotted
with chalets, a cosy little domain hidden away from the busy
world in a cloistered nook among giant precipices topped
with snowy peaks that seemed to float like islands above the
curling surf of the sea of vapor that severed them from the
lower world. Down from vague and vaporous heights, little
ruffled zigzag milky currents came crawling, and found their
way to the verge of one of those tremendous overhanging

walls, whence they plunged, a shaft of silver, shivered to
a t o m s in mid-descent
and turned to an airy
puff of luminous d u s t.
Here and there, in groov-
ed depressions among the
snowy desolations of the
upper a l t i t u d e s, one
glimpsed the extremity of
a glacier, with i t s sea-
green and honey-combed
battlements of ice.

Up the valley, under a
dizzy precipice, nestled
t h e village of Kander-
steg, our halting place
for the night. We were
soon there, and housed
i n the hotel. .B u t the
waning day had such an
inviting influence that we
did not remain housed
many moments, but struck
out and followed a roar-
ing torrent of ice water
up to its far source in a
sort of little grass-carpet-
ed parlor, walled in all
around by vast precipices
and overlooked by cluster-
ing summits of ice. This
was t h e snuggest little
croquet ground imagina-

A MOUNTAIN CASCADE.

ble; it was perfectly level, and not more than a mile long
by half a mile wide. The walls around it were so gigantic,
and everything about it was on so mighty a scale that it was

belittled, by contrast, to what I have likened it to,—a cosy and carpeted parlor. It was so high above the Kandersteg

valley that there was nothing between it and the snow peaks. I had never been in such intimate relations with the high altitudes before; the snow peaks had always been remote and unapproachable grandeurs, hitherto, but now we were hob-a-nob,—if one may use such a seemingly irreverent expression about creations so august as these.

We could see the streams which fed the torrent we had followed issuing from

THE GASTERNTHAL.   under the greenish ramparts of glaciers ; but two or three of these, instead of flowing over the precipices, sank down into the rock and sprang in big jets out of holes in the mid-face of the walls.

The green nook which I have been describing is called the Gasternthal. The glacier streams gather and flow through it in a broad and rushing brook to a narrow cleft between lofty precipices; here the rushing brook becomes a mad torrent and goes booming and thundering down toward Kandersteg, lashing and thrashing its way over and among monster bowlders, and hurling chance roots and logs about like straws. There was no lack of cascades along this route. The path by the side of the torrent was so narrow that one had to look sharp, when he heard a cow bell, and hunt for a place that was wide enough to accommodate a cow and a Christian side by side, and such places were not always to be had at an instant's notice. The cows wear church bells, and that is a good idea in the cows, for where that torrent is, you couldn't hear an ordinary cow-bell any further than you could hear the ticking of a watch.

I needed exercise, so I employed my

EXHILARATING SPORT.

agent in setting stranded logs and dead trees adrift, and I sat on a bowlder and watched them go whirling and leaping head

over heels down the boiling torrent. It was a wonderfully
exhilarating spectacle. When I had had exercise enough, I
made the agent take some, by running a race with one of
those logs. I made a trifle by betting on the log.

After dinner we had a walk up and down the quiet Kandersteg valley, in the soft gloaming, with the spectacle of
the dying lights of day playing about the crests and pinnacles of the still and solemn upper realm for contrast, and
text for talk. There were no sounds but the dulled com-
plaining of the torrent and the occasional tinkling of a distant bell. The spirit of the place was a sense of deep, pervading peace; one might dream his life tranquilly away
there, and not miss it or mind it when it was gone.

The summer departed with the sun, and winter came with
the stars. It grew to be a bitter night in that little hotel,
backed up against a precipice that had no visible top to it,
but we kept warm, and woke in time in the morning to find
that everybody else had left for the Gemmi three hours
before,—so our little plan of helping that German family
(principally the old man,) over the Pass, was a blocked
generosity.

CHAPTER XXXIV.

WE hired the only guide left, to lead us on our way. He was over seventy, but he could have given me nine-tenths of his strength and still had all his age entitled him to. He shouldered our satchels, overcoats, and alpenstocks, and we set out up the steep path. It was hot work. The old man soon begged us to hand over our coats and waistcoats to him to carry, too, and we did it: one could not refuse so little a thing to a poor old man like that; he should have had them if he had been a hundred and fifty.

When we began that ascent, we could see a microscopic chalet perched away up against heaven on what seemed to be the highest mountain near us. It was on our right, across the narrow head of the valley. But when we got up abreast it on its own level, mountains were towering high above on every hand, and we saw that its altitude was just about that of the little Gasternthal which we had visited the evening before. Still it seemed a long way up in the air, in that waste and lonely wilderness of rocks. It had an unfenced grass-plot in front of it which seemed about as big as a billiard table, and this grass plot slanted so sharply downwards, and was so brief, and ended so exceedingly soon at the verge of the absolute precipice, that it was a shuddery thing to think of a person's venturing to trust his foot on an incline so situated at all. Suppose a man stepped on an orange peel in that yard: there would be nothing for him to seize; nothing could keep him from rolling; five revolutions would bring him to the edge, and over he would go. What a frightful distance he would fall!—for there are very few birds that fly as high as his starting-point. He would strike and bounce, two or three times, on his way down, but this would be no advantage to him. I would as soon take an airing on the slant of a rainbow as in such a front yard.

WHAT MIGHT BE.

I would rather, in fact, for the distance down would be about the same, and it is pleasanter to slide than to bounce. I could not see how the peasants got up to that chalet,—the region seemed too steep for anything but a balloon.

As we strolled on climbing up higher and higher, we were continually bringing neighboring peaks into view and lofty prominence which had been hidden behind lower peaks before; so by and by, while standing before a group of these giants, we looked around for the chalet again: there it was, away down below us, apparently on an inconspicuous ridge in the valley! It was as far below us, now, as it had been above us when we were beginning the ascent.

After a while the path led us along a railed precipice, and we looked over—far beneath us was the snug parlor again, the little Gasternthal, with its water jets spouting from the face of its rock walls. We could have dropped a stone into it. We had been finding the top of the world all along—and always finding a still higher top stealing into view in a disappointing way just ahead: when we looked down into the Gasternthal we felt pretty sure that we had reached the genuine top at last, but it was not so; there were much higher altitudes to be scaled yet. We were still in the pleasant shade of forest t r e e s, we were still in a re-gio n which was cushioned w i t h beautiful mosses a n d aglow with t h e many-tinted lustre of innumer-able wild flowers.

We found, i n-deed, more inter-est i n the wild flowers t h a n in anything e l s e. W e gathered a specimen or two o f every kind w h i c h we were u n a c q u a i n t e d with; so we had sumptuous b o u-

AN ALPINE BOUQUET.

quets. But one of the chief interests lay in chasing the seasons of the year up the mountain, and determining them by the presence of flowers and berries which we were ac-quainted with. For instance, it was the end of August at the level of the sea; in the Kandersteg valley at the base of the Pass, we found flowers which would not be due at the sea level for two or three weeks; higher up, we entered October, and gathered fringed gentians. I made no notes, and have forgotten the details, but the construction of the floral calendar was very entertaining while it lasted.

In the high regions we found rich store of the splendid red flower called the Alpine rose, but we did not find any examples of the ugly Swiss favorite called *Edelweiss*. Its name seems to indicate that it is a noble flower and that it is white. It may be noble enough, but it is not attractive, and it is not white. The fuzzy blossom is the color of bad cigar ashes, and appears to be made of a cheap quality of gray plush. It has a noble and distant way of confining itself to the high altitudes, but that is probably on account of its looks; it apparently has no monopoly of those upper altitudes, however, for they are sometimes intruded upon by some of the loveliest of the valley families of wild flowers. Everybody in the Alps wears a sprig of Edelweiss in his hat. It is the native's pet, and also the tourist's.

All the morning, as we loafed along, having a good time, other pedestrians went staving by us with vigorous strides, and with the intent and determined look of men who were walking for a wager. These wore loose knee-breeches, long yarn stockings, and hob-nailed high-laced walking shoes. They were gentlemen who would go home to England or Germany and tell how many miles they had beaten the guidebook every day. But I doubted if they ever had much real fun, outside of the mere magnificent exhilaration of the tramp through the green valleys and the breezy heights; for they were almost always alone, and even the finest scenery loses incalculably when there is no one to enjoy it with.

All the morning an endless double procession of mule-mounted tourists filed past us along the narrow path,—the one procession going, the other coming. We had taken a good deal of trouble to teach ourselves the kindly German custom of saluting all strangers with doffed hat, and we resolutely clung to it, that morning, although it kept us bareheaded most of the time and was not always responded to. Still we found an interest in the thing, because we naturally

liked to know who were English and Americans among the
passers-by. All continental natives responded, of course;
so did some of the English and Americans, but as a general
thing these two races gave no sign. Whenever a man or a
woman showed us cold neglect, we spoke up confidently in
our own tongue and asked for such information as we happened to need, and we always got a reply in the same language.
The English and American folk are not less kindly than
other races, they are only more reserved, and that comes of
habit and education. In one dreary, rocky waste, away above
the line of vegetation, we met a procession of twenty-five
mounted young men, all from America. We got answering
bows enough from these, of course, for they were of an age to

learn to do
in Rome as
Rome does,
without
much effort.

THE END OF THE WORLD.

At one extremity of this patch of desolation, overhung by
bare and forbidding crags which husbanded drifts of everlasting snow in their shaded cavities, was a small stretch of thin
and discouraged grass, and a man and a family of pigs were
actually living here in some shanties. Consequently this

place could be really reckoned as " property ; " it had a money value, and was doubtless taxed.   I think it must have marked the limit of real estate in this world.   It would be hard to set a money value upon any piece of earth that lies between that spot and the empty realm of space.   That man may claim the distinction of owning the end of the world, for if there is any definite end to the world he has certainly found it.

From here forward we moved through a storm-swept and smileless desolation.   All about us rose gigantic masses, crags, and ramparts of bare and dreary rock, with not a vestige or semblance of plant or tree or flower anywhere, or glimpse of any creature that had life.   The frost and the tempests of unnumbered ages had battered and hacked at these cliffs, with a deathless energy, destroying them piecemeal ; so all the region about their bases was a tumbled chaos of great fragments which had been split off and hurled to the ground. Soiled and aged banks of snow lay close about our path. The ghastly desolation of the place was as tremendously complete as if Doré had furnished the working plans for it.   But every now and then, through the stern gateways around us we caught a view of some neighboring majestic dome, sheathed with glittering ice, and displaying its white purity at an elevation compared to which ours was groveling and plebeian, and this spectacle always chained one's interest and admiration at once, and made him forget there was anything ugly in the world.

I have just said that there was nothing but death and desolation in these hideous places, but I forgot.   In the most forlorn and arid and dismal one of all, where the racked and splintered debris was thickest, where the ancient patches of snow lay against the very path, where the winds blew bitterest and the general aspect was mournfulest and dreariest, and furthest from any suggestion of cheer or hope, I found a solitary wee forget-me-not flourishing away, not a droop about it anywhere, but holding its bright blue star up with the prettiest and gallantest air in the world, the only happy spirit, the only smiling thing, in all that grisly desert. She seemed to say, " Cheer up!—as long as we are here, let us make the best of it." I judged she had earned a right to a more hospitable place; so I plucked her up and sent her to America to a friend who would respect her for the fight she had made, all by her small self, to make a whole vast despondent Alpine desolation stop breaking its heart over the unalterable, and

THE FORGET-ME-NOT.

hold up its head and look at the bright side of things for once.

We stopped for a nooning at a strongly built little inn called the Schwarenbach. It sits in a lonely spot among the peaks, where it is swept by the trailing fringes of the cloud-rack, and is rained on, snowed on, and pelted and persecuted by the storms, nearly every day of its life. It was the only habitation in the whole Gemmi Pass.

Close at hand, now, was a chance for a blood-curdling Alpine adventure. Close at hand was the snowy mass of the Great Altels cooling its top-knot in the sky and daring us to an ascent. I was fired with the idea, and immediately made up my mind to procure the necessary guides, ropes, etc., and undertake it. I instructed Harris to go to the landlord of the inn and set him about our preparations. Meantime I went diligently to work to read up and find out what this much-talked-of mountain-climbing was like, and how one should go about it,—for in these matters I was ignorant. I opened Mr. Hinchliff's " Summer Months among the Alps,"

(published 1857,) and selected his account of his ascent of
Monte Rosa. It began,—

"It is very difficult to free the mind from excitement on
the evening before a grand expedition,—"

I saw that I was too calm ; so I walked the room a while
and worked myself into a high excitement; but the book's
next remark,—that the adventurer must get up at two in 'he
morning,—came as near as anything to flatting it all out
again. However, I reinforced it, and read on, about how
Mr. Hinchliff dressed by candle-light and was "soon down
among the guides, who were bustling about in the passage,
packing provisions, and making every preparation for the
start ;" and how he glanced out into the cold clear night and
saw that—

"The whole sky was blazing with stars, larger and brighter
than they appear through the dense atmosphere breathed by
inhabitants of the lower parts of the earth. They seemed actually suspended from the dark vault of heaven, and their gentle light shed a fairy like gleam over the snow-fields around
the foot of the Matterhorn, which raised its stupendous pinnacle on high, penetrating to the heart of the Great Bear, and
crowning itself with a diadem of his magnificent stars. Not
a sound disturbed the deep tranquillity of the night, except
the distant roar of streams which rush from the high plateau
of the St. Theodule glacier, and fall headlong over precipitous rocks till they lose themselves in the mazes of the Gorner glacier."

He took his hot toast and coffee, and then about half past
three his caravan of ten men filed away from the Riffel Hotel,
and began the steep climb. At half past five he happened to
turn around, and "beheld the glorious spectacle of the Matterhorn, just touched by the rosy-fingered morning, and looking like a huge pyramid of fire rising out of the barren ocean
of ice and rock around it." Then the Breithorn and the
Dent Blanche caught the radiant glow ; but "the intervening
mass of Monte Rosa made it necessary for us to climb many

A NEEDLE OF ICE.

hours before we could hope to see the sun himself, yet the whole air soon grew warmer after the splendid birth of day."

He gazed at the lofty crown of Monte Rosa and the wastes of snow that guarded its steep approaches, and the chief guide delivered the opinion that no man could conquer their awful heights and put his foot upon that summit. But the adventurers moved steadily on, nevertheless.

They toiled up, and up, and still up; they passed the Grand Plateau; then toiled up a steep shoulder of the mountain, clinging like flies to its rugged face; and now they were confronted by a tremendous wall from

CLIMBING THE MOUNTAIN.

which great blocks of ice and snow were evidently in the

habit of falling. They turned aside to skirt this wall, and

SNOW CREVASSES.

gradually ascended until their way was barred by a " maze of gigantic snow crevasses,"—so they turned aside again, and "began a long climb of sufficient steepness to make a zigzag course necessary."

Fatigue compelled them to halt frequently, for a moment or two. At one of these halts somebody called out, "Look at Mont Blanc!" and " we were at once made aware of the very great height we had attained by actually seeing the monarch of the Alps and his attendant satellites right over the top of the Breithorn, itself at least 14,000 feet high!"

These people moved in single file, and were all tied to a strong rope, at regular distances apart, so that if one of them slipped, on those giddy heights, the others could brace themselves on their alpenstocks and save him from darting into the valley, thousands of feet below. By and by they came to an ice-coated ridge which was tilted up at a sharp angle, and had a precipice on one side of it. They had to climb this, so the guide in the lead cut steps in the ice with his hatchet, and as fast as he took his toes out of one of these slight holes, the toes of the man behind him occupied it.

"Slowly and steadily we kept on our way over this dangerous part of the ascent, and I daresay it was fortunate for some of us that attention was distracted from the head by the paramount necessity of looking after the feet; *for, while on the left the incline of ice was so steep that it would be impossible for any man to save himself in case of a slip, unless the others could hold him up, on the right we might drop a pebble from the hand over precipices of unknown extent down upon the tremendous glacier below.*

"Great caution, therefore, was absolutely necessary, and in this exposed situation we were attacked by all the fury of that grand enemy of aspirants to Monte Rosa—a severe and bitterly cold wind from the north. The fine powdery snow was driven past us in clouds, penetrating the interstices of our clothes, and the pieces of ice which flew from the blows of Peter's axe were whisked into the air, and then dashed over the precipice. We had quite enough to do to prevent ourselves from being served in the same ruthless fashion, and now and then, in the more violent gusts of wind, were glad to stick our alpenstocks into the ice and hold on hard."

Having surmounted this perilous steep, they sat down and took a brief rest with their backs against a sheltering rock and their heels dangling over a bottomless abyss; then they climbed to the base of another ridge,—a more difficult and dangerous one still:

"The whole of the ridge was exceedingly narrow, and the fall on each side desperately steep, but the ice in some of these intervals between the masses of rock assumed the form of a mere sharp edge, almost like a knife; these places, though not more than three or four short paces in length, looked uncommonly awkward; but, like the sword leading true believers to the gates of Paradise, they must needs be passed before we could attain to the summit of our ambition. These were in one or two places so narrow, that in stepping over them with toes well turned out for greater security, *one end of the foot projected over the awful precipice on the right, while the other was on the beginning of the icy slope on the left, which was scarcely less steep than the rocks.* On these occasions Peter would take my hand, and each of us stretching as far as we could, he was thus enabled to get a firm footing two paces or rather more from me, whence a spring would probably bring him to the rock on the other side; then, turning round, he called to me to come, and taking a couple of steps carefully, I was met at the third by his outstretched hand ready to clasp mine, and in a moment stood by his side. The others followed in much the same fashion. Once my right foot slipped on the side towards the precipice, but I threw out my left arm in a moment so that it caught the icy edge under my armpit as I fell, and supported me considerably; at the same instant I cast my eyes down the side on which I had slipped, and contrived to plant my right foot on a piece of rock as large as a cricket ball, which chanced to protrude through the ice, on the very edge of the precipice. Being thus anchored fore and aft, as it were, I believe I could easily have recovered myself, even if I had been alone, though it must be confessed the situation would have been an awful one; as it was, however, a jerk from Peter settled the matter very soon, and I was on my legs all right in an instant. The rope is an immense help in places of this kind."

Now they arrived at the base of a great knob or dome veneered with ice and powdered with snow—the utmost summit, the last bit of solidity between them and the hollow vault of heaven. They set to work with their hatchets, and were soon creeping, insect-like, up its surface, with their heels projecting over the thinnest kind of nothingness, thickened up a little with a few wandering shreds and films of cloud moving in lazy procession far below. Presently one man's toe-hold broke and he fell! There he dangled in mid-air at the end of the rope, like a spider, till his friends above hauled him into place again.

CUTTING STEPS.

A little bit later, the party stood upon the wee pedestal of the very summit, in a driving wind, and looked out upon the vast green expanses of Italy and a shoreless ocean of billowy Alps.

When I had read thus far, Harris burst into the room in a noble excitement and said the ropes and the guides were secured, and asked if I was ready. I said I believed I wouldn't ascend the Altels this time. I said Alp-climbing was a different thing from what I had supposed it was, and so I judged we had better study its points a little more before we went definitely into it. But I told him to retain the guides and order them to follow us to Zermatt, because I meant to use

them there. I said I could feel the spirit of adventure
beginning to stir in me, and was sure that the fell fascination
of Alp-climbing would soon be upon me. I said he could
make up his mind to it that we would do a deed before we
were a week older which would make the hair of the timid
curl with fright.

This made Harris happy, and filled him with ambitious
anticipations. He went at once to tell the guides to follow
us to Zermatt and bring all their paraphernalia with them.

CHAPTER XXXV.

A GREAT and priceless thing is a new interest! How it takes possession of a man! how it clings to him, how it rides him! I strode onward from the Schwarenbach hostelry a changed man, a reorganized personality. I walked in a new world, I saw with new eyes. I had been looking aloft at the giant snow-peaks only as things to be worshiped for their grandeur and magnitude, and their unspeakable grace of form; I looked up at them now, as also things to be conquered and climbed. My sense of their grandeur and their noble beauty was neither lost nor impaired; I had gained a new interest in the mountains without losing the old ones. I followed the steep lines up, inch by inch, with my eye, and noted the possibility or impossibility of following them with my feet. When I saw a shining helmet of ice projecting above the clouds, I tried to imagine I saw files of black specks toiling up it roped together with a gossamer thread.

We skirted the lonely little lake called the Daubensee, and presently passed close by a glacier on the right,—a thing like a great river frozen solid in its flow and broken square off like a wall at its mouth. I had never been so near a glacier before.

Here we came upon a new board shanty, and found some men engaged in building a stone house; so the Schwarenbach was soon to have a rival. We bought a bottle or so of

381

beer here; at any rate they called it beer, but I knew by the price that it was dissolved jewelry, and I perceived by the taste that dissolved jewelry is not good stuff to drink.

We were surrounded by a hideous desolation. We stepped forward to a sort of jumping-off place, and were confronted by a startling contrast: we seemed to look down into fairyland. Two or three thousand feet below us was a bright

VIEW FROM THE CLIFF.

green level, with a pretty town in its midst, and a silvery stream winding among the meadows; the charming spot was walled in on all sides by gigantic precipices clothed with pines; and over the pines, out of the softened distances, rose the snowy domes and peaks of the Monte Rosa region. How exquisitely green and beautiful that little valley down there was! The distance was not great enough to obliterate details, it only made them little, and mellow, and dainty, like landscapes and towns seen through the wrong end of a spyglass.

GEMMI PASS AND LAKE DAUBENSEE.

Right under us a narrow ledge rose up out of the valley, with a green, slanting, bench-shaped top, and grouped about upon this green-baize bench were a lot of black and white sheep which looked merely like over-sized worms. The bench seemed lifted well up into our neighborhood, but that was a deception,—it was a long way down to it.

We began our descent, now, by the most remarkable road I have ever seen. It wound in corkscrew curves down the face of the colossal precipice,—a narrow way, with always the solid rock wall at one elbow, and perpendicular nothingness at the other. We met an everlasting procession of guides, porters, mules, litters, and tourists climbing up this steep and muddy path, and there was no room to spare when you had to pass a tolerably fat mule. I always took the inside, when I heard or saw the mule coming, and flattened myself against the wall. I preferred the inside, of course, but I should have had to take it anyhow, because the mule prefers the outside. A mule's preference,—on a precipice —is a thing to be respected. Well, his choice is always the outside. His life is mostly devoted to carrying bulky paniers and packages which rest against his body,—therefore he is habituated to taking the outside edge of mountain paths, to keep his bundles from rubbing against rocks or banks on the other. When he goes into the passenger business he absurdly clings to his old habit, and keeps one leg of his passenger always dangling over the great deeps of the lower world while that passenger's heart is in the highlands, so to speak. More than once I saw a mule's hind foot cave over the outer edge and send earth and rubbish into the bottomless abyss; and I noticed that upon these occasions the rider, whether male or female, looked tolerably unwell.

There was one place where an 18-inch breadth of light masonry had been added to the verge of the path, and as there was a very sharp turn, here, a panel of fencing had been set up there at some ancient time, as a protection. This panel was old and gray and feeble, and the light masonry had been

23

loosened by recent rains.   A young American girl came along
on a mule, and in making the turn the mule's hind foot

caved all
the loose
masonry
and one of
the fence
posts over
board; the
mule gave
a violent
lurch in-
board to
save him-
self, and
succeed-
ed in the
effort, but
that girl turned as white as the snows
of Mont Blanc for a moment.

ALMOST A TRAGEDY.

The path here was simply a groove
cut into the face of the precipice;
there was a four-foot breadth of solid
rock under the traveler, and a four-foot
breadth of solid rock just above his head, like the roof of a
narrow porch; he could look out from this gallery and see
a sheer summitless and bottomless wall of rock before him,
across a gorge or crack a biscuit's toss in width,—but he could
not see the bottom of his own precipice unless he lay down
and projected his nose over the edge.   I did not do this,
because I did not wish to soil my clothes.

Every few hundred yards, at particularly bad places, one
came across a panel or so of plank fencing; but they were
always old and weak, and they generally leaned out over the
chasm and did not make any rash promises to hold up people
who might need support.   There was one of these panels

which had only its upper board left; a pedestrianizing English youth came tearing down the path, was seized with an
impulse to look over the precipice, and without an instant's
thought he threw his weight upon that crazy board. It bent
outward a foot! I never made a gasp before that came so
near suffocating me. The English youth's face simply showed a lively surprise, but nothing more. He went swinging
along valleywards again, as if he did not know he had just
swindled a coroner by the closest kind of a shave.

The Alpine litter is sometimes like a cushioned box made
fast between the middles of two long poles, and sometimes it
is a chair with a back to it and a support for the feet. It is

THE ALPINE LITTER.

carried by relays of strong porters. The motion is easier
than that of any other conveyance. We met a few men and
a great many ladies in litters; it seemed to me that most of
the ladies looked pale and nauseated; their general aspect
gave me the idea that they were patiently enduring a horri-
ble suffering. As a rule, they looked at their laps, and left
the scenery to take care of itself.

But the most frightened creature I saw, was a led horse
that overtook us. Poor fellow, he had been born and reared
in the grassy levels of the Kandersteg valley and had never
seen anything like this hideous place before. Every few
steps he would stop short, glance wildly out from the dizzy

height, and then spread his red nostrils wide and pant as violently as if he had been running a race; and all the while he quaked from head to heel as with a palsy. He was a handsome

A STRANGE SITUATION.

fellow, and he made a fine statuesque picture of terror, but it was pitiful to see him suffer so.

This dreadful path has had its tragedy. Baedeker, with his customary over-terseness, begins and ends the tale thus: " The descent on horseback should be avoided. In 1861 a Comtesse d' Herlincourt fell from her saddle over the precipice and was killed on the spot."

We looked over the precipice there, and saw the monument which commemorates the event. It stands in the bottom of the gorge, in a place which has been hollowed out of the rock to protect it from the torrent and the storms. Our old guide never spoke but when spoken to, and then limited himself to a syllable or two ; but when we asked him about this tragedy he showed a strong interest in the matter. He said the Countess was very pretty, and very young,—hardly out of her girlhood, in fact. She was newly married, and was on her bridal tour. The young husband

DEATH OF A COUNTESS.

—

was riding a little in advance; one guide was leading the husband's horse, another was leading the bride's. The old man continued,—

" The guide that was leading the husband's horse happened to glance back, and there was that poor young thing sitting up staring out over the precipice; and her face began to bend downward a little, and she put up her two hands slowly and met it,—so,—and put them flat against her eyes,—so,—and then she sunk out of the saddle, with a sharp shriek, and one caught only the flash of a dress, and it was all over."

Then after a pause,—

" Ah yes, that guide saw these things,—yes, he saw them all. He saw them all, just as I have told you."

After another pause,—

" Ah yes, he saw them all. My God, that was *me*. I was that guide ! "

This had been the one event of the old man's life; so one may be sure he had forgotten no detail connected with it. We listened to all he had to say about what was done and what happened and what was said after the sorrowful occurrence, and a painful story it was.

When we had wound down toward the valley until we were about on the last spiral of the corkscrew, Harris's hat blew over the last remaining bit of precipice,—a small cliff a hundred or a hundred and fifty feet high,—and sailed down towards a steep slant composed of rough chips and fragments which the weather had flaked away from the precipices. We went leisurely down there, expecting to find it without any trouble, but we had made a mistake, as to that. We hunted during a couple of hours,—not because the old straw hat was valuable, but out of curiosity to find out how such a thing could manage to conceal itself in open ground where there was nothing for it to hide behind. When one is reading in bed, and lays his paper-knife down, he cannot find it again if it is smaller than a sabre; that hat was as stubborn as any paper-knife could have been, and we

finally had to give it up; but we found a fragment that had
once belonged to an opera glass, and by digging around and
turning over the rocks we gradually collected all the lenses
and the cylinders and the various odds and ends that go to
make up a complete opera glass. We afterwards had the
thing reconstructed, and the owner can have his adventurous long-lost property by submitting proofs and paying costs
of rehabilitation. We had hopes of finding the owner there,
distributed around amongst. the rocks, for it would have made
an elegant paragraph ; but we were disappointed. Still, we
were far from being disheartened, for there was a considerable area which we had not thoroughly searched; we were
satisfied he was there, somewhere, so we resolved to wait
over a day at Leuk and come back and get him. Then we
sat down to polish off the perspiration and arrange about
what we would do with him when we got him. Harris was
for contributing him to the British Museum; but I was for
mailing him to his widow. That is the difference between
Harris and me : Harris is all for display, I am all for the
simple right, even though I lose money by it. Harris argued
in favor of his proposition and against mine, I argued in
favor of mine and against his. The discussion warmed into
a dispute; the dispute warmed into a quarrel. I finally said,
very decidedly,—

" My mind is made up. He goes to the widow."

Harris answered sharply,—

"And *my* mind is made up. He goes to the Museum."

I said, calmly,—

" The Museum may whistle when it gets him."

Harris retorted,—

" The widow may save herself the trouble of whistling, for
I will see that she never gets him."

After some angry bandying of epithets, I said,—

" It seems to me that you are taking on a good many airs
about these remains. I don't quite see what *you've* got to
say about them ? "

"*I?* I've got *all* to say about them. They'd never have been thought of if I hadn't found their opera glass. The corpse belongs to me, and I'll do as I please with him."

I was leader of the Expedition, and all discoveries achieved by it naturally belonged to me. I was entitled to these remains, and could have enforced my right; but rather than have bad blood about the matter, I said we would toss up for them. I threw heads and won, but it was a barren victory, for although we spent all the next day searching, we never found a bone. I cannot imagine what could ever have become of that fellow.

The town in the valley is called Leuk or Leukerbad, we pointed our course toward it, down a verdant slope which was adorned with fringed gentians and other flowers, and presently entered the narrow alleys of the outskirts and waded toward the middle of the town through liquid "fertilizer." They ought to either pave that village or organize a ferry.

Harris's body was simply a chamois-pasture; his person was populous with the little hungry pests; his skin, when he stripped, was splotched like a scarlet fever patient's; so, when we were about to enter one of the Leukerbad inns, and he noticed its sign, "Chamois Hotel," he refused to stop there. He said the chamois was plentiful enough, without hunting up hotels where they made a specialty of it. I was indifferent, for the chamois is a creature that will neither bite me nor abide with me: but to calm Harris, we went to the Hotel des Alpes.

At the table d'hote we had this, for an incident. A very grave man,—in fact his gravity amounted to solemnity, and almost to austerity,—sat opposite us and he was "tight," but doing his best to appear sober. He took up a *corked* bottle of wine, tilted it over his glass a while, then sat it out of the way, with a contented look, and went on with his dinner.

Presently he put his glass to his mouth, and of course

found it empty. He looked puzzled, and glanced furtively and suspiciously out of the corner of his eye at a benignant and unconscious old lady who sat at his right. Shook his head, as much as to say, "No, she couldn't have done it."

He tilted the corked bottle over his glass again, meantime searching around with his watery eye to see if anybody was watching him. He ate a few mouthfuls, raised his glass to his lips, and of course it was still empty. He bent an injured and accusing side gaze upon that unconscious old lady, which was a study to see. She went on eating and gave no sign. He took up his glass and his bottle, with a wise private nod of his head, and set them gravely on the left hand side of his plate,—poured himself another imaginary drink, —went to work with his knife and fork once more,—presently lifted his glass with good confidence, and found it empty, as usual.

"THEY'VE GOT IT ALL."

This was almost a petrifying surprise. He straightened himself up in his chair and deliberately and sorrowfully inspected the busy old ladies at his elbows, first one and then the other. At last he softly pushed his plate away, set his glass directly in front of him, held on to it with his left hand, and proceeded to pour with his right. This time he observed that nothing came. He turned the bottle clear upside down; still nothing issued from it; a plaintive look came into his face, and he said, as if to himself, "*'ic!* They've got it all!*" Then he set the bottle down, resignedly, and took the rest of his dinner dry.

It was at that table d'hôte, too, that I had under inspection the largest lady I have ever seen in private life. She was over seven feet high, and magnificently proportioned. What had first called my attention to her, was my stepping on an outlying flange of her foot, and hearing, from up toward the ceiling, a deep " Pardon, m'sieu, but you encroach ! "

That was when we were coming through the hall, and the place was dim, and I could see her only vaguely. The thing which called my attention to her the second time, was, that at a table beyond ours were two very pretty girls, and this great lady came in and sat down between them and me and blotted out the view. She had a handsome face, and she was very finely formed, —perfectly formed, I should say. But she made everybody around her look trivial and commonplace. Ladies near her looked like children, and the men about her looked mean. They looked like failures ; and they looked as if they felt so, too. She sat with her back to us.

MODEL FOR AN EMPRESS.

I never saw such a back in my life. I would have so liked to see the moon rise over it. The whole congregation waited, under one pretext or another, till she finished her dinner and went out; they wanted to see her at her full altitude, and they found it worth tarrying for. She filled one's idea of what an empress ought to be, when she rose up in her unapproachable grandeur and moved superbly out of that place.

We were not at Leuk in time to see her at her heaviest

weight. She had suffered from corpulence and had come there to get rid of her extra flesh in the baths. Five weeks of soaking,—five uninterrupted hours of it every day,—had accomplished her purpose and reduced her to the right proportions.

Those baths remove fat, and also skin-diseases. The patients remain in the great tanks hours at a time. A dozen gentlemen and ladies occupy a tank together, and amuse themselves with rompings and various games. They have floating desks and tables, and they read or lunch or play chess in water that is breast deep. The tourist can step in and view this novel spectacle if he chooses. There's a poor-box, and he will have to contribute. There are several of these

BATH HOUSES AT LEUKE.

big bathing houses, and you can always tell when you are near one of them by the romping noises and shouts of laughter that proceed from it. The water is running water, and changes all the time, else a patient with a ringworm might

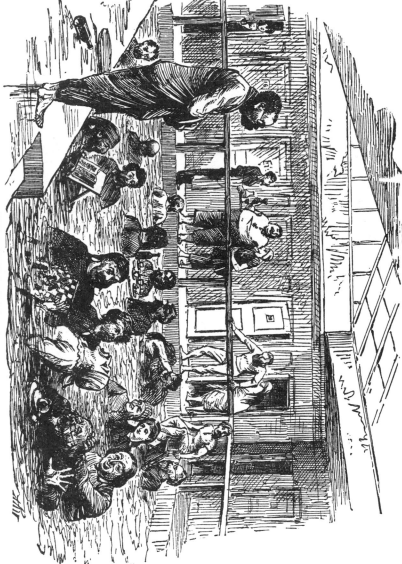

THE BATHERS AT LEUKE.

take the bath with only a partial success, since while he was
ridding himself of his ringworm, he might catch the itch.

The next morning we wandered back up the green valley,
leisurely, with the curving walls of those bare and stupendous precipices rising into the clouds before us. I had never
seen a clean, bare precipice stretching up five thousand feet
above me before, and I never shall expect to see another one.
They exist, perhaps, but not in places where one can easily
get close to them. This pile of stone is peculiar. From its
base to the soaring tops of its mighty towers, all its lines and
all its details vaguely suggest human architecture. There
are rudimentary bow windows, cornices, chimneys, demarca-
tions of stories, etc. One could sit and stare up there and
study the features and exquisite graces of this grand structure,
bit by bit, and day after day, and never weary his interest.
The termination, toward the town, observed in profile, is the
perfection of shape. It comes down out of the clouds in a
succession of rounded, colossal, terrace-like projections, —a
stairway for the gods; at its head spring several lofty storm-
scarred towers, one above another, with faint films of vapor
curling always about them like spectral banners. If there
were a king whose realms included the whole world, here
would be the palace meet and proper for such a monarch.
He would only need to hollow it out and put in the electric
light. He could give audience to a nation at a time under
its roof.

Our search for those remains having failed, we inspected
with a glass the dim and distant track of an old-time avalanche
that once swept down from some pine-grown summits behind
the town and swept away the houses and buried the people;
then we struck down the road that leads toward the Rhone,
to see the famous *Ladders*. These perilous things are built
against the perpendicular face of a cliff two or three hundred
feet high. The peasants, of both sexes, were climbing up and
down them, with heavy loads on their backs. I ordered
Harris to make the ascent, so I could put the thrill and

horror of it in my book, and he accomplished the feat successfully, through a sub-agent for three francs, which I paid. It
makes me shudder yet when I think of what I felt when I
was clinging there between heaven and earth in the person
of that proxy. At times the world swam around me, and I
could hardly keep from letting go, so dizzying was the appal-
ing danger. Many a person would have given up and descended, but I stuck to my task, and would not yield until I
had accomplished it. I felt a just pride in my exploit, but
I would not have repeated it for the wealth of the world. I
shall break my neck yet with some such fool-hardy performance, for warnings never seem to have any lasting effect
upon me. When the people of the hotel found that I had
been climbing those crazy Ladders, it made me an object of
considerable distinction.

Next morning, early, we drove to the Rhone valley and
took the train for Visp. There we shouldered our knapsacks
and things, and set out on foot, in a tremendous rain, up the
winding gorge, toward Zermatt. Hour after hour we slopped along, by the roaring torrent, and under noble Lesser
Alps which were clothed in rich velvety green all the way
up and had little atomy Swiss homes perched upon grassy
benches along their mist-dimmed heights.

The rain continued to pour and the torrent to boom, and
we continued to enjoy both. At the one spot where this
torrent tossed its white mane highest, and thundered loudest,
and lashed the big boulders fiercest, the canton had done itself the honor to build the flimsiest wooden bridge that exists
in the world. While we were walking over it, along with a
party of horsemen, I noticed that even the larger rain-drops
made it shake. I called Harris's attention to it, and he noticed it, too. It seemed to me that if I owned an elephant
that was a keepsake, and I thought a good deal of him, I
would think twice before I would ride him over that bridge.

We climbed up to the village of St. Nicholas, about half
past four in the afternoon, waded ankle deep through the

fertilizer-juice, and stopped at a new and nice hotel close by the little church. We stripped and went to bed, and sent our clothes down to be baked. All the horde of soaked tourists did the same. That chaos of clothing got mixed in the kitchen, and there were consequences. I did not get back the same drawers I sent down, when our things came up at 6:15; I got a pair on a new plan. They were merely a pair of white ruffle-cuffed absurdities, hitched together at the top with a narrow band, and they did not come quite down to my knees. They were pretty enough, but they made me feel like two people, and disconnected at that. The man must have been an idiot that got himself up like that, to rough it

RATHER MIXED UP.

in the Swiss mountains. The shirt they brought me was shorter than the drawers, and hadn't any sleeves to it,—at least it hadn't anything more than what Mr. Darwin would call "rudimentary" sleeves; these had "edging" around them, but the bosom was ridiculously plain. The knit silk undershirt they brought me was on a new plan, and was really a sensible thing; it opened behind, and had pockets in it to put your shoulder blades in; but they did not seem to fit mine, and so I found it a sort of uncomfortable garment. They gave my bob-tail coat to somebody else, and sent me an ulster suitable for a giraffe. I had to tie my collar on, because there was no button behind on that foolish little shirt which I described a while ago.

When I was dressed for dinner at 6.30, I was too loose in some places and too tight in others, and altogether I felt slovenly and ill conditioned. However, the people at the table d'hôte were no better off than I was; they had everybody's clothes but their own on. A long stranger recognized his ulster as soon as he saw the tail of it following me in, but nobody claimed my shirts or my drawers, though I described them as well as I was able. I gave them to the chambermaid that night when I went to bed, and she probably found the owner, for my own things were on a chair outside my door in the morning.

There was a lovable English clergyman who did not get to the table d'hôte at all. His breeches had turned up missing, and without any equivalent. He said he was not more particular than other people, but he had noticed that a clergyman at dinner without any breeches was almost sure to excite remark.

CHAPTER XXXVI.

WE did not oversleep at St. Nicholas. The church bell began to ring at 4:30 in the morning, and from the length of time it continued to ring I judged that it takes the Swiss sinner a good while to get the invitation through his head. Most church bells in the world are of poor quality, and have a harsh and rasping sound which upsets the temper and produces much sin, but the St. Nicholas bell is a good deal the worst one that has been contrived yet, and is peculiarly maddening in its operation. Still, it may have its right and its excuse to exist, for the community is poor and not every citizen can afford a clock, perhaps; but there cannot be any excuse for our church bells at home, for there is no family in America without a clock, and consequently there is no fair pretext for the usual Sunday medley of dreadful sounds that issues from our steeples. There is much more profanity in America on Sunday than in all the other six days of the week put together, and it is of a more bitter and malignant character than the week-day profanity, too. It is produced by the cracked-pot clangor of the cheap church bells.

We build our churches almost without regard to cost; we rear an edifice which is an adornment to the town, and we gild it, and fresco it, and mortgage it, and do everything we can think of to perfect it, and then spoil it all by putting a bell on it which afflicts everybody who hears it, giving some the headache, others St. Vitus's dance, and the rest the blind-staggers.

401

An American village at ten o'clock on a summer Sunday is the quietest and peacefulest and holiest thing in nature; but it is a pretty different thing half an hour later. Mr. Poe's poem of the "Bells" stands incomplete to this day; but it

is well enough that it is so, for the public reciter or "reader" who goes around trying to imitate the sounds of the various sorts of bells with his voice would find himself "up a stump" when he got to the church bell—as Joseph Addison would say. The church is always trying to get other people to reform; it might not be a bad idea to reform itself a little, by way of example. It is still clinging to one or two things which were useful once, but which are not useful now, neither are they ornamental. One is the bell-ringing to remind a clock-caked town that it is church time, and another is the reading from the pulpit of a tedious list of "notices" which everybody who is interested has already read in the newspaper. The clergyman even reads the hymn through,—a relic of an ancient time when hymn books were scarce and costly; but

A SUNDAY MORNING'S DEMON. everybody has a hymn book, now, and so the public reading is no longer necessary. It is not merely unnecessary, it is generally painful; for the average clergyman could not fire into his congregation with a shot-gun and hit a worse reader than himself, unless the weapon scattered shamefully. I am not meaning to be flippant and irreverent, I am only meaning to be truthful. The average clergyman, in all countries and of all denominations, is a very bad reader. One would think he would at least learn how to read the Lord's Prayer, by and by, but it is not so. He races through it as if he thought the quicker he got it in, the sooner it would be answered. A person who does not appreciate the exceeding value of pauses, and does not know how to measure their duration judiciously, cannot render the grand simplicity and dignity of a composition like that effectively.

We took a tolerably early breakfast, and tramped off toward Zermatt through the reeking lanes of the village, glad to get away from that bell. By and by we had a fine spectacle on our right. It was the wall-like butt-end of a huge glacier, which looked down on us from an Alpine height which was well up in the blue sky. It was an astonishing amount of ice to be compacted together in one mass. We ciphered upon it and decided that it was not less than several hundred feet from the base of the wall of solid ice to the top of it,—Harris believed it was really twice that. We judged that if St. Paul's, St. Peter's, the Great Pyramid, the Strasburg Cathedral and the Capitol at Washington were clustered against that wall, a man sitting on its upper edge could not hang his hat on the top of any one of them without reaching down three or four hundred feet,—a thing which of course no man could do.

To me, that mighty glacier was very beautiful. I did not imagine that anybody could find fault with it; but I was mistaken. Harris had been snarling for several days. He was a rabid Protestant, and he was always saying,—

"In the Protestant cantons you never see such poverty and dirt and squalor as you do in this Catholic one; you never see the lanes and alleys flowing with foulness; you never see such wretched little sties of houses; you never see an inverted tin turnip on top of a church for a dome; and as for a church bell, why you never hear a church bell at all."

All this morning he had been finding fault, straight along. First it was with the mud. He said, "It ain't muddy in a

24

Protestant canton when it rains." Then it was with the dogs: "They don't have those lop-eared dogs in a Protestant canton." Then it was with the roads: "They don't leave the roads to make themselves in a Protestant canton, the people make them,—and they make a road that *is* a road, too." Next it was the goats: "You never see a goat shedding tears in a Protestant canton—a goat, there, is one of the cheerfulest objects in nature." Next it was the chamois: "You never see a Protestant chamois act like one of these, —they take a bite or two and go; but these fellows camp with you and stay." Then it was the guide-boards: "In a Protestant canton you couldn't get lost if you wanted to, but you never see a guide-board in a Catholic canton." Next, "You never see any flower-boxes in the windows, here,— never anything but now and then a cat,—a torpid one; but you take a Protestant canton: windows perfectly lovely with flowers,—and as for cats, there's just acres of them. These folks in this canton leave a road to make itself, and then fine you three francs if you 'trot' over it—as if a horse could trot over such a sarcasm of a road." Next about the goitre: "*They* talk about goitre!—I haven't seen a goitre in this whole canton that I couldn't put in a hat."

He had growled at everything, but I judged it would puzzle him to find anything the matter with this majestic glacier. I intimated as much; but he was ready, and said with surly discontent,—

"You ought to see them in the Protestant cantons."

This irritated me. But I concealed the feeling, and asked, "What is the matter with this one?"

"Matter? Why, it ain't in any kind of condition. They never take any care of a glacier here. The moraine has been spilling gravel around it, and got it all dirty."

"Why, man, *they* can't help that."

"*They?* You're right. That is, they *won't*. They could if they wanted to. You never see a speck of dirt on a Protestant glacier. Look at the Rhone glacier. It is fifteen miles long, and seven hundred feet thick. If this was a Protestant glacier you wouldn't see it looking like this, I can tell you."

"That is nonsense. What would they do with it?"

"They would whitewash it. They always do."

I did not believe a word of this, but rather than have trouble I let it go; for it is a waste of breath to argue with a bigot. I even doubted if the Rhone glacier *was* in a Protestant canton; but I did not know, so I could not make anything by contradicting a man who would probably put me down at once with manufactured evidence.

About nine miles from St. Nicholas we crossed a bridge over the raging torrent of the Visp, and came to a long strip of flimsy fencing which was pretending to secure people from tumbling over a perpendicular wall forty feet high and into the river. Three children were approaching; one of them, a little girl about eight years old, was running; when pretty close to us she stumbled and fell, and her feet shot under the rail of the fence and for a moment projected over the stream. It gave us a sharp shock, for we thought she was gone, sure, for the ground slanted steeply, and to save herself seemed a sheer impossibility; but she managed to scramble up, and ran by us laughing.

We went forward and examined the place and saw the long tracks which her feet had made in the dirt when they darted over the verge. If she had finished her trip she would have struck some big rocks in the edge of the water, and then the torrent would have snatched her down stream among the half covered boulders and she would have been pounded to pulp in two minutes. We had come exceedingly near witnessing her death.

And now Harris's contrary nature and inborn selfishness were strikingly manifested. He has no spirit of self-denial. He began straight off, and continued for an hour, to express his gratitude that the child was not destroyed. I never saw such a man. That was the kind of person he was; just so *he* was gratified, he never cared anything about anybody else.

I had noticed that trait in him, over and over again. Often, of course, it was mere heedlessness, mere want of reflection. Doubtless this may have been the case in most instances, but it was not the less hard to bear on that account,—and after all, its bottom, its groundwork, was selfishness. There is no avoiding that conclusion. In the instance under consideration, I did think the indecency of running on in that way

JUST SAVED.

might occur to him; but no, the child was saved and he was glad, that was sufficient,—he cared not a straw for *my* feelings, or my loss of such a literary plum, snatched from my very mouth at the instant it was ready to drop into it. His

VIEW IN VALLEY OF ZERMATT.

selfishness was sufficient to place his own gratification in being spared suffering clear before all concern for me, his friend. Apparently he did not once reflect upon the valuable details which would have fallen like a windfall to me: fishing the child out,—witnessing the surprise of the family and the stir the thing would have made among the peasants, —then a Swiss funeral,—then the roadside monument, to be paid for by us and have our names mentioned in it. And we should have gone into Baedeker and been immortal. I was silent. I was too much hurt to complain. If he could act so, and be so heedless and so frivolous at such a time, and actually seem to glory in it, after all I had done for him, I would have cut my hand off before I would let him see that I was wounded.

We were approaching Zermatt; consequently we were approaching the renowned Matterhorn. A month before, this mountain had been only a name to us, but latterly we had been moving through a steadily thickening double row of pictures of it, done in oil, water, chromo, wood, steel, copper, crayon, and photography, and so it had at length become a shape to us,—and a very distinct, decided, and familiar one, too. We were expecting to recognize that mountain whenever or wherever we should run across it. We were not deceived. The monarch was far away when we first saw him, but there was no such thing as mistaking him. He has the rare peculiarity of standing by himself; he is peculiarly steep, too, and is also most oddly shaped. He towers into the sky like a colossal wedge, with the upper third of its blade bent a little to the left. The broad base of this monster wedge is planted upon a grand glacier-paved Alpine platform whose elevation is ten thousand feet above sea level; as the wedge itself is some five thousand feet high, it follows that its apex is about fifteen thousand feet above sea level. So the whole bulk of this stately piece of rock, this sky-cleaving monolith, is above the line of eternal snow. Yet while all its giant neighbors have the look of being built of solid snow, from their waists up, the Matterhorn stands black and naked and forbidding, the year round, or merely powdered or streaked with white in places, for its sides are so steep that the snow cannot stay there. Its strange form, its august isolation, and its majestic unkinship with its own kind, make it,—so to speak,—the Napoleon of the mountain world. " Grand, gloomy, and peculiar," is a phrase which fits it as aptly as it fitted the great captain.

Think of a monument a mile high, standing on a pedestal two miles high! This is what the Matterhorn is,—a monument. Its office, henceforth, for all time, will be to keep watch and ward over the secret resting-place of the young Lord Douglas, who, in 1865, was precipitated from the summit over a precipice 4,000 feet high, and never seen again. No man ever had such a monument as this before; the most imposing of the world's other monuments are but atoms compared to it; and they will perish, and their places will pass from memory, but this will remain.*

A walk from St. Nicholas to Zermatt is a wonderful experience. Nature is built on a stupendous plan in that region. One marches continually between walls that are piled into the skies, with their upper heights broken into a confusion of sublime shapes that gleam white and cold against the background of blue; and here and there one sees a big glacier displaying its grandeurs on the top of a precipice, or a graceful cascade leaping and flashing down the green declivities. There is nothing tame, or cheap, or trivial,—it is all magnificent. That short valley is a picture gallery of a notable kind, for it contains no mediocrities; from end to end the Creator has hung it with His masterpieces.

---

* The accident which cost Lord Douglas his life, (see chapter 41) also cost the lives of three other men. These three fell four-fifths of a mile, and their bodies were afterwards found, lying side by side, upon a glacier, whence they were borne to Zermatt and buried in the churchyard. The remains of Lord Douglas have never been found. The secret of his sepulture, like that of Moses, must remain a mystery always.

ARRIVAL AT ZERMATT.

We made Zermatt at 3 in the afternoon, nine hours out from St. Nicholas. Distance, by guide-book, 12 miles, by pedometer 72. We were in the heart and home of the mount-ain-climbers, now, as all visible things testified. The snow-peaks did not hold themselves aloof, in aristocratic reserve, they nestled close around, in a friendly, sociable way; guides, with the ropes and axes, and other implements of their fear-ful calling slung about their persons, roosted in a long line upon a stone wall in front of the hotel, and waited for cus-tomers; sunburned climbers, in mountaineering costume, and followed by their guides and porters, arrived from time to time, from break-neck expeditions among the peaks and glaciers of the High Alps; male and female tourists, on mules, filed by, in a continuous procession, hotelward-bound from wild adventures which would grow in grandeur every time they were described at the English or American fireside, and at last outgrow the possible itself.

We were not dreaming; this was not a make-believe home of the Alp-climber, created by our heated imaginations: no, for here was Mr. Girdlestone himself, the famous Englishman who hunts his way to the most formidable Alpine summits without a guide. I was not equal to imagining a Girdlestone; it was all I could do to even realize him, while looking straight at him at short range. I would rather face whole Hyde Parks of artillery than the ghastly forms of death which he has faced among the peaks and precipices of the mountains. There is probably no pleasure equal to the pleas-ure of climbing a dangerous Alp; but it is a pleasure which is confined strictly to people who can find pleasure in it. I have not jumped to this conclusion; I have traveled to it per gravel train, so to speak. I have thought the thing all out, and am quite sure I am right. A born climber's appetite for climbing is hard to satisfy; when it comes upon him he is like a starving man with a feast before him; he may have other business on hand, but it must wait. Mr. Girdlestone had had his usual summer holiday in the Alps, and had spent it in his usual way, hunting for unique chances to break his neck; his vacation was over, and his luggage packed for England, but all of a sudden a hunger had come upon him to climb the tremendous Weisshorn once more, for he had heard of a new and utterly impossible route up it. His baggage was unpacked at once, and now he and a friend, laden with knapsacks, ice-axes, coils of rope, and canteens of milk, were just setting out. They would spend the night high up among the snows, somewhere, and get up at 2 in the morning and finish the enterprise. I had a strong desire to go with them, but forced it down,—a feat which Mr. Girdlestone, with all his fortitude, could not do.

Even ladies catch the climbing mania, and are unable to throw it off. A famous climber, of that sex, had attempted the Weisshorn a few days before our arrival, and she and her guides had lost their way in a snowstorm high up among the peaks and glaciers and been forced to wander around a good while before they could find a way down. When this lady reached the bottom, she had been on her feet twenty-three hours!

Our guides, hired on the Gemmi, were already at Zermatt when we reached there. So there was nothing to interfere with our getting up an adventure whenever we should choose the time and the object. I resolved to devote my first evening in Zermatt to studying up the subject of Alpine climbing, by way of preparation.

I read several books, and here are some of the things I found out. One's shoes must be strong and heavy, and have pointed hob-nails in them. The alpenstock must be of the best wood, for if it should break, loss of life might be the result. One should carry an axe, to cut steps in the ice with, on the great heights. There must be a ladder, for there are steep bits of rock which can be surmounted with this instrument,—or this utensil,—but could not be surmounted without it; such an obstruction has compelled the tourist to waste hours hunting another route, when a ladder would **have** saved him all trouble. One must have from 150 to 500 feet of strong rope, to be used in lowering the party down steep declivities which are too steep and smooth to be traversed in any other way. One must have a steel hook, on another rope,—a very useful thing; for when one is ascending and comes to a low bluff which is yet too high for the ladder, h e swings this rope aloft like a lasso, the hook catches at the top of the bluff, and then the tourist climbs the rope, hand over hand, —being always particular to try and forget that if the hook gives way he will never stop falling till h e arrives in some part of Switzerland where they are not expecting him. Another important thing— there must be a rope

FITTED OUT.

to tie the whole party together with, so that if one falls from a mountain or down a bottomless chasm in a glacier, the others may brace back on the rope and save him. One must have a silk veil, to protect his face from snow, sleet, hail and gale, and colored goggles to protect his eyes from that dangerous enemy, snow-blindness. Finally, there must be some porters, to carry provisions, wine and scientific instruments, and also blanket bags for the party to sleep in.

I closed my readings with a fearful adventure which **Mr.** **Whymper** once had on the Matterhorn when he was prowling around alone, 5,000 above the town of Breil. He was edging his way gingerly around the corner of a precipice where the upper edge of a sharp declivity of ice-glazed snow joined it. This declivity swept down a couple of hundred feet, into a gully which curved around and ended at a precipice 800 feet high, overlooking a glacier. His foot slipped, and he fell. He says:

"My knapsack brought my head down first, and I pitched into some rocks about a dozen feet below; they caught something, and tumbled me off the edge, head over heels, into the gully; the baton was dashed from my hands, and I whirled downwards in a series of bounds, each longer than the last; now over ice, now into rocks, striking my head four or five times, each time with increased force. The last bound sent me spinning through the air in a leap of fifty or sixty feet, from one side of the gully to the other, and I struck the rocks, luckily, with the whole of my left side. They caught my clothes for a moment, and I fell back on to the snow with motion arrested. My head fortunately came the right side up, and a few frantic catches brought me to a halt, in the neck of the gully and on the verge of the precipice. Baton, hat, and veil skimmed by and disappeared, and the crash of the rocks—which I had started—as they fell on to the glacier, told how narrow had been the escape from utter destruction. As it was, I fell nearly 200 feet in seven or eight bounds. Ten feet more would have taken me in one gigantic leap of 800 feet on to the glacier below.

"The situation was sufficiently serious. The rocks could not be let go for a moment, and the blood was spirting out of more than twenty cuts. The most serious ones were in the head, and I vainly tried to close them with one hand, whilst holding on with the other. It was useless; the blood gushed out in blinding jets at each pulsation. At last, in a moment of inspiration, I kicked out a big lump of snow and stuck it as plaster on my head. The idea was a happy one, and the flow of blood diminished. Then, scrambling up, I got, not a moment too soon, to a place of safety, and fainted

A FEARFUL FALL.

away. The sun was setting when consciousness returned, and it was pitch dark before the Great Staircase was descended; but by a combination of luck and care, the whole 4700 feet of descent to Breil was accomplished without a slip, or once missing the way."

His wounds kept him abed some days. Then he got up and climbed that mountain again. That is the way with a true Alp-climber; the more fun he has, the more he wants.

CHAPTER XXXVII.

AFTER I had finished my readings, I was no longer myself; I was tranced, uplifted, intoxicated, by the almost incredible perils and adventures I had been following my authors through, and the triumphs I had been sharing with them. I sat silent some time, then turned to Harris and said,—

"My mind is made up."

Something in my tone struck him; and when he glanced at my eye and read what was written there, his face paled perceptibly. He hesitated a moment, then said,—

"Speak."

I answered, with perfect calmness,—

"I WILL ASCEND THE RIFFELBERG."

If I had shot my poor friend he could not have fallen from his chair more suddenly. If I had been his father he could not have pleaded harder to get me to give up my purpose. But I turned a deaf ear to all he said. When he perceived at last that nothing could alter my determination, he ceased to urge, and for a while the deep silence was broken only by his sobs. I sat in marble resolution, with my eyes fixed upon vacancy, for in spirit I was already wrestling with the perils of the mountains, and my friend sat gazing at me in adoring admiration through his tears. At last he threw himself upon me in a loving embrace and exclaimed in broken tones:

"Your Harris will never desert you. We will die together!"

I cheered the noble fellow with praises, and soon his fears were forgotten and he was eager for the adventure. He wanted to summon the guides at once and leave at 2 in the morning, as he supposed the custom was; but I explained that nobody was looking, at that hour; and that the start in the dark was not usually made from the village but from the first night's resting place on the mountain side. I said we would leave the village at 3 or 4 p. m. on the morrow; meantime he could notify the guides, and also let the public know of the attempt which we proposed to make.

I went to bed, but not to sleep. No man can sleep when he is about to undertake one of these Alpine exploits. I tossed feverishly all night long, and was glad enough when I heard the clock strike half past eleven and knew it was time to get up for dinner. I rose jaded and rusty, and went to the noon meal, where I found myself the centre of interest and curiosity; for the news was already abroad. It is not easy to eat calmly when you are a lion, but it is very pleasant, nevertheless.

As usual, at Zermatt, when a great ascent is about to be undertaken, everybody, native and foreign, laid aside his own projects and took up a good position to observe the start. The expedition consisted of 198 persons, including the mules; or 205, including the cows. As follows:

CHIEFS OF SERVICE.		SUBORDINATES.	
	Myself.	1	Veterinary Surgeon.
	Mr. Harris.	1	Butler.
17	Guides.	12	Waiters.
4	Surgeons.	1	Footman.
1	Geologist.	1	Barber.
1	Botanist.	1	Head Cook.
3	Chaplains.	9	Assistants.
2	Draftsmen.	4	Pastry Cooks.
15	Barkeepers.	1	Confectionery Artist.
1	Latinist.		

TRANSPORTATION, etc.

27	Porters.	3	Coarse Washers and Ironers.
44	Mules.	1	Fine ditto.
44	Muleteers.	7	Cows.
		2	Milkers.

Total, 154 men, 51 animals.　Grand Total, 205.

RATIONS, etc.		APPARATUS.	
16	Cases Hams.	25	Spring Mattrasses.
2	Barrels Flour.	2	Hair ditto.
22	Barrels Whiskey.		Bedding for same.
1	Barrel Sugar	2	Mosquito Nets.
1	Keg Lemons.	29	Tents.
2,000	Cigars.		Scientific Instruments.
1	Barrel Pies.	97	Ice-axes.
1	Ton of Pemmican.	5	Cases Dynamite.
143	Pair Crutches.	7	Cans Nitro-glycerine.
2	Barrels Arnica.	22	40-foot Ladders.
1	Bale of Lint.	2	Miles of Rope.
27	Kegs Paregoric.	154	Umbrellas.

It was full four o'clock in the afternoon before my cavalcade was entirely ready. At that hour it began to move. In point of numbers and spectacular effect, it was the most imposing expedition that had ever marched from Zermatt.

I commanded the chief guide to arrange the men and animals in single file, twelve feet apart, and lash them all together on a strong rope. He objected that the first two miles was a dead level, with plenty of room, and that the rope was never used except in very dangerous places. But I would not listen to that. My reading had taught me that many serious accidents had happened in the Alps simply from not having the people tied up soon enough; I was not going to add one to the list. The guide then obeyed my order.

When the procession stood at ease, roped together, and ready to move, I never saw a finer sight. It was 3,122 feet long—over half a mile; every man but Harris and me was on foot, and had on his green veil and his blue goggles, and his white rag around his hat, and his coil of rope over one shoulder and under the other, and his ice-axe in his belt, and carried his alpenstock in his left hand, his umbrella (closed,) in his right, and his crutches slung at his back.   The burdens of the pack mules, and the horns of the cows, were decked with the Edelweiss and the Alpine rose.

I and my agent were the only persons mounted.   We were in the post of danger in the extreme rear, and tied securely to five guides apiece.   Our armor-bearers carried our ice-axes, alpenstocks and other implements for us.   We were mount-

ALL READY.

ed upon very small donkeys, as a measure of safety; in time of peril we could straighten our legs and stand up, and let the donkey walk from under.   Still, I cannot recommend this sort of animal, —at least for excursions of mere pleasure,— because his ears interrupt the view.   I and my agent possess-ed the regulation mountaineering costumes, but concluded to leave them behind.   Out of respect for the great numbers of tourists of both sexes who would be assembled in front of the hotels to see us pass, and also out of respect for the many tourists, whom we expected to encounter on our expedition, we decided to make the ascent in evening dress.

At 15 minutes past 4 I gave the command to move, and my subordinates passed it along the line. The great crowd in front of the Monte Rosa hotel parted in twain, with a cheer, as the procession approached; and as the head of it was filing by I gave the order,—" Unlimber—make ready —HOIST!"

—and with one impulse up went my half mile of umbrellas. It was a beautiful sight, and a total surprise to the spectators. Nothing like that had ever been seen in the Alps before. The applause it brought forth was deeply gratifying to me, and I rode by with my plug hat in my hand to testify my appreciation of it. It was the only testimony I could offer, for I was too full to speak.

We watered the caravan at the cold stream which rushes down a trough

THE MARCH.

near the end of the village, and soon afterward left the haunts

THE CARAVAN.

of civilization behind us. About half past 5 o'clock **we ar-**rived at a bridge which spans the Visp, and after throwing over a detachment to see if it was safe, the caravan crossed without accident. The way now led, by a gentle ascent, car-peted with fresh green grass, to the church of Winkelmatten. Without stopping to examine this edifice, I executed a flank movement to the right and crossed the bridge over the Findel-enbach, after first testing its strength. Here I deployed to the right again, and presently entered an inviting stretch of meadow land which was unoccupied save by a couple of deserted huts toward its furthest extremity. These meadows offered an excellent camping place. We pitched our tents, supped, established a proper guard, recorded the events of the day, and then went to bed.

We rose at 2 in the morning and dressed by candle light. It was a dismal and chilly business. A few stars were shin-ing, but the general heavens were overcast, and the great shaft of the Matterhorn was draped in a sable pall of clouds. The chief guide advised a delay; he said he feared it was going to rain. We waited until nine o'clock, and then got away in tolerably clear weather.

Our course led up some terrific steeps, densely wooded with larches and cedars, and traversed by paths which the rains had guttered and which were obstructed by loose stones. To add to the danger and inconvenience, we were constantly meeting returning tourists on foot or horseback, and as con-stantly being crowded and battered by ascending tourists who were in a hurry and wanted to get by.

Our troubles thickened. About the middle of the after-noon the seventeen guides called a halt and held a consulta-tion. After consulting an hour they said their first suspicion remained intact,—that is to say, they believed they were lost. I asked if they did not *know* it? No, they said, they *couldn't* absolutely know whether they were lost or not, because none of them had ever been in that part of the country before. They had a strong instinct that they were lost, but they had

25

no proofs,—except that they did not know where they were. They had met no tourists for some time, and they considered that a suspicious sign.

Plainly we were in an ugly fix. The guides were naturally unwilling to go alone and seek a way out of the difficulty; so we all went together. For better security we moved slow and cautiously, for the forest was very dense. We did not move up the mountain, but around it, hoping to strike across the old trail. Toward nightfall, when we were about tired out, we came up against a rock as big as a cottage. This barrier took all the remaining spirit out of the men, and a panic of fear and despair ensued. They moaned and wept, and said they should never see their homes and their dear ones again. Then they began to upbraid me for bringing them upon this fatal expedition. Some even muttered threats against me.

Clearly it was no time to show weakness. So I made a speech in which I said that other Alp-climbers had been in as perilous a position as this, and yet by courage and perseverance had escaped. I promised to stand by them, I promised to rescue them. I closed by saying we had plenty of provisions to maintain us for quite a siege,—and did they suppose Zermatt would allow half a mile of men and mules to mysteriously disappear during any considerable time, right above their noses, and make no inquiries? No, Zermatt would send out searching-expeditions and we should be saved.

This speech had a great effect. The men pitched the tents with some little show of cheerfulness, and we were snugly under cover when the night shut down. I now reaped the reward of my wisdom in providing one article which is not mentioned in any book of Alpine adventure but this. I refer to the paregoric. But for that beneficent drug, not one of those men would have slept a moment during that fearful night. But for that gentle persuader they must have tossed, unsoothed, the night through; for the whisky was for me. Yes, they would have risen in the morning unfitted for their heavy task. As it was, everybody slept but my agent and me,—only we two and the barkeepers. I would not permit myself to sleep at such a time. I considered myself responsible for all those lives. I meant to be on hand and ready, in case of avalanches. I am aware now, that there were no avalanches up there, but I did not know it then.

We watched the weather all through that awful night, and kept an eye on the barometer, to be prepared for the least change. There was not the slightest change recorded by the instrument, during the whole time. Words cannot describe the comfort that that friendly, hopeful, steadfast thing was to me in that season of trouble. It was a defective barometer, and had no hand but the stationary brass pointer, but I did not know that until afterward. If I should be in such a situation again, I should not wish for any barometer but that one.

All hands rose at 2 in the morning and took breakfast, and as soon as it was light we roped ourselves together and went at that rock. For some time we tried the hook-rope and other means of scaling it, but without success. That is without perfect success. The hook caught once, and Harris started

THE HOOK.

up it hand over hand, but the hold broke and if there had not happened to be a chaplain sitting underneath at the time, Harris would certainly have been crippled. As it was, it was the chaplain. He took to his crutches, and I ordered the hook-rope to be laid aside. It was too dangerous an implement where so many people were standing around.

We were puzzled for a while; then somebody thought of the ladders. One of these was leaned against the rock, and the men went up it tied together in couples. Another ladder was sent up for use in descending. At the end of half an hour everybody was over, and that rock was conquered. We gave our first grand shout of triumph. But the joy was short-lived, for somebody asked how we were going to get the animals over.

THE DISABLED CHAPLAIN.

This was a serious difficulty; in fact it was an impossibility. The courage of the men began to waver immediately; once more we were threatened with a panic. But when the danger was most imminent, we were saved in a mysterious way. A mule which had attracted attention from the beginning by its disposition to experiment, tried to eat a five-pound can of nitro-glycerine. This happened right along-side the rock. The explosion threw us all to the ground, and covered us with dirt and débris; it frightened us extremely, too, for

TRYING EXPERIMENTS.

the crash it made was deafening, and the violence of the shock made the ground tremble. However, we were grateful, for the rock was gone. Its place was occupied by a new cellar, about thirty feet across, by fifteen feet deep. The explosion was heard as far as Zermatt; and an hour and a half after-ward, many citizens of that town were knocked down and quite seriously injured by descending portions of mule meat, frozen solid. This shows, better than any estimate in figures how high the experimenter went.

We had nothing to do, now, but bridge the cellar and pro-ceed on our way. With a cheer the men went at their work. I attended to the engineering, myself. I appointed a strong detail to cut down trees with ice-axes and trim them for piers to support the bridge. This was a slow business, for ice-axes are not good to cut wood with. I caused my piers to be firm-ly set up in ranks in the cellar, and upon them I laid six of my forty-foot ladders, side by side, and laid six more on top of them. Upon this bridge I caused a bed of boughs to be spread, and on top of the boughs a bed of earth six inches deep. I stretched ropes upon either side to serve as railings, and then my bridge was complete. A train of elephants could have crossed it in safety and comfort. By nightfall the cara-van was on the other side and the ladders taken up.

Next morning we went on in good spirits for a while, though our way was slow and difficult, by reason of the steep and rocky nature of the ground and the thickness of the for-est; but at last a dull despondency crept into the men's faces and it was apparent that not only they, but even the guides, were now convinced that we were lost. The fact that we still met no tourists was a circumstance that was but too signifi-cant. Another thing seemed to suggest that we were not only lost, but very badly lost: for there must surely be search-ing-parties on the road before this time, yet we had seen no sign of them.

Demoralization was spreading; something must be done, and done quickly, too. Fortunately, I am not unfertile in expedients. I contrived one now which commended itself to all, for it promised well. I took three-quarters of a mile of rope and fastened one end of it around the waist of a guide, and told him to go and find the road, whilst the

caravan waited. I instructed him to guide himself back by
the rope, in case of failure; in case of success, he was to give
the rope a series of violent jerks, whereupon the Expedition
would go to him at once. He departed, and in two minutes
had disappeared among the trees. I payed out the rope myself, while everybody watched the crawling thing with eager
eyes. The rope crept away quite slowly, at times, at other
times with some briskness. Twice or thrice we seemed to
get the signal, and a shout was just ready to break from the
men's lips when they perceived it was a false alarm. But at
last, when over half a mile of rope had slidden away it stopped gliding and stood absolutely still,—one minute,—two

SAVED! SAVED!

minutes,—three,—while we held
our breath and watched.

Was the guide resting? Was he
scanning the country from some
high point? Was he inquiring of
a chance mountaineer? Stop,—
had he fainted from excess of fatigue and anxiety?

This thought gave us a shock.
I was in the very act of detailing
an expedition to succor him, when
the cord was assailed with a series
of such frantic jerks that I could
hardly keep hold of it. The huzza
that went up, then, was good to hear. "Saved! saved!"
was the word that rang out, all down the long rank of the
caravan.

We rose up and started at once. We found the route to
be good enough for a while, but it began to grow difficult,
by and by, and this feature steadily increased. When we
judged we had gone half a mile, we momently expected to
see the guide; but no, he was not visible anywhere; neither
was he waiting, for the rope was still moving, consequently
he was doing the same. This argued that he had not found

the road, yet, but was marching to it with some peasant. There was nothing for us to do but plod along,—and this we did. At the end of three hours we were still plodding. This was not only mysterious, but exasperating. And very fatiguing, too ; for we had tried hard, along at first, to catch up with the guide, but had only fagged ourselves, in vain ; for although he was traveling slowly he was yet able to go faster than the hampered caravan over such ground.

At three in the afternoon we were nearly dead with exhaustion,—and still the rope was slowly gliding out. The murmurs against the guide had been growing, steadily, and at last they were become loud and savage. A mutiny ensued. The men refused to proceed. They declared that we had been traveling over and over the same ground all day, in a kind of circle. They demanded that our end of the rope be made fast to a tree, so as to halt the guide until we could overtake him and kill him. This was not an unreasonable requirement, so I gave the order.

As soon as the rope was tied, the Expedition moved forward with that alacrity which the thirst for vengeance usually inspires. But after a tiresome march of almost half a mile,

TWENTY MINUTES' WORK.

we came to a hill covered thick with a crumbly rubbish of stones, and so steep that no man of us all was now in a condition to climb it. Every attempt failed, and ended in crippling somebody. Within twenty minutes I had five men on crutches. Whenever a climber tried to assist himself by the rope, it yielded and let him tumble backwards. The frequency of this result suggested an idea to me. I ordered the caravan to ' bout face and form in marching order; I then made the tow-rope fast to the rear mule, and gave the command,—

"Mark time—by the right flank—forward—march!"

The procession began to move, to the impressive strains of a battle-chant, and I said to myself, "Now, if the rope don't break I judge *this* will fetch that guide into the camp." I watched the rope gliding down the hill, and presently when I was all fixed for triumph I was confronted by a bitter disappointment: there was no guide tied to the rope, it was only a very indignant old black ram. The fury of the baffled Expedition exceeded all bounds. They even wanted to wreak their unreasoning vengeance on this innocent dumb brute. But I prey, stood between them and their menaced by a bristling wall of ice-axes and alpenstocks, and proclaimed that there was but one road to this murder, and it was directly over my corse. Even as I spoke I saw that my doom was sealed, except a miracle supervened to divert these madmen from their fell purpose. I see that sickening wall of weapons now; I see that advancing host as I saw it then, I see the hate in those cruel eyes; I remember how I drooped my head upon my breast, I feel again the sudden earthquake shock in my rear, administered by the very ram I was sacrificing myself to save, I hear once more the typhoon of laughter that

burst from the assaulting column as I clove it from van to
rear like a Sepoy shot from a Rodman gun.

I was saved. Yes, I was saved, and by the merciful instinct of ingratitude which nature had planted in the breast
of that treacherous beast. The grace which eloquence had
failed to work in those
men's hearts, had been
wrought by a laugh. The
ram was set free and my
life was
spared.

We lived
to find out
that that
guide had
deserted us
as soon as he
had placed a half mile between himself and us. To avert
suspicion, he had judged it best that the line should continue
to move; so he caught that ram, and at the time that he
was sitting on it making the rope fast to it, we were imagining that he was lying in a swoon, overcome by fatigue and
distress. When he allowed the ram to get up it fell to
plunging around, trying to rid itself of the rope, and this
was the signal which we had risen up with glad shouts to
obey. We had followed this ram round and round in a circle
all day—a thing which was proven by the discovery that we
had watered the Expedition seven times at one and the same
spring in seven hours. As expert a woodman as I am, I had
somehow failed to notice this until my attention was called
to it by a hog. This hog was always wallowing there, and
as he was the only hog we saw, his frequent repetition, together with his unvarying similarity to himself, finally
caused me to reflect that he must be the same hog, and this
led me to the deduction that this must be the same spring,
also,—which indeed it was.

THE MIRACLE.

I made a note of this curious thing, as showing in a striking manner the relative difference between glacial action and
the action of the hog.   It is now a well established fact, that
glaciers move; I consider that my observations go to show,
with equal conclusiveness, that a hog in a spring does not
move.   I shall be glad to receive the opinions of other observers upon this point.

To return, for an explanatory moment, to that guide, and
then I shall be done with him.   After leaving the ram tied
to the rope, he had wandered at large a while, and then happened to run across a cow.   Judging that a cow would naturally know more than a guide, he took her by the tail, and
the result justified his judgment.   She nibbled her leisurely
way down hill till it was near milking time, then she struck
for home and towed him into Zermatt.

CHAPTER XXXVIII.

WE went into camp on that wild spot to which that ram had brought us. The men were greatly fatigued. Their conviction that we were lost was forgotten in the cheer of a good supper, and before the reaction had a chance to set in, I loaded them up with paregoric and put them to bed.

Next morning I was considering in my mind our desperate situation and trying to think of a remedy, when Harris came to me with a Baedeker map which showed conclusively that the mountain we were on was still in Switzerland,—yes, every part of it was in Switzerland. So we were not lost, after all. This was an immense relief; it lifted the weight of two such mountains from my breast. I immediately had the news disseminated and the map exhibited. The effect was wonderful. As soon as the men saw with their own eyes that they knew where they were, and that it was only the summit that was lost and not themselves, they cheered up instantly and said with one accord, let the summit take care of itself, they were not interested in its troubles.

Our distresses being at an end, I now determined to rest the men in camp and give the scientific department of the Expedition a chance. First, I made a barometric observation, to get our altitude, but I could not perceive that there was any result. I knew, by my scientific reading, that either thermometers or barometers ought to be boiled, to make them accurate; I did not know which it was, so I boiled both. There was still no result; so I examined these instruments and discovered that they possessed radical blemishes: the barometer had no hand but the brass pointer and the ball of the thermometer was stuffed with tin foil. I might have boiled those things to rags, and never found out anything.

I hunted up another barometer; it was new and perfect. I boiled it half an hour in a pot of bean soup which the cooks were making. The result was unexpected: the instrument was not affected at all, but there was such a strong barometer taste to the soup that the head cook, who was a most consci-

entious person, changed its name in the bill of fare. The dish was so greatly liked by all, that I ordered the cook to have barometer soup every day. It was believed that the barometer might eventually be injured, but I did not care for that. I had demonstrated to my satisfaction that it could not tell how high a mountain was, therefore I had no real use

SCIENTIFIC RESEARCHES.

for it. Changes of the weather I could take care of without it; I did not wish to know when the weather was going to be good, what I wanted to know was when it was going to be bad, and this I could find out from Harris's corns. Harris had had his corns tested and regulated at the government observatory in Heidelberg, and one could depend upon them with confidence. So I transferred the new barometer to the cooking department, to be used for the official mess. It was found that even a pretty fair article of soup could be made with the defective barometer; so I allowed that one to be transferred to the subordinate messes.

I next boiled the thermometer, and got a most excellent result; the mercury went up to about 200° Farenheit. In the opinion of the other scientists of the Expedition, this seemed to indicate that we had attained the extraordinary altitude of 200,000 feet above sea level. Science places the line of eternal snow at about 10,000 feet above sea level. There was no snow where we were, consequently it was proven that the eternal snow line ceases somewhere above the 10,000 foot level and does not begin any more. This was an interesting fact, and one which had not been observed by any observer before. It was as valuable as interesting, too, since it would open up the deserted summits of the highest Alps to population and agriculture. It was a proud thing to be where we were, yet it caused us a pang to reflect that but for that ram we might just as well have been 200,000 feet higher.

The success of my last experiment induced me to try an experiment with my photographic apparatus. I got it out, and boiled one of my cameras, but the thing was a failure: it made the wood swell up and burst, and I could not see that the lenses were any better than they were before.

I now concluded to boil a guide. It might improve him, it could not impair his usefulness. But I was not allowed to proceed. Guides have no feeling for science, and this one would not consent to be made uncomfortable in its interest.

In the midst of my scientific work, one of those needless accidents happened which are always occurring among the ignorant and thoughtless. A porter shot at a chamois and missed it and crippled the Latinist. This was not a serious matter to me, for a Latinist's duties are as well performed on crutches as otherwise,—but the fact remained that if the Latinist had not happened to be in the way a mule would have got that load. That would have been quite another matter, for when it comes down to a question of value there is a palpable difference between a Latinist and a mule. I could not depend on having a Latinist in the right place every time; so, to make things safe, I ordered that in future the chamois must not be hunted within the limits of the camp with any other weapon than the forefinger.

My nerves had hardly grown quiet after this affair when they got another shake-up,—one which utterly unmanned me for a moment: a rumor swept suddenly through the camp that one of the barkeepers had fallen over a precipice!

However, it turned out that it was only a chaplain. I had laid in an extra force of chaplains, purposely to be prepared for emergencies like this, but by some unaccountable oversight had come away rather short-handed in the matter of barkeepers.

On the following morning we moved on, well refreshed and in good spirits. I remember this day with peculiar pleasure, because it saw our road restored to us. Yes, we found our road again, and in quite an extraordinary way. We had plodded along some two hours and a half, when we came up against a solid mass of rock about twenty feet high. I did not need to be instructed by a mule this time.—I was already beginning to know more than any mule in the Expedition.— I at once put in a blast of dynamite, and lifted that rock out of the way. But to my surprise and mortification, I found that there had been a chalet on top of it.

I picked up such members of the family as fell in my vicinity, and subordinates of my corps collected the rest. None of these poor people were injured, happily, but they were much annoyed. I explained to the head chaleteer just how the thing happened, and that I was only searching for the road, and would certainly have given him timely notice if I had known he was up there. I said I had meant no harm, and hoped I had not lowered myself in his estimation by raising him a few rods in the air. I said many other judicious things, and finally when I offered to rebuild his chalet, and pay for breakages, and throw in the cellar, he was mollified and satisfied. He hadn't any cellar at all, before; he would not have as good a view, now, as formerly, but what he had lost in view he had gained in cellar, by exact measurement.

He said there wasn't another hole like that in the mountains,
—and he would have been right if the late mule had not
tried to eat
up the nitro-
glycerine.

I put a
b u n d r e d
and sixteen
m e n a t
work, a n d
they rebuilt
t h e chalet
from its own
debris in fif-
teen m i n -
u t e s. I t
was a good
deal m o r e
picturesque
than it was
before, too.
T h e m a n
said we were
now on the
F e l i-Stutz,
a b o v e the
S c h w e g-
matt,— i n -
form a t i o n
which I was
glad to get,
since it gave

MOUNTAIN CHALET.

us our position to a degree of particularity which we had not
been accustomed to for a day or so. We also learned that
we were standing at the foot of the Riffelberg proper, and
that the initial chapter of our work was completed.

We had a fine view, from here, of the energetic Visp, as it makes its first plunge into the world from under a huge arch of solid ice, worn through the foot-wall of the great Gorner Glacier; and we could also see the Furggenbach, which is the outlet of the Furggen Glacier.

The mule-road to the summit of the Riffelberg passed right in front of the chalet, a circumstance which we almost immediately noticed, because a procession of tourists was filing along it pretty much all the time*. The chaleteer's business consisted in furnishing refreshments to tourists. My blast had interrupted this trade for a few minutes, by breaking all the bottles on the place; but I gave the man a lot of whisky to sell for Alpine champaign, and a lot of vinegar which would answer for Rhine wine, consequently trade was soon as brisk as ever.

Leaving the Expedition outside to rest, I quartered myself in the chalet, with Harris, purposing to correct my journals and scientific observations before continuing the ascent. I had hardly begun my work when a tall, slender, vigorous American youth of about twenty-three, who was on his way down the mountain, entered and came toward me with that breezy self-complacency which is the adolescent's idea of the well bred ease of the man of the world. His hair was short and parted accurately in the middle, and he had all the look of an American person who would be likely to begin his signature with an initial, and spell his middle name out. He introduced himself, smiling a smirky smile borrowed from the courtiers of the stage, extended a fair-skinned talon, and whilst he gripped my hand in it he bent his body forward three times at the hips, as the stage-courtier does, and said in the airiest and most condescending and patronizing way, —I quote his exact language,—

"Very glad to make your acquaintance, 'm sure; very glad indeed, assure you. I've read all your little efforts and

---

* "Pretty much" may not be elegant English, but it is high time it was. There is no elegant word or phrase which means just what it means.—M. T.

greatly admired them, and when I heard you were here,
I....."

I indicated a chair, and he sat down. This grandee
was the grandson of an American of considerable note in his
day, and not wholly forgotten yet,—a man who came so near

being a great man
that he was quite
generally accoun-
ted one while he
lived.

I slowly paced
the floor, ponder-
ing scientific
problems, and
heard this con-
versation:

Grandson.
First visit to Eu-
rope?

Harris. Mine?
Yes.

G. S. (With
a soft reminiscent
sigh suggestive of
by-gone joys that
may be tasted in
their freshness
but once.) Ah, I

THE GRANDSON.

know what it is to you. A first visit!—ah, the romance
of it! I wish I could feel it again.

H. Yes, I find it exceeds all my dreams. It is enchantment. I go....

G. S. (With a dainty gesture of the hand signifying,
"Spare me your callow enthusiasms, good friend.") Yes, *I*
know, I know; you go to cathedrals, and exclaim; and you
drag through league-long picture galleries and exclaim; and

26

you stand here, and there, and yonder, upon historic ground, and continue to exclaim; and you are permeated with your first crude conceptions of Art, and are proud and happy. Ah, yes, proud and happy—that expresses it. Yes-yes, enjoy it —it is right,—it is an innocent revel.

H. And you? Don't you do these things now?

G. S. I! O, that is *very* good! My dear sir, when you are as old a traveler as I am, you will not ask such a question as that. *I* visit the regulation gallery, moon around the regulation cathedral, do the worn round of the regulation sights, *yet?*—Excuse me!

H. Well what *do* you do, then?

G. S. Do? I flit,—and flit,—for I am ever on the wing, —but I avoid the herd. To-day I am in Paris, to-morrow in Berlin, anon in Rome; but you would look for me in vain in the galleries of the Louvre or the common resorts of the gazers in those other capitals. If you would find me, you must look in the unvisited nooks and corners where others never think of going. One day you will find me making myself at home in some obscure peasant's cabin, another day you will find me in some forgotten castle worshiping some little gem of art which the careless eye has overlooked and which the unexperienced would despise; again you will find me a guest in the inner sanctuaries of palaces while the herd is content to get a hurried glimpse of the unused chambers by feeing a servant.

H. You are a *guest* in such places?

G. S. And a welcome one.

H. It is surprising. How does it come?

G. S. My grandfather's name is a passport to all the courts in Europe. I have only to utter that name and every door is open to me. I flit from court to court at my own free will and pleasure, and am always welcome. I am as much at home in the palaces of Europe as you are among your relatives. I know every titled person in Europe, I think. I have my pockets full of invitations all the time.

I am under promise now, to go to Italy, where I am to be the guest of a succession of the noblest houses in the land. In Berlin my life is a continued round of gayety in the imperial palace. It is the same, wherever I go.

H. It must be very pleasant. But it must make Boston seem a little slow when you are at home.

G. S. Yes, of course it does. But I don't go home much. There's no life there—little to feed a man's higher nature. Boston's very narrow, you know. She doesn't know it, and you couldn't convince her of it—so I say nothing when I'm there: where's the use? Yes, Boston is very narrow, but she has such a good opinion of herself that she can't see it. A man who has traveled as much as I have, and seen as much of the world, sees it plain enough, but he can't cure it, you know, so the best way is to leave it and seek a sphere which is more in harmony with his tastes and culture. I run across there, once a year, perhaps, when I have nothing important on hand, but I'm very soon back again. I spend my time in Europe.

H. I see. You map out your plans and.....

G. S. No, excuse me. I don't map out any plans. I simply follow the inclination of the day. I am limited by no ties, no requirements, I am not bound in any way. I am too old a traveler to hamper myself with deliberate purposes. I am simply a traveler—an inveterate traveler—a man of the world, in a word,—I can call myself by no other name. I do not say, "I am going here, or I am going there"—I say nothing at all, I only act. For instance, next week you may find me the guest of a grandee of Spain, or you may find me off for Venice, or flitting toward Dresden. I shall probably go to Egypt presently; friends will say to friends, "He is at the Nile cataracts"—and at that very moment they will be surprised to learn that I'm away off yonder in India somewhere. I am a constant surprise to people. They are always saying, "Yes, he was in Jerusalem when we heard of him last, but goodness knows where he is now."

Presently the Grandson rose to leave—discovered he had an appointment with some Emperor, perhaps. He did his graces over again: gripped me with one talon, at arm's length, pressed his hat against his stomach with the other, bent his body in the middle three times, murmuring,—

"Pleasure, 'm sure; great pleasure, 'm sure. 'Wish you much success."

Then he removed his gracious presence. It is a great and solemn thing to have a grandfather.

I have not purposed to misrepresent this boy in any way, for what little indignation he excited in me soon passed and left nothing behind it but compassion. One cannot keep up a grudge against a vacuum. I have tried to repeat the lad's very words; if I have failed anywhere I have at least not failed to reproduce the marrow and meaning of what he said. He and the innocent chatterbox whom I met on the Swiss lake are the most unique and interesting specimens of Young America I came across during my foreign tramping. I have

OCCASIONALLY MET WITH.

made honest portraits of them, not caricatures. The Grandson of twenty-three referred to himself five or six times as an "old traveler," and as many as three times, (with a serene complacency which was maddening,) as a "man of the world."

There was something very delicious about his leaving Boston to her "narrowness," unreproved and uninstructed.

I formed the caravan in marching order, presently, and after riding down the line to see that it was properly roped together, gave the command to proceed. In a little while the road carried us to open, grassy land. We were above the troublesome forest, now, and had an uninterrupted view, straight before us, of our summit,—the summit of the Riffelberg.

We followed the mule road, a zigzag course, now to the right, now to the left, but always up, and always crowded and incommoded by going and coming files of reckless tourists who were never, in a single instance, tied together. I was obliged to exert the utmost care and caution, for in many places the road was not two yards wide, and often the lower side of it sloped away in slanting precipices eight and even nine feet deep. I had to encourage the men constantly, to keep them from giving way to their unmanly fears.

We might have made the summit before night, but for a delay caused by the loss of an umbrella. I was for allowing the umbrella to remain lost, but the men murmured, and with reason, for in this exposed region we stood in peculiar need of protection against avalanches; so I went into camp and detached a strong party to go after the missing article.

The difficulties of the next morning were severe, but our courage was high, for our goal was near. At noon we conquered the last impediment—we stood at last upon the summit, and without the loss of a single man except the mule that ate the glycerine. Our great achievement was achieved—the possibility of the impossible was demonstrated, and Harris and I walked proudly into the great dining room of the Riffelberg Hotel and stood our alpenstocks up in the corner.

Yes, I had made the grand ascent; but it was a mistake to do it in evening dress. The plug hats were battered, the swallow-tails were fluttering rags, mud added no grace, the general effect was unpleasant and even disreputable.

There were about seventy-five tourists at the hotel,—mainly ladies and little children,—and they gave us an admiring welcome which paid us for all our privations and sufferings. The ascent had been made, and the names and

SUMMIT OF THE GORNER GRAT.

dates now stand recorded on a stone monument there to prove it to all future tourists.

I boiled a thermometer and took an altitude, with a most curious result: *the summit was not as high as the point on the mountain side where I had taken the first altitude.* Suspecting that I had made an important discovery, I prepared to verify it. There happened to be a still higher summit (called the Gorner Grat,) above the hotel, and notwithstanding the fact that it overlooks a glacier from a dizzy height, and that the ascent is difficult and dangerous, I resolved to venture up there and boil a thermometer. So I sent a strong party, with some borrowed hoes, in charge of two chiefs of service, to dig a stairway in the soil all the way, and this I ascended, roped to the guides. This breezy height was the summit proper—so I accomplished even more than I had originally purposed to do. This fool-hardy exploit is record-ed on another stone monument.

I boiled my thermometer, and sure enough, this spot, which purported to be 2,000 feet higher than the locality of the hotel, turned out to be 9,000 feet *lower*. Thus the fact

CHIEFS OF THE ADVANCE GUARD.

was clearly demonstrated, that, *above a certain point, the high-er a point seems to be, the lower it actually is.* Our ascent it-self was a great achievement, but this contribution to science was an inconceivably greater matter.

Cavilers object that water boils at a lower and lower tem-perature the higher and higher you go, and hence the appar-ent anomaly. I answer that I do not base my theory upon what the boiling water does, but upon what a boiled ther-mometer says. You can't go behind the thermometer.

I had a magnificent view of Monte Rosa, and apparently
all the rest of the Alpine world, from that high place. All
the circling horizon was piled high with a mighty tumult of
snowy crests. One might have imagined he saw before him
the tented camps of a beleaguering host of Brobdignagians.

MY PICTURE OF THE MATTERHORN.

But lonely, conspicuous, and superb, rose that wonderful
upright wedge, the Matterhorn. Its precipitous sides were
powdered over with snow, and the upper half hidden in
thick clouds which now and then dissolved to cobweb films

NOTE.—I had the very unusual luck to catch one little momentary glimpse
of the Matterhorn wholly unencumbered by clouds. I leveled my photographic apparatus at it without the loss of an instant, and should have got
an elegant picture if my donkey had not interfered. It was my purpose to
draw this photograph all by myself for my book, but was obliged to put
the mountain part of it into the hands of the professional artist because I
found I could not do landscape well.

and gave brief glimpses of the imposing tower as through a veil. A little later the Matterhorn took to himself the semblance of a volcano; he was stripped naked to his apex—around this circled vast wreaths of white cloud which strung slowly out and streamed away slantwise toward the sun, a twenty-mile stretch of rolling and tumbling vapor, and looking just as if it were pouring out of a crater. Later again, one of the mountain's sides was clean and clear, and another side densely clothed from base to summit in thick smoke-like cloud which feathered off and blew around the shaft's sharp edge like the smoke around the corners of a burning building. The Matterhorn is always experimenting, and always gets up fine effects, too. In the sunset, when all the lower world is palled in gloom, it points toward heaven out of the pervading blackness like a finger of fire. In the sunrise—well, they say it is very fine in the sunrise.

Authorities agree that there is no such tremendous "layout" of snowy Alpine magnitude, grandeur and sublimity to be seen from any other accessible point as the tourist may see from the summit of the Riffelberg. Therefore, let the tourist rope himself up and go there; for I have shown that with nerve, caution, and judgment, the thing can be done.

I wish to add one remark, here,—in parentheses, so to speak,—suggested by the word "snowy," which I have just used. We have all seen hills and mountains and levels with snow on them, and so we think we know all the aspects and effects produced by snow. But indeed we do not, until we have seen the Alps. Possibly mass and distance add something,—at any rate something *is* added. Among other noticeable things, there is a dazzling, intense whiteness about the distant Alpine snow, when the sun is on it, which one recognizes as peculiar, and not familiar to the eye. The snow which one is accustomed to, has a tint to it,—painters usually give it a bluish cast,—but there is no perceptible tint to the distant Alpine snow when it is trying to look its whitest. As to the unimaginable splendor of it when the sun is blazing down on it,—well, it simply *is* unimaginable.

CHAPTER XXXIX.

A GUIDE book is a queer thing. The reader has just seen what a man who undertakes the great ascent from Zermatt to the Riffelberg hotel must experience. Yet Baedeker makes these strange statements concerning this matter:

1. Distance,—3 hours.
2. The road cannot be mistaken.
3. Guide unnecessary.
4. Distance from Riffelberg hotel to the Gorner Grat, one hour and a half.
5. Ascent simple and easy. Guide unnecessary.
6. Elevation of Zermatt above sea level, 5,315 feet.
7. Elevation of Riffelberg hotel above sea level, 8,429 feet.
8. Elevation of the Gorner Grat above sea level, 10,289 feet.

I have pretty effectually throttled these errors by sending him the following demonstrated facts:

1. Distance from Zermatt to Riffelberg hotel, 7 days.
2. The road *can* be mistaken. If I am the first that did it, I want the credit of it, too.
3. Guides *are* necessary, for none but a native can read those finger-boards.
4. The estimate of the elevation of the several localities above sea level is pretty correct—for Baedeker. He only

450

misses it about a hundred and eighty or ninety thousand feet.

I found my arnica invaluable. My men were suffering excruciatingly, from the friction of sitting down so much. During two or three days, not one of them was able to do more than lie down or walk about; yet so effective was the arnica, that on the fourth all were able to sit up. I consider, that, more than to anything else, I owe the success of our great undertaking to arnica and paregoric.

My men being restored to health and strength, my main perplexity, now, was how to get them down the mountain again. I was not willing to expose the brave fellows to the perils, fatigues, and hardships of that fearful route again if it could be helped. First I thought of balloons; but of course I had to give that idea up, for balloons were not procurable. I thought of several other expedients, but upon consideration discarded them, for cause. But at last I hit it. I was aware that the movement of glaciers is an established fact, for I had read it in Baedeker; so I resolved to take passage for Zermatt on the great Gorner Glacier.

Very good. The next thing was, how to get down to the glacier comfortably,—for the mule-road to it was long, and winding, and wearisome. I set my mind at work, and soon thought out a plan. One looks straight down upon the vast frozen river called the Gorner Glacier, from the Gorner Grat, a sheer precipice 1200 feet high. We had 154 umbrellas, —and what is an umbrella but a parachute?

I mentioned this noble idea to Harris, with enthusiasm, and was about to order the Expedition to form on the Gorner Grat, with their umbrellas, and prepare for flight by platoons, each platoon in command of a guide, when Harris stopped me and urged me not to be too hasty. He asked me if this method of descending the Alps had ever been tried before. I said no, I had not heard of an instance. Then, in his opinion, it was a matter of considerable gravity; in his opinion it would not be well to send the whole command over the cliff at once: a better way would be to send down a single individual, first, and see how he fared.

I saw the wisdom of this idea instantly. I said as much, and thanked my agent cordially, and told him to take his umbrella and try the thing right away, and wave his hat when he got down, if he struck in a soft place, and then I would ship the rest right along.

Harris was greatly touched with this mark of confidence, and said so, in a voice that had a perceptible tremble in it; but at the same time he said he did not feel himself worthy of so conspicuous a favor; that it might cause jealousy in the command, for there were plenty who would not hesitate to say he had used underhand means to get the appointment, whereas his conscience would bear him witness that he had not sought it at all, nor even, in his secret heart, desired it.

I said these words did him extreme credit, but that he must not throw away the imperishable distinction of being the first man to descend an Alp per parachute, simply to save the feelings of some envious underlings. No, I said, he *must* accept the appointment,—it was no longer an invitation, it was a command.

He thanked me with effusion, and said that putting the thing in this form removed every objection. He retired, and soon returned with his umbrella, his eyes flaming with gratitude and his cheeks pallid with joy. Just then the head guide passed along. Harris's expression changed to one of infinite tenderness, and he said,—

"That man did me a cruel injury four days ago, and I said in my heart he should live to perceive and confess that the only noble revenge a man can take upon his enemy is to return good for evil. I resign in his favor. Appoint him."—

I threw my arms around the generous fellow and said,—

"Harris, you are the noblest soul that lives. You shall not regret this sublime act, neither shall the world fail to know of it. You shall have opportunities far transcending this one, too, if I live,—remember that."

I called the head guide to me and appointed him on the spot. But the thing aroused no enthusiasm in him. He did not take to the idea at all. He said,—

"Tie myself to an umbrella and jump over the Gorner Grat! Excuse me, there are a great many pleasanter roads to the devil than that."

Upon a discussion of the subject with him, it appeared that he considered the project distinctly and decidedly dangerous. I was not convinced, yet I was not willing to try the experiment in any risky way—that

EVERYBODY HAD AN EXCUSE.

is, in a way that might cripple the strength and efficiency of the Expedition. I was about at my wits' end when it occurred to me to try it on the Latinist.

He was called in. But he declined, on the plea of inexperience, diffidence in public, lack of curiosity, and I don't know what all. Another man declined on account of a cold in the head; thought he ought to avoid exposure. Another could not jump well—never *could* jump well—did not believe he could jump so far without long and patient practice. Another was afraid it was going to rain, and his umbrella had a hole in it. Everybody had an excuse. The result was what the reader has by this time guessed: the most magnificent idea that was ever conceived had to be abandoned, from sheer lack of a person with enterprise enough to carry it out. Yes, I actually had to give that thing up,—whilst doubtless I should live to see somebody use it and take all the credit from me.

Well, I had to go overland—there was no other way. I marched the Expedition down the steep and tedious mule-path and took up as good a position as I could upon the middle of the Glacier—because Baedeker said the middle part travels the fastest. As a measure of economy, however, I put some of the heavier baggage on the shoreward parts, to go as slow freight.

I waited and waited, but the Glacier did not move. Night was coming on, the darkness began to gather—still we did not budge. It occurred to me then, that there might be a time-table in Baedeker: it would be well to find out the hours of starting. I called for the book—it could not be found. Bradshaw would certainly contain a time-table: but no Bradshaw could be found.

Very well, I must make the best of the situation. So I pitched the tents, picketed the animals, milked the cows, had supper, paregoricked the men, established the watch, and went to bed—with orders to call me as soon as we came in sight of Zermatt.

I awoke about half past ten, next morning, and looked around. We hadn't budged a peg! At first I could not understand it: then it occurred to me that the old thing must be aground. So I cut down some trees and rigged a spar on

the starboard and another on the port side, and fooled away
upwards of three hours trying to spar her off. But it was
no use. She was half a mile wide and fifteen or twenty miles
long, and there was no telling just whereabouts she *was*
aground. The men began to show uneasiness, too, and presently they came flying to me with ashy faces, saying she had
sprung a leak.

Nothing but my cool behavior at this critical time saved
us from another panic. I ordered them to show
me the place. They led me to a spot where a
huge boulder lay in a deep pool
of clear and brilliant water.
It did look like a pretty bad leak,
but I kept that to my- self. I
made a pump and set the men
to work to pump out
the glacier.
We made a
success of
it. I per-
ceived,
then,
that it

SPRUNG A LEAK.

was not a leak at all. This boulder had descended from a
precipice and stopped on the ice in the middle of the glacier,
and the sun had warmed it up, every day, and consequently

it had melted its way deeper and deeper into the ice, until at last it reposed, as we had found it, in a deep pool of the clearest and coldest water.

Presently Baedeker was found again, and I hunted eagerly for the time-table. There was none. The book simply said the glacier was moving all the time. This was satisfactory, so I shut up the book and chose a good position to view the scenery as we passed along. I stood there some time enjoying the trip, but at last it occurred to me that we did not seem to be gaining any on the scenery. I said to myself, "This confounded old thing's aground again, sure,"—and opened Baedeker to see if I could run across any remedy for these annoying interruptions. I soon found a sentence which threw a dazzling light upon the matter. It said, "The Gorner Glacier travels at an average rate of a little less than an inch a day." I have seldom felt so outraged. I have seldom had my confidence so wantonly betrayed. I made a small calculation: 1 inch a day, say 30 feet a year; estimated distance to Zermatt, 3 1-18 miles. Time required to go by glacier, *a little over five hundred years!* I said to myself, "I can *walk* it quicker—and before I will patronize such a fraud as this, I will do it."

When I revealed to Harris the fact that the passenger-part of this glacier,—the central part,—the lightning-express part, so to speak,—was not due in Zermatt till the summer of 2378, and that the baggage, coming along the slow edge, would not arrive until some generations later, he burst out with,—

"That is European management, all over! An inch a day —think of that! Five hundred years to go a trifle over three miles! But I am not a bit surprised. It's a Catholic glacier. You can tell by the look of it. And the management."

I said, no, I believed nothing but the extreme end of it was in a Catholic canton.

"Well, then, it's a government glacier," said Harris. "It's all the same. Over here the government runs everything,— so everything's slow; slow, and ill managed. But with us, everything's done by private enterprise—and then there ain't much lolling around, you can depend on it. I wish Tom Scott could get his hands on this torpid old slab once,—you'd see it take a different gait from this."

I said I was sure he would increase the speed, if there was trade enough to justify it.

"He'd *make* trade," said Harris. "That's the difference between governments and individuals. Governments don't care, individuals do. Tom Scott would take all the trade; in two years Gorner stock would go to 200, and inside of two more you would see all the other glaciers under the hammer for taxes." After a reflective pause, Harris added, "A little less than an inch a day; a little less than an *inch*, mind you. Well, I'm losing my reverence for glaciers."

I was feeling much the same way myself. I have traveled by canal boat, ox-wagon, raft, and by the Ephesus and Smyrna railway; but when it comes down to good solid honest slow motion, I bet my money on the glacier. As a means of passenger transportation, I consider the glacier a failure; but as a vehicle for slow freight, I think she fills the bill. In the matter of putting the fine shades on that line of business, I judge she could teach the Germans something.

I ordered the men to break camp and prepare for the land journey to Zermatt. At this moment a most interesting find was made; a dark object, bedded in the glacial ice, was cut out with the ice-axes, and it proved to be a piece of the undressed skin of some animal,—a hair trunk, perhaps; but a close inspection disabled the hair trunk theory, and further discussion and examination exploded it entirely,—that is, in the opinion of all the scientists except the one who had advanced it. This one clung to his theory with the affectionate fidelity characteristic of originators of scientific theories, and afterwards won many of the first scientists of the age to his view, by a very able pamphlet which he wrote, entitled, " Evidences going to show that the hair trunk, in a wild state, belonged to the early glacial period, and roamed the wastes of chaos in company with the cave bear, primeval man, and the other Oolitics of the Old Silurian family."

27

Each of our scientists had a theory of his own, and put forward an animal of his own as a candidate for the skin. I sided with the geologist of the Expedition in the belief that

this patch of skin had once helped to cover a Siberian elephant, in some old forgotten age—but we divided there, the geologist believing that this discovery proved that Siberia had formerly been located where Switzerland is now, whereas I held the opinion that it merely proved that the primeval Swiss was not the dull savage he is represented to have been, but was a being of high intellectual development, who liked to go to the menagerie.

A SCIENTIFIC QUESTION.

We arrived that evening, after many hardships and adventures, in some fields close to the great ice-arch where the mad Visp boils and surges out from under the foot of the great Gorner Glacier, and here we camped, our perils over and our magnificent undertaking successfully completed. We marched into Zermatt the next day, and were received with the most lavish honors and applause. A document, signed and sealed by all the authorities, was given to me which established and endorsed the fact that I had made the ascent of the Riffelberg. This I wear around my neck, and it will be buried with me when I am no more.

CHAPTER XL.

I AM not so ignorant about glacial movement, now, as I was when I took passage on the Gorner Glacier. I have "read up," since. I am aware that these vast bodies of ice do not travel at the same rate of speed: whilst the Gorner Glacier makes less than an inch a day, the Unter-Aar Glacier makes as much as eight; and still other glaciers are said to go twelve, sixteen, and even twenty inches a day. One writer says that the slowest glacier travels 25 feet a year, and the fastest 400.

What is a glacier? It is easy to say it looks like a frozen river which occupies the bed of a winding gorge or gully between mountains. But that gives no notion of its vastness. For it is sometimes 600 feet thick, and we are not accustomed to rivers 600 feet deep; no, our rivers are 6 feet, 20 feet, and sometimes 50 feet deep; we are not quite able to grasp so large a fact as an ice-river 600 feet deep.

The glacier's surface is not smooth and level, but has deep swales and swelling elevations, and sometimes has the look of a tossing sea whose turbulent billows were frozen hard in the instant of their most violent motion; the glacier's surface is not a flawless mass, but is a river with cracks or crevasses, some narrow, some gaping wide. Many a man, the victim of a slip or a misstep, has plunged down one of these and met his death. Men have been fished out of them alive, but

459

it was when they did not go to a great depth; the cold of the great depths would quickly stupefy a man, whether he was hurt or unhurt. These cracks do not go straight down; one can seldom see more than twenty to forty feet down them; consequently men who have disappeared in them have been sought for, in the hope that they had stopped within helping distance, whereas their case, in most instances, had really been hopeless from the beginning.

In 1864 a party of tourists was descending Mont Blanc, and while picking their way over one of the mighty glaciers of that lofty region, roped together, as was proper, a young porter disengaged himself from the line and started across an ice-bridge which spanned a crevasse. It broke under him with a crash, and he disappeared. The others could not see how deep he had gone, so it might be worth while to try and rescue him. A brave young guide named Michel Payot volunteered.

Two ropes were made fast to his leather belt and he bore the end of a third one in his hand to tie to the victim in case he found him. He was lowered into the crevasse, he descended deeper and deeper between the clear blue walls of solid ice, he approached a bend in the crack and disappeared under it. Down, and still down, he went, into this profound grave; when he had reached a depth of 80 feet he passed under another bend in the crack, and thence descended 80 feet lower, as between perpendicular precipices. Arrived at this stage of 160 feet below the surface of the glacier, he peered through the twilight dimness and perceived that the chasm took another turn and stretched away at a steep slant to unknown deeps, for its course was lost in darkness. What a place that was to be in—especially if that leather belt should break! The compression of the belt threatened to suffocate the intrepid fellow; he called to his friends to draw him up, but could not make them hear. They still lowered him, deeper and deeper. Then he jerked his third cord as vigorously as he could; his friends understood, and dragged him out of those icy jaws of death.

Then they attached a bottle to a cord and sent it down 200 feet, but it found no bottom. It came up covered with congelations—evidence enough that even if the poor porter reached the bottom with unbroken bones, a swift death from cold was sure, anyway.

A glacier is a stupendous, ever progressing, resistless plow. It pushes ahead of it masses of boulders which are packed together, and they stretch across the gorge, right in front of

A TERMINAL MORAINE.

it, like a long grave or a long, sharp roof. This is called a moraine. It also shoves out a moraine along each side of its course.

Imposing as the modern glaciers are, they are not so huge as were some that once existed. For instance, Mr. Whymper says:

"At some very remote period the Valley of Aosta was occupied by a vast glacier, which flowed down its entire length from Mont Blanc to the plain of Peidmont, remained stationary, or nearly so, at its mouth for many centuries, and deposited there enormous masses of debris. The length of this glacier exceeded *eighty miles*, and it drained a basin 25 to 35 miles across, bounded by the highest mountains in the Alps. The great peaks rose several thousand feet above the glaciers, and then, as now, shattered by sun and frost, poured down their showers of rocks and stones, in witness of which there are the immense piles of angular fragments that constitute the moraines of Ivria.

"The moraines around Ivria are of extraordinary dimen-

FRONT OF GLACIER.

sions. That which was on the left bank of the glacier is about *thirteen miles* long, and in some places rises to a height of *two thousand one hundred and thirty feet* above the floor of the valley! The terminal moraines (those which are pushed in front of the glaciers), cover something like twenty square miles of country. At the mouth of the Valley of the Aosta, the thickness of the glacier must have been at least *two thousand* feet, and its width, at that part, *five miles and a quarter.*"

It is not easy to get at a comprehension of a mass of ice like that. If one could cleave off the butt end of such a glacier—an oblong block two or three miles wide by five and a

AN OLD MORAINE.

quarter long and 2,000 feet thick he could completely hide the city of New York under it, and Trinity steeple would only stick up into it relatively as far as a shingle nail would stuck up into the bottom of a Saratoga trunk.

"The boulders from Mont Blanc, upon the plain below Ivria, assure us that the glacier which transported them existed for a prodigious length of time. Their present distance

GLACIER OF ZAMATT WITH LATERAL MORAINE.

from the cliffs from which they were derived is about 420,000 feet, and if we assume that they traveled at the rate of 400 feet per annum, their journey must have occupied them no less than 1055 years! In all probability they did not travel so fast."

Glaciers are sometimes hurried out of their characteristic snail-pace. A marvelous spectacle is presented then. Mr. Whymper refers to a case which occurred in Iceland in 1721:

"It seems that in the neighborhood of the mountain Kotlugja, large bodies of water formed underneath, or within the glaciers (either on account of the interior heat of the earth, or from other causes,) and at length acquired irresistible power, tore the glaciers from their mooring on the land, and swept them over every obstacle into the sea. Prodigious masses of ice were thus borne for a distance of about ten miles over land in the space of a few hours; and their bulk was so enormous that they covered the sea for seven miles from the shore, and remained aground in 600 feet of water! The denudation of the land was upon a grand scale. All superficial accumulations were swept away, and the bed-rock was exposed. It was described, in graphic language, how all irregularities and depressions were obliterated, and a smooth surface of several miles area laid bare, and that this area had the appearance of having been *planed by a plane.*"

The account translated from the Icelandic says that the mountain-like ruins of this majestic glacier so covered the sea that as far as the eye could reach no open water was discoverable, even from the highest peaks. A monster wall or barrier of ice was built across a considerable stretch of land, too, by this strange irruption:

"One can form some idea of the altitude of this barrier of ice when it is mentioned that from Hofdabrekka farm, which lies high up on a fjeld, one could not see Hjorleifshofdi opposite, which is a fell 640 feet in height; but in order to do so had to clamber up a mountain slope east of Hofdabrekka 1,200 feet high."

These things will help the reader to understand why it is that a man who keeps company with glaciers comes to feel tolerably insignificant by and by. The Alps and the glaciers together are able to take every bit of conceit out of a man and reduce his self-importance to zero if he will only remain within the influence of their sublime presence long enough to give it a fair and reasonable chance to do its work.

The Alpine glaciers move—that is granted, now, by everybody. But there was a time when people scoffed at the idea; they said you might as well expect leagues of solid rock to crawl along the ground as expect solid leagues of ice to do it.

But proof after proof was furnished, and finally the world had to believe.

The wise men not only said the glacier moved, but they timed its movement. They ciphered out a glacier's gait, and then said confidently that it would travel just so far in so many years. There is record of a striking and curious example of the accuracy which may be attained in these reckonings.

In 1820 the ascent of Mont Blanc was attempted by a Russian and two Englishmen, with seven guides. They had reached a prodigious altitude, and were approaching the summit, when an avalanche swept several of the party down a sharp slope of two hundred feet and hurled five of them (all guides,) into one of the crevasses of a glacier. The life of one of the five was saved by a long barometer which was strapped to his back—it bridged the crevasse and suspended him until help came. The alpenstock or baton of another saved its owner in a similar way. Three men were lost— Pierre Balmat, Pierre Carrier, and Auguste Tairraz. They had been hurled down into the fathomless great deeps of the crevasse.

Dr. Forbes, the English geologist, had made frequent visits to the Mont Blanc region, and had given much attention to the disputed question of the movement of glaciers. During one of these visits he completed his estimates of the rate of movement of the glacier which had swallowed up the three guides, and uttered the prediction that the glacier would deliver up its dead at the foot of the mountain thirty-five years from the time of the accident, or possibly forty.

A dull, slow journey—a movement imperceptible to any eye—but it was proceeding, nevertheless, and without cessation. It was a journey which a rolling stone would make in a few seconds—the lofty point of departure was visible from the village below in the valley.

The prediction cut curiously close to the truth; forty-one years after the catastrophe, the remains were cast forth at the foot of the glacier.

I find an interesting account of the matter in the "Histoire du Mont Blanc, by Stephen d'Arve." I will condense this account, as follows:

On the 12th of August, 1861, at the hour of the close of mass, a guide arrived out of breath at the mairie of Chamonix, and bearing on his shoulders a very lugubrious burden. It was a sack filled with human remains which he had gathered from the orifice of a crevasse in the Glacier des Bossons. He conjectured that these were remains of the victims of the catastrophe of 1820, and a minute inquest, immediately instituted by the local authorities, soon demonstrated the correctness of his supposition. The contents of the sack were spread upon a long table, and officially inventoried, as follows:

Portions of three human skulls. Several tufts of black and blonde hair. A human jaw, furnished with fine white teeth. A fore-arm and hand, all the fingers of the latter intact. The flesh was white and fresh, and both the arm and hand preserved a degree of flexibility in the articulations.

The ring-finger had suffered a slight abrasion, and the stain of the blood was still visible and unchanged after forty-one years. A left foot, the flesh white and fresh.

Along with these fragments were portions of waistcoats, hats, hob-nailed shoes and other clothing ; a wing of a pigeon, with black feathers ; a fragment of an alpenstock ; a tin lantern ; and lastly, a boiled leg of mutton, the only flesh among all the remains that exhaled an unpleasant odor. The guide said that the mutton had no odor when he took it from the glacier ; an hour's exposure to the sun had already begun the work of decomposition upon it.

Persons were called for, to identify these poor pathetic relics, and a touching scene ensued. Two men were still living who had witnessed the grim catastrophe of nearly half a century before,—Marie Couttet, (saved by his bâton,) and Julien Davouassoux, (saved by the barometer). These aged men entered and approached the table. Davouassoux, more than eighty years old, contemplated the mournful remains mutely and with a vacant eye, for his intelligence and his memory were torpid with age; but Couttet's faculties were still perfect at 72, and he exhibited strong emotion. He said,—

"Pierre Balmat was fair; he wore a straw hat. This bit of skull, with the tuft of blond hair, was his; this is his hat. Pierre Carrier was very dark; this skull was his, and this felt hat. This is Balmat's hand, I remember it so well!" and the old man bent down and kissed it reverently, then closed his fingers upon it in an affectionate grasp, crying out, "I could never have dared to believe that before quitting this

UNEXPECTED MEETING OF FRIENDS.

world it would be granted me to press once more the hand of one of those brave comrades, the hand of my good friend Balmat."

There is something wierdly pathetic about the picture of that white-haired veteran greeting with his loving hand-shake this friend who had been dead forty years. When these hands had met last, they were alike in the softness and fresh-ness of youth; now, one was brown and wrinkled and horny with age, while the other was still as young and fair and blemishless as if those forty years had come and gone in a single moment, leaving no mark of their passage. Time had gone on, in the one case; it had stood still in the other. A man who has not seen a friend for a generation, keeps him in mind always as he saw him last, and is somehow surprised, and is also shocked, to see the aging change the years have wrought when he sees him again. Marie Couttet's experience, in finding his friend's hand unaltered from the image of it which he had carried in his memory for forty years, is an experience which stands alone in the history of man, perhaps.

Couttet identified other relics:

"This hat belonged to Auguste Tairraz. He carried the cage of pigeons which we proposed to set free upon the summit. Here is the wing of one of those pigeons. And here is the fragment of my broken bâton: 'it was by grace of that bâton that my life was saved. Who could have told me that I should one day have the satisfaction to look again upon this bit of wood that supported me above the grave that swallowed up my unfortunate companions!"

No portions of the body of Tairraz had been found. A diligent search was made, but without result. However, another search was instituted a year later, and this had better success. Many fragments of clothing which had belonged to the lost guides were discovered; also, part of a lantern, and a green veil, with blood stains on it. But the interesting feature was this:

One of the searchers came suddenly upon a sleeved arm projecting from a crevice in the ice-wall, with the hand outstretched as if offering greeting! "The nails of this white hand were still rosy, and the pose of the extended fingers seemed to express an eloquent welcome to the long lost light of day."

The hand and arm were alone; there was no trunk. After being removed from the ice the flesh tints quickly faded out and the rosy nails took on the alabaster hue of death.

This was the third *right* hand found : therefore, all three of the lost men were accounted for, beyond cavil or question.

Dr. Hamel was the Russian gentleman of the party which made the ascent at the time of the famous disaster. He left Chamonix as soon as he conveniently could after the descent; and as he had shown a chilly indifference about the calamity, and offered neither sympathy nor assistance to the widows and orphans, he carried with him the cordial execrations of the whole community. Four months before the first remains were found, a Chamonix guide named Balmat,—a relative of one of the lost men,—was in London, and one day encountered a hale old gentleman in the British museum, who said,—

"I overheard your name. Are you from Chamonix, Monsieur Balmat ? "

" Yes, sir."

" Haven't they found the bodies of my three guides, yet ? I am Dr. Hamel."

" Alas, no, monsieur."

" Well, you'll find them, sooner or later."

" Yes, it is the opinion of Dr. Forbes and Mr. Tyndal, that the glacier will sooner or later restore to us the remains of the unfortunate victims."

" Without a doubt, without a doubt. And it will be a great thing for Chamonix, in the matter of attracting tourists. You can get up a museum with those remains that will draw ! "

This savage idea has not improved the odor of Dr. Hamel's name in Chamonix by any means. But after all, the man was sound on human nature. His idea was conveyed to the public officials of Chamonix, and they gravely discussed it around the official council table. They were only prevented from carrying it into execution by the determined opposition of the friends and descendants of the lost guides, who insisted on giving the remains Christian burial, and succeeded in their purpose.

A close watch had to be kept upon all the poor remnants and fragments, to prevent embezzlement. A few accessory odds and ends were sold. Rags and scraps of the coarse clothing were parted with at a rate equal to about twenty dollars a yard; a piece of a lantern and one or two other trifles brought nearly their weight in gold; and an Englishman offered a pound sterling for a single breeches-button.

VILLAGE OF CHAMONIX.

CHAPTER XLI.

ONE of the most memorable of all the Alpine catastrophes was that of July 1865, on the Matterhorn,—already slightly referred to, a few pages back. The details of it are scarcely known in America. To the vast majority of readers they are not known at all. Mr. Whymper's account is the only authentic one. I will import the chief portion of it into this book, partly because of its intrinsic interest, and partly because it gives such a vivid idea of what the perilous pastime of Alp-climbing is. This was Mr. Whymper's *ninth* attempt during a series of years, to vanquish that steep and stubborn pillar of rock; it succeeded, the other eight were failures. No man had ever accomplished the ascent before, though the attempts had been numerous.

MR. WHYMPER'S NARRATIVE.

We started from Zermatt on the 13th of July, at half past 5, on a brilliant and perfectly cloudless morning. We were eight in number—Croz, (guide,) old Peter Taugwalder, (guide,) and his two sons; Lord F. Douglas, Mr. Hadow, Rev. Mr. Hudson, and I. To ensure steady motion, one tourist and one native walked together. The youngest Taugwalder fell to my share. The wine-bags also fell to my lot to carry, and throughout the day, after each drink, I replenished them secretly with water, so that at the next halt they were found fuller than before! This was considered a good omen, and little short of miraculous.

473

On the first day we did not intend to ascend to any great height, and we mounted, accordingly, very leisurely. Before 12 o'clock we had found a good position for the tent, at a height of 11,000 feet. We passed the remaining hours of daylight—some basking in the sunshine, some sketching, some collecting; Hudson made tea, I coffee, and at length we retired, each one to his blanket-bag.

We assembled together before dawn on the 14th and started directly it was light enough to move. One of the young Taugwalders returned to Zermatt. In a few minutes we turned the rib which had intercepted the view of the eastern face from our tent platform. The whole of this great slope was now revealed, rising for 3,000 feet like a huge natural staircase. Some parts were more, and others were less easy, but we were not once brought to a halt by any serious impediment, for when an obstruction was met in front it could always be turned to the right or to the left. For the greater part of the way there was no occasion, indeed, for the rope, and sometimes Hudson led, sometimes myself. At 6:20 we had attained a height of 12,800 feet, and halted for half an hour; we then continued the ascent without a break until 9:55, when we stopped for 50 minutes, at a height of 14,000 feet.

We had now arrived at the foot of that part which, seen from the Riffelberg, seems perpendicular or overhanging. We could no longer continue on the eastern side. For a little distance we ascended by snow upon the arête--that is, the ridge—then turned over to the right, or northern side. The work became difficult, and required caution. In some places there was little to hold; the general slope of the mountain was *less* than 40°, and snow had accumulated in, and had filled up, the interstices of the rock-face, leaving only occasional fragments projecting here and there. These were at times covered with a thin film of ice. It was a place which any fair mountaineer might pass in safety. We bore away nearly horizontally for about 400 feet, then ascended directly

ONE VIEW OF THE MATTEHORN.

toward the summit for about 60 feet, then doubled back to the ridge which descends toward Zermatt. A long stride round a rather awkward corner brought us to snow once more. The last doubt vanished! The Matterhorn was ours! Nothing but 200 feet of easy snow remained to be surmounted.

The higher we rose, the more intense became the excitement. The slope eased off, at length we could be detached, and Croz and I, dashing away, ran a neck-and-neck race, which ended in a dead heat. At 1: 40 p. m., the world was at our feet, and the Matterhorn was conquered!

The others arrived. Croz now took the tent-pole, and planted it in the highest snow. "Yes" we said, "there is the flag-staff, but where is the flag?" "Here it is," he an-

ON THE SUMMIT.

swered, pulling off his blouse and fixing it to the stick. It made a poor flag, and there was no wind to float it out, yet it was seen all around. They saw it at Zermatt—at the Riffel —in the Val Tournanche. * * *

We remained on the summit for one hour—

<blockquote>"One crowded hour of glorious life."</blockquote>

It passed away too quickly, and we began to prepare for the descent.

28

Hudson and I consulted as to the best and safest arrangement of the party. We agreed that it was best for Croz to go first, and Hadow second; Hudson, who was almost equal to a guide in sureness of foot, wished to be third; Lord Douglas was placed next, and old Peter, the strongest of the remainder, after him. I suggested to Hudson that we should attach a rope to the rocks on our arrival at the difficult bit, and hold it as we descended, as an additional protection. He approved the idea, but it was not definitely decided that it should be done. The party was being arranged in the above order whilst I was sketching the summit, and they had finished, and were waiting for me to be tied in line, when some one remembered that our names had not been left in a bottle. They requested me to write them down, and moved off while it was being done.

A few minutes afterwards I tied myself to young Peter, ran down after the others, and caught them just as they were commencing the descent of the difficult part. Great care was being taken. Only one man was moving at a time; when he was firmly planted the next advanced, and so on. They had not, however, attached the additional rope to rocks, and nothing was said about it. The suggestion was not made for my own sake, and I am not sure that it even occurred to me again. For some little distance we two followed the others, detached from them, and should have continued so had not Lord Douglas asked me, about 3 p. m., to tie on to old Peter, as he feared, he said, that Taugwalder would not be able to hold his ground if a slip occurred.

A few minutes later, a sharp-eyed lad ran into the Monte Rosa hotel, at Zermatt, saying that he had seen an avalanche fall from the summit of the Matterhorn on to the Matterhorn glacier. The boy was reproved for telling idle stories; he was right, nevertheless, and this was what he saw.

Michel Croz had laid aside his axe, and in order to give Mr. Hadow greater security, was absolutely taking hold of his legs, and putting his feet, one by one, into their proper

THE CATASTROPHE ON THE MATTERHORN, 1865.

positions. As far as I know, no one was actually descending. I cannot speak with certainty, because the two leading men were partially hidden from my sight by an intervening mass of rock, but it is my belief, from the movements of their shoulders, that Croz, having done as I have said, was in the act of turning round to go down a step or two himself; at this moment Mr. Hadow slipped, fell against him, and knocked him over. I heard one startled exclamation from Croz, then saw him and Mr. Hadow flying downwards; in another moment Hudson was dragged from his steps, and Lord Douglas immediately after him. All this was the work of a moment. Immediately we heard Croz's exclamation, old Peter and I planted ourselves as firmly as the rocks would permit: the rope was taut between us, and the jerk came on us both as on one man. We held; but the rope broke midway between Taugwalder and Lord Francis Douglas. For a few seconds we saw our unfortunate companions sliding downwards on their backs, and spreading out their hands, endeavoring to save themselves. They passed from our sight uninjured, disappeared one by one, and fell from precipice to precipice on to the Matterhorn glacier below, a distance of nearly 4,000 feet in height. From the moment the rope broke it was impossible to help them. So perished our comrades!

* * * * *

For more than two hours afterwards I thought almost every moment that the next would be my last; for the Taugwalders, utterly unnerved, were not only incapable of giving assistance, but were in such a state that a slip might have been expected from them at any moment. After a time we were able to do that which should have been done at first, and fixed rope to firm rocks, in addition to being tied together. These ropes were cut from time to time, and were left behind. Even with their assurance the men were afraid to proceed, and several times old Peter turned, with ashy face and faltering limbs, and said, with terrible emphasis, "*I cannot!*"

About 6 p. m., we arrived at the snow upon the ridge de-

descending towards Zermatt, and all peril was over. We frequently looked, but in vain, for traces of our unfortunate companions; we bent over the ridge and cried to them, but no sound returned. Convinced at last that they were neither within sight nor hearing, we ceased from our useless efforts; and, too cast down for speech, silently gathered up our things, and the little effects of those who were lost, and then completed the descent.

Such is Mr. Whymper's graphic and thrilling narrative. Zermatt gossip darkly hints that the elder Taugwalder cut the rope, when the accident occurred, in order to preserve himself from being dragged into the abyss; but Mr. Whymper says that the ends of the rope showed no evidence of cutting, but only of breaking. He adds that if Taugwalder had had the disposition to cut the rope, he would not have had time to do it, the accident was so sudden and unexpected.

Lord Douglas's body has never been found. It probably lodged upon some inaccessible shelf in the face of the mighty precipice. Lord Douglas was a youth of 19. The three other victims fell nearly 4,000 feet, and their bodies lay together upon the glacier when found by Mr. Whymper and the other searchers the next morning. Their graves are beside the little church in Zermatt.

CHAPTER XLII.

SWITZERLAND is simply a large, humpy, solid rock, with a thin skin of grass stretched over it. Consequently, they do not dig graves, they blast them out with powder and fuse. They cannot afford to have large graveyards, the grass skin is too circumscribed and too valuable. It is all required for the support of the living.

The graveyard in Zermatt occupies only about one-eighth of an acre. The graves are sunk in the living rock, and are very permanent; but occupation of them is only temporary; the occupant can only stay till his grave is needed by a later subject, he is removed, then, for they do not bury one body on top of another. As I understand it, a family owns a grave, just as it owns a house. A man dies, and leaves his house to his son,—and at the same time, this dead father succeeds to his own father's grave. He moves out of the house and into the grave, and his predecessor moves out of the grave and into the cellar of the chapel. I saw a black box lying in the churchyard, with skull and cross-bones painted on it, and was told that this was used in transferring remains to the cellar.

In that cellar the bones and skulls of several hundreds of former citizens were compactly corded up. They made a pile 18 feet long, 7 feet high, and 8 feet wide. I was told that in some of the receptacles of this kind in the Swiss villages, the skulls were all marked, and if a man wished to find the skulls of his ancestors for several generations back, he could do it by these marks, preserved in the family records.

STORAGE OF ANCESTORS.

An English gentleman who had lived some years in this region, said it was the cradle of compulsory education. But he said that the English idea that compulsory education would reduce bastardy and intemperance was an error—it has not that effect. He said there was more seduction in the Protestant than in the Catholic cantons, because the confessional protected the girls. I wonder why it doesn't protect married women in France and Spain?

This gentleman said that among the poorer peasants in the Valaïs, it was common for the brothers in a family to cast lots to determine which of them should have the coveted privilege of marrying. Then the lucky one got married, and his brethren—doomed bachelors,—heroically banded themselves together to help support the new family.

We left Zermatt in a wagon—and in a rain storm, too,—for St. Nicholas about ten o'clock one morning. Again we passed between those grass-clad prodigious cliffs, specked with wee dwellings peeping over at us from velvety, green walls ten and twelve hundred feet high. It did not seem possible that the imaginary chamois even, could climb those precipices. Lovers on opposite cliffs probably kiss through a spyglass, and correspond with a rifle.

In Switzerland the farmer's plow is a wide shovel, which scrapes up and turns over the thin earthy skin of his native rock —and there the man of the plow is a hero. Now here, by our St. Nicholas road, was a grave, and it had a tragic story. A plowman was skinning his farm one morning,—not the steepest part of it, but still a steep part—that is, he was not skinning the front of his farm, but the roof of it, near the eaves,— when he absent-mindedly let go of the plow-handles to moisten his hands, in the usual way: he lost his balance and fell out of his farm

FALLING OUT OF HIS FARM.

backwards; poor fellow, he never touched anything till he struck bottom, 1500 feet below.* We throw a halo of heroism around the life of the soldier and the sailor, because of the deadly dangers they are facing all the time. But we are

---

* This was on a Sunday. M. T.

not used to looking upon farming as a heroic occupation. This is because we have not lived in Switzerland.

From St. Nicholas we struck out for Visp,—or Vispach —on foot. The rain storms had been at work during several days, and had done a deal of damage in Switzerland and Savoy. We came to one place where a stream had changed its course and plunged down the mountain in a new place, sweeping everything before it. Two poor but precious farms by the roadside were ruined. One was washed clear away, and the bed-rock exposed; the other was buried out of sight under a tumbled chaos of rocks, gravel, mud, and rubbish. The resistless might of water was well exemplified. Some saplings which had stood in the way were bent to the ground, stripped clean of their bark, and buried under rocky debris. The road had been swept away, too.

In another place, where the road was high up on the mountain's face, and its outside edge protected by flimsy masonry, we frequently came across spots where this mason- ry had caved off and left dangerous gaps for mules to get over; and with still more frequency we found the masonry slightly crumbled, and marked by mule-hoofs, thus showing that there had been danger of an accident to somebody. When at last we came to a badly ruptured bit of masonry, with hoof-prints evidencing a desperate struggle to regain the lost foot-hold, I looked quite hopefully over the dizzy precipice. But there was nobody down there.

They take exceedingly good care of their rivers in Switz- erland and other portions of Europe. They wall up both banks with slanting solid stone masonry—so that from end to end of these rivers the banks look like the wharves at St. Louis and other towns on the Mississippi river.

It was during this walk from St. Nicholas, in the shadow of the majestic Alps, that we came across some little children amusing themselves in what seemed, at first, a most odd and original way—but it wasn't: it was in simply a natural and characteristic way. They were roped together with a string, they had mimic alpenstocks and ice-axes, and were climbing a meek and lowly manure pile with a most blood-curdling amount of care and caution. The "guide" at the head of the line cut imaginary steps, in a laborious and painstaking way, and not a monkey budged till the step above him was vacated. If we had waited we should have witnessed an imaginary accident, no doubt; and we should have heard the intrepid band hurrah when they made the summit and looked around upon the "magnificent view," and seen them throw themselves down in exhausted attitudes for a rest in that commanding situation.

In Nevada I used to see the children play at silver mining. Of course the great thing was an accident in a mine, and there were two "star" parts: that of the man who fell down the mimic shaft, and that of the daring hero who was lowered

CHILD-LIFE IN SWITZERLAND.

into the depths to bring him up. I knew one small chap who always insisted on playing *both* of these parts,—and he carried his point. He would tumble into the shaft and die, and then come to the surface and go back after his own remains.

It is the smartest boy that gets the hero-part, everywhere: he is head guide in Switzerland, head miner in Nevada, head bull-fighter in Spain, etc., but I knew a preacher's son, seven years old, who once selected a part for himself compared to which those just mentioned are tame and unimpressive. Jimmy's father stopped him from driving imaginary horse-cars one Sunday—stopped him from playing captain of an imaginary steamboat next Sunday—stopped him from leading an imaginary army to battle the following Sunday—and so on. Finally the little fellow said,—

"I've tried everything, and they won't any of them do. What *can* I play?"

"I hardly know, Jimmy; but you *must* play only things that are suitable to the Sabbath day."

Next Sunday the preacher stepped softly to a back room door to see if the children were rightly employed. He peeped in. A chair occupied the middle of the room, and on the back of it hung Jimmy's cap; one of the little sisters took

A SUNDAY PLAY.

the cap down, nibbled at it, then passed it to another small sister and said, "Eat of this fruit, for it is good." The Reverend took in the situation—alas, they were playing the

Expulsion from Eden! Yet he found one little crumb of comfort. He said to himself, "For once Jimmy has yielded the chief rōle—I have been wronging him, I did not believe there was so much modesty in him: I should have expected him to be either Adam or Eve." This crumb of comfort lasted but a very little while; he glanced around and discovered Jimmy standing in an imposing attitude in a corner, with a dark and deadly frown on his face. What that meant was very plain—*he was personating the Deity!* Think of the guileless sublimity of that idea.

We reached Vispach at 8 p. m., only about seven hours out from St. Nicholas. So we must have made fully a mile and a half an hour, and it was all down hill, too, and very muddy at that. We staid all night at the Hotel du Soliel; I remember it because the landlady, the portier, the waitress, and the chambermaid, were not separate persons, but were all contained in one neat and chipper suit of spotless muslin, and she was the prettiest young creature I saw in all that region. She was the landlord's daughter. And

THE COMBINATION.

I remember that the only native match to her I saw in all Europe was the young daughter of the landlord of a village inn in the Black Forest. Why don't more people in Europe marry and keep hotel?

Next morning we left with a family of English friends and went by train to Brevet, and thence by boat across the lake to Ouchy (Lausanne.)

Ouchy is memorable to me, not on account of its beautiful

situation and lovely surroundings,—although these would make it stick long in one's memory,—but as the place where I caught the London *Times* dropping into humor. It was not aware of it, though. It did not do it on purpose. An English friend called my attention to this lapse, and cut out the reprehensible paragraph for me. Think of encountering a grin like this on the face of that grim journal:

ERRATUM.—We are requested by Reuter's Telegram Company to correct an erroneous announcement made in their Brisbane telegram of the 2d inst., published in our impression of the 5th inst., stating that "Lady Kennedy had given birth to twins, the eldest being a son." The Company explain that the message they received contained the words "Governor of Queensland, *twins first son.*" Being, however, subsequently informed that Sir Arthur Kennedy was unmarried and that there must be some mistake, a telegraphic repetition was at once demanded. It has been received to-day (11th inst.) and shows that the words really telegraphed by Reuter's agent were "Governor Queensland *turns first sod,*" alluding to the Maryborough-Gympic Railway in course of construction. The words in italics were mutilated by the telegraph in transmission from Australia, and reaching the company in the form mentioned above gave rise to the mistake.

I had always had a deep and reverent compassion for the sufferings of the "prisoner of Chillon," whose story Byron has told in such moving verse; so I took the steamer and made pilgrimage to the dungeons of the Castle of Chillon, to see the place where poor Bonivard endured his dreary captivity 300 years ago. I am glad I did that, for it took away some of the pain I was feeling on the prisoner's account. His dungeon was a nice, cool, roomy place, and I cannot see why he should have been so dissatisfied with it. If he had been imprisoned in a St. Nicholas private dwelling, where the fertilizer prevails, and the goat sleeps with the guest, and the chickens roost on him, and the cow comes in and bothers him when he wants to muse, it would have been another matter altogether; but he surely could not have had a very cheerless time of it in that pretty dungeon. It has romantic window-slits that let in generous bars of light, and it has tall, noble columns, carved apparently from the living rock; and what is more, they are written all over with thousands of names; some of them,—like Byron's and Victor Hugo's,—of the first celebrity. Why didn't he amuse himself reading these names? Then there are the couriers and tourists—swarms of them every day—what was to hinder him from having a good time with them? I think Bonivard's sufferings have been overrated.

Next, we took the train and went to Martigny, on the way to Mont Blanc. Next morning we started, about 8 o'clock, on foot. We had plenty of company, in the way of wagon-

CHILLON.

loads and mule-loads of tourists—and dust. This scattering procession of travelers was perhaps a mile long. The road was up hill—interminably up hill,—and tolerably steep. The weather was blistering hot, and the man or woman who had to sit on a creeping mule, or in a crawling wagon, and broil

in the beating sun, was an object to be pitied. We could dodge among the bushes, and have the relief of shade, but those people could not. They paid for a conveyance, and to get their money's worth they rode.

THE TETE NOIR.

We went by the way of the Tête Noir, and after we reached

AIGUILLE DU DRU AND AIGUILLE VERTE, IN THE MONT BLANC CHAIN.

high ground there was no lack of fine scenery. In one place the road was tunneled through a shoulder of the mountain; from there one looked down into a gorge with a rushing torrent in it, and on every hand was a charming view of rocky buttresses and wooded heights. There was a liberal allowance of pretty water-falls, too, on the Tête Noir route.

About half an hour before we reached the village of Argentiere a vast dome of snow with the sun blazing on it, drifted into view and framed itself in a strong V-shaped gateway of the mountains, and we recognized Mont Blanc, the "monarch of the Alps." With every step, after that, this stately dome rose higher and higher into the blue sky, and at last seemed to occupy the zenith.

Some of Mont Blanc's neighbors—bare, light-brown, steeple-like rocks,—were very peculiarly shaped. Some were whittled to a sharp point, and slightly bent at the upper end, like a lady's finger; one monster sugar-loaf resembled a bishop's hat; it was too steep to hold snow on its sides, but had some in the division.

While we were still on very high ground, and before the descent toward Argentiere began, we looked up toward a neighboring mountain-top, and saw exquisite prismatic colors playing about some white clouds which were so delicate as to almost resemble gossamer webs. The faint pinks and greens were peculiarly beautiful; none of the colors were deep, they were the lightest shades. They were bewitchingly commingled. We sat down to study and enjoy this singular spectacle. The tints remained during several minutes —flitting, changing, melting into each other; paling almost away, for a moment, then re-flushing,—a shifting, restless, unstable succession of soft opaline gleams, shimmering over that airy film of white cloud, and turning it into a fabric dainty enough to clothe an angel with.

By and by we perceived what those super-delicate colors, and their continuous play and movement, reminded us of: it is what one sees in a soap-bubble that is drifting along, catching changes of tint from the objects it passes. A soap-bubble is the most beautiful thing, and the most exquisite, in nature: that lovely phantom fabric in the sky was suggestive of a soap-bubble split open, and spread out in the sun. I wonder how much it would take to buy a soap-bubble,

AN EXQUISITE THING.

if there was only one in the world? One could buy a hat-full of Koh-i-Noors with the same money, no doubt.

We made the tramp from Martigny to Argentiere in eight hours. We beat all the mules and wagons; we didn't usually do that. We hired a sort of open baggage-wagon for the trip down the valley to Chamonix, and then devoted an hour to dining. This gave the driver time to get drunk. He had a friend with him, and this friend also had had time to get drunk.

When we drove off, the driver said all the tourists had arrived and gone by while we were at dinner; "but," said he, impressively, "be not disturbed by that—remain tranquil —give yourselves no uneasiness—Their dust rises far before us, you shall see it fade and disappear far behind us—rest you tranquil, leave all to me—I am the king of drivers. Behold!"

Down came his whip, and away we clattered. I never had

such a shaking up in my life. The recent flooding rains had washed the road clear away in places, but we never stopped, we never slowed down, for any thing. We tore right along, over rocks, rubbish, gullies, open fields—sometimes with one or two wheels on the ground, but generally with none. Every

A WILD RIDE.

now and then that calm, good-natured madman would bend a majestic look over his shoulder at us and say, "Ah, you perceive? It is as I have said—I am the king of drivers." Every time we just missed going to destruction, he would say, with tranquil happiness, "Enjoy it, gentlemen, it is very rare, it is very unusual—it is given to few to ride with the king of drivers—and observe, it is as I have said, *I* am he."

He spoke in French, and punctuated with hiccups. His friend was French, too, but spoke in German—using the same system of punctuation, however. The friend called himself the "Captain of Mont Blanc," and wanted us to make the ascent with him. He said he had made more ascents than any other man,—47,—and his brother had made 37. His brother was the best guide in the world, except himself—

29

but he, yes, observe him well,—he was the " Captain of Mont
Blanc"—that title belonged to none other.

The "king" was as good as his word—he overtook that
long procession of tourists and went by it like a hurricane.
The result was that we got choicer rooms at the hotel in Chamonix than we should have done if his majesty had been a
slower artist—or rather, if he hadn't most providentially
got drunk before he left Argentiere.

CHAPTER XLIII.

EVERYBODY was out of doors; everybody was in the principal street of the village,—not on the sidewalks, but all over the street; everybody was lounging, loafing, chatting, waiting, alert, expectant, interested,—for it was train-time. That is to say, it was diligence-time—the half dozen big diligences would soon be arriving from Geneva, and the village was interested, in many ways, in knowing how many people were coming and what sort of folk they might be. It was altogether the livest looking street we had seen in any village on the continent.

The hotel was by the side of a booming torrent, whose music was loud and strong; we could not see this torrent, for it was dark, now, but one could locate it without a light. There was a large enclosed yard in front of the hotel, and this was filled with groups of villagers waiting to see the diligences arrive, or to hire themselves to excursionists for the morrow A telescope stood in the yard, with its huge barrel canted up toward the lustrous evening star. The long porch of the hotel was populous with tourists, who sat in shawls and wraps under the vast overshadowing bulk of Mont Blanc, and gossiped or meditated.

Never did a mountain seem so close; its big sides seemed at one's very elbow, and its majestic dome, and the lofty cluster of slender minarets that were its neighbors, seemed

499

to be almost over one's head. It was night in the streets, and the lamps were sparkling everywhere; the broad bases and shoulders of the mountains were in a deep gloom, but their summits swam in a strange rich glow which was really daylight, and yet had a mellow something about it which was very different from the hard white glare of the kind of daylight I was used to. Its radiance was strong and clear, but at the same time it was singularly soft, and spiritual, and benignant. No, it was not our harsh, aggressive, realistic daylight; it seemed properer to an enchanted land—or to heaven.

I had seen moonlight and daylight together before, but I had not seen daylight and black night elbow to elbow before. At least I had not seen the daylight resting upon an object sufficiently close at hand, before, to make the contrast startling and at war with nature.

The daylight passed away. Presently the moon rose up behind some of those sky-piercing fingers or pinnacles of bare rock of which I have spoken—they were a little to the left of the crest of Mont Blanc, and right over our heads,—but she couldn't manage to climb high enough toward heaven to get entirely above them. She would show the glittering arch of her upper third, occasionally, and scrape it along behind the comb-like row; sometimes a pinnacle stood straight up, like a statuette of ebony, against that glittering white shield, then seemed to glide out of it by its own volition and power, and become a dim spectre, whilst the next pinnacle glided into its place and blotted the spotless disk with the black exclamation point of its presence. The top of one pinnacle took the shapely, clean-cut form of a rabbit's head, in the inkiest silhouette, while it rested against the moon. The unillumined peaks and minarets, hovering vague and phantom-like above us while the others were painfully white and strong with snow and moonlight, made a peculiar effect.

But when the moon, having passed the line of pinnacles, was hidden behind the stupendous white swell of Mont Blanc, the masterpiece of the evening was flung on the canvas. A rich greenish radiance sprang into the sky from behind the

STREET IN CHAMONIX.

mountain, and in this some airy shreds and ribbons of vapor
floated about, and being flushed with that strange tint, went
waving to and fro like pale green flames.   After a while, radiating bars,—vast broadening fan-shaped shadows,—grew
up and stretched away to the zenith from behind the mountain.   It was a spectacle to take one's breath, for the wonder
of it, and the sublimity.

Indeed, those mighty bars of alternate light and shadow
streaming up from behind that dark and prodigious form and
occupying the half of the dull and opaque heavens, was the
most imposing and impressive marvel I had ever looked upon.
There is no simile for it, for nothing is like it.   If a child
had asked me what it was, I should have said, " Humble yourself, in this presence, it is the glory flowing from the hidden
head of the Creator."   One falls shorter of the truth than
that, sometimes, in trying to explain mysteries to the little
people.   I could have found out the cause of this awe-com-
pelling miracle by inquiring, for it is not infrequent at **Mont
Blanc**,—but I did not wish to know.   We have not the reverent feeling for the rainbow that a savage has, because we
know how it is made.   We have lost as much as we gained
by prying into that matter.

We took a walk down street, a block or two, and at a place
where four streets met and the principal shops were clustered,
found the groups of men in the roadway thicker than ever—
for this was the Exchange of Chamonix.   These men were
in the costumes of guides and porters, and were there to be
hired.

The office of that great personage, the Guide-in-Chief of
the Chamonix Guild of Guides, was near by.   This guild is
a close corporation, and is governed by strict laws.   There
are many excursion-routes, some dangerous and some not,
some that can be made safely without a guide, and some that
cannot.   The bureau determines these things.   Where it de-
cides that a guide is necessary, you are forbidden to go without one.   Neither are you allowed to be a victim of extortion; the law states what you are to pay.   The guides **serve**

in rotation; you cannot select the man who is to take your life into his hands, you must take the worst in the lot, if it is his turn.

A guide's fee ranges all the way up from a half dollar (for some trifling excursion of a few rods,) to twenty dollars, according to the distance traversed and the nature of the ground. A guide's fee for taking a person to the summit of Mont Blanc and back, is twenty dollars—and he earns it. The time employed is usually three days, and there is enough early rising in it to make a man far more "healthy and wealthy and wise" than any one man has any right to be. The porter's fee for the same trip is ten dollars. Several fools,—no, I mean several tourists,—usually go together, and divide up the expense, and thus make it light; for if only

THE PROUD GERMAN.

one f—tourist, I mean — went, he would have to have several guides and porters, and that would made the matter costly.

We went into the Chief's office. There were maps of mountains on the walls; also one or two lithographs of celebrated guides, and a portrait of the scientist De Saussure.

In glass cases were some labeled fragments of boots and batons, and other suggestive relics and remembrancers of casualities on Mont Blanc. In a book was a record of all the ascents which have ever been made, beginning with Nos. 1 and 2,—being those of Jacques Balmat and De Saussure, in 1787, and ending with No. 685, which wasn't cold yet. In fact No. 685 was standing by the official table waiting to receive the precious official diploma which should prove to his German household and to his descendants that he had once been indiscreet enough to climb to the top of Mont Blanc. He looked very happy when he got his document; in fact, he spoke up and said he *was* happy.

I tried to buy a diploma for an invalid friend at home who had never traveled, and whose desire all his life has been to ascend Mont Blanc, but the Guide-in-Chief rather insolently refused to sell me one. I was very much offended. I said I did not propose to be discriminated against on account of my nationality; that he had just sold a diploma to this German gentleman, and my money was as good as his; I would see to it that he couldn't keep shop for Germans and deny his produce to Americans; I would have his license taken away from him at the dropping of a handkerchief; if France refused to break him, I would make an international matter of it and bring on a war; the soil should be drenched with blood; and not only that, but I would set up an opposition shop and sell diplomas at half price.

For two cents I would have done these things, too; but nobody offered me the two cents. I tried to move that German's feelings, but it could not be done; he would not give

THE INDIGNANT TOURIST.

me his diploma, neither would he sell it to me. I *told* him my friend was sick and could not come himself, but he said he did not care a verdammtes pfennig, he wanted his diploma for himself—did I suppose he was going to risk his neck for that thing and then give it to a sick stranger? Indeed he wouldn't, so he wouldn't. I resolved, then, that I would do all I could to injure Mont Blanc.

In the record book was a list of all the fatal accidents which had happened on the mountain. It began with the one in 1820 when the Russian Dr. Hamel's three guides were lost in a crevasse of the glacier, and it recorded the delivery of the remains in the valley by the slow-moving glacier 41 years later. The latest catastrophe bore date 1877.

We stepped out and roved about the village a while. In front of the little church was a monument to the memory of the bold guide Jacques Balmat, the first man who ever stood upon the summit of Mont Blanc. He made that wild trip solitary and alone. He accomplished the ascent a number of times afterward. A stretch of nearly half a century lay between his first ascent and his last one. At the ripe old age of 72 he was climbing around a corner of a lofty precipice of the Pic du Midi—nobody with him—when he slipped and fell. So he died in the harness.

He had grown very avaricious in his old age, and used to go off stealthily to hunt for non-existent and impossible gold among those perilous peaks and precipices. He was on a quest of that kind when he lost his life. There was a statue to him, and another to De Saussure, in the hall of our hotel, and a metal plate on the door of a room up stairs bore an inscription to the effect that that room had been occupied by Albert Smith. Balmat and De Saussure discovered Mont Blanc—so to speak—but it was Smith who made it a paying property. His articles in Blackwood and his lectures on Mont Blanc in London advertised it and made people as anxious to see it as if it owed them money.

As we strolled along the road we looked up and saw a red signal light glowing in the darkness of the mountain side. It seemed but a trifling way up,—perhaps a hundred yards, a climb of ten minutes. It was a lucky piece of sagacity in us that we concluded to stop a man whom we met and get a light for our pipes from him instead of continuing the climb to that lantern to get a light, as had been our purpose. The man said that that lantern was on the Grands Mulets, some

6,500 feet above the valley! I know by our Riffelberg experience, that it would have taken us a good part of a week to go up there. I would sooner not smoke at all, than take all that trouble for a light.

Even in the daytime the foreshortening effect of the mountain's close proximity creates curious deceptions. For instance, one sees with the naked eye a cabin up there beside the glacier, and a little above and beyond he sees the spot where that red light was located; he thinks he could throw a stone from the one place to the other. But he couldn't, for the difference between the two altitudes is more than 3,000 feet. It looks impossible, from below, that this can be true, but it is true, nevertheless.

While strolling about, we kept the run of the moon all the time, and we still kept an eye on her after we got back to the hotel portico. I had a theory that the gravitation of refraction, being subsidiary to atmospheric compensation, the refrangibility of the earth's surface would emphasize this effect in regions where great mountain ranges occur, and possibly so even-handedly impact the odic and idyllic forces together, the one upon the other, as to prevent the moon from rising higher than 12,200 feet above sea level. This daring theory had been received with frantic scorn by some of my fellow-scientists, and with an eager silence by others. Among the former I may mention Prof. H——y; and among the latter Prof. T——l. Such is professional jealousy; a scientist will never show any kindness for a theory which he did not start himself. There is no feeling of brotherhood among these people. Indeed, they always resent it when I call them brother. To show how far their ungenerosity can carry them, I will state that I offered to let Prof. H——y publish my great theory as his own discovery; I even begged him to do it; I even proposed to print it myself as his theory. Instead of thanking me, he said that if I tried to fasten that theory on him he would sue me for slander. I was going to offer it to Mr Darwin, whom I understood to be a man without prejudices, but it occurred to me that perhaps he would not be interested in it since it did not concern heraldry.

But I am glad, now, that I was forced to father my intrepid theory myself, for on the night of which I am writing, it was triumphantly justified and established. Mont Blanc is nearly 16,000 feet high; he hid the moon utterly; near him is a peak which is 12,216 feet high; the moon slid along behind the pinnacles, and when she approached that one I watched her with intense interest, for my reputation as a scientist must stand or fall by its decision. I cannot describe the emotions which surged like tidal waves through my breast when I saw the moon glide behind that lofty needle and pass it by without exposing more than two feet four inches of her upper rim above it! I was secure, then. I knew she could rise no higher, and I was right. She sailed behind all the peaks and never succeded in hoisting her disk above a single one of them.

While the moon was behind one of those sharp fingers, its shadow was flung athwart the vacant heavens—a long, slanting, clean-cut, dark ray—with a streaming and energetic suggestion of *force* about it, such as the ascending jet of water from a powerful fire engine affords. It was curious to see a good strong shadow of an earthly object cast upon so intangible a field as the atmosphere.

We went to bed, at last, and went quickly to sleep, but I woke up, after about three hours, with throbbing temples, and a head which was physically sore, outside and in. I was dazed, dreamy, wretched, seedy, unrefreshed. I recognized the occasion of all this; it was that torrent. In the mountain villages of Switzerland, and along the roads, one has always the roar of the torrent in his ears. He imagines it is music, and he thinks poetic things about it; he lies in his comfortable bed and is lulled to sleep by it. But by and by he begins to notice that his head is very sore—he cannot account for it; in solitudes where the profoundest silence reigns, he notices a sullen, distant, continuous roar in his ears, which

MUSIC OF SWITZERLAND.

is like what he would experience if he had sea shells pressed against them—he cannot account for it; he is drowsy and absent minded; there is no tenacity to his mind, he cannot keep hold of a thought and follow it out; if he sits down to write, his vocabulary is empty, no suitable words will come, he forgets what he started to do, and remains there, pen in hand, head tilted up, eyes closed, listening painfully to the muffled roar of a distant train in his ears; in his soundest sleep, the strain continues, he goes on listening, always listening, intently, anxiously, and wakes at last, harrassed, irritable, unrefreshed. He cannot manage to account for these things. Day after day he feels as if he had spent his nights in a sleeping car. It actually takes him weeks to find out that it is those persecuting torrents that have been making all the mischief. It is time for him to get out of Switzerland, then, for as soon as he has discovered the cause, the misery is magnified several fold.

The roar of the torrent is maddening, then, for his imagination is assisting; the physical pain it inflicts is exquisite. When he finds he is approaching one of those streams, his dread is so lively that he is disposed to fly the track and avoid the implacable foe.

Eight or nine months after the distress of the torrents had departed from me, the roar and thunder of the streets of Paris brought it all back again. I moved to the sixth story of the hotel to hunt for peace. About midnight the noises dulled away, and I was sinking to sleep, when I heard a new and curious sound; I listened: evidently some joyous lunatic was

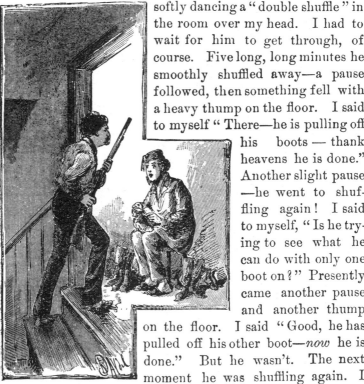

ONLY A MISTAKE.

softly dancing a "double shuffle" in the room over my head. I had to wait for him to get through, of course. Five long, long minutes he smoothly shuffled away—a pause followed, then something fell with a heavy thump on the floor. I said to myself "There—he is pulling off his boots — thank heavens he is done." Another slight pause —he went to shuffling again! I said to myself, "Is he trying to see what he can do with only one boot on?" Presently came another pause and another thump on the floor. I said "Good, he has pulled off his other boot—*now* he is done." But he wasn't. The next moment he was shuffling again. I said, "Confound him, he is at it in his slippers!" After a little came that same old pause, and right after it that thump on the floor once more. I said,

"Hang him, he had on *two* pair of boots!" For an hour that magician went on shuffling and pulling off boots till he had shed as many as twenty-five pair, and I was hovering on the verge of lunacy. I got my gun and stole up there. The fellow was in the midst of an acre of sprawling boots, and he had a boot in his hand, shuffling it—no I mean *polishing* it. The mystery was explained. He hadn't been dancing. He was the " Boots " of the hotel, and was attending to business.

CHAPTER XLIV.

AFTER breakfast, that next morning in Chamonix, we went out in the yard and watched the gangs of excursionizing tourists arriving and departing with their mules and guides and porters; then we took a look through the telescope at the snowy hump of Mont Blanc. It was brilliant with sunshine, and the vast smooth bulge seemed hardly five hundred yards away. With the naked eye we could dimly make out the house at the Pierre Pointue, which is located by the side of the great glacier, and is more than 3,000 feet above the level of the valley; but with the telescope we could see all its details. While I looked, a woman rode by the house on a mule, and I saw her with sharp distinctness; I could have described her dress. I saw her nod to the people of the house, and rein up her mule, and put her hand up to shield her eyes from the sun. I was not used to telescopes; in fact I never had looked through a good one before; it seemed incredible to me that this woman could be so far away. I was satisfied that I could see all these details with my naked eye; but when I tried it, that mule and those vivid people had wholly vanished, and the house itself was become small and vague. I tried the telescope again, and again everything was vivid. The strong black shadows of the mule and the woman were flung against the side of the house, and I saw the mule's silhouette wave its ears.

PREPARING FOR THE START.

The telescopulist,—or the telescopulariat,—I do not know which is right,—said a party were making the grand ascent, and would come in sight on the remote upper heights, presently ; so we waited to observe this performance.

Presently I had a superb idea. I wanted to stand with a party on the summit of Mont Blanc, merely to be able to say I had done it, and I believed the telescope could set me within seven feet of the uppermost man. The telescoper assured me that it could. I then asked him how much I owed him for as far as I had got? He said, one franc. I asked him how much it would cost me to make the entire ascent? Three francs. I at once determined to make the entire ascent. But first I inquired if there was any danger? He said no,—not by telescope; said he had taken a great many parties to the summit, and never lost a man. I asked what he would charge to let my agent go with me, together with such guides and porters as might be necessary? He said he would let Larris go for two francs; and that unless we were unusually timid, he should consider guides and porters unnecessary; it was not customary to take them, when going by telescope, for they were rather an incumbrance than a help. He said that the party now on the mountain were approaching the most difficult part, and if we hurried we should overtake them within ten minutes, and could then join them and have the benefit of their guides and porters without their knowledge, and without expense to us.

I then said we would start immediately. I believe I said it calmly, though I was conscious of a shudder and of a paling cheek, in view of the nature of the exploit I was so unreflectingly engaging in. But the old dare-devil spirit was upon me, and I said that as I had committed myself I would not back down; I would ascend Mont Blanc if it cost me my life. I told the man to slant his machine in the proper direction and let us be off.

Harris was afraid and did not want to go, but I heartened him up and said I would hold his hand all the way; so he gave his consent, though he trembled a little at first. I took a last pathetic look upon the pleasant summer scene about me, then boldly put my eye to the glass and prepared to mount among the grim glaciers and the everlasting snows.

We took our way carefully and cautiously across the great Glacier des Bossons, over yawning and terrific crevasses and amongst imposing crags and buttresses of ice which were fringed with icicles of gigantic proportions. The desert of ice that stretched far and wide about us was wild and desolate beyond description, and the perils which beset us were so great that at times I was minded to turn back. But I pulled my pluck together and pushed on.

We passed the glacier safely and began to mount the steeps beyond, with great celerity. When we were seven minutes out from the starting point, we reached an altitude where the scene took a new aspect; an apparently limitless continent of gleaming snow was tilted heavenward before our faces. As my eye followed that awful acclivity far away up into the remote skies, it seemed to me that all I had ever seen before of sublimity and magnitude was small and insignificant compared to this.

We rested a moment, and then began to mount with speed. Within three minutes we caught sight of the party ahead of us, and stopped to observe them. They were toiling up a long, slanting ridge of snow—twelve persons, roped together some fifteen feet apart, marching in single file, and strongly marked against the clear blue sky. One was a woman. We could see them lift their feet and put them down; we saw them swing their alpenstocks forward in unison, like so many pendulums, and then bear their weight upon them; we saw the lady wave her handkerchief. They dragged themselves upward in a worn and weary way, for they had been climbing steadily from the Grands Mulets, on the Glacier des Bossons, since three in the morning, and it was eleven, now. We saw them sink down in the snow and rest, and drink something from a bottle. After a while they moved on, and as they approached the final short dash of the home-stretch we closed up on them and joined them.

Presently we all stood together on the summit! What a view was spread out below! Away off under the north-western horizon rolled the silent billows of the Farnese Oberland, their snowy crests glinting softly in the subdued lights of distance; in the north rose the giant form of the Wobblehorn, draped from peak to shoulder in sable thunder-clouds; beyond him, to the right, stretched the grand pro-cessional summits of the Cisalpine Cordillera, drowned in a sensuous haze; to the east loomed the colossal masses of the Yodelhorn, the Fuddlehorn and the Dinnerhorn, their cloud-less summits flashing white and cold in the sun; beyond them shimmered the faint far line of the Ghauts of Jub-belpore and the Aiguilles des Alleghenies; in the south towered the smoking peak of Popocatapetl and the unap-

"WE ALL RAISED A TREMENDOUS SHOUT."

proachable altitudes of the peerless Scrabblehorn; in the west-south-west the stately range of the Himmalayas lay dreaming in a purple gloom; and thence all around the

30

curving horizon the eye roved over a troubled sea of sun-
kissed Alps, and noted, here and there, the noble proportions
and soaring domes of the Bottlehorn, and the Saddlehorn,
and the Shovelhorn, and the Powderhorn, all bathed in the
glory of noon and mottled with softly-gliding blots, the
shadows flung from drifting clouds.

Overcome by the scene, we all raised a triumphant, tremendous shout, in unison. A startled man at my elbow
said,—

"Confound you, what do you yell like that, for, right here
in the street?"

That brought me down to Chamonix, like a flirt. I gave
that man some spiritual advice and disposed of him, and
then paid the telescope man his full fee, and said that we
were charmed with the trip and would remain down, and
not re-ascend and require him to fetch us down by telescope. This pleased him very much, for of course we could
have stepped back to the summit and put him to the trouble
of bringing us home if we had wanted to.

I judged we could get diplomas, now, anyhow; so we
went after them, but the Chief Guide put us off, with one
pretext or another, during all the time we staid in Chamonix, and we ended by never getting them at all. So much
for his prejudice against people's nationality. However, we
worried him enough to make him remember us and our ascent
for some time. He even said, once, that he wished there
was a lunatic asylum in Chamonix. This shows that he
really had fears that we were going to drive him mad. It
was what we intended to do, but lack of time defeated it.

I cannot venture to advise the reader one way or the other,
as to ascending Mont Blanc. I say only this: if he is at all
timid, the enjoyments of the trip will hardly make up for
the hardships and sufferings he will have to endure. But if
he has good nerve, youth, health, and a bold, firm will, and
could leave his family comfortably provided for in case the
worst happened, he would find the ascent a wonderful

experience, and the view from the top a vision to dream about, and tell about, and recall with exultation all the days of his life.

While I do not advise such a person to attempt the ascent, I do not advise him against it. But if he elects to attempt it, let him be warily careful of two things: choose a calm clear day; and do not pay the telescope man in advance. There are dark stories of his getting advance-payers on the summit and then leaving them there to rot.

A frightful tragedy was once witnessed through the Chamonix telescopes. Think of questions and answers like these, on an inquest:

Coroner. You saw deceased lose his life?

Witness. I did.

C. Where was he, at the time?

W. Close to the summit of Mont Blanc.

C. Where were you?

W. In the main street of Chamonix.

C. What was the distance between you?

W. *A little over five miles,* as the bird flies.

This accident occurred in 1866, a year and a month after the disaster on the Matterhorn. Three adventurous English gentlemen,* of great experience in mountain climbing, made up their minds to ascend Mont Blanc without guides or porters. All endeavors to dissuade them from their project failed. Powerful telescopes are numerous in Chamonix. These huge brass tubes, mounted on their scaffoldings and pointing skyward from every choice vantage-ground, have the formidable look of artillery, and give the town the general aspect of getting ready to repel a charge of angels. The reader may easily believe that the telescopes had plenty of custom on that August morning in 1866, for everybody knew of the dangerous undertaking which was on foot, and all had fears that misfortune would result. All the morning the tubes

---

* Sir George Young and his brothers James and Albert.

remained directed toward the mountain heights, each with its anxious group around it; but the white deserts were vacant.

At last, toward eleven o'clock, the people who were looking through the telescopes cried out "There they are!"—and sure enough, far up, on the loftiest terraces of the Grand Plateau, the three pygmies appeared, climbing with remarkable vigor and spirit. They disappeared in the "Corridor," and were lost to sight during an hour. Then they reappeared, and were presently seen standing together upon the extreme summit of Mont Blanc. So far, all was well. They remained a few minutes on that highest point of land in Europe, a target for all the telescopes, and were then seen to begin the descent. Suddenly all three vanished. An instant after, they appeared again, *two thousand feet below!*

Evidently they had tripped and been shot down an almost perpendicular slope of ice to a point where it joined the border of the upper glacier. Naturally the distant witnesses supposed they were now looking upon three corpses; so they could hardly believe their eyes when they presently saw two of the men rise to their feet and bend over the third. During two hours and a half they watched the two busying themselves over the extended form of their brother, who seemed entirely inert. Chamonix's affairs stood still; everybody was in the street, all interest was centered upon what was going on upon that lofty and isolated stage five miles away. Finally the two,—one of them walking with great difficulty, —were seen to begin the descent, abandoning the third, who was no doubt lifeless. Their movements were followed, step by step, until they reached the "Corridor" and disappeared behind its ridge. Before they had had time to traverse the "Corridor" and reappear, twilight was come, and the power of the telescopes was at an end.

The survivors had a most perilous journey before them in the gathering darkness, for they must get down to the Grands Mulets before they would find a safe stopping place—a long and tedious descent, and perilous enough even in good day-light. The oldest guides expressed the opinion that they could not succeed; that all the chances were that they would lose their lives.

Yet those brave men did succeed. They reached the Grands Mulets in safety. Even the fearful shock which their nerves had sustained was not sufficient to overcome their coolness and courage. It would appear from the official account that

THE GRANDS MULETS.

they were threading their way down through those dangers from the closing in of twilight until 2 o'clock in the morning, or later, because the rescuing party from Chamonix reached the Grands Mulets about 3 in the morning and moved thence toward the scene of the disaster under the leadership of Sir George Young, " who had only just arrived."

After having been on his feet twenty-four hours, in the exhausting work of mountain-climbing, Sir George began the re-ascent at the head of the relief party of six guides, to recover the corpse of his brother. This was considered a new imprudence, as the number was too few for the service required. Another relief party presently arrived at the cabin on the Grands Mulets and quartered themselves there to await

CABIN ON THE GRANDS MULETS.

events. Ten hours after Sir George's departure toward the summit, this new relief were still scanning the snowy altitudes above them from their own high perch among the ice-deserts 10,000 feet above the level of the sea, but the whole forenoon had passed without a glimpse of any living thing appearing up there.

This was alarming. Half a dozen of their number set out, then, early in the afternoon, to seek and succor Sir George and his guides. The persons remaining at the cabin saw these disappear, and then ensued another distressing wait. Four hours passed, without tidings. Then at 5 o'clock another relief, consisting of three guides, set forward from the cabin. They carried food and cordials for the refreshment of their predecessors; they took lanterns with them, too; night was coming on, and to make matters worse, a fine, cold rain had begun to fall.

At the same hour that these three began their dangerous ascent, the official Guide-in-Chief of the Mont Blanc region undertook the dangerous descent to Chamonix, all alone, to get reinforcements. However, a couple of hours later, at 7 p. m., the anxious solicitude came to an end, and happily. A bugle note was heard, and a cluster of black specks was distinguishable against the snows of the upper heights. The watchers counted these specks eagerly—14,—nobody was missing. An hour and a half later they were all safe under the roof of the cabin. They had brought the corpse with them. Sir George Young tarried there but a few minutes, and then began the long and troublesome descent from the cabin to Chamonix. He probably reached there about 2 or 3 o'clock in the morning, after having been afoot among the rocks and glaciers during two days and two nights. His endurance was equal to his daring.

The cause of the unaccountable delay of Sir George and the relief parties among the heights where the disaster had happened was a thick fog—or, partly that and partly the slow and difficult work of conveying the dead body down the perilous steeps.

The corpse, upon being viewed at the inquest, showed no bruises, and it was sometime before the surgeons discovered that the neck was broken. One of the surviving brothers had sustained some unimportant injuries, but the other had suffered no hurt at all. How these men could fall 2,000 feet, almost perpendicularly, and live afterward, is a most strange and unaccountable thing.

A great many women have made the ascent of Mont Blanc. An English girl, Miss Stratton, conceived the daring idea, two or three years ago, of attempting the ascent in the middle of winter. She tried it—and she succeeded. Moreover, she froze two of her fingers on the way up, she fell in love with her guide on the summit, and she married him when she got to the bottom again. There is nothing in romance, in the way of a striking "situation," which can beat this love-scene in mid-heaven on an isolated ice-crest with the thermometer at zero and an Arctic gale blowing.

KEEPING WARM.

The first woman who ascended Mont Blanc was a girl aged 22— Mlle. Maria Paradis—1809. Nobody was with her but her sweetheart, and he was not a guide. The sex then took a rest for about 30 years, when a Mlle. d'Angeville made the ascent—1838. In Chamonix I picked up a rude old lithograph of that day which pictured her " in the act. However, I value it less as a work of art than as a fashion plate. Miss d'Angeville put on a pair of men's pantaloons to climb in, which was wise; but she cramped their utility by adding her petticoat, which was idiotic.

One of the mournfulest calamities which men's disposition to climb dangerous mountains has resulted in, happened on Mont Blanc in September, 1870. Mr. d'Arve tells the story briefly in his " Histoire du Mont Blanc." In the next chapter I will copy its chief features.

CHAPTER XLV.

ON the 5th of September, 1870, a caravan of eleven persons departed from Chamonix to make the ascent of Mont Blanc. Three of the party were tourists : Messrs. Randall and Bean, Americans, and Mr. George Corkindale, a Scotch gentleman ; there were three guides and five porters. The cabin on the Grands Mulets was reached that day ; the ascent was resumed early the next morning, Sept. 6. The day was fine and clear, and the movements of the party were observed through the telescopes of Chamonix ; at 2 o'clock in the afternoon they were seen to reach the summit. A few minutes later they were seen making the first steps of the descent ; then a cloud closed around them and hid them from view.

Eight hours passed, the cloud still remained, night came, no one had returned to the Grands Mulets. Sylvain Couttet, keeper of the cabin there, suspected a misfortune, and sent down to the valley for help. A detachment of guides went up, but by the time they had made the tedious trip and reached the cabin, a raging storm had set in. They had to wait ; nothing could be attempted in such a tempest.

The wild storm lasted *more than a week*, without ceasing ; but on the 17th, Couttet, with several guides, left the cabin and succeeded in making the ascent. In the snowy wastes near the summit they came upon five bodies, lying upon their sides in a reposeful attitude which suggested that possibly they had fallen asleep, there, while exhausted with fatigue and hunger, and benumbed with cold, and never knew when death stole upon them. Couttet moved a few steps further and discovered five more bodies. The eleventh corpse,—that of a porter,—was not found, although diligent search was made for it.

In the pocket of Mr. Bean, one of the Americans, was found a note-book in which had been penciled some sentences which admit us, in flesh and spirit, as it were, to the presence of these men during their last hours of life, and to the grisly horrors which their fading vision looked upon and their failing consciousness took cognizance of:

Tuesday, Sept. 6. I have made the ascent of Mont Blanc, with ten persons—eight guides, and Mr. Corkindale and Mr. Randall. We reached the summit at half past 2. Immediately after quitting it, we were enveloped in clouds of snow. We passed the night in a grotto hollowed in the snow, which afforded but poor shelter, and I was ill all night.

Sept. 7—*Morning.* The cold is excessive. The snow falls heavily and without interruption. The guides take no rest.

Evening. My Dear Hessie, we have been two days on Mont Blanc, in the midst of a terrible hurricane of snow, we have lost our way, and are in a hole scooped in the snow, at an altitude of 15,000 feet. I have no longer any hope of descending.

They had wandered around, and around, in that blinding snow storm, hopelessly lost, in a space only a hundred yards square ; and when cold and fatigue vanquished them at last, they scooped their cave and lay down there to die by inches, *unaware that five steps more would have brought them into the true path.* They were so near to life and safety as that, and did not suspect it. The thought of this gives the sharpest pang that the tragic story conveys.

The author of the " Histoire du Mont Blanc " introduces the closing sentences of Mr. Bean's pathetic record thus :

" Here the characters are large and unsteady ; the hand which traces them is become chilled and torpid ; but the

spirit survives, and the faith and resignation of the dying
man are expressed with a sublime simplicity."

Perhaps this note book will be found and sent to you. We have nothing
to eat, my feet are already frozen, and I am exhausted; I have strength to
write only a few words more. I have left means for C.'s education;
I know you will employ them wisely. I die with faith in God, and with
loving thoughts of you. Farewell to all. We shall meet again, in
Heaven.   *   *   *   I think of you always.

It is the way of the Alps to deliver death to their victims
with a merciful swiftness, but here the rule failed. These
men suffered the bitterest death that has been recorded in
the history of those mountains, freighted as that history is
with grisly tragedies.

CHAPTER XLVI.

MR. HARRIS and I took some guides and porters and ascended to the Hotel des Pyramides, which is perched on the high moraine which borders the Glacier des Bossons. The road led sharply up hill, all the way, through grass and flowers and woods, and was a pleasant walk, barring the fatigue of the climb.

From the hotel we could view the huge glacier at very close range. After a rest we followed down a path which had been made in the steep inner frontage of the moraine, and stepped upon the glacier itself. One of the shows of the place was a tunnel-like cavern, which had been hewn in the glacier. The proprietor of this tunnel took candles and conducted us into it. It was three or four feet wide and about six feet high. Its walls of pure and solid ice emitted a soft and rich blue light that produced a lovely effect, and suggested enchanted caves, and that sort of thing. When we had proceeded some yards and were entering darkness, we turned about and had a dainty sun-lit picture of distant woods and heights framed in the strong arch of the tunnel and seen through the tender blue radiance of the tunnel's atmosphere.

The cavern was nearly a hundred yards long, and when we reached its inner limit the proprietor stepped into a branch tunnel with his candles and left us buried in the bowels of the glacier, and in pitch darkness. We judged his purpose

was murder and robbery ; so we got out our matches and prepared to sell our lives as dearly as possible by setting the glacier on fire if the worst came to the worst—but we soon perceived that this man had changed his mind ; he began to sing,
in a deep, melodious voice, and woke some curious and pleasing echoes.   By and by he came back and pretended that that
was what he had gone behind there, for.   We believed as
much of that as we wanted to.

Thus our lives had been once more in imminent peril, but
by the exercise of the swift sagacity and cool courage which
had saved us so often, we had added another escape to the
long list.   The tourist should visit that ice-cavern, by all
means, for it is well worth the trouble ; but I would advise
him to go only with a strong and well armed force.   I do not
consider artillery necessary, yet it would not be unadvisable
to take it along, if convenient.   The journey, going and coming, is about three miles and a half, three of which are on lev-

el ground.   We made it in
less than a day, but I would
counsel the unpracticed,—if
not pressed for time,— to
a l l o w themselves t w o .
Nothing is gained in the
Alps b y   o v e r-exertion ;
nothing is gained by crowding two day's work into one
for the poor sake of being
able to boast of the exploit
afterward. It will be found
much better, in the long
run, to do the thing in two
days, and then subtract one

TAKE IT EASY.

of them from the narrative.   This saves fatigue, and does
not injure the narrative.   All the more thoughtful among
the Alpine tourists do this.

We now called upon the Guide-in-Chief, and asked for a

squadron of guides and porters for the ascent of the Montanvert. This idiot glared at us, and said,—

"You don't need guides and porters to go to the Montanvert."

"What do we need, then?"

"Such as *you?*—an ambulance!"

I was so stung by this brutal remark that I took my custom elsewhere.

Betimes, next morning, we had reached an altitude of
5,000 feet above the level of the sea. Here we camped and
breakfasted. There was a cabin there—the spot is called the
Caillet—and a spring of ice-cold water. On the door of the
cabin was a sign, in French, to the effect that "One may here
see a living chamois for 50 centimes." We did not invest;
what we wanted was to see a dead one.

A little after noon we ended the ascent and arrived at the
new hotel on the Montanvert, and had a view of six miles,
right up the great glacier, the famous Mer de Glace. At this
point it is like a sea whose deep swales and long, rolling
swells have been caught in mid-movement and frozen solid;
but further up it is broken up into wildly-tossing billows of
ice.

We descended a ticklish path in the steep side of the moraine, and invaded the glacier. There were tourists of both
sexes scattered far and wide over it, everywhere, and it had
the festive look of a skating rink.

The Empress Josephine came this far, once. She ascended the Montanvert in 1810—but not alone; a small army of
men preceded her to clear the path—and carpet it, perhaps,
—and she followed, under the protection of *sixty-eight* guides.

Her successor visited Chamonix later, but in far different
style. It was seven weeks after the first fall of the Empire,
and poor Marie Louise, ex-Empress, was a fugitive. She
came at night, and in a storm, with only two attendants, and
stood before a peasant's hut, tired, bedraggled, soaked with
rain, "the red print of her lost crown still girdling her brow,"

THE MER DE GLACE (MONT BLANC.)

and implored admittance—and was refused! A few days before, the adulations and applauses of a nation were sounding in her ears, and now she was come to this!

We crossed the Mer de Glace in safety, but we had misgivings. The crevasses in the ice yawned deep and blue and mysterious, and it made one nervous to traverse them. The huge round waves of ice were slippery and difficult to climb, and the chances of tripping and sliding down them and darting into a crevasse were too many to be comfortable.

In the bottom of a deep swale between two of the biggest of the ice-waves, we found a fraud who pretended to be cut-

TAKING TOLL.

ting steps to insure the safety of tourists. He was "soldiering" when we came upon him, but he hopped up and chipped out a couple of steps about big enough for a cat, and charged us a franc or two for it. Then he sat down again, to doze till the next party should come along. He had collected black mail from two or three hundred people already, that day, but had not chipped out ice enough to impair the glacier perceptibly. I have heard of a good many soft sinecures, but it seems to me that keeping toll-bridge on a glacier is the softest one I have encountered yet.

That was a blazing hot day, and it brought a persistent and persecuting thirst with it. What an unspeakable luxury it was to slake that thirst with the pure and limpid ice-water of the glacier! Down the sides of every great rib of ice poured limpid rills in gutters carved by their own attrition; better still, wherever a rock had lain, there was now a bowl-shaped hole, with smooth white sides and bottom of ice, and this bowl was brimming with water of such absolute clearness that the careless observer would not see it at all, but would think the bowl was empty. These fountains had such an alluring look that I often stretched myself out when I was not thirsty and dipped my face in and drank till my teeth ached. Everywhere among the Swiss mountains we had at hand the blessing—not to be found in Europe *except* in the mountains—of water capable of quenching thirst. Everywhere in the Swiss highlands brilliant little rills of exquisitely cold water went dancing along by the roadsides, and my comrade and I were always drinking and always delivering our deep gratitude.

But in Europe everywhere except in the mountains, the water is flat and insipid beyond the power of words to describe. It is served lukewarm; but no matter, ice could not help it; it is incurably flat, incurably insipid. It is only good to wash with; I wonder it doesn't occur to the average inhabitant to try it for that. In Europe the people say contemptuously, "Nobody drinks water here." Indeed they have a sound and sufficient reason. In many places they even have what may be called prohibitory reasons. In Paris and Munich, for instance, they say, "Don't drink the water, it is simply poison."

Either America is healthier than Europe, notwithstanding her "deadly" indulgence in ice water, or she does not keep the run of her death-rate as sharply as Europe does. I think we do keep up the death-statistics accurately: and if we do, our cities are healthier than the cities of Europe. Every month the German government tabulates the death-rate of the world and publishes it. I scrap-booked these reports during several months, and it was curious to see how regular and persistently each city repeated its same death-rate month after month. The tables might as well have been stereotyped, they varied so little. These tables were based upon weekly reports showing the average of deaths in each 1,000 of population for a year. Munich was always present with her 33 deaths in each 1,000 of her population (yearly average,) Chicago was as constant with her 15 or 17, Dublin with her 48—and so on.

Only a few American cities appear in these tables, but they are scattered so widely over the country that they furnish a good general average of *city* health in the United States; and I think it will be granted that our towns and villages are healthier than our cities

Here is the average of the only American cities reported in the German tables:

Chicago, deaths in 1,000 of population annually, 16; Philadelphia, 18; St. Louis, 18; San Francisco, 19; New York, (the Dublin of America,) 23.

See how the figures jump up, as soon as one arrives at the transatlantic list:

Paris, 27; Glasgow, 27; London, 28; Vienna, 28; Augsburg, 28; Braunschweig, 28; Königsberg, 29; Colonge, 29; Dresden, 29; Hamburg, 29; Berlin, 30; Bombay, 30; Warsaw, 31; Breslau, 31; Odessa, 32; Munich, 33; Strasburg, 33; Pesth, 35; Cassel, 35; Lisbon, 36; Liverpool, 36; Prague, 37; Madras, 37; Bucharest, 39; St. Petersburg, 40; Triest, 40; Alexandria, (Egypt,) 43; Dublin, 48; Calcutta, 55.

Edinburg is as healthy as New York—23; but there is no *city* in the entire list which is healthier, except Frankfort-on-the-Main—20. But Frankfort is not as healthy as Chicago, San Francisco, St. Louis, or Philadelphia.

Perhaps a strict average of the world might develop the fact that where 1 in 1,000 of America's population dies, 2 in 1,000 of the other populations of the earth succumb.

I do not like to make insinuations, but I do think the above

31

statistics darkly suggest that these people over here drink this detestable water " on the sly."

We climbed the moraine on the opposite side of the glacier, and then crept along its sharp ridge a hundred yards or

so, in pretty constant danger of a tumble to the glacier below. The fall would have been only 100 feet, but it would have closed me out as effectually as 1,000, therefore I respected the distance accordingly, and was glad when the trip was done. A moraine is an ugly thing to assault head-first. At a distance it looks like an endless grave of fine sand, accurately shaped and nicely smoothed; but close by, it is found to be made mainly of rough boulders of all sizes, from that of a man's head to that of a cottage.

By and by we came to the *Mauvais Pas,*

A DESCENDING TOURIST.

or, the Villainous Road, to translate it feelingly. It was a break-neck path around the face of a precipice forty or fifty feet high, and nothing to hang on to but some iron railings. I got along, slowly, safely, and uncomfortably, and finally reached the middle. My hopes began to rise a little, but they were quickly blighted ; for there I met a hog—a long-nosed, bristly fellow, that held up his snout and worked his nostrils at me inquiringly. A hog on a pleasure excursion in Switzerland—think of it. It is striking and unusual; a body might write a poem about it. He could not retreat, if he had been disposed to do it. It would have been foolish to stand upon our dignity in a place where there was hardly room to stand upon our feet, so we did nothing of the sort. There were twenty or thirty ladies and gentlemen behind us; we all turned about and went back, and the hog followed behind. The creature did not seem set up by what he had done; he had probably done it before.

We reached the restaurant on the height called the Chapeau at 4 in the afternoon. It was a memento-factory, and the stock was large, cheap and varied. I bought the usual paper-cutter to remember the place by, and had Mont Blanc, the Mauvais Pas, and the rest of the region branded on my alpenstock; then we descended to the valley and walked

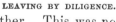
LEAVING BY DILIGENCE.

home without being tied together. This was not dangerous, for the valley was five miles wide, and quite level.

We reached the hotel before 9 o'clock. Next morning we left for Geneva on top of the diligence, under shelter of a gay awning. If I remember rightly, there were more than twenty people up there. It was so high that the ascent was made by ladder. The huge vehicle was full everywhere, inside and out. Five other diligences left at the same time, all full. We had engaged our seats two days beforehand, to make sure, and paid the regulation price, five dollars each; but the rest of the company were wiser; they had trusted Baedeker, and waited; consequently some of them got their seats for one or two dollars. Baedeker knows all about hotels, railway and diligence companies, and speaks his mind freely. He is a trustworthy friend of the traveler.

We never saw Mont Blanc at his best until we were many miles away; then he lifted his majestic proportions high into the heavens, all white and cold and solemn, and made the rest of the world seem little and plebeian, and cheap and trivial.

As he passed out of sight at last, an old Englishman settled himself in his seat and said,—

"Well, I am satisfied, I have seen the principal features of Swiss scenery—Mont Blanc and the goitre—now for home!"

CHAPTER XLVII.

WE spent a few pleasant restful days at Geneva, that delightful city where accurate time-pieces are made for all the rest of the world, but whose own clocks never give the correct time of day by any accident.

Geneva is filled with pretty little shops, and the shops are filled with the most enticing gimcrackery, but if one enters one of these places he is at once pounced upon, and followed up, and so persecuted to buy this, that, and the other thing, that he is very grateful to get out again, and is not at all apt to repeat his experiment. The shopkeepers of the smaller sort, in Geneva, are as troublesome and persistent as are the salesmen of that monster hive in Paris, the Grands Magasins du Louvre—an establishment where ill-mannered pestering, pursuing and insistance have been reduced to a science.

In Geneva, prices in the smaller shops are very elastic— that is another bad feature. I was looking in at a window at a very pretty string of beads, suitable for a child. I was only admiring them; I had no use for them; I hardly ever wear beads. The shopwoman came out and offered them to me for 35 francs. I said it was cheap, but I did not need them.

"Ah, but monsieur, they are so beautiful!"

I confessed it, but said they were not suitable for one of my age and simplicity of character. She darted in and brought them out and tried to force them into my hands, saying,—

"Ah, but only see how lovely they are! Surely monsieur will take them; monsieur shall have them for 30 francs. There, I have said it—it is a loss, but one must live."

I dropped my hands, and tried to move her to respect my unprotected situation. But no, she dangled the beads in the sun before my face, exclaiming, "Ah, monsieur *cannot* resist them!" She hung them on my coat button, folded her hands resignedly, and said, "Gone,—and for 30 francs, the lovely things—it is incredible!—but the good God will sanctify the sacrifice to me."

I removed them gently, returned them, and walked away,

HIGH PRESSURE.

shaking my head and smiling a smile of silly embarrassment while the passers-by halted to observe. The woman leaned out of her door, shook the beads, and screamed after me,—

"Monsieur shall have them for 28!"

I shook my head.

"Twenty-seven! It is a cruel loss, it is ruin—but take them, only take them."

I still retreated, still wagging my head.

"Mon Dieu, they shall even go for 26! There, I have said it. Come!"

I wagged another negative. A nurse and a little English girl had been near me, and were following me, now. The shopwoman ran to the nurse, thrust the beads into her hands, and said,—

"Monsieur shall have them for 25! Take them to the hotel—he shall send me the money to-morrow—next day—when he likes." Then to the child: "When thy father sends me the money, come thou also, my angel, and thou shalt have something oh so pretty!"

I was thus providentially saved. The nurse refused the beads squarely and firmly, and that ended the matter.

The "sights" of Geneva are not numerous. I made one attempt to hunt up the houses once inhabited by those two disagreeable people, Rousseau and Calvin, but had no success. Then I concluded to go home. I found it was easier to propose to do that than to do it; for that town is a bewildering place. I got lost in a tangle of narrow and crooked streets, and staid lost for an hour or two. Finally I found a street which looked somewhat familiar, and said to myself, "Now I am at home, I judge." But I was wrong; this was "*Hell* street." Presently I found another place which had a familiar look, and said to myself, "Now I am at home, sure." It was another error. This was "*Purgatory* street." After a little I said, "*Now* I've got to the right place, anyway....... no, this is '*Paradise* street;' I'm further from home than I was in the beginning." Those were queer names—Calvin was the author of them, likely. "Hell" and "Purgatory" fitted those two streets like a glove, but the "Paradise" appeared to be sarcastic.

I came out on the lake front, at last, and then I knew where

I was. I was walking along before the glittering jewelry shops when I saw a curious performance. A lady passed by, and a trim dandy lounged across the walk in such an apparently carefully-timed way as to bring himself exactly in front of her when she got to him; he made no offer to step out of the way; he did not apologize; he did not even notice her. She had to stop still and let him lounge by.

NO APOLOGY.

I wondered if he had done that piece of brutality purposely. He strolled to a chair and seated himself at a small table; two or three other males were sitting at similar tables sipping sweetened water. I waited; presently a youth came by, and this fellow got up and served him the same trick. Still, it did not

NONE ASKED.

seem possible that any one could do such a thing deliberately. To satisfy my curiosity I went around the block, and sure enough, as I approached, at a good round speed, he got up and lounged lazily across my path, fouling my course exactly at the right moment to receive all my weight. This proved that his previous performances had not been accidental, but intentional.

I saw that dandy's curious game played afterwards, in Paris, but not for amusement; not with a motive of any sort, indeed, but simply from a selfish indifference to other people's comfort and rights. One does not see it as frequently in Paris as he might expect to, for there the law says, in effect, "it is the business of the weak to get out of the way of the strong." We fine a cabman if he runs over a citizen; Paris fines the citizen for being run over. At least so everybody says—but I saw something which caused me to doubt; I saw a horseman run over an old woman one day,—the police arrested him and took him away. That looked as if they meant to punish him.

It will not do for me to find merit in American manners —for are they not the standing butt for the jests of critical and polished Europe? Still I must venture to claim one little matter of superiority in our manners: a lady may traverse our streets all day, going and coming as she chooses, and she will never be molested by any man; but if a lady, unattended, walks abroad in the streets of London, even at noonday, she will be pretty likely to be accosted and insulted— and not by drunken sailors, but by men who carry the look and wear the dress of gentlemen. It is maintained that these people are not gentlemen, but are a lower sort, disguised as gentlemen. The case of Colonel Valentine Baker obstructs that argument, for a man cannot become an officer in the British army except he hold the rank of gentleman. This person, finding himself alone in a railway compartment with an unprotected girl,—but it is an atrocious story, and doubtless the reader remembers it well enough. London must have been more or less accustomed to Bakers, and the ways of Bakers, else London would have been offended, and excited. Baker was "imprisoned"—in a parlor; and he could not have been more visited, or more overwhelmed with attentions, if he had committed six murders and then—while the gallows was preparing—"got religion"—after the manner of the holy Charles Peace, of saintly memory. Arkansaw—it seems a little indelicate to be trumpeting forth our own superiorities, and comparisons are always odious, but still—Arkansaw would certainly have hanged Baker. I do not say she would have tried him first, but she would have hanged him, anyway.

Even the most degraded woman can walk our streets unmolested, her sex and her weakness being her sufficient protection. She will encounter less polish than she would in the old world, but she will run across enough humanity to make up for it.

The music of a donkey awoke us early in the morning, and we rose up and made ready for a pretty formidable walk— to Italy; but the road was so level that we took the train. We lost a good deal of time by this, but it was no matter, we were not in a hurry. We were four hours going to Chambery. The Swiss trains go upwards of three miles an hour, in places, but they are quite safe.

That aged French town of Chambery was as quaint and crooked as Heilbronn. A drowsy reposeful quiet reigned in the back streets which made strolling through them very pleasant, barring the almost unbearable heat of the sun. In one of these streets which was eight feet wide, gracefully curved, and

A LIVELY STREET.

built up with small antiquated houses, I saw three fat hogs lying asleep, and a boy (also asleep), taking care of them. From queer old-fashioned windows along the curve, projected boxes of bright flowers, and over the edge of one of these boxes hung the head and shoulders of a cat—asleep. The five sleeping creatures were the only living things visible in that street. There was not a sound; absolute stillness

prevailed. It was Sunday; one is not used to such dreamy
Sundays on the Continent. In our part of the town it
was different that night. A regiment of brown and battered
soldiers had arrived home from Algiers, and I judged they
got thirsty on the way. They sang and drank till dawn, in
the pleasant open air.

We left for Turin at 10 the next morning by a railway

HAVING HER FULL RIGHTS.

which was profusely decorated with tunnels. We forgot to
take a lantern along, consequently we missed all the scenery.
Our compartment was full. A ponderous tow-headed Swiss
woman who put on many fine-lady airs, but was evidently
more used to washing linen than wearing it, sat in a corner
seat and put her legs across into the opposite one, propping
them intermediately with her up-ended valise. In the seat
thus pirated, sat two Americans, greatly incommoded by that
woman's majestic coffin-clad feet. One of them begged her,

politely, to remove them. She opened her wide eyes and
gave him a stare, but answered nothing. By and by he preferred his request again, with great respectfulness. She said,
in good English, and in a deeply offended tone, that she had
paid her passage and was not going to be bullied out of her
"rights" by ill-bred foreigners, even if she *was* alone and
unprotected.

"But I have rights, also, madam. My ticket entitles me
to a seat, but you are occupying half of it."

"I will not talk with you, sir. What right have you to
speak to me? I do not know you. One would know you
came from a land where there are no gentlemen. No *gentleman* would treat a lady as you have treated me."

"I come from a region where a lady would hardly give
me the same provocation."

"You have insulted me, sir! You have intimated that I
am not a lady—and I hope I am *not* one, after the pattern of
your country."

"I beg that you will give yourself no alarm on that head,
madam; but at the same time I must insist—always respectfully—that you let me have my seat."

Here the fragile laundress burst into tears and sobs.

"I never was so insulted before! Never, never! It is
shameful, it is brutal, it is base, to bully and abuse an unprotected lady who has lost the use of her limbs and cannot put
her feet to the floor without agony!"

"Good heavens, madam, why didn't you say that at first!
I offer a thousand pardons. And I offer them most sincerely.
I did not know—I *could* not know—that anything was the
matter. You are most welcome to the seat, and would have
been from the first if I had only known. I am truly sorry
it all happened, I do assure you."

But he couldn't get a word of forgiveness out of her. She
simply sobbed and snuffled in a subdued but wholly unap-
peasable way for two long hours, meantime crowding the man
more than ever with her undertaker-furniture and paying no

sort of attention to his frequent and humble little efforts to do something for her comfort. Then the train halted at the Italian line and she hopped up and marched out of the car with as firm a leg as any washerwoman of all her tribe! And how sick I was, to see how she had fooled me.

HOW SHE FOOLED US.

Turin is a very fine city. In the matter of roominess it transcends anything that was ever dreamed of before, I fancy. It sits in the midst of a vast dead-level, and one is obliged to imagine that land may be had for the asking, and no taxes to pay, so lavishly do they use it. The streets are extravagantly wide, the paved squares are prodigious, the houses are huge and handsome, and compacted into uniform blocks that stretch away as straight as an arrow, into the distance. The sidewalks are about as wide as ordinary European *streets*, and are covered over with a double arcade supported on great stone piers or columns. One walks from one end to the other of these spacious streets, under shelter all the time, and all his course is lined with the prettiest of shops and the most inviting dining-houses.

There is a wide and lengthy court, glittering with the most wickedly-enticing shops, which is roofed with glass, high aloft over head, and paved with soft-toned marbles laid in graceful figures; and at night when this place is brilliant with gas and populous with a sauntering and chatting and laughing multitude of pleasure-seekers, it is a spectacle worth seeing.

Everything is on a large scale; the public buildings, for instance—and they are architecturally imposing, too, as well as large. The big squares have big bronze monuments in them. At the hotel they gave us rooms that were alarming, for size, and a parlor to match. It was well the weather required no fire in the parlor, for I think one might as well have tried to warm a park. The place would have a warm look, though, in any weather, for the window curtains were of red silk damask, and the walls were covered with the same fire-hued goods—so, also, were the four sofas and the brigade of chairs. The furniture, the ornaments, the chandeliers, the carpets, were all new and bright and costly. We did not need a parlor, at all, but they said it belonged to the two bedrooms and we might use it if we chose. Since it was to cost nothing, we were not averse from using it, of course.

Turin must surely read a good deal, for it has more book stores to the square rod than any other town I know of. And it has its own share of military folk. The Italian officers' uniforms are very much the most beautiful I have ever seen; and as a general thing the men in them were as handsome as the clothes. They were not large men, but they had fine forms, fine features, rich olive complexions and lustrous black eyes.

For several weeks I had been culling all the information I could about Italy, from tourists. The tourists were all agreed upon one thing—one must expect to be cheated at every turn by the Italians. I took an evening walk in Turin, and presently came across a little Punch and Judy show in one of the great squares. Twelve or fifteen people constituted the audience. This minature theatre was not much bigger than a man's coffin stood on end; the upper part was open and displayed a tinseled parlor—a good-sized handkerchief would have answered for a drop-curtain; the footlights consisted of a couple of candle-ends an inch long; various manikins the size of dolls appeared on the stage and made long speeches at each other, gesticulating a good deal, and they generally had a fight before they got through. They were worked by strings from above, and the illusion was not perfect, for one saw not only the strings but the brawny hand that manipulated them—and the actors and actresses all talked in the same voice, too. The audience stood in front of the theatre, and seemed to enjoy the performance heartily.

When the play was done, a youth in his shirt-sleeves started around with a small copper saucer to make a collection. I did not know how much to put in, but thought I would be guided by my predecessors. Unluckily I only had two of these and they did not help me much because they did not put in anything. I had no Italian money, so I put in a small Swiss coin worth about ten cents. The youth finished his collection-trip and emptied the result on the stage; he had some very animated talk with the concealed manager, then he came working his way through the little crowd—seeking me, I thought. I had a mind to slip away, but concluded I wouldn't; I would stand my ground, and confront the villainy, whatever it was. The youth stood before me and held up that Swiss coin, sure enough, and said something. I did not understand him, but I judged he was requiring Italian money of me. The crowd gathered close, to listen. I was irritated, and said,—in English, of course,—

"I know it's Swiss, but you'll take that or none. I haven't any other."

He tried to put the coin in my hand, and spoke again. I drew my hand away, and said,—

"*No*, sir. I know all about you people. You can't play any of your fraudful tricks on me. If there is a discount on that coin, I am sorry, but I am not going to make it good. I noticed that some of the audience didn't pay you anything at all. You let them go, without a word, but you come after me because you think I'm a stranger and will put up with an extortion rather than have a scene. But you are mistaken this time—you'll take that Swiss money or none."

The youth stood there with the coin in his fingers nonplussed, and bewildered; of course he had not understood a word. An English-speaking Italian spoke up, now, and said,—

"You are misunderstanding the boy. He does not mean any harm. He did not suppose you gave him so much money purposely, so he hurried back to return you the coin lest you might get away before you discovered your mistake.

"YOU'LL TAKE THAT OR NONE."

Take it, and give him a penny—that will make everything smooth again."

I probably blushed, then, for there was occasion. Through the interpreter I begged the boy's pardon, but I nobly refused to take back the ten cents. I said I was accustomed to squandering large sums in that way—it was the kind of person I was. Then I retired to make a note to the effect that in Italy, persons connected with the drama do not cheat.

The episode with the showman reminds me of a dark chapter in my history. I once robbed an aged and blind beggar-woman of four dollars—in a church. It happened in this way. When I was out with the Innocents Abroad, the ship stopped in the Russian port of Odessa, and I went ashore, with others, to view the town. I got separated from the rest, and wandered about, alone, until late in the afternoon, when I entered a Greek church to see what it was like. When I was ready to leave, I observed two wrinkled old women standing stiffly upright against the inner wall, near the door, with their brown palms open to receive alms. I contributed to the nearer one, and passed out. I had gone fifty yards, perhaps, when it occurred to me that I must remain ashore all night, as I had heard that the ship's business would carry her away at 4 o'clock and keep her away until morning. It was a little after 4, now. I had come ashore with only two pieces of money, both about the same size, but differing largely in value—one was a French gold piece worth four dollars, the other a Turkish coin worth two cents and a half. With a sudden and horrified misgiving, I put my hand in my pocket, now, and, sure enough, I fetched out that Turkish penny!

Here was a situation. A hotel would require pay in advance—I must walk the streets all night, and perhaps be arrested as a suspicious character. There was but one way out of the difficulty—I flew back to the church, and softly entered. There stood the old woman yet, and in the palm of the nearest one still lay my gold piece. I was grateful. I crept close, feeling unspeakably mean; I got my Turkish penny ready, and was extending a trembling hand to make the nefarious exchange, when I heard a cough behind me. I jumped back as if I had been accused, and stood quaking while a worshiper entered and passed up the aisle.

I was there a year trying to steal that money; that is, it seemed a year, though of course it must have been much less. The worshipers went and came; there were hardly ever three in the church at once, but there was always one or more.

32

Every time I tried to commit my crime somebody came in or somebody started out, and I was prevented; but at last my opportunity came; for one moment there was nobody in the church but the two beggar-women and me. I whipped the gold piece out of the poor old pauper's palm and dropped my Turkish penny in its place. Poor old thing, she murmured her thanks—they smote me to the heart. Then I sped away in a guilty hurry, and even when I was a mile from the church I was still glancing back, every moment, to see if I was being pursued.

That experience has been of priceless value and benefit to me; for I resolved then, that as long as I lived I would never again rob a blind beggar-woman in a church; and I have always kept my word. The most permanent lessons in morals are those which come, not of booky teaching, but of experience.

CHAPTER XLVIII.

IN Milan we spent most of our time in the vast and beautiful Arcade or Gallery, or whatever it is called. Blocks of tall new buildings of the most sumptuous sort, rich with decoration and graced with statues, the streets between these blocks roofed over with glass at a great height, the pavements all of smooth and variegated marble, arranged in tasteful patterns—little tables all over these marble streets, people sitting at them, eating, drinking, or smoking—crowds of other people strolling by—such is the Arcade. I should like to live in it all the time. The windows of the sumptuous restaurants stand open, and one breakfasts there and enjoys the passing show.

We wandered all over the town, enjoying whatever was going on in the streets. We took one omnibus ride, and as I did not speak Italian and could not ask the price, I held out some copper coins to the conductor, and he took two. Then he went and got his tariff-card and showed me that he had taken only the right sum. So I made a note—Italian omnibus conductors do not cheat.

Near the Cathedral I saw another instance of probity. An old man was peddling dolls and toy fans. Two small American children bought fans, and one gave the old man a franc and three copper coins, and both started away; but they were called back, and the franc and one of the coppers were restored to them. Hence it is plain that in Italy, parties connected with the drama and with the omnibus and

toy interests do not cheat.

The stocks of goods in the shops were not extensive, generally. In the vestibule of what seemed to be a clothing store, we saw eight or ten wooden dummies grouped together, clothed in

DISHONEST ITALY.

woolen business-suits and each suit marked with its price. One suit was marked 45 francs—nine dollars. Harris stepped in and said he wanted a suit like that. Nothing easier:

the old merchant dragged in the dummy, brushed him off with a broom, stripped him, and shipped the clothes to the hotel. He said he did not keep two suits of the same kind in stock, but manufactured a second when it was needed to re-clothe the dummy.

In another quarter we found six Italians engaged in a violent quarrel. They danced fiercely about, gesticulating with their heads, their arms, their legs, their whole bodies; they would rush forward occasionally

STOCK IN TRADE.

in a sudden access of passion and shake their fists in each

other's very faces. We lost half an hour there, waiting to help cord up the dead, but th‥ finally embraced each other affectionately, and the trouble was all over. The episode was interesting, but we could not have afforded all that time to it if we had known nothing was going to come of it but a reconciliation. Note made—in Italy, people who quarrel cheat the spectator.

We had another disappointment, afterward. We approached a deeply interested crowd, and in the midst of it found a fellow wildly chattering and gesticulating over a box on the ground which was covered with a piece of old blanket. Every little while he would bend down and take hold of the edge of the blanket with the extreme tips of his fingers, as if to show there was no deception—chattering away all the while,—but always, just as I was expecting to see a wonderful feat of legerdemain, he would let go the blanket and rise to explain further. However, at last he uncovered the box and got out a spoon with a liquid in it, and held it fair and frankly around, for people to see that it was all right and he was taking no advantage—his chatter became more excited than ever. I supposed he was going to set fire to the liquid and swallow it, so I was greatly wrought up and interested. I got a cent ready in one hand and a florin in the other, intending to give him the former if he survived and the latter if he killed himself—for his loss would be my gain in a literary way, and I was willing to pay a fair price for the item—but this impostor ended his intensely moving performance by simply adding some powder to the liquid and polishing the spoon! Then he held it aloft, and he could not have shown a wilder exultation if he had achieved an immortal miracle. The crowd applauded in a gratified way, and it seemed to me that history speaks the truth when it says these children of the south are easily entertained.

We spent an impressive hour in the noble cathedral, where long shafts of tinted light were cleaving through the solemn dimness from the lofty windows and falling on a pillar here, a picture there, and a kneeling worshiper yonder. The organ was muttering, censers were swinging, candles were glinting on the distant altar, and robed priests were filing silently past them; the scene was one to sweep all frivolous thoughts away and steep the soul in a holy calm.   A trim

STYLE.

young American lady paused a yard or two from me, fixed her eyes on the mellow sparks flecking the far-off altar, bent her head reverently a moment, then straightened up, kicked her train into the air with her heel, caught it deftly in her hand, and marched briskly out.

We visited the picture galleries and the other regulation "sights" of Milan—not because I wanted to write about them again, but to see if I had learned anything in twelve years. I afterwards visited the great galleries of Rome and Florence for the same purpose. I found I had learned one thing. When I wrote about the Old Masters before, I said the copies were better than the originals. That was a mistake of large dimensions.   The Old Masters were still unpleasing to me, but they were truly divine contrasted with the copies. The copy is to the original as the pallid, smart, inane new wax work-group is to the vigorous, earnest, dignified group of living men and women whom it professes to duplicate. There is a mellow richness, a subdued color, in the old pictures,

which is to the eye what muffled and mellowed sound is to
the ear. That is the merit which is most loudly praised in
the old picture, and is the one which the copy most conspicuously lacks, and which the copyist must not hope to
compass. It was generally conceded by the artists with
whom I talked, that that subdued splendor, that mellow
richness, is imparted to the picture by *age*. Then why
should we worship the Old Master for it, who didn't impart it, instead of worshiping Old Time, who did? Perhaps
the picture was a clanging bell, until Time muffled it and
sweetened it.

In conversation with an artist in Venice, I asked,—

"What is it that people see in the Old Masters? I have
been in the Dogés' Palace and I saw several acres of very
bad drawing, very bad perspective, and very incorrect proportions. Paul Veronese's dogs do not resemble dogs ; all

SPECIMENS FROM OLD MASTERS.

the horses look like bladders on legs; one man had a *right*
leg on the left side of his body ; in the large picture where
the Emperor (Barbarossa?) is prostrate before the Pope,
there are three men in the foreground who are over thirty
feet high, if one may judge by the size of a kneeling little
boy in the centre of the foreground ; and according to the
same scale, the Pope is 7 feet high and the Doge is a shriv-
eled dwarf of 4 feet."

The artist said,—

" Yes, the Old Masters often drew badly ; they did not
care much for truth and exactness in minor details; but
after all, in spite of bad drawing, bad perspective, bad proportions, and a choice of subjects which no longer appeal to
people as strongly as they did three hundred years ago,
there is a *something* about their pictures which is divine—a
something which is above and beyond the art of any epoch
since—a something which would be the despair of artists but
that they never hope or expect to attain it, and therefore do
not worry about it."

That is what he said—and he said what he believed ; and
not only believed, but felt.

Reasoning,—especially reasoning without technical knowledge,—must be put aside, in cases of this kind.   It cannot
assist the inquirer.   It will lead him, in the most logical
progression, to what, in the eyes of artists, would be a most
illogical conclusion.   Thus : bad drawing, bad proportion, bad
perspective, indifference to truthful detail, color which gets its
merit from time, and not from the artist—these things constitute the Old Master ; conclusion, the Old Master was a bad
painter, the Old Master was not an Old Master at all, but an
Old Apprentice.   Your friend the artist will grant your
premises, but deny your conclusion ; he will maintain that
notwithstanding this formidable list of confessed defects,
there is still a something that is divine and unapproachable
about the Old Master, and that there is no arguing the fact
away by any system of reasoning whatever.

I can believe that.   There are women who have an indefinable charm in their faces which makes them beautiful to
their intimates ; but a cold stranger who tried to reason the
matter out and find this beauty would fail.   He would say
of one of these women : This chin is too short; this nose is
too long, this forehead is too high, this hair is too red, this
complexion is too pallid, the perspective of the entire composition is incorrect ; conclusion, the woman is not beautiful.

But her nearest friend might say, and say truly, "Your premises are right, your logic is faultless, but your conclusion is wrong, nevertheless; she is an Old Master—she is beau-

AN OLD MASTER.

tiful, but only to such as know her; it is a beauty which cannot be formulated, but it is there, just the same."

I found more pleasure in contemplating the Old Masters this time than I did when I was in Europe in former years, but still it was a calm pleasure; there was nothing over-heated about it. When I was in Venice before, I think I found no picture which stirred me much, but this time there were two which enticed me to the Doge's palace day after day, and kept me there hours at a time. One of these was Tintoretto's three-acre picture in the Great Council Chamber. When I saw it twelve years ago I was not strongly attracted to it—the guide told me it was an insurrection in heaven—but this was an error.

The movement of this great work is very fine. There are ten thousand figures, and they are all doing something. There is a wonderful "go" to the whole composition. Some of the figures are diving headlong downward, with clasped hands, others are swimming through the cloud-shoals,—some on their faces, some on their backs—great processions of bishops, martyrs and angels are pouring swiftly centerwards from various outlying directions—everywhere is enthusiastic joy, there is rushing movement everywhere.   There are fifteen or twenty figures scattered here and there, with books, but they cannot keep their attention on their reading—they offer

the books to others, but no one wishes to read, now.   The Lion of St. Mark is there with his book; St. Mark is there with his pen uplifted; he and the Lion are looking each other earnestly in the face, disputing about the way to spell a word—the Lion looks up in wrapt admiration while St. Mark spells. This is wonderfully interpreted by the artist. It is the master-stroke of this incomparable painting.

THE LION OF ST. MARK.

I visited the place daily, and never grew tired of looking at that grand picture. As I have intimated, the movement is almost unimaginably vigorous; the figures are singing, hosannahing, and many are blowing trumpets. So vividly is noise suggested, that spectators who become absorbed in the picture almost always fall to shouting comments in each other's ears, making ear-trumpets of their curved hands, fearing they may not otherwise be heard.   One often sees a tourist, with the eloquent tears pouring down his cheeks, funnel his hands at his wife's ear, and hears him roar through them, "O, TO BE THERE AND AT REST!"

None but the supremely great in art can produce effects like these with the silent brush.

Twelve years ago I could not have appreciated this picture.

One year ago I could not have appreciated it. My study of
Art in Heidelberg has been a noble education to me. All
that I am to-day in Art, I
owe to that.

The other great work which
fascinated me was Bassano's
immortal Hair Trunk. This
is in the Chamber of the Council of Ten. It is in one of the
three forty-foot pictures which
decorate the walls of the room.
The composition of this picture is beyond praise. The
Hair Trunk is not hurled at
the stranger's head,—so to
speak—as the chief feature of
an immortal work so often is;
no, it is carefully guarded
from prominence, it is subordinated, it is restrained, it is
most deftly and cleverly held
in reserve, it is most cautiously
and ingeniously led up to, by

OH, TO BE AT REST.

the master, and consequently when the spectator reaches it
at last, he is taken unawares, he is unprepared, and it bursts
upon him with a stupefying surprise.

One is lost in wonder at all the thought and care which
this elaborate planning must have cost. A general glance
at the picture could never suggest that there was a hair trunk
in it; the Hair Trunk is not mentioned in the title even,—
which is, " Pope Alexander III and the Doge Ziani, the Con-
queror of the Emperor Frederick Barbarossa; " you see, the
title is actually utilized to help divert attention from the
Trunk; thus, as I say, nothing suggests the presence of the
Trunk, by any hint, yet everything studiedly leads up to it,
step by step. Let us examine into this, and observe the exquisitely artful artlessness of the plan.

At the extreme left end of the picture are a couple of women, one of them with a child looking over her shoulder at a wounded man sitting with bandaged head on the ground. These people seem needless, but no, they are there for a purpose; one cannot look at them without seeing the gorgeous procession of grandees, bishops, halberdiers, and banner-bearers which is passing along behind them; one cannot see the procession without feeling a curiosity to follow it and learn whither it is going; it leads him to the Pope, in the center of the picture, who is talking with the bonnetless Doge—talking tranquilly, too, although within 12 feet of them a man is beating a drum, and not far from the drummer two persons are blowing horns, and many horsemen are plunging and rioting about—indeed, 22 feet of this great work is all a deep and happy holiday serenity and Sunday School procession, and then we come suddenly upon 11½ feet of turmoil and racket and insubordination. This latter state of things is not an accident, it has its purpose. But for it, one would linger upon the Pope and the Doge, thinking them t be the motive and supreme feature of the picture; whereas one is drawn along, almost unconsciously, to see what the trouble is about. Now at the very *end* of this riot, within 4 feet of the end of the picture, and full 36 feet from the beginning of it, the Hair Trunk bursts with an electrifying suddenness upon the spectator, in all its matchless perfection, and the great master's triumph is sweeping and complete. From that moment no other thing in those forty feet of canvas has any charm; one sees the Hair Trunk, and the Hair Trunk only. —and to see it is to worship it. Bassano even placed objects in the immediate vicinity of the Supreme Feature whose pretended purpose was to divert attention from it yet a little longer and thus delay and augment the surprise; for instance, to the right of it he has placed a stooping man with a cap so red that it is sure to hold the eye for a moment—to the left of it, some 6 feet away, he has placed a red-coated man on an inflated horse, and that coat plucks your eye to that locality the next moment—then, between the Trunk and the red horse-man he has intruded a man, naked to his waist, who is carry-ing a fancy flour sack on the middle of his back instead of on his shoulder—this admirable feat interests you, of course—keeps you at bay a little longer, like a sock or a jacket thrown to the pursuing wolf—but at last, in spite of all distractions and detentions, the eye of even the most dull and heedless spectator is sure to fall upon the World's Masterpiece, and in that moment he totters to his chair or leans upon his guide for support.

Descriptions of such a work as this must necessarily be im-perfect, yet they are of value. The top of the Trunk is arch-ed; the arch is a perfect half circle, in the Roman style of architecture, for in the then rapid decadence of Greek art, the rising influence of Rome was already beginning to be felt

THE WORLD'S MASTERPIECE.

in the art of the Republic. The Trunk is bound or bordered with leather all around where the lid joins the main body. Many critics consider this leather too cold in tone; but I consider this its highest merit, since it was evidently made so to emphasize by contrast the impassioned fervor of the hasp. The high lights in this part of the work are cleverly managed, the *motif* is admirably subordinated to the ground tints, and the *technique* is very fine. The brass nail-heads are in the purest style of the early renaissance. The strokes, here, are very firm and bold—every nail-head is a portrait. The handle on the end of the Trunk has evidently been re-touched—I think, with a piece of chalk—but one can still see the inspiration of the Old Master in the tranquil, almost too tranquil, hang of it. The hair of this Trunk is *real* hair—

so to speak—white in patches, brown in patches. The details are finely worked out; the repose proper to hair in a recumbent and inactive attitude is charmingly expressed. There is a feeling about this part of the work which lifts it to the highest altitudes of art; the sense of sordid realism vanishes away—one recognizes that there is *soul* here. View this Trunk as you will, it is a gem, it is a marvel, it is a miracle. Some of the effects are very daring, approaching even to the boldest flights of the rococo, the sirocco, and the Byzantine schools—yet the master's hand never falters—it moves on, calm, majestic, confident,—and with that art which conceals art, it finally casts over the *tout ensemble*, by mysterious methods of its own, a subtle something which refines, subdues, etherealizes the arid components and endues them with the deep charm and gracious witchery of poesy.

Among the art treasures of Europe there are pictures which approach the Hair Trunk—there are two which may be said to equal it, possibly—but there is none that surpasses it. So perfect is the Hair Trunk that it moves even persons who ordinarily have no feeling for art. When an Erie baggage-master saw it two years ago, he could hardly keep from checking it; and once when a customs inspector was brought into its presence, he gazed upon it in silent rapture for some moments, then slowly and unconsciously placed one hand behind him with the palm uppermost, and got out his chalk with the other. These facts speak for themselves.

CHAPTER XLIX.

ONE lingers about the Cathedral a good deal, in Venice. There is a strong fascination about it—partly because it is so old, and partly because it is so ugly. Too many of the world's famous buildings fail of one chief virtue—harmony; they are made up of a methodless mixture of the ugly and the beautiful; this is bad; it is confusing, it is unrestful. One has a sense of uneasiness, of distress, without knowing why. But one is calm before St. Mark, one is calm within it, one would be calm on top of it, calm in the cellar; for its details are masterfully ugly, no misplaced and impertinent beauties are intruded anywhere; and the consequent result is a grand harmonious whole, of soothing, entrancing, tranquilizing, soul-satisfying ugliness. One's admiration of a perfect thing always grows, never declines; and this is the surest evidence to him that it *is* perfect. St. Mark is perfect. To me it soon grew to be so nobly, so augustly ugly, that it was difficult to stay away from it, even for a little while. Every time its squat domes disappeared from my view, I had a despondent feeling; whenever they reappeared, I felt an honest rapture—I have not known any happier hours than those I daily spent in front of Florian's, looking across the Great Square at it. Propped on its long row of low thick-leggèd columns, its back knobbed with domes, **it** seemed like a vast warty bug taking a meditative walk.

St. Mark is not the oldest building in the world, of course, but it seems the oldest, and looks the oldest—especially inside. When the ancient mosaics in its walls become damaged, they are repaired but not altered; the grotesque old pattern is preserved. Antiquity has a charm of its own, and to smarten it up would only damage it. One day I was sitting on a red marble bench in the vestibule looking up at an ancient piece of apprentice-work, in mosaic, illustrative of the command to "multiply and replenish the earth." The Cathedral itself had seemed very old; but this picture was illustrating a period in history which made the building seem young by comparison. But I presently found an antique which was older than either the battered Cathedral or the date assigned to that piece of history; it was a spiral-shaped fossil as large as the crown of a hat; it was embedded in the marble bench, and had been sat upon by tourists until it was worn smooth. Contrasted with the inconceivable antiquity of this modest fossil, those other things were flippantly modern—jejune—mere matters of day-before-yesterday. The sense of the oldness of the Cathedral vanished away under the influence of this truly venerable presence.

St. Mark's is monumental; it is an imperishable remembrancer of the profound and simple piety of the Middle Ages. Whoever could ravish a column from a pagan temple, did it and contributed his swag to this Christian one. So this fane is upheld by several hundred acquisitions procured in that peculiar way. In our day it would be immoral to go on the highway to get bricks for a church, but it was no sin in the old times. St. Mark's was itself the victim of a curious robbery, once. The thing is set down in the history of Venice, but it might be smuggled into the Arabian Nights and not seem out of place there:

Nearly four hundred and fifty years ago, a Candian named Stammato, in the suite of a prince of the house of Este, was allowed to view the riches of St. Mark. His sinful eye was dazzled and he hid himself behind an altar, with an evil purpose in his heart, but a priest discovered him and turned him out. Afterward he got in again—by false keys, this time. He went there, night after night, and worked hard and patiently, all alone, overcoming difficulty after difficulty with his toil, and at last succeeded in removing a great block of the marble paneling which walled the lower part of the treasury ; this block he fixed so that he could take it out and put it in at will. After that, for weeks, he spent all his midnights in his magnificent mine, inspecting it in security, gloating over its marvels at his leisure, and always slipping back to his obscure lodgings before dawn, with a duke's ransom under his cloak. He did not need to grab, haphazard, and run—there was no hurry. He could make deliberate and well-considered selections ; he could consult his æsthetic tastes. One comprehends how undisturbed he was,

ÆSTHETIC TASTES.

and how safe from any danger of interruption, when it is stated that he even carried off a unicorn's horn—a mere curiosity—which would not pass through the egress entire, but had to be sawn in two—a bit of work which cost him hours of tedious labor. He continued to store up his treasures

33

at home until his occupation lost the charm of novelty
and became monotonous; then he ceased from it, contented.
Well he might be; for his collection, raised to modern values,
represented nearly $50,000,000 !

He could have gone home much the richest citizen of his
country, and it might have been years before the plunder
was missed; but he was human—he could not enjoy his
delight alone, he must have somebody to talk about it with.
So he exacted a solemn oath from a Candian noble
named Crioni, then led him to his lodgings and nearly took
his breath away with a sight of his glittering hoard.   He
detected a look in his friend's face which excited his suspicion, and was about to slip a stiletto into him when Crioni
saved himself by explaining that that look was only an expression of supreme and happy astonishment.   Stammato
made Crioni a present of one of the State's principal jewels—a huge carbuncle, which afterward figured in the Ducal
cap of state—and the pair parted.   Crioni went at once to
the palace, denounced the criminal, and handed over the carbuncle as evidence.   Stammato was arrested, tried, and condemned, with the old-time Venetian promptness.   He was
hanged between the two great columns in the Piazza—with a
gilded rope, out of compliment to his love of gold, perhaps.
He got no good of his booty at all—it was *all* recovered.

In Venice we had a luxury which very seldom fell to our
lot on the continent—a home dinner, with a private family.
If one could always stop with private families, when traveling, Europe would have a charm which it now lacks.   As it
is, one must live in the hotels, of course, and that is a sorrowful business.   A man accustomed to American food and
American domestic cookery would not starve to death suddenly in Europe; but I think he would gradually waste
away, and eventually die.

He would have to do without his accustomed morning
meal.   That is too formidable a change altogether; he would
necessarily suffer from it.   He could get the shadow, the

sham, the base counterfeit of that meal; but that would do him no good, and money could not buy the reality.

To particularize: the average American's simplest and commonest form of breakfast consists of coffee and beef-steak; well, in Europe, coffee is an unknown beverage. You can get what the European hotel keeper thinks is coffee, but it resembles the real thing as hypocrisy resembles holiness. It is a feeble, characterless, uninspiring sort of stuff, and almost as undrinkable as if it had been made in

A PRIVATE FAMILY BREAKFAST.

an American hotel. The milk used for it is what the French call "Christian" milk,—milk which has been baptized.

After a few months' acquaintance with European "coffee," one's mind weakens, and his faith with it, and he begins to wonder if the rich beverage of home, with its clotted layer of yellow cream on top of it is not a mere dream, after all, and a thing which never existed.

Next comes the European bread,—fair enough, good enough, after a fashion, but cold; cold and tough, and unsympathetic; and never any change, never any variety,—always the same tiresome thing.

Next, the butter,—the sham and tasteless butter; no salt in it, and made of goodness knows what.

Then there is the beefsteak. They have it in Europe, but they don't know how to cook it. Neither will they cut it right. It comes on the table in a small, round, pewter platter. It lies in the centre of this platter, in a bordering bed of grease-soaked potatoes; it is the size, shape, and thickness of a man's hand with the thumb and fingers cut off. It is a little overdone, is rather dry, it tastes pretty insipidly, it rouses no enthusiasm.

Imagine a poor exile contemplating that inert thing; and imagine an angel suddenly sweeping down out of a better land and setting before him a mighty porter-house steak an inch and a half thick, hot and sputtering from the griddle; dusted with fragrant pepper; enriched with little melting bits of butter of the most unimpeachable freshness and genuineness; the precious juices of the meat trickling out and joining the gravy, archipelagoed with mushrooms; a township or two of tender, yellowish fat gracing an outlying district of this ample county of beefsteak; the long white bone which divides the sirloin from the tenderloin still in its place; and imagine that the angel also adds a great cup of American home-made coffee, with the cream a-froth on top, some real butter, firm and yellow and fresh, some smoking hot biscuits, a plate of hot buckwheat cakes, with transparent syrup,—could words describe the gratitude of this exile?

The European dinner is better than the European breakfast, but it has its faults and inferiorities, it does not satisfy. He comes to the table eager and hungry; he swallows his soup,—there is an undefinable lack about it somewhere; thinks the fish is going to be the thing he wants,—eats it and isn't sure; thinks the next dish is perhaps the one that will hit the hungry place,—tries it, and is conscious that there was a something wanting about it, also. And thus he goes on, from dish to dish, like a boy after a butterfly which just misses getting caught every time it alights, but somehow doesn't get caught after all; and at the end the exile and the boy have fared about alike: the one is full, but grievously unsatisfied, the other has had plenty of exercise, plenty of

interest, and a fine lot of hopes, but he hasn't got any butterfly. There is here and there an American who will say
he can remember rising from a European table d' hôte perfectly satisfied; but we must not overlook the fact that there
is also here and there an American who will lie.

The number of dishes is sufficient; but then it is such a
monotonous variety of *unstriking* dishes. It is an inane dead
level of "fair-to-middling." There is nothing to *accent* it.
Perhaps if the roast of mutton or of beef,—a big generous
one,—were brought on the table and carved in full view of
the client, that might give the right sense of earnestness and
reality to the thing; but they don't do that, they pass the
sliced meat around on a dish, and so you are perfectly calm,
it does not stir you in the least. Now a vast roast turkey,
stretched on the broad of his back, with his heels in the air
and the rich juices oozing from his fat sides.......but I may

as well stop there,
for they would not
know how to cook
him. They can't even
cook a chicken re-
spectably; and as for
carving it, they do
that with a hatchet.

This is about the
customary table d'
hôte bill in summer:
Soup, (character-
less.)

Fish — sole, sal-
mon, or whiting—
usually tolerably
good.

EUROPEAN CARVING.

Roast—mutton or beef—tasteless—and some last year's
potatoes.

A pâté, or some other made-dish—usually good—"considering."

One vegetable—brought on in state, and all alone—usually insipid lentils, or string beans, or indifferent asparagus.

Roast chicken, as tasteless as paper.

Lettuce-salad—tolerably good.

Decayed strawberries or cherries.

Sometimes the apricots and figs are fresh, but this is no advantage, as these fruits are of no account anyway.

The grapes are generally good, and sometimes there is a tolerably good peach, by mistake.

The variations of the above bill are trifling. After a fortnight one discovers that the variations are only apparent, not real; in the third week you get what you had the first, and in the fourth week you get what you had the second. Three or four months of this weary sameness will kill the robustest appetite.

It has now been many months, at the present writing, since I have had a nourishing meal, but I shall soon have one,—a modest, private affair, all to myself. I have selected a few dishes, and made out a little bill of fare, which will go home in the steamer that precedes me, and be hot when I arrive —as follows:

Radishes. Baked apples, with cream.
Fried oysters; stewed oysters. Frogs.
American coffee, with real cream.
American butter.
Fried chicken, Southern style.
Porter-house steak.
Saratoga potatoes.
Broiled chicken, American style.
Hot biscuits, Southern style.
Hot wheat-bread, Southern style.
Hot buckwheat cakes.
American toast. Clear maple syrup.
Virginia bacon, broiled.
Blue-points, on the half shell.
Cherry-stone clams.
San Francisco mussels, steamed.
Oyster soup. Clam soup.
Philadelphia Terapin soup.

Oysters roasted in shell—Northern style.
Soft-shell crabs. Connecticut shad.
Baltimore perch.
Brook trout, from Sierra Nevadas.
Lake trout, from Tahoe.
Sheep-head and croakers, from New Orleans.
Black bass from the Mississippi.
American roast beef.
Roast turkey, Thanksgiving style.
Cranberry sauce. Celery.
Roast wild turkey. Woodcock.
Canvas-back-duck, from Baltimore.
Prairie hens, from Illinois.
Missouri partridges, broiled.
'Possum. Coon.
Boston bacon and beans.

Bacon and greens, Southern style.
Hominy. Boiled onions. Turnips.
Pumpkin. Squash. Asparagus.
Butter beans. Sweet potatoes.
Lettuce. Succotash. String beans.
Mashed potatoes. Catsup.
Boiled potatoes, in their skins.
New potatoes, minus the skins.
Early rose potatoes, roasted in the ashes, Southern style, served hot.
Sliced tomatoes, with sugar or vinegar. Stewed tomatoes.
Green corn, cut from the ear and served with butter and pepper.

Green corn, on the ear.
Hot corn-pone, with chitlings, Southern style.
Hot hoe-cake, Southern style.
Hot egg-bread, Southern style.
Hot light-bread, Southern style.
Buttermilk. Iced sweet milk.
Apple dumplings, with real cream.
Apple pie. Apple fritters.
Apple puffs, Southern style.
Peach cobbler, Southern style
Peach pie. American mince pie.
Pumpkin pie. Squash pie.
All sorts of American pastry.

Fresh American fruits of all sorts, including strawberries which are not to be doled out as if they were jewelry, but in a more liberal way.

Ice-water—not prepared in the ineffectual goblet, but in the sincere and capable refrigerator.

Americans intending to spend a year or so in European hotels, will do well to copy this bill and carry it along. They will find it an excellent thing to get up an appetite with, in the dispiriting presence of the squalid table d' hôte.

Foreigners cannot enjoy our food, I suppose, any more than we can enjoy theirs. It is not strange; for tastes are made, not born. I might glorify my bill of fare until I was tired; but after all, the Scotchman would shake his head and say, " Where's your haggis ? " and the Fijian would sigh and say, " Where's your missionary ? "

I have a neat talent in matters pertaining to nourishment. This has met with professional recognition. I have often furnished recipes for cook-books. Here are some designs for pies and things, which I recently prepared for a friend's projected cook-book, but as I forgot to furnish diagrams and perspectives, they had to be left out, of course:

Recipe for an Ash-Cake.

Take a lot of water and add to it a lot of coarse Indian meal and about a quarter of a lot of salt. Mix well together, knead into the form of a " pone," and let the pone stand a while,—not on its edge, but the other way. Rake away a place among the embers, lay it there, and cover it an inch deep with hot ashes. When it is done, remove it; blow off all the ashes but one layer; butter that one and eat.

N. B. No household should ever be without this talisman. It has been noticed that tramps never return for another ash-cake.

Recipe for New England Pie.

To make this excellent breakfast dish, proceed as follows: Take a sufficiency of water and a sufficiency of flour, and construct a bullet-proof dough. Work this into the form of a disk, with the edges turned up some three-fourths of an inch. Toughen and kiln-dry it a couple of days in a mild but unvarying temperature. Construct a cover for this redoubt in the same way and of the same material. Fill with stewed dried apples; aggravate with cloves, lemon peel and slabs of citron; add two portions of New Orleans sugar, then solder on the lid and set in a safe place till it petrifies. Serve cold at breakfast and invite your enemy.

Recipe for German Coffee.

Take a barrel of water and bring it to a boil; rub a chiccory berry against a coffee berry, then convey the former into the water. Continue the boiling and evaporation until the intensity of the flavor and aroma of the coffee and chiccory has been diminished to a proper degree; then set aside to cool. Now unharness the remains of a once cow from the plow, insert them in a hydraulic press, and when you shall have acquired a teaspoonful of that pale blue juice which a German superstition regards as milk, modify the malignity of its strength in a bucket of tepid water and ring up the breakfast. Mix the beverage in a cold cup, partake with moderation, and keep a wet rag around your head to guard against over-excitement.

To Carve Fowls in the German Fashion.

Use a club, and avoid the joints.

CHAPTER L.

I WONDER why some things are? For instance, Art is allowed as much indecent license to-day as in earlier times—but the privileges of Literature in this respect have been sharply curtailed within the past eighty or ninety years. Fielding and Smollet could portray the beastliness of their day in the beastliest language; we have plenty of foul subjects to deal with in our day, but we are not allowed to approach them very near, even with nice and guarded forms of speech. But not so with Art. The brush may still deal freely with any subject, however revolting or indelicate. It makes a body ooze sarcasm at every pore, to go about Rome and Florence and see what this last generation has been doing with the statues. These works, which had stood in innocent nakedness for ages, are all fig-leaved now. Yes, every one of them. Nobody noticed their nakedness before, perhaps; nobody can help noticing it now, the fig-leaf makes it so conspicuous. But the comical thing about it all, is, that the fig-leaf is confined to cold and pallid marble, which would be still cold and unsuggestive without this sham and ostentatious symbol of modesty, whereas warm-blooded paintings which do really need it have in no case been furnished with it.

At the door of the Ufizzi, in Florence, one is confronted by statues of a man and a woman, noseless, battered, black with accumulated grime,—they hardly suggest human beings

—yet these ridiculous creatures have been thoughtfully and conscientiously fig-leaved by this fastidious generation. You enter, and proceed to that most-visited little gallery that exists in the world—the Tribune—and there, against the wall, without obstructing rag or leaf, you may look your fill upon the foulest, the vilest, the obscenest picture the world possesses—Titian's Venus. It isn't that she is naked and stretched out on a bed—no, it is the attitude of one of her arms and hand. If I ventured to describe that attitude, there would be a fine howl—but there the Venus lies, for anybody to gloat over that wants to—and there she has a right to lie, for she is a work of art, and Art has its privileges. I saw young girls stealing furtive glances at her; I saw young men gaze long and absorbedly at her; I saw aged, infirm men hang upon her charms with a pathetic interest. How I should like to describe her—just to see what a holy indignation I could stir up in the world—just to hear the unreflecting average man deliver himself about my grossness and coarseness, and all that. The world says that no worded description of a moving spectacle is a hundredth part as moving as the same spectacle seen with one's own eyes—yet the world is willing to let its son and its daughter and itself look at Titian's beast, but won't stand a description of it in words. Which shows that the world is not as consistent as it might be.

There are pictures of nude women which suggest no impure thought—I am well aware of that. I am not railing at such. What I am trying to emphasize is the fact that Titian's Venus is very far from being one of that sort. Without any question it was painted for a bagnio and it was probably refused because it was a trifle too strong. In truth it is too strong for any place but a public Art Gallery. Titian has two Venuses in the Tribune; persons who have seen them will easily remember which one I am referring to.

In every gallery in Europe there are hideous pictures of blood, carnage, oozing brains, putrefaction—pictures portraying intolerable suffering—pictures alive with every conceivable horror, wrought out in dreadful detail—and similar pictures are being put on the canvas every day and publicly exhibited—without a growl from anybody—for they are innocent, they are inoffensive, being works of art. But suppose a literary artist ventured to go into a pains-taking and elaborate description of one of these grisly things—the critics would skin him alive. Well, let it go, it cannot be helped ; Art retains her privileges, Literature has lost hers. Somebody else may cipher out the whys and the wherefores and the consistencies of it—I haven't got time.

Titian's Venus defiles and disgraces the Tribune, there is no softening that fact, but his "Moses" glorifies it. The simple truthfulness of this noble work wins the heart and the applause of every visitor, be he learned or ignorant. After wearying oneself with the acres of stuffy, sappy, expressionless babies that populate the canvases of the Old Masters in Italy, it is refreshing to stand before this peerless child and feel that thrill which tells you you are at last in the presence of the real thing. This is a human child, this is genuine. You have seen him a thousand times—you have seen him just as he is here—and you confess, without reserve, that Titian *was* a Master. The doll-faces of other painted babes may mean one thing, they may mean another, but with the "Moses" the case is different. The most famous of all the art critics has said, "There is no room for doubt, here—plainly this child is in trouble."

I consider that the "Moses" has no equal among the works of the Old Masters, except it be the divine Hair Trunk of Bassano. I feel sure that if all the other Old Masters were lost and only these two preserved, the world would be the gainer by it.

My sole purpose in going to Florence was to see this immortal "Moses," and by good fortune I was just in time, for they were already preparing to remove it to a more private and better protected place because a fashion of robbing the great galleries was prevailing in Europe at the time.

I got a capable artist to copy the picture; Pannemaker,

the engraver of Dorè's books, engraved it for me, and I have the pleasure of laying it before the reader in this volume.*

We took a turn to Rome and some other Italian cities—then to Munich, and thence to Paris—partly for exercise, but mainly because these things were in our projected program, and it was only right that we should be faithful to it.

From Paris I branched out and walked through Holland and Belgium, procuring an occasional lift by rail or canal when tired, and I had a tolerably good time of it " by and large." I worked Spain and other regions through agents to save time and shoe leather.

We crossed to England, and then made the homeward passage in the Cunarder, *Gallia*, a very fine ship. I was glad to get home—immeasurably glad; so glad, in fact, that it did not seem possible that anything could ever get me out of the country again. I had not enjoyed a pleasure abroad which seemed to me to compare with the pleasure I felt in seeing New York harbor again. Europe has many advantages which we have not, but they do not compensate for a good many still more valuable ones which exist nowhere but in our own country. Then we are such a homeless lot when we are over there! So are Europeans themselves, for that matter. They live in dark and chilly vast tombs,—costly enough, may be, but without conveniences. To be condemned to live as the average European family lives would make life a pretty heavy burden to the average American family.

On the whole, I think that short visits to Europe are better for us than long ones. The former preserve us from becoming Europeanized; they keep our pride of country intact, and at the same time they intensify our affection for our country and our people; whereas long visits have the effect of dulling those feelings,—at least in the majority of cases. I think that one who mixes much with Americans long resident abroad must arrive at this conclusion.

* See Frontispiece.

THE END.

APPENDIX.

Nothing gives such weight and
dignity to a book as an Appendix.

Herodotus.

APPENDIX A.

THE PORTIER.

Omar Khayam, the poet-prophet of Persia, writing more than eight hundred years ago, has said:

"In the four parts of the earth are many that are able to write learned books, many that are able to lead armies, and many also that are able to govern kingdoms and empires; but few there be that can keep hotel."

A word about the European hotel *portier*. He is a most admirable invention, a most valuable convenience. He always wears a conspicuous uniform; he can always be found when he is wanted, for he sticks closely to his post at the front door; he is as polite as a duke; he speaks from four to ten languages; he is your surest help and refuge in time of trouble or perplexity. He is not the clerk, he is not the landlord; he ranks above the clerk, and represents the landlord, who is seldom seen. Instead of going to the clerk for information, as we do at home, you go to the portier. It is the pride of our average hotel clerk to know nothing whatever; it is the pride of the portier to know everything. You ask the portier at what hours the trains leave,—he tells you instantly; or you ask him who is the best physician in town; or what is the hack tariff; or how many children the mayor has; or what days the galleries are open, and whether a permit is required, and where you are to get it, and what you must pay for it; or when the theatres open and close, what the plays are to be, and the price of seats; or what is the newest thing in hats; or how the bills of mortality average; or "who struck Billy Patterson." It does not matter what you ask him: in nine cases out of ten he knows, and in the tenth case he will find out for you before you can turn around three times. There is nothing he will not put his hand to. Suppose you tell him you wish to go from Hamburg to Peking by the way of Jericho, and are ignorant of routes and prices,—the next morning he will hand you a piece of paper with the whole thing worked out on it to the last detail. Before you have been long on European soil, you find yourself still *saying* you are relying on Providence, but when you come to look closer you will see that in reality you are relying on the portier. He discovers what is puzzling you, or what is troubling you, or what your need is, before you can get the half of it out, and he promptly says, "Leave that to me." Consequently you easily drift into the habit of leaving everything to him. There is a certain embarrassment about applying to the average American hotel clerk, a certain hesitancy, a sense of insecurity against rebuff; but you feel no embarrassment in your intercourse with the portier; he receives your propositions with an enthusiasm which cheers, and plunges into their accomplishment with an alacrity which almost inebriates. The more requirements you can pile upon him, the better he likes it. Of course the result is that you cease from doing anything for yourself. He calls a hack when you want one; puts you into it; tells the driver whither to take you; receives you like a long lost child when you return; sends you about your business, does all the quarreling with the hackman himself, and pays him his money out of his own pocket. He sends for your theatre tickets, and pays for them; he sends for any possible article you can require, be it a doctor, an elephant, or a postage stamp; and when you leave, at last, you will find a subordinate seated with the cab driver who will put you in your railway compartment, buy your tickets, have your baggage weighed, bring you the printed tags, and tell you everything is in your bill and paid for. At home you get such elaborate, excellent, and willing service as this only in the best hotels of our large cities; but in Europe you get it in the mere back country towns just as well.

What is the secret of the portier's devotion? It is very simple: he gets *fees, and no salary.* His fee is pretty closely regulated, too. If you stay a week in the house, you give him five marks— a dollar and a quarter, or about eighteen cents a day. If you stay a month, you reduce this average somewhat. If you stay two or three months or longer, you cut it down half, or even more than half. If you stay only one day, you give the portier a mark.

The head waiter's fee is a shade less than the portier's; the Boots, who not only blacks your boots and brushes your clothes, but is usually the porter and handles your baggage, gets a somewhat smaller fee than the head waiter; the chambermaid's fee ranks below that of the Boots. You fee only these four, and no one else. A German gentleman told me that when he remained a week in a hotel, he gave the portier five marks, the head waiter four, the Boots three, and the chambermaid two; and if he staid three months he divided ninety marks among them, in about the above proportions. Ninety marks make $22.50.

None of these fees are ever paid until you leave the hotel, though it be a year,—except one of these four servants should go away in the meantime; in that case he will be sure to come and bid you good-bye and give you the opportunity to pay him what is fairly coming to him. It is considered very bad policy to fee a servant while you are still to remain longer in the hotel, because if you gave him too little he might neglect you afterward, and if you gave him too much he might neglect somebody else to attend to you. It is considered best to keep his expectations "on a string" until your stay is concluded.

I do not know whether hotel servants in New York get any wages or not, but I do know that in some of the hotels there the feeing system in vogue is a heavy burden. The waiter expects a quarter at breakfast,—and gets it. You have a different waiter at luncheon, and so he gets a quarter. Your waiter at dinner is another stranger,—consequently he gets a quarter. The boy who carries your satchel to your room and lights your gas, fumbles around and hangs around significantly, and you fee him to get rid of him. Now you may ring for ice water; and ten minutes later for a lemonade; and ten minutes afterwards, for a cigar; and by and by for a newspaper,—and what is the result? Why, a new boy has appeared every time and fooled and fumbled around until you have paid him something. Suppose you boldly put your foot down, and say it is the hotel's business to pay its servants?—and suppose you stand your ground and stop feeing? You will have to ring your bell ten or fifteen times before you get a servant there; and when he goes off to fill your order you will grow old and infirm before you see him again. You may struggle nobly for twenty-four hours, maybe, if you are an ada-

mantine sort of person, but in the meantime you will have been
so wretchedly served, and so insolently, that you will haul down
your colors, and go to impoverishing yourself with fees.

A TWENTY-FOUR HOUR FIGHT.

It seems to me that it would be a happy idea to import the
European feeing system into America. I believe it would result
in getting even the bells of the Philadelphia hotels answered, and
cheerful service rendered.

The greatest American hotels keep a number of clerks and a
cashier, and pay them salaries which mount up to a considerable
total in the course of a year. The great continental hotels keep a
cashier on a trifling salary, and a portier *who pays the hotel a salary.*
By the latter system both the hotel and the public save money
and are better served than by our system. One of our consuls
told me that the portier of a great Berlin hotel paid $5,000 a year
for his position, and yet cleared $6,000 for himself. The position
of portier in the chief hotels of Saratoga, Long Branch, New
York, and similar centers of resort, would be one which the holder
could afford to pay even more than $5,000 for, perhaps.

When we borrowed the feeing fashion from Europe a dozen
years ago, the salary system ought to have been discontinued, of
course. We might make this correction now, I should think.
And we might add the portier, too. Since I first began to study
the portier, I have had opportunities to observe him in the chief

34

cities of Germany, Switzerland, and Italy; and the more I have seen of him the more I have wished that he might be adopted in America, and become there, as he is in Europe, the stranger's guardian angel.

Yes, what was true eight hundred years ago, is just as true to-day: "Few there be that can keep hotel." Perhaps it is because the landlords and their subordinates have in too many cases taken up their trade without first learning it. In Europe the trade of hotel-keeper is taught. The apprentice begins at the bottom of the ladder and masters the several grades one after the other. Just as in our country printing-offices the apprentice first learns how to sweep out and bring water; then learns to "roll"; then to sort "pi"; then to set type; and finally rounds and completes his education with job-work and press-work: so the landlord-apprentice serves as call-boy; then as under-waiter; then as a parlor-waiter; then as head-waiter, in which position he often has to make out all the bills; then as clerk or cashier; then as portier. His trade is learned now, and by and by he will assume the style and dignity of landlord, and be found conducting a hotel of his own.

Now in Europe, the same as in America, when a man has kept a hotel so thoroughly well during a number of years as to give it a great reputation, he has his reward. He can live prosperously on that reputation. He can let his hotel run down to the last degree of shabbiness and yet have it full of people all the time. For instance, there is the Hotel de Ville, in Milan. It swarms with mice and fleas, and if the rest of the world were destroyed it could furnish dirt enough to start another one with. The food would create an insurrection in a poor-house; and yet if you go outside to get your meals that hotel makes up its loss by over-charging you on all sorts of trifles,—and without making any denials or excuses about it, either. But the Hotel de Ville's old excellent reputation still keeps its dreary rooms crowded with travelers who would be elsewhere if they had only had some wise friend to warn them.

B.

HEIDELBERG CASTLE.

Heidelberg Castle must have been very beautiful before the French battered and bruised and scorched it two hundred years ago. The stone is brown, with a pinkish tint, and does not seem to stain easily. The dainty and elaborate ornamentation upon its two chief fronts is as delicately carved as if it had been intended for the interior of a drawing-room rather than for the outside of a house. Many fruit and flower-clusters, human heads and grim projecting lion's heads are still as perfect in every detail as if they were new. But the statues which are ranked between the windows have suffered. These are life-size statues of old-time emperors, electors, and similar grandees, clad in mail and bearing ponderous swords. Some have lost an arm, some a head, and one poor fellow is chopped off at the middle. There is a saying that if a stranger will pass over the draw-bridge and walk across the court to the castle front without saying anything, he can make a wish and it will be fulfilled. But they say that the truth of this thing has never had a chance to be proved, for the reason that before any stranger can walk from the drawbridge to the appointed place, the beauty of the palace front will extort an exclamation of delight from him.

A ruin must be rightly situated, to be effective. This one could not have been better placed. It stands upon a commanding elevation, it is buried in green woods, there is no level ground about it, but on the contrary there are wooded terraces upon terraces, and one looks down through shining leaves into profound chasms and abysses where twilight reigns and the sun cannot intrude. Nature knows how to garnish a ruin to get the best effect. One of these old towers is split down the middle, and one half has tumbled aside. It tumbled in such a way as to establish itself in a picturesque attitude. Then all it lacked was a fitting drapery, and Nature has furnished that; she has robed the rugged mass in flowers and verdure, and made it a charm to the eye. The standing half exposes its arched and cavernous rooms to you, like open, toothless mouths; there, too, the vines and flowers have done their work of grace. The rear portion of the tower has not been neglected, either, but is clothed with a clinging garment of polished ivy which hides the wounds and stains of time. Even the top is not left bare, but is crowned with a flourishing group of trees and shrubs. Misfortune has done for this old tower what it has done for the human character sometimes—improved it.

A gentleman remarked, one day, that it might have been fine to live in the castle in the day of its prime, but that we had one advantage which its vanished inhabitants lacked—the advantage of having a charming ruin to visit and muse over. But that was a hasty idea. Those people had the advantage of *us*. They had the fine castle to live in, and they could cross the Rhine valley and muse over the stately ruin of Trifels besides. The Trifels people, in their day, five hundred years ago, could go and muse over majestic ruins which have vanished, now, to the last stone. There have always been ruins, no doubt; and there have always been pensive people to sigh over them, and asses to scratch upon them their names and the important date of their visit. Within a hundred years after Adam left Eden, the guide probably gave the usual general flourish with his hand and said: "Place where the animals were named, ladies and gentlemen; place where the tree of the forbidden fruit stood; exact spot where Adam and Eve first met; and here, ladies and gentlemen, adorned and hallowed by the names and addresses of three generations of tourists, we have the crumbling remains of Cain's altar,—fine old ruin!" Then, no doubt, he taxed them a shekel apiece and let them go.

An illumination of Heidelberg Castle is one of the sights of Europe. The Castle's picturesque shape; its commanding situation, midway up the steep and wooded mountain side; its vast size,—these features combine to make an illumination a most effective spectacle. It is necessarily an expensive show, and consequently rather infrequent. Therefore whenever one of these exhibitions is to take place, the news goes about in the papers and Heidelberg is sure to be full of people on that night. I and my agent had one of these opportunities, and improved it.

About half past seven on the appointed evening we crossed the lower bridge, with some American students, in a pouring rain, and started up the road which borders the Neunheim side of the river. This roadway was densely packed with carriages and foot passengers; the former of all ages, and the latter of all ages and both sexes. This black and solid mass was struggling painfully onward, through the slop, the darkness, and the deluge. We waded along for three-quarters of a mile, and finally took up a position in an unsheltered beer garden directly opposite the Castle. We could not *see* the Castle,—or anything else, for that matter,—but we could dimly discern the outlines of the mountain over the way, through the pervading blackness, and knew whereabouts the Castle was located. We stood on one of the hundred benches in the garden, under our umbrellas; the other ninety-nine were occupied by standing men and women, and they also had umbrellas. All the region round about, and up and down the river-road, was a dense wilderness of humanity hidden under an unbroken pavement of carriage tops and umbrellas. Thus we stood during two drenching hours. No rain fell on my head, but the converging whalebone points of a dozen neighboring umbrellas poured little cooling streams of water down my neck, and sometimes into my ears, and thus kept me from getting hot and impatient. I had the rheumatism, too, and had heard that this was good for it. Afterward, however, I was led to believe that the water treatment is *not* good for rheumatism. There were even little girls in that dreadful place. A man held one in his arms, just in front of me, for as much as an hour, with umbrella-drippings soaking into her clothing all the time.

In the circumstances, two hours was a good while for us to have to wait, but when the illumination did at last come, we felt repaid. It came unexpectedly, of course,—things always do, that have been long looked and longed for. With a perfectly breath-taking suddenness several vast sheaves of vari-colored rockets were vomited skyward out of the black throats of the castle towers, accompanied by a thundering crash of sound, and instantly

every detail of the prodigious ruin stood revealed against the
mountain side and glowing with an almost intolerable splendor of
fire and color. For some little time the whole building was a
blinding crimson mass, the towers continued to spout thick columns of rockets aloft, and overhead the sky was radiant with
arrowy bolts which clove their way to the zenith, paused, curved
gracefully downward, then burst into brilliant fountain sprays of
richly colored sparks. The red fires died slowly down, within
the castle, and presently the shell grew nearly black outside; the
angry glare that shone out through the broken arches and innumerable sashless windows, now, reproduced the aspect which the
Castle must have borne in the old time when the French spoilers
saw the monster bonfire which they had made there fading and
smouldering toward extinction.

While we still gazed and enjoyed, the ruin was suddenly enveloped in rolling and tumbling volumes of vaporous green fire;
then in dazzling purple ones; then a mixture of many colors followed, and drowned the great fabric in its blended splendors.
Meantime the nearest bridge had been illuminated, and from
several rafts anchored in the river, meteor showers of rockets,
Roman candles, bombs, serpents, and Catharine wheels were being
discharged in wasteful profusion into the sky,—a marvelous sight
indeed to a person as little used to such spectacles as I was. For
a while the whole region about us seemed as bright as day, and
yet the rain was falling in torrents all the time. The evening's
entertainment presently closed, and we joined the innumerable
caravan of half-drowned spectators, and waded home again.

The Castle grounds are very ample and very beautiful; and as
they joined the Hotel grounds, with no fences to climb, but only
some nobly shaded stone stairways to descend, we spent a part of
nearly every day in idling through their smooth walks and leafy
groves. There was an attractive spot among the trees where
were a great many wooden tables and benches; and there one
could sit in the shade and pretend to sip at his foamy beaker of
beer while he inspected the crowd. I say pretend, because I
only pretended to sip, without really sipping. That is the polite
way; but when you are ready to go, you empty the beaker at a
draught. There was a brass band, and it furnished excellent
music every afternoon. Sometimes so many people came that

every seat was occupied, every table filled. And never a rough in the assemblage,—all nicely dressed fathers and mothers, young gentlemen and ladies and children ; and plenty of university students and glittering officers; with here and there a gray professor, or a peaceful old lady with her knitting; and always a sprinkling of gawky foreigners. Everybody had his glass of beer before him, or his cup of coffee, or his bottle of wine, or his hot cutlet and potatoes; young ladies chatted, or fanned themselves, or wrought at their crotcheting or embroidering; the students fed sugar to their dogs, or discussed duels, or illustrated new fencing-tricks with their little canes; and everywhere was comfort and enjoyment, and everywhere peace and good-will to men. The trees were jubilant with birds, and the paths with rollicking children. One could have a seat in that place and plenty of music, any afternoon, for about eight cents, or a family ticket for the season for two dollars.

For a change, when you wanted one, you could stroll to the castle, and burrow among its dungeons, or climb about its ruined towers, or visit its interior shows,—the great Heidelberg Tun, for instance. Everybody has heard of the great Heidelberg Tun, and most people have seen it, no doubt. It is a wine cask as big as a cottage, and some traditions say it holds eighteen hundred thousand bottles, and other traditions say it holds eighteen hundred million barrels. I think it likely that one of these statements is a mistake, and the other one a lie. However, the mere matter of capacity is a thing of no sort of consequence, since the cask is empty, and indeed has always been empty, history says. An empty cask the size of a cathedral could excite but little emotion in me. I do not see any wisdom in building a monster cask to hoard up emptiness in, when you can get a better quality, outside, any day, free of expense. What could this cask have been built for? The more one studies over that, the more uncertain and unhappy he becomes. Some historians say that thirty couples, some say thirty thousand couples, can dance on the head of this cask at the same time. Even this does not seem to me to account for the building of it. It does not even throw light on it. A profound and scholarly Englishman,—a specialist,—who had made the great Heidelberg Tun his sole study for fifteen years. told me he had at last satisfied himself that the ancients built it to make

German cream in. He said that the average German cow yielded from one to two and a half teaspoonfuls of milk, when she was

GREAT HEIDELBERG TUN.

not worked in the plow or the hay wagon more than eighteen or nineteen hours a day. This milk was very sweet and good, and of a beautiful transparent bluish tint; but in order to get cream from it in the most economical way, a peculiar process was necessary. Now he believed that the habit of the ancients was to collect several milkings in a teacup, pour it into the Great Tun, fill up with water, and then skim off the cream from time to time as the needs of the German Empire demanded.

This began to look reasonable. It certainly began to account for the German cream which I had encountered and marveled over in so many hotels and restaurants. But a thought struck me,—

" Why did not each ancient dairyman take his own teacup of milk and his own cask of water, and mix them, without making a government matter of it ? "

"Where could he get a cask large enough to contain the right proportion of water?"

Very true. It was plain that the Englishman had studied the matter from all sides. Still I thought I might catch him on one point; so I asked him why the modern empire did not make the nation's cream in the Heidelberg Tun, instead of leaving it to rot away unused. But he answered as one prepared,—

"A patient and diligent examination of the modern German cream has satisfied me that they do not use the Great Tun now, because they have got a *bigger* one hid away somewhere. Either that is the case or they empty the spring milkings into the mountain torrents and then skim the Rhine all summer."

There is a museum of antiquities in the castle, and among its most treasured relics are ancient manuscripts connected with German history. There are hundreds of these, and their dates stretch back through many centuries. One of them is a decree signed and sealed by the hand of a successor of Charlmagne, in the year 896. A signature made by a hand which vanished out of this life near a thousand years ago, is a more impressive thing than even a ruined castle. Luther's wedding ring was shown me; also a fork belonging to a time anterior to our era, and an early bootjack. And there was a plaster cast of the head of a man who was assassinated about sixty years ago. The stab-wounds in the face were duplicated with unpleasant fidelity. One or two real hairs still remained sticking in the eyebrows of the cast. That trifle seemed to almost change the counterfeit into a corpse.

There are many aged portraits,—some valuable, some worthless; some of great interest, some of none at all. I bought a couple,— one a gorgeous duke of the olden time, and the other a comely blue-eyed damsel, a princess, may be. I bought them to start a portrait gallery of my ancestors with. I paid a dollar and a half for the duke and two and a half for the princess. One can lay in ancestors at even cheaper rates than these, in Europe, if he will mouse among old picture shops and look out for chances.

C.

THE COLLEGE PRISON.

It seems that the student may break a good many of the public laws without having to answer to the public authorities. His case must come before the University for trial and punishment. If a policeman catches him in an unlawful act and proceeds to arrest him, the offender proclaims that he is a student, and perhaps shows his matriculation card, whereupon the officer asks for his address, then goes his way, and reports the matter at headquarters. If the offense is one over which the city has no jurisdiction, the authorities report the case officially to the University, and give themselves no further concern about it. The University court send for the student, listen to the evidence, and pronounce judgment. The punishment usually inflicted is imprisonment in the University prison. As I understand it, a student's case is often tried without his being present at all. Then something like this happens: A constable in the service of the University visits the lodgings of the said student, knocks, is invited to come in, does so, and says politely,—

"If you please, I am here to conduct you to prison."

"Ah," says the student, "I was not expecting it. What have I been doing?"

"Two weeks ago the public peace had the honor to be disturbed by you."

"It is true; I had forgotten it. Very well: I have been complained of, tried, and found guilty—is that it?"

"Exactly. You are sentenced to two days' solitary confinement in the College prison, and I am sent to fetch you."

Student. "O, I can't go to-day!"

Officer. "If you please,—why?"

Student. "Because I've got an engagement."

Officer. "To-morrow, then, perhaps?"

Student. "No, I am going to the opera, to-morrow."

Officer. "Could you come Friday?"

Student. (Reflectively.) "Let me see,—Friday—Friday. I don't seem to have anything on hand Friday."

Officer. "Then, if you please, I will expect you on Friday."

Student. "All right, I'll come around Friday."

Officer. "Thank you. Good day, sir."

Student. "Good day."

So on Friday the student goes to the prison of his own accord, and is admitted.

It is questionable if the world's criminal history can show a custom more odd than this. Nobody knows, now, how it originated. There have always been many noblemen among the students, and it is presumed that all students are gentlemen; in the old times it was usual to mar the convenience of such folk as little as possible; perhaps this indulgent custom owes its origin to this.

One day I was listening to some conversation upon this subject when an American student said that for some time he had been under sentence for a slight breach of the peace and had promised the constable that he would presently find an unoccupied day and betake himself to prison. I asked the young gentleman to do me the kindness to go to jail as soon as he conveniently could, so that I might try to get in there and visit him, and see what college-captivity was like. He said he would appoint the very first day he could spare.

His confinement was to endure twenty-four hours. He shortly chose his day, and sent me word. I started immediately. When I reached the University Place, I saw two gentlemen talking together, and as they had portfolios under their arms, I judged they were tutors or elderly students; so I asked them in English to show me the college jail. I had learned to take it for granted that anybody in Germany who knows anything, knows English, so I had stopped afflicting people with my German. These gentlemen seemed a trifle amused,—and a trifle confused, too,—but one of them said he would walk around the corner with me and show me the place. He asked me why I wanted to get in there, and I said to see a friend,—and for curiosity. He doubted if I would be admitted, but volunteered to put in a word or two for me with the custodian.

He rang the bell, a door opened, and we stepped into a paved way and then into a small living-room, where we were received by a hearty and good natured German woman of fifty. She threw up her hands with a surprised "Ach Gott, Herr Professor!" and exhibited a mighty deference for my new acquaintance. By the sparkle in her eye I judged she was a good deal amused, too. The "Herr Professor" talked to her in German, and I understood enough of it to know that he was bringing very plausible reasons to bear for admitting me. They were successful. So the Herr Professor received my earnest thanks and departed. The old dame got her keys, took me up two or three flights of stairs, unlocked a door, and we stood in the presence of the criminal. Then she went into a jolly and eager description of all that had occurred down stairs, and what the Herr Professor had said, and so forth and so on. Plainly she regarded it as quite a superior joke that I had waylaid a Professor and employed him in so odd a service. But I wouldn't have done it if I had known he was a Professor; therefore my conscience was not disturbed.

Now the dame left us to ourselves. The cell was not a roomy one; still it was a little larger than an ordinary prison cell. It had a window of good size, iron-grated; a small stove; two wooden chairs; two oaken tables, very old and most elaborately carved with names, mottoes, faces, armorial bearings, etc.,—the work of several generations of imprisoned students; and a narrow wooden bedstead with a villainous old straw mattress, but no sheets, pillows, blankets or coverlets,—for these the student must furnish at his own cost if he wants them. There was no carpet, of course.

The ceiling was completely covered with names, dates, and monograms, done with candle smoke. The walls were thickly covered with pictures and portraits (in profile), some done with ink, some with soot, some with a pencil, and some with red, blue, and green chalks; and wherever an inch or two of space had remained between the pictures, the captives had written plaintive verses, or names and dates. I do not think I was ever in a more elaborately frescoed apartment.

Against the wall hung a placard containing the prison laws. I made a note of one or two of these. For instance: The prisoner must pay, for the "privilege" of entering, a sum equivalent to 20 cents of our money; for the privilege of leaving, when his term has expired, 20 cents; for every day spent in the prison, 12 cents; for fire and light, 12 cents a day. The jailor furnishes coffee, mornings, for a small sum; dinners and suppers may be ordered from outside if the prisoner chooses,—and he is allowed to pay for them, too.

Here and there, on the walls, appeared the names of American students, and in one place the American arms and motto were displayed in colored chalks.

With the help of my friend I translated many of the inscriptions. Some of them were cheerful, others the reverse. I will give the reader a few specimens:

"In my tenth semestre, (my best one,) I am cast here through the complaints of others. Let those who follow me take warning."

"III Tage ohne Grund angeblich aus Neugierde."* Which is to say, he had a curiosity to know what prison-life was like; so he made a breach in some law and got three days for it. It is more

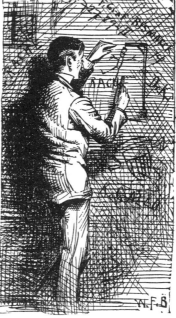

BISMARCK IN PRISON.

than likely that he never had the same curiosity again.

(*Translation.*) "E. Glinicke, four days for being too eager a spectator of a row."

"F. Graf Bismarck,—27–29, II, '74." Which means that Count Bismark, son of the great statesman, was a prisoner two days in 1874.

(*Translation.*)   "R. Diergandt,—for Love,—4 days."   Many people in this world have caught it heavier than that for the same indiscretion.

This one is terse.   I translate:

"Four weeks for *misinterpreted gallantry.*"

I wish the sufferer had explained a little more fully.   A four weeks' term is a rather serious matter.

There were many uncomplimentary references, on the walls, to a certain unpopular college dignitary.   One sufferer had got three days for not saluting him.   Another had "here two days slept and three nights lain awake," on account of this same " Dr. K."   In one place was a picture of Dr. K. hanging on a gallows.

Here and there, lonesome prisoners had eased the heavy time by altering the records left by predecessors.   Leaving the name standing, and the date and length of the captivity, they had erased the description of the misdemeanor, and written in its place, in staring capitals, "FOR THEFT!" or "FOR MURDER!" or some other gaudy crime.   In one place, all by itself, stood this blood-curdling word:

."RACHE!"*

There was no name signed, and no date.   It was an inscription well calculated to pique curiosity.   One would greatly like to know the nature of the wrong that had been done, and what sort of vengeance was wanted, and whether the prisoner ever achieved it or not.   But there was no way of finding out these things.

Occasionally a name was followed simply by the remark, "II days, for disturbing the peace," and without comment upon the justice or injustice of the sentence.

In one place was a hilarious picture of a student of the green-cap corps with a bottle of champagne in each hand; and below was the legend: "These make an evil fate endurable."

There were two prison cells, and neither had space left on walls or ceiling for another name or portrait or picture.   The inside surfaces of the two doors were completely covered with cartes de visite of former prisoners, ingeniously let into the wood and protected from dirt and injury by glass.

I very much wanted one of the sorry old tables which the pris-

---

* " Revenge ! "

oners had spent so many years in ornamenting with their pocket knives, but red tape was in the way. The custodian could not sell one without an order from a superior; and that superior would have to get it from *his* superior; and this one would have to get it from a higher one,—and so on up and up until the faculty should sit on the matter and deliver final judgment. The system was right, and nobody could find fault with it; but it did not seem justifiable to bother so many people, so I proceeded no further. It might have cost me more than I could afford, anyway; for one of those prison tables, which was at that time in a private museum in Heidelberg, was afterwards sold at auction for two hundred and fifty dollars. It was not worth more than a dollar, or possibly a dollar and a half, before the captive students began their work on it. Persons who saw it at the auction said it was so curiously and wonderfully carved that it was worth the money that was paid for it.

Among the many who have tasted the college prison's dreary hospitality was a lively young fellow from one of the Southern States of America, whose first year's experience of German university life was rather peculiar. The day he arrived in Heidelberg he enrolled his name on the college books, and was so elated with the fact that his dearest hope had found fruition and he was actually a student of the old and renowned university, that he set to work that very night to celebrate the event by a grand lark in company with some other students. In the course of his lark he managed to make a wide breach in one of the university's most stringent laws. Sequel: before noon, next day, he was in the college prison,—booked for three months. The twelve long weeks dragged slowly by, and the day of deliverance came at last. A great crowd of sympathizing fellow-students received him with a rousing demonstration as he came forth, and of course there was another grand lark,—in the course of which he managed to make a wide breach in one of the *city's* most stringent laws. Sequel: before noon, next day, he was safe in the city lock-up,—booked for three months. This second tedious captivity drew to an end in the course of time, and again a great crowd of sympathizing fellow-students gave him a rousing reception as he came forth; but his delight in his freedom was so boundless that he could not proceed soberly and calmly, but must go hopping and skipping and jumping down the sleety street from sheer excess of joy. Sequel: he slipped and broke his leg, and actually lay in the hospital during the next three months !

When he at last became a free man again, he said he believed he would hunt up a brisker seat of learning; the Heidelberg lectures might be good, but the opportunities of attending them were too rare, the educational process too slow; he said he had come to Europe with the idea that the acquirement of an education was only a matter of time, but if he had averaged the Heidelberg system correctly, it was rather a matter of eternity.

D.

THE AWFUL GERMAN LANGUAGE.

A little learning makes the whole world kin.—Proverbs xxxii, 7.

I went often to look at the collection of curiosities in Heidelberg Castle, and one day I surprised the keeper of it with my German. I spoke entirely in that language. He was greatly interested; and after I had talked awhile he said my German was very rare, possibly a "unique;" and wanted to add it to his museum.

If he had known what it had cost me to acquire my art, he would also have known that it would break any collector to buy it. Harris and I had been hard at work on our German during several weeks at that time, and although we had made good progress, it had been accomplished under great difficulty and annoyance, for three of our teachers had died in the meantime. A person who has not studied German can form no idea of what a perplexing language it is.

Surely there is not another language that is so slip-shod and systemless, and so slippery and elusive to the grasp. One is washed about in it, hither and hither, in the most helpless way; and when at last he thinks he has captured a rule which offers firm ground to take a rest on amid the general rage and turmoil of the ten parts of speech, he turns over the page and reads, "Let the pupil make careful note of the following *exceptions*." He runs his eye down and finds that there are more exceptions to the rule than instances of it. So overboard he goes again, to hunt for another Ararat and find another quicksand. Such has been, and continues to be,

35

my experience. Every time I think I have got one of these four confusing "cases" where I am master of it, a seemingly insignificant preposition intrudes itself into my sentence, clothed with an awful and unsuspected power, and crumbles the ground from under me. For instance, my book inquires after a certain bird —(it is always inquiring after things which are of no sort of consequence to anybody): "Where is the bird?" Now the answer to this question,—according to the book,—is that the bird is waiting in the blacksmith shop on account of the rain. Of course no bird would do that, but then you must stick to the book. Very well, I begin to cipher out the German for that answer. I begin at the wrong end, necessarily, for that is the German idea. I say to myself, "*Regen*, (rain,) is masculine—or maybe it is feminine— or possibly neuter—it is too much trouble to look, now. Therefore, it is either *der* (the) Regen, or *die* (the) Regen, or *das* (the) Regen, according to which gender it may turn out to be when I look. In the interest of science, I will cipher it out on the hypothesis that it is masculine. Very well—then *the* rain is *der* Regen, if it is simply in the quiescent state of being *mentioned*, without enlargement or discussion—Nominative case; but if this rain is lying around, in a kind of a general way on the ground, it is then definitely located, it is *doing something*—that is, *resting*, (which is one of the German grammar's ideas of doing something,) and this throws the rain into the Dative case, and makes it *dem* Regen. However, this rain is not resting, but is doing something *actively*,—it is falling,—to interfere with the bird, likely,—and this indicates *movement*, which has the effect of sliding it into the Accusative case and changing *dem* Regen into *den* Regen." Having completed the grammatical horoscope of this matter, I answer up confidently and state in German that the bird is staying in the blacksmith shop "wegen (on account of) *den* Regen." Then the teacher lets me softly down with the remark that whenever the word "wegen" drops into a sentence, it *always* throws that subject into the *Genitive* case, regardless of consequences—and that therefore this bird staid in the blacksmith shop "wegen *des* Regens."

N. B. I was informed, later, by a higher authority, that there was an "exception" which permits one to say "wegen *den* Regen" in certain peculiar and complex circumstances, but that this exception is not extended to anything *but* rain.

There are ten parts of speech, and they are all troublesome. An average sentence, in a German newspaper, is a sublime and impressive curiosity; it occupies a quarter of a column; it contains all the ten parts of speech—not in regular order, but mixed; it is built mainly of compound words constructed by the writer on the spot, and not to be found in any dictionary—six or seven words compacted into one, without joint or seam—that is, without hyphens; it treats of fourteen or fifteen different subjects, each enclosed in a parenthesis of its own, with here and there extra parentheses which re-enclose three or four of the minor parentheses, making pens within pens; finally, all the parentheses and re-parentheses are massed together between a couple of king-parentheses, one of which is placed in the first line of the majestic sentence and the other in the middle of the last line of it—*after which comes the* VERB, and you find out for the first time what the man has been talking about; and after the verb—merely by way of ornament, as far as I can make out,—the writer shovels in "*haben sind gewesen gehabt haben geworden sein*," or words to that effect, and the monument is finished. I suppose that this closing hurrah is in the nature of the flourish to a man's signature—not necessary, but pretty. German books are easy enough to read when you hold them before the looking-glass or stand on your head,—so as to reverse the construction,—but I think that to learn to read and understand a German newspaper is a thing which must always remain an impossibility to a foreigner.

Yet even the German books are not entirely free from attacks of the Parenthesis distemper—though they are usually so mild as to cover only a few lines, and therefore when you at last get down to the verb it carries some meaning to your mind because you are able to remember a good deal of what has gone before.

Now here is a sentence from a popular and excellent German novel,—with a slight parenthesis in it. I will make a perfectly literal translation, and throw in the parenthesis-marks and some hyphens for the assistance of the reader,—though in the original there are no parenthesis-marks or hyphens, and the reader is left to flounder through to the remote verb the best way he can:

"But when he, upon the street, the (in-satin-and-silk-covered-

now-very-unconstrainedly-after-the-newest-fashion-dressed) govern‐
ment counsellor's wife *met*," etc., etc.*

That is from "The Old Mamselle's Secret," by Mrs. Marlitt.
And that sentence is constructed upon the most approved German
model.   You observe how far that verb is from the reader's base
of operations; well, in a German newspaper they put their verb
away over on the next page; and I have heard that sometimes
after stringing along on exciting preliminaries and parentheses
for a column or two, they get in a hurry and have to go to press
without getting to the verb at all.   Of course, then, the reader is
left in a very exhausted and ignorant state.

We have the Parenthesis disease in our literature, too; and one
may see cases of it every day in our books and newspapers: but
with us it is the mark and sign of an unpractised writer or a cloudy
intellect, whereas with the Germans it is doubtless the mark and
sign of a practised pen and of the presence of that sort of luminous
intellectual fog which stands for clearness among these people.
For surely it is *not* clearness,—it necessarily can't be clearness.
Even a jury would have penetration enough to discover that.   A
writer's ideas must be a good deal confused, a good deal out of
line and sequence, when he starts out to say that a man met a
counsellor's wife in the street, and then right in the midst of this
so simple undertaking halts these approaching people and makes
them stand still until he jots down an inventory of the woman's
dress.   That is manifestly absurd.   It reminds a person of those
dentists who secure your instant and breathless interest in a tooth
by taking a grip on it with the forceps, and then stand there and
drawl through a tedious anecdote before they give the dreaded
jerk.   Parentheses in literature and dentistry are in bad taste.

The Germans have another kind of parenthesis, which they
make by splitting a verb in two and putting half of it at the be‐
ginning of an exciting chapter and the *other half* at the end of it.
Can any one conceive of anything more confusing than that?
These things are called "separable verbs."   The German grammar
is blistered all over with separable verbs; and the wider the two
portions of one of them are spread apart, the better the author of

---

* Wenn er aber auf der Strasse der in Sammt und Seide gehüllten jetz
sehr ungenirt nach der neusten mode gekleideten Regierungsrathin begeg‐
net."

the crime is pleased with his performance. A favorite one is *reiste ab*,—which means, *departed.* Here is an example which I culled from a novel and reduced to English:

"The trunks being now ready, he DE- after kissing his mother and sisters, and once more pressing to his bosom his adored Gretchen, who, dressed in simple white muslin, with a single tube-rose in the ample folds of her rich brown hair, had tottered feebly down the stairs, still pale from the terror and excitement of the past evening, but longing to lay her poor aching head yet once again upon the breast of him whom she loved more dearly than life itself, PARTED."

However, it is not well to dwell too much on the separable verbs. One is sure to lose his temper early; and if he sticks to the subject, and will not be warned, it will at last either soften his brain or petrify it. Personal pronouns and adjectives are a fruitful nuisance in this language, and should have been left out. For instance, the same sound, *sie*, means *you*, and it means *she*, and it means *her*, and it means *it*, and it means *they*, and it means *them.* Think of the ragged poverty of a language which has to make one word do the work of six,—and a poor little weak thing of only three letters at that. But mainly, think of the exaspera-tion of never knowing which of these meanings the speaker is trying to convey. This explains why, whenever a person says *sie* to me, I generally try to kill him, if a stranger.

Now observe the Adjective. Here was a case where simplicity would have been an advantage; therefore, for no other reason, the inventor of this language complicated it all he could. When we wish to speak of our "good friend or friends," in our enlightened tongue, we stick to the one form and have no trouble or hard feeling about it; but with the German tongue it is different. When a German gets his hands on an adjective, he declines it, and keeps on declining it until the common sense is all declined out of it. It is as bad as Latin. He says, for instance:

SINGULAR:

Nominative—Mein guter Freund, my good friend.
Genitive—Meines guten Freundes, of my good friend.
Dative—Meinem guten Freund, to my good friend.
Accusative—Meinen guten Freund, my good friend.

N.—Meine guten Freunde, my good friends.

G.—Meiner guten Freunde, of my good friends.

D.—Meinen guten Freunden, to my good friends.

A.—Meine guten Freunde, my good friends.

Now let the candidate for the asylum try to memorize those variations, and see how soon he will be elected.   One might better go without friends in Germany than take all this trouble about them.   I have shown what a bother it is to decline a good (male) friend; well, this is only a third of the work, for there is a variety of new distortions of the adjective to be learned when the object is feminine, and still another when the object is neuter.   Now there are more adjectives in this language than there are black cats in Switzerland, and they must all be as elaborately declined as the examples above suggested.   Difficult ?—troublesome ?— these words cannot describe it.   I heard a Californian student in Heidelberg, say, in one of his calmest moods, that he would rather decline two drinks than one German adjective.

The inventor of the language seems to have taken pleasure in complicating it in every way he could think of.   For instance, if one is casually referring to a house, *Haus*, or a horse, *Pferd*, or a dog, *Hund*, he spells these words as I have indicated; but if he is referring to them in the Dative case, he sticks on a foolish and unnecessary *e* and spells them Hause, Pferde, Hunde.   So, as an added *e* often signifies the plural, as the *s* does with us, the new student is likely to go on for a month making twins out of a Dative dog before he discovers his mistake; and on the other hand, many a new student who could ill afford loss, has bought and paid for two dogs and only got one of them, because he ignorantly bought that dog in the Dative singular when he really supposed he was talking plural,—which left the law on the seller's side, of course, by the strict rules of grammar, and therefore a suit for recovery could not lie.

In German, all the Nouns begin with a capital letter.   Now that is a good idea; and a good idea, in this language, is necessarily conspicuous from its lonesomeness.   I consider this capitalizing of nouns a good idea, because by reason of it you are almost always able to tell a noun the minute you see it.   You fall into error occasionally, because you mistake the name of a person for the name of a thing, and waste a good deal of time trying to dig a meaning out of it. German names almost always do mean something, and this helps to deceive the student. I translated a passage one day, which said that "the infuriated tigress broke loose and utterly ate up the unfortunate fir-forest," (*Tannenwald.*) When I was girding up my loins to doubt this, I found out that Tannenwald, in this instance, was a man's name.

Every noun has a gender, and there is no sense or system in the distribution; so the gender of each must be learned separately and by heart. There is no other way. To do this, one has to have a memory like a memorandum book. In German, a young lady has no sex, while a turnip has. Think what overwrought reverence that shows for the turnip, and what callous disrespect for the girl. See how it looks in print—I translate this from a conversation in one of the best of the German Sunday-school books:

"*Gretchen.* Wilhelm, where is the turnip?

"*Wilhelm.* She has gone to the kitchen.

"*Gretchen.* Where is the accomplished and beautiful English maiden?

"*Wilhelm.* It has gone to the opera."

To continue with the German genders: a tree is male, its buds are female, its leaves are neuter; horses are sexless, dogs are male, cats are female,—Tom-cats included, of course; a person's mouth, neck, bosom, elbows, fingers, nails, feet, and body, are of the male sex, and his head is male or neuter according to the word selected to signify it, and *not* according to the sex of the individual who wears it,—for in Germany all the women wear either male heads or sexless ones; a person's nose, lips, shoulders, breast, hands, hips, and toes are of the female sex; and his hair, ears, eyes, chin, legs, knees, heart, and conscience, haven't any sex at all. The inventor of the language probably got what he knew about a conscience from hearsay.

Now, by the above dissection, the reader will see that in Germany a man may *think* he is a man, but when he comes to look into the matter closely, he is bound to have his doubts; he finds that in sober truth he is a most ridiculous mixture; and if he ends by trying to comfort himself with the thought that he can at least depend on a third of this mess as being manly and masculine, the humiliating second thought will quickly remind him that in this respect he is no better off than any woman or cow in the land.

In the German it is true that by some oversight of the inventor of the language, a Woman is a female; but a Wife, (*Weib,*) is not,—which is unfortunate. A Wife, here, has no sex; she is neuter; so, according to the grammar, a fish is *he*, his scales are *she*, but a fishwife is neither. To describe a wife as sexless, may be called under-description; that is bad enough, but over-description is surely worse. A German speaks of an Englishman as the *Engländer;* to change the sex, he adds *inn*, and that stands for Englishwoman,—*Engländerinn*. That seems descriptive enough, but still it is not exact enough for a German; so he precedes the word with that article which indicates that the creature to follow is feminine, and writes it down thus: "*die* Englanderinn,"—which means "the *she-Englishwoman*." I consider that that person is over-described.

Well, after the student has learned the sex of a great number of nouns, he is still in a difficulty, because he finds it impossible to persuade his tongue to refer to things as "*he*" and "*she*," and "*him*" and "*her*," which it has been always accustomed to refer to as "*it*." When he even frames a German sentence in his mind, with the hims and hers in the right places, and then works up his courage to the utterance-point, it is no use,—the moment he begins to speak his tongue flies the track and all those labored males and females come out as "*its*." And even when he is reading German to himself, he always calls those things "*it;*" whereas he ought to read in this way:

Tale of the Fishwife and Its Sad Fate.*

It is a bleak Day. Hear the Rain, how he pours, and the Hail, how he rattles; and see the Snow, how he drifts along, and oh the Mud, how deep he is! Ah the poor Fishwife, it is stuck fast in the Mire; it has dropped its Basket of Fishes; and its Hands have been cut by the Scales as it seized some of the falling Creatures; and one Scale has even got into its Eye, and it cannot get her out. It opens its Mouth to cry for Help; but if any Sound comes out of him, alas he is drowned by the raging of the Storm.

---

*I capitalize the nouns, in the German (and ancient English) fashion.

And now a Tomcat has got one of the Fishes and she will surely escape with him. No, she bites off a Fin, she holds her in her Mouth,—will she swallow her? No, the Fishwife's brave Mother-Dog deserts his Puppies and rescues the Fin,—which he eats, himself, as his Reward. O, horror, the Lightning has struck the Fishbasket; he sets him on Fire; see the Flame, how she licks the doomed Utensil with her red and angry Tongue; now she attacks the helpless Fishwife's Foot,—she burns him up, all but the big Toe and even *she* is partly consumed; and still she spreads, still she waves her fiery Tongues; she attacks the Fishwife's Leg and destroys *it;* she attacks its Hand and destroys *her;* she attacks its poor worn Garment and destroys *her* also; she attacks its Body and consumes *him;* she wreathes herself about its Heart and *it* is consumed; next about its Breast, and in a Moment *she* is a Cinder; now she reaches its Neck,—*he* goes; now its Chin,—*it* goes; now its Nose,—*she* goes. In another Moment, except Help come, the Fishwife will be no more. Time presses,—is there none to succor and save? Yes! Joy, joy, with flying Feet the she-Englishwoman comes! But alas, the generous she-Female is too late: where now is the fated Fishwife? It has ceased from its Sufferings, it has gone to a better Land; all that is left of it for its loved Ones to lament over, is this poor smouldering Ash-heap. Ah, woful, woful Ash-heap! Let us take him up tenderly, reverently, upon the lowly Shovel, and bear him to his long Rest, with the Prayer that when he rises again it will be in a Realm where he will have one good square responsible Sex, and have it all to himself, instead of having a mangy lot of assorted Sexes scattered all over him in Spots.

There, now, the reader can see for himself that this pronoun-business is a very awkward thing for the unaccustomed tongue.

I suppose that in all languages the similarities of look and sound between words which have no similarity in meaning are a fruitful source of perplexity to the foreigner. It is so in our tongue, and it is notably the case in the German. Now there is that troublesome word *vermählt:* to me it has so close a resemblance,—either real or fancied,—to three or four other words, that I never know whether it means despised, painted, suspected, or married; until I look in the dictionary, and then I find it means the latter. There are lots of such words, and they are a great torment. To increase the difficulty there are words which *seem* to resemble each other, and yet do not; but they make just as much trouble as if they did. For instance, there is the word *vermiethen*, (to let, to lease, to hire); and the word *verheirathen*, (another way of saying to *marry*.) I heard of an Englishman who knocked at a man's door in Heidelberg and proposed, in the best German he could command, to "verheirathen" that house. Then there are some words which mean one thing when you emphasize the first syllable, but mean something very different if you throw the emphasis on the last syllable. For instance, there is a word which means a runaway, or the act of glancing through a book, according to the placing of the emphasis; and another word which signifies to *associate* with a man, or to *avoid* him, according to where you put the emphasis,—and you can generally depend on putting it in the wrong place and getting into trouble.

There are some exceedingly useful words in this language. *Schlag*, for example; and *Zug*. There are three-quarters of a column of Schlags in the dictionary, and a column and a half of Zugs. The word Schlag means Blow, Stroke, Dash, Hit, Shock, Clap, Slap, Time, Bar, Coin, Stamp, Kind, Sort, Manner, Way, Apoplexy, Wood-Cutting, Enclosure, Field, Forest-Clearing. This is its simple and *exact* meaning,—that is to say, its restricted, its fettered meaning; but there are ways by which you can set it free, so that it can soar away, as on the wings of the morning, and never be at rest. You can hang any word you please to its tail, and make it mean anything you want to. You can begin with *Schlag-ader*, which means artery, and you can hang on the whole dictionary, word by word, clear through the alphabet to *Schlag-wasser*, which means bilge-water,—and including *Schlag-mutter*, which means mother-in-law.

Just the same with *Zug*. Strictly speaking, Zug means Pull, Tug, Draught, Procession, March, Progress, Flight, Direction, Expedition, Train, Caravan, Passage, Stroke, Touch, Line, Flourish, Trait of Character, Feature, Lineament, Chess-move, Organ-stop, Team, Whiff, Bias, Drawer, Propensity, Inhalation, Disposition: but that thing which it does *not* mean,—when all its legitimate pendants have been hung on, has not been discovered yet.

One cannot over-estimate the usefulness of Schlag and Zug. Armed just with these two, and the word *Also*, what cannot the foreigner on German soil accomplish ? The German word *Also* is the equivalent of the English phrase "You know," and does not mean anything at all,—in *talk*, though it sometimes does in print. Every time a German opens his mouth an *Also* falls out; and every time he shuts it he bites one in two that was trying to *get* out.

Now, the foreigner, equipped with these three noble words, is master of the situation. Let him talk right along, fearlessly; let him pour his indifferent German forth, and when he lacks for a word, let him heave a *Schlag* into the vacuum; all the chances are, that it fits it like a plug; but if it doesn't, let him promptly heave a *Zug* after it; the two together can hardly fail to bung the hole; but if, by a miracle, they *should* fail, let him simply say *Also!* and this will give him a moment's chance to think of the needful word. In Germany, when you load your conversational gun it is always best to throw in a *Schlag* or two and a *Zug* or two; because it doesn't make any difference how much the rest of the charge may scatter, you are bound to bag something with *them*. Then you blandly say *Also*, and load up again. Nothing gives such an air of grace and elegance and unconstraint to a German or an English conversation as to scatter it full of "Also's" or "You-knows."

In my note-book I find this entry:

July 1.—In the hospital, yesterday, a word of thirteen syllables was successfully removed from a patient,—a North-German from near Hamburg; but as most unfortunately the surgeons had opened him in the wrong place, under the impression that he contained a panorama, he died. The sad event has cast a gloom over the whole community.

That paragraph furnishes a text for a few remarks about one of the most curious and notable features of my subject,—the length of German words. Some German words are so long that they have a perspective. Observe these examples:

Freundschaftsbezeigungen.

Dilletantenaufdringlichkeiten.

Stadtverordnetenversammlungen.

These things are not words, they are alphabetical processions. And they are not rare; one can open a German newspaper any time and see them marching majestically across the page,—and if he has any imagination he can see the banners and hear the music, too. They impart a martial thrill to the meekest subject. I take a great interest in these curiosities. Whenever I come across a good one, I stuff it and put it in my museum. In this way I have made quite a valuable collection. When I get duplicates, I exchange with other collectors, and thus increase the variety of my stock. Here are some specimens which I lately bought at an auction sale of the effects of a bankrupt bric-a-brac hunter:

GENERALSTAATSVERORDNETENVERSAMMLUNGEN.

ALTERTHUMSWISSENSCHAFTEN.

KINDERBEWAHRUNGSANSTALTEN.

UNABHAENGIGKEITSERKLAERUNGEN.

WIEDERHERSTELLUNGSBESTREBUNGEN.

WAFFENSTILLSTANDSUNTERHANDLUNGEN.

Of course when one of these grand mountain ranges goes stretching across the printed page, it adórns and ennobles that

A COMPLETE WORD.

literary landscape,—but at the same time it is a great distress to the new student, for it blocks up his way; he cannot crawl under it, or climb over it or tunnel through it. So he resorts to the dictionary for help; but there is no help there. The dictionary must draw the line somewhere,—so it leaves this sort of words out. And it is right, because these long things are hardly legitimate words, but are rather combinations of words, and the inventor of them ought to have been killed. They are compound words, with the hyphens left out. The various words used in building them are in the dictionary, but in a very scattered condition; so you can hunt the materials out, one by one, and get at the meaning at last, but it is a tedious and harrassing business. I have tried this process upon some of the above examples. 'Freundschaftsbezeigungen" seems to be "Friendship demonstrations," which is only a foolish and clumsy way of saying "demonstrations of friendship." "Unabhaengigkeitserklaerungen" seems to be "Independencedeclarations," which is no improvement upon "Declarations of Independence," as far as I can see. "Generalstaatsverordnetenversammlungen" seems to be "Generalstatesrepresentativesmeetings," as nearly as I can get at it,—a mere rhythmical, gushy euphuism for "meetings of the legislature," I judge. We used to have a good deal of this sort of crime in our literature, but it has gone out, now. We used to speak of a thing as a "never-to-be-forgotten" circumstance, instead of cramping it into the simple and sufficient word "memorable" and then going calmly about our business as if nothing had happened. In those days we were not content to embalm the thing and bury it decently, we wanted to build a monument over it.

But in our newspapers the compounding-disease lingers a little to the present day, but with the hyphens left out, in the German fashion. This is the shape it takes: instead of saying "Mr. Simmons, clerk of the county and district courts, was in town yesterday," the new form puts it thus: "Clerk of the County and District Court Simmons was in town yesterday." This saves neither time nor ink, and has an awkward sound besides. One often sees a remark like this in our papers: "*Mrs.* Assistant District Attorney Johnson returned to her city residence yesterday for the season." That is a case of really unjustifiable compounding; because it not only saves no time or trouble, but confers a title on Mrs. Johnson which she has no right to. But these little instances are trifles indeed, contrasted with the ponderous and dismal German system of piling jumbled compounds together. I wish to submit the following local item, from a Mannheim journal, by way of illustration:

"In the daybeforeyesterdayshortlyaftereleveno'clock Night, the inthistownstandingtavern called "The Wagoner" was downburnt. When the fire to the onthedownburninghouseresting Stork's Nest reached, flew the parent Storks away. But when the bytheraging, firesurrounded Nest *itself* caught Fire, straightway plunged the quickreturning Mother-Stork into the Flames and died, her Wings over her young ones outspread."

Even the cumbersome German construction is not able to take the pathos out of that picture,—indeed it somehow seems to strengthen it. This item is dated away back yonder months ago. I could have used it sooner, but I was waiting to hear from the Father-Stork. I am still waiting.

"*Also!*" If I have not shown that the German is a difficult language, I have at least intended to do it. I have heard of an American student who was asked how he was getting along with his German, and who answered promptly: "I am not getting along at all. I have worked at it hard for three level months, and all I have got to show for it is one solitary German phrase,— '*Zwei glas,*'" (two glasses of beer.) He paused a moment, reflectively, then added with feeling, "But I've got that *solid!*"

And if I have not also shown that German is a harassing and infuriating study, my execution has been at fault, and not my intent. I heard lately of a worn and sorely tried American student who used to fly to a certain German word for relief when he could bear up under his aggravations no longer,—the only word in the whole language whose sound was sweet and precious to his ear and healing to his lacerated spirit. This was the word *Damit.* It was only the *sound* that helped him, not the meaning*; and so, at last, when he learned that the emphasis was not on the first syllable, his only stay and support was gone, and he faded away and died.

I think that a description of any loud, stirring, tumultuous episode must be tamer in German than in English. Our descriptive words of this character have such a deep, strong, resonant sound, while their German equivalents do seem so thin and mild and energyless. Boom, burst, crash, roar, storm, bellow, blow, thunder, explosion; howl, cry, shout, yell, groan; battle, hell. These are magnificent words; they have a force and magnitude of sound befitting the things which they describe. But their German equivalents would be ever so nice to sing the children to sleep with, or else my awe-inspiring ears were made for display and not for superior usefulness in analyzing sounds. Would any man

---

* It merely means, in its general sense, "*herewith.*"

want to die in a battle which was called by so tame a term as a *Schlacht?* Or would not a consumptive feel too much bundled up, who was about to go out, in a shirt collar and a seal ring, into a storm which the bird-song word *Gewitter* was employed to describe? And observe the strongest of the several German equivalents for explosion,—*Ausbruch.* Our word Toothbrush is more powerful than that. It seems to me that the Germans could do worse than import it into their language to describe particularly tremendous explosions with. The German word for hell,—Hölle, —sounds more like *helly* than anything else; therefore, how necessarily chipper, frivolous and unimpressive it is. If a man were told in German to go there, could he really rise to the dignity of feeling insulted?

Having now pointed out, in detail, the several vices of this language, I now come to the brief and pleasant task of pointing out its virtues. The capitalizing of the nouns, I have already mentioned. But far before this virtue stands another,—that of spelling a word according to the sound of it. After one short lesson in the alphabet, the student can tell how any German word is pronounced, without having to ask; whereas in our language if a student should inquire of us " What does B, O, W, spell?" we should be obliged to reply, " Nobody can tell what it spells, when you set it off by itself,—you can only tell by referring to the context and finding out what it signifies,—whether it is a thing to shoot arrows with, or a nod of one's head, or the forward end of a boat."

There are some German words which are singularly and powerfully effective. For instance, those which describe lowly, peaceful and affectionate home life; those which deal with love, in any and all forms, from mere kindly feeling and honest good will toward the passing stranger, clear up to courtship; those which deal with out-door Nature, in its softest and loveliest aspects,—with meadows, and forests, and birds and flowers, the fragrance and sunshine of summer, and the moonlight of peaceful winter nights; in a word, those which deal with any and all forms of rest, repose, and peace; those also which deal with the creatures and marvels of fairyland; and lastly and chiefly, in those words which express pathos, is the language surpassingly rich and effective. There are German songs which can make a stranger to the language cry. That shows that the *sound* of the words is correct,—it interprets the meanings with truth and with exactness; and so the ear is informed, and through the ear, the heart.

The Germans do not seem to be afraid to repeat a word when it is the right one. They repeat it several times, if they choose. That is wise. But in English when we have used a word a couple of times in a paragraph, we imagine we are growing tautological, and so we are weak enough to exchange it for some other word which only approximates exactness, to escape what we wrongly fancy is a greater blemish. Repetition may be bad, but surely inexactness is worse.

There are people in the world who will take a great deal of trouble to point out the faults in a religion or a language, and then go blandly about their business without suggesting any remedy. I am not that kind of a person. I have shown that the German language needs reforming. Very well, I am ready to reform it. At least I am ready to make the proper suggestions. Such a course as this might be immodest in another; but I have devoted upwards of nine full weeks, first and last, to a careful and critical study of this tongue, and thus have acquired a confidence in my ability to reform it which no mere superficial culture could have conferred upon me.

In the first place, I would leave out the Dative Case. It confuses the plurals; and besides, nobody ever knows when he is in the Dative Case, except he discover it by accident,—and then he does not know when or where it was that he got into it, or how long he has been in it, or how he is ever going to get out of it again. The Dative Case is but an ornamental folly,—it is better to discard it.

In the next place, I would move the Verb further up to the front. You may load up with ever so good a Verb, but I notice that you never really bring down a subject with it at the present German range,—you only cripple it. So I insist that this important part of speech should be brought forward to a position where it may be easily seen with the naked eye.

Thirdly, I would import some strong words from the English

tongue,—to swear with, and also to use in describing all sorts of vigorous things in a vigorous way.*

Fourthly, I would reorganize the sexes, and distribute them according to the will of the Creator. This as a tribute of respect, if nothing else.

Fifthly, I would do away with those great long compounded words; or require the speaker to deliver them in sections, with intermissions for refreshments. To wholly do away with them would be best, for ideas are more easily received and digested when they come one at a time than when they come in bulk. Intellectual food is like any other; it is pleasanter and more beneficial to take it with a spoon than with a shovel.

Sixthly, I would require a speaker to stop when he is done, and not hang a string of those useless "haben sind gewesen gehabt haben geworden seins" to the end of his oration. This sort of gew-gaws undignify a speech, instead of adding a grace. They are therefore an offense, and should be discarded.

Seventhly, I would discard the Parenthesis. Also the re-Parenthesis, the re-re-parenthesis, and the re-re-re-re-re-re-parentheses, and likewise the final wide-reaching all-enclosing King-parenthesis. I would require every individual, be he high or low, to unfold a plain straightforward tale, or else coil it and sit on it and hold his peace. Infractions of this law should be punishable with death.

And eighthly and lastly, I would retain *Zug* and *Schlag*, with their pendants, and discard the rest of the vocabulary. This would simplify the language.

I have now named what I regard as the most necessary and important changes. These are perhaps all I could be expected to

---

* "*Verdammt*," and its variations and enlargements, are words which have plenty of meaning, but the *sounds* are so mild and ineffectual that German ladies can use them without sin. German ladies who could not be induced to commit a sin by any persuasion or compulsion, promptly rip out one of these harmless little words when they tear their dresses or don't like the soup. It sounds about as wicked as our "My gracious." German ladies are constantly saying, "Ach! Gott!" "Mein Gott!" "Gott in Himmel!" "Herr Gott!" "Der Herr Jesus!" etc. They think our ladies have the same custom, perhaps, for I once heard a gentle and lovely old German lady say to a sweet young American girl, "The two languages are so alike—how pleasant that is; we say 'Ach! Gott!' you say 'Goddam.'"

name for nothing; but there are other suggestions which I can and will make in case my proposed application shall result in my being formally employed by the government in the work of reforming the language.

My philological studies have satisfied me that a gifted person ought to learn English (barring spelling and pronouncing), in 30 hours, French in 30 days, and German in 30 years. It seems manifest, then, that the latter tongue ought to be trimmed down and repaired. If it is to remain as it is, it ought to be gently and reverently set aside among the dead languages, for only the dead have time to learn it.

A FOURTH OF JULY ORATION IN THE GERMAN TONGUE, DELIVERED AT A BANQUET OF THE ANGLO-AMERICAN CLUB OF STUDENTS BY THE AUTHOR OF THIS BOOK.

GENTLEMEN: Since I arrived, a month ago, in this old wonderland, this vast garden of Germany, my English tongue has so often proved a useless piece of baggage to me, and so troublesome to carry around, in a country where they haven't the checking system for luggage, that I finally set to work, last week, and learned the German language. Also! Es freũt mich dass dies so ist, denn es muss, in ein hauptsächlich degree, höflich sein, dass man aũf ein occasion like this, sein Rede in die Sprache des Landes worin he boards, aũssprechen soll. Dafür habe ich, aũs reinische Verlegenheit,—no Vergangenheit,—no, I mean Höflichkeit,—aũs reinische Höflichkeit habe ich resolved to tackle this business in the German language, ũm Gottes willen! Also! Sie müssen so freũndlich sein, ũnd verzeih mich die interlarding von ein oder zwei Englischer Worte, hie ũnd da, denn ich finde dass die deũtche is not a very copious language, and so when you've really got anything to say, you've got to draw on a language that can stand the strain.

Wenn aber man kann nicht meinem Rede verstehen, so werde ich ihm später dasselbe übersetz, wenn er solche Dienst verlangen wollen haben werden sollen sein hätte. (I don't know what wollen haben werden sollen sein hätte means, but I notice they always put it at the end of a German sentence—merely for general literary gorgeousness, I suppose.)

This is a great and justly honored day,—a day which is worthy of the veneration in which it is held by the true patriots of all climes and nationalities,—a day which offers a fruitful theme for thought and speech; ŭnd meinem Freŭnde,—no, meinen Freŭden, —meines Freŭndes,—well, take your choice, they're all the same price; I don't know which one is right,—also! ich habe gehabt haben worden gewesen sein, as Goethe says, in his Paradise Lost, —ich,—ich,—that is to say,—ich,—but let us change cars.

Also! Die Anblick so viele Grossbrittanischer ŭnd Amerikan-ischer hier zusammengetroffen in Bruderliche concord, ist zwar a welcome and inspiriting spectacle. And what has moved you to it? Can the terse German tongue rise to the expression of this impulse? Is it Freŭndschaftsbezeigŭngenstadtverordnetenver-sammlungenfamilieneigenthümlichkeiten? Nein, o nein! This is a crisp and noble word, but it fails to pierce the marrow of the impulse which has gathered this friendly meeting and produced diese Anblick,—eine Anblick welche ist gŭt zu sehen,—gŭt für die Aŭgen in a foreign land and a far country,—eine Anblick solche als in die gewönliche Heidelberger phrase nennt man ein "schönes Aussicht!" Ja, freilich natürlich wahrscheinlich eben-sowohl! Also! Die Aussicht aŭf dem Königstuhl mehr gröss-erer ist, aber geistlische sprechend nicht so schön, lob' Gott! Because sie sind hier zusammengetroffen, in Bruderlichem con-cord, ein grossen Tag zu feiern, whose high benefits were not for one land and one locality only, but have conferred a measure of good upon all lands that know liberty to day, and love it. Hŭn-dert Jahre vorüber, waren die Engländer ŭnd die Amerikaner Feinde; aber heŭte sind sie herzlichen Freŭnde, Gott sei Dank! May this good fellowship endure; may these banners here blended in amity, so remain; may they never any more wave over oppos-ing hosts, or be stained with blood which was kindred, is kindred, and always will be kindred, until a line drawn upon a map shall be able to say, "*This* bars the ancestral blood from flowing in the veins of the descendant!"

E.

LEGEND OF THE CASTLES.

CALLED THE "SWALLOWS NEST" AND "THE BROTHERS," AS CONDENSED FROM THE CAPTAIN'S TALE.

In the neighborhood of three hundred years ago the Swallow's Nest and the larger castle between it and Neckarsteinach were owned and occupied by two old knights who were twin brothers, and bachelors. They had no relatives. They were very rich. They had fought through the wars and retired to private life—covered with honorable scars. They were honest, honorable men in their dealings, but the people had given them a couple of nicknames which were very suggestive,—Herr Givenaught and Herr Heartless. The old knights were so proud of these names that if a burgher called them by their right ones they would correct him.

The most renowned scholar in Europe, at that time, was the Herr Doctor Franz Reikmann, who lived in Heidelberg. All Germany was proud of the venerable scholar, who lived in the simplest way, for great scholars are always poor. He was poor, as to money, but very rich in his sweet young daughter Hildegarde and his library. He had been all his life collecting his library, book by book, and he loved it as a miser loves his hoarded gold. He said the two strings of his heart were rooted, the one in his daughter, the other in his books; and that if either were severed he must die. Now in an evil hour, hoping to win a marriage portion for his child, this simple old man had entrusted his small savings to a sharper to be ventured in a glittering speculation. But that was not the worst of it: he signed a paper,—without reading it. That is the way with poets and scholars, they always sign without reading. This cunning paper made him responsible for heaps of things. The result was, that one night he found himself in debt to the sharper eight thousand pieces of gold!

(620)

—an amount so prodigious that it simply stupefied him to think of it. It was a night of woe in that house.

"I must part with my library,—I have nothing else. So perishes one heartstring," said the old man.

"What will it bring, father?" asked the girl.

"Nothing! It is worth seven hundred pieces of gold; but by auction it will go for little or nothing."

"Then you will have parted with the half of your heart and the joy of your life to no purpose, since so mighty a burden of debt will remain behind."

"There is no help for it, my child. Our darlings must pass under the hammer. We must pay what we can."

"My father, I have a feeling that the dear Virgin will come to our help. Let us not lose heart."

"She cannot devise a miracle that will turn *nothing* into eight thousand gold pieces, and lesser help will bring us little peace."

"She can do even greater things, my father. She will save us, I know she will."

Toward morning, while the old man sat exhausted and asleep in his chair where he had been sitting before his books as one who watches by his beloved dead and prints the features on his memory for a solace in the aftertime of empty desolation, his daughter sprang into the room and gently woke him, saying,—

"My presentiment was true! She will save us. Three times has she appeared to me in my dreams, and said, 'Go to the Herr Givenaught, go to the Herr Heartless, ask them to come and bid.' There, did I not tell you she would save us, the thrice blesséd Virgin!"

Sad as the old man was, he was obliged to laugh.

"Thou mightest as well appeal to the rocks their castles stand upon as to the harder ones that lie in those men's breasts, my child. *They* bid on books writ in the learned tongues!—they can scarce read their own."

But Hildegarde's faith was in no wise shaken. Bright and early she was on her way up the Neckar road, as joyous as a bird.

Meantime Herr Givenaught and Herr Heartless were having an early breakfast in the former's castle,—the Sparrow's Nest,—and flavoring it with a quarrel; for although these twins bore a love for each other which almost amounted to worship, there was

one subject upon which they could not touch without calling each
other hard names,—and yet it was the subject which they oftenest
touched upon.

"I tell you," said Givenaught, "you will beggar yourself yet,
with your insane squanderings of money upon what you choose
to consider poor and worthy objects. All these years I have
implored you to stop this foolish custom and husband your means,
but all in vain. You are always lying to me about these secret
benevolences, but you never have managed to deceive me yet.
Every time a poor devil has been set upon his feet I have detected
your hand in it—incorrigible ass!"

"Every time you didn't set him on his feet yourself, you mean.
Where I give one unfortunate a little private lift, you do the same
for a dozen. The idea of *your* swelling around the country and
petting yourself with the nickname of Givenaught,—intolerable
humbug! Before I would be such a fraud as that, I would cut
my right hand off. Your life is a continual lie. But go on, I
have tried *my* best to save you from beggaring yourself by your
riotous charities,—now for the thousandth time I wash my hands
of the consequences. A maundering old fool! that's what you are."

"And you a blethering old idiot!" roared Givenaught, spring-
ing up.

"I won't stay in the presence of a man who has no more delicacy than to call me such names. Mannerless swine!"

So saying, Herr Heartless sprang up, in a passion. But some
lucky accident intervened, as usual, to change the subject, and the
daily quarrel ended in the customary daily loving reconciliation.
The grey-headed old eccentrics parted, and Herr Heartless walked
off to his own castle.

Half an hour later, Hildegarde was standing in the presence of
Herr Givenaught. He heard her story, and said,—

"I am sorry for you, my child, but I am very poor, I care nothing for bookish rubbish, I shall not be there."

He said the hard words kindly, but they nearly broke poor
Hildegarde's heart, nevertheless. When she was gone the old
heart-breaker muttered, rubbing his hands,—

"It was a good stroke. I have saved my brother's pocket this
time, in spite of him. Nothing else would have prevented his
rushing off to rescue the old scholar, the pride of Germany, from

his troubles. The poor child won't venture near *him* after the rebuff she has received from his brother the Givenaught."

But he was mistaken. The Virgin had commanded, and Hildegarde would obey. She went to Herr Heartless and told her story. But he said coldly,—

"I am very poor, my child, and books are nothing to me. I wish you well, but I shall not come."

When Hildegarde was gone, he chuckled and said,—

"How my fool of a soft-headed soft-hearted brother would rage if he knew how cunningly I have saved his pocket. How he would have flown to the old man's rescue! But the girl won't venture near him now."

When Hildegarde reached home, her father asked her how she had prospered. She said,—

"The Virgin has promised, and she will keep her word; but not in the way I thought. She knows her own ways, and they are best.

The old man patted her on the head, and smiled a doubting smile, but he honored her for her brave faith, nevertheless.

II.

Next day the people assembled in the great hall of the Ritter tavern, to witness the auction,—for the proprietor had said the treasure of Germany's most honored son should be bartered away in no meaner place. Hildegarde and her father sat close to the books, silent and sorrowful, and holding each other's hands. There was a great crowd of people present. The bidding began,—

"How much for this precious library, just as it stands, all complete?" called the auctioneer.

"Fifty pieces of gold!"

"A hundred!"

"Two hundred!"

"Three!"

"Four!"

"Five hundred!"

"Five twenty-five!"

A brief pause.

"Five forty!"

A longer pause, while the auctioneer redoubled his persuasions.

"Five forty-five!"

A heavy drag—the auctioneer persuaded, pleaded, implored,—it was useless, everybody remained silent,—

"Well, then,—going, going,—one,—two,—"

"Five hundred and fifty!"

This in a shrill voice, from a bent old man, all hung with rags, and with a green patch over his left eye. Everybody in his vicinity turned and gazed at him. It was Givenaught in disguise. He was using a disguised voice, too.

"Good!" cried the auctioneer. "Going, going,—one,—two,—"

"Five hundred and sixty!"

This, in a deep harsh voice, from the midst of the crowd at the other end of the room. The people near by turned, and saw an old man, in a strange costume, supporting himself on crutches. He wore a long white beard, and blue spectacles. It was Herr Heartless, in disguise, and using a disguised voice.

"Good again! Going, going,—one,—"

"Six hundred!"

Sensation. The crowd raised a cheer, and some one cried out, "Go it, Green-patch!" This tickled the audience and a score of voices shouted, "Go it, Green-patch!"

"Going,—going,—going,—third and last call,—one, two,—"

"Seven hundred!"

"Huzzah!—well done, Crutches!" cried a voice. The crowd took it up, and shouted altogether, "Well done, Crutches!"

"Splendid, gentlemen! you are doing magnificently. Going, going,—"

"A thousand!"

"Three cheers for Green-patch! Up and at him, Crutches!"

"Going,—going,—"

"Two thousand!"

And while the people cheered and shouted, "Crutches" muttered, "Who can this devil be, that is fighting so to get these useless books?—But no matter, he shan't have them. The pride of Germany shall have his books if it beggars me to buy them for him."

"Going, going, going,—"

"Three thousand!"

"Come, everybody—give a rouser for Green-patch!"

And while they did it, "Green-patch" muttered, "This cripple is plainly a lunatic; but the old scholar shall have his books, nevertheless, though my pocket sweat for it."

"Going,—going,—"

"Four thousand!"

"Huzza!"

"Five thousand!"

"Huzza!"

"Six thousand!"

"Huzza!"

"Seven thousand!"

"Huzza!"

"*Eight* thousand!"

"We are saved, father! I told you the Holy Virgin would keep her word!" "Blessed be her sacred name!" said the old scholar, with emotion. The crowd roared, "Huzza, huzza, huzza, —at him again, Green-patch!"

"Going,—going,—"

"Ten thousand!" As Givenaught shouted this, his excitement was so great that he forgot himself and used his natural voice. His brother recognized it, and muttered, under cover of the storm of cheers,—

"Aha, you are there, are you, besotted old fool? Take the books, I know what you'll do with them!"

So saying, he slipped out of the place and the auction was at an end. Givenaught shouldered his way to Hildegarde, whispered a word in her ear, and then he, also, vanished. The old scholar and his daughter embraced, and the former said, "Truly the Holy Mother has done more than she promised, child, for she has given you a splendid marriage portion,—think of it, two thousand pieces of gold!"

"And more still," cried Hildegarde, "for she has given you back your books; the stranger whispered me that he would none of them,—'the honored son of Germany must keep them,' so he said. I would I might have asked his name and kissed his hand and begged his blessing; but he was Our Lady's angel, and it is not meet that we of earth should venture speech with them that dwell above."

F.

GERMAN JOURNALS.

The daily journals of Hamburg, Frankfort, Baden, Munich and Augsburg are all constructed on the same general plan. I speak of these because I am more familiar with them than with any other German papers. They contain no " editorials " whatever; no "personals,"—and this is rather a merit than a demerit, perhaps; no funny-paragraph column; no police court reports; no reports of proceedings of higher courts; no information about prize fights or other dog fights, horse races, walking-matches, yachting contests, rifle-matches, or other sporting matters of any sort; no reports of banquet-speeches; no department of curious odds and ends of floating fact and gossip; no "rumors" about anything or anybody; no prognostications or prophecies about anything or anybody; no lists of patents granted or sought, or any reference to such things; no abuse of public officials, big or little, or complaints against them, or praises of them; no religious column Saturdays, no rehash of cold sermons Mondays; no "weather indications;" no "local item" unveilings of what is happening in town,—nothing of a local nature, indeed, is mentioned, beyond the movements of some prince or the proposed meeting of some deliberative body.

After so formidable a list of what one can't find in a German daily, the question may well be asked, What *can* be found in it? It is easily answered: A child's handful of telegrams, mainly about European national and international political movements; letter-correspondence about the same things; market reports. There you have it. That is what a German daily is made of. A German daily is the slowest and saddest and dreariest of the inventions of man. Our own dailies infuriate the reader, pretty often;

(626)

the German daily only stupefies him. Once a week the German daily of the highest class lightens up its heavy columns,—that is, it thinks it lightens them up,—with a profound, an abysmal, book criticism; a criticism which carries you down, down, down, into the scientific bowels of the subject,—for the German critic is nothing if not scientific,—and when you come up at last and scent the fresh air and see the bonny daylight once more, you resolve without a dissenting voice that a book-criticism is a mistaken way to lighten up a German daily. Sometimes, in place of the criticism, the first-class daily gives you what it thinks is a gay and chipper essay,—about ancient Grecian funeral customs, or the ancient Egyptian method of tarring a mummy, or the reasons for believing that some of the peoples who existed before the flood did not approve of cats. These are not unpleasant subjects; they are not uninteresting subjects; they are even exciting subjects,— until one of these massive scientists gets hold of them. He soon convinces you that even these matters can be handled in such a way as to make a person low-spirited.

As I have said, the average German daily is made up solely of correspondence,—a trifle of it by telegraph, the rest of it by mail. Every paragraph has the side-head, " London," " Vienna," or some other town, and a date. And always, before the name of the town, is placed a letter or a sign, to indicate who the correspondent is, so that the authorities can find him when they want to hang him. Stars, crosses, triangles, squares, half-moons, suns,— such are some of the signs used by correspondents.

Some of the dailies move too fast, others too slowly. For instance, my Heidelberg daily was always twenty-four hours old when it arrived at the hotel; but one of my Munich evening papers used to come a full twenty-four hours before it was due.

Some of the less important dailies give one a tablespoonful of a continued story every day; it is strung across the bottom of the page, in the French fashion. By subscribing for the paper for five years I judge that a man might succeed in getting pretty much all of the story.

If you ask a citizen of Munich which is the best Munich daily journal, he will always tell you that there is only one good Munich daily, and that it is published in Augsburg, forty or fifty miles away. It is like saying that the best daily paper in New York is published out in New Jersey somewhere. Yes, the Augsburg *Allgemeine Zeitung* is "the best Munich paper," and it is the one I had in my mind when I was describing a "first-class German daily" above. The entire paper, opened out, is not quite as large as a single page of the New York *Herald*. It is printed on both sides, of course; but in such large type that its entire contents could be put, in *Herald* type, upon a single page of the *Herald*,—and there would still be room enough on the page for the *Zeitung's* "supplement" and some portion of the *Zeitung's* next day's contents.

Such is the first-class daily. The dailies actually printed in Munich are all called second-class by the public. If you ask which is the best of these second-class papers they say there is no difference, one is as good as another. I have preserved a copy of one of them; it is called the *Münchener Tages-Anzeiger*, and bears date January 25, 1879. Comparisons are odious, but they need not be malicious; and without any malice I wish to compare this journal, published in a German city of 170,000 inhabitants with journals of other countries. I know of no other way to enable the reader to "size" the thing.

A column of an average daily paper in America contains from 1800 to 2500 words; the reading matter in a single issue consists of from 25,000 to 50,000 words. The reading matter in my copy of the Munich journal consists of a total of 1,654 words, —for I counted them. That would be nearly a column of one of our dailies. A single issue of the bulkiest daily newspaper in the world,—the London *Times*,—often contains 100,000 words of reading matter. Considering that the *Daily Anzeiger* issues the usual 26 numbers per month, the reading matter in a single number of the London *Times* would keep it in "copy" two months and a half!

The *Anzeiger* is an eight-page paper; its page is one inch wider and one inch longer than a foolscap page; that is to say, the dimensions of its page are somewhere between those of a school-boy's slate and a lady's pocket handkerchief. One-fourth of the first page is taken up with the heading of the journal; this gives it a rather top-heavy appearance; the rest of the first page is reading matter; all of the second page is reading matter; the other six pages are devoted to advertisements.

The reading matter is compressed into two hundred and five

small pica lines, and is lighted up with eight pica head-lines. The bill of fare is as follows: First, under a pica head-line, to enforce attention and respect, is a four line sermon urging mankind to remember that although they are pilgrims here below, they are yet heirs of heaven; and that " When they depart from earth they soar to heaven." Perhaps a four-line sermon in a Saturday paper is the sufficient German equivalent of the eight or ten columns of sermons which the New Yorkers get in their Monday morning papers. The latest news (two days old), follows the four-line sermon, under the pica head-line " Telegrams,"—these are "telegraphed" with a pair of scissors out of the *Augsburger Zeitung* of the day before. These telegrams consist of fourteen and two-thirds lines from Berlin, fifteen lines from Vienna, and two and five-eighths lines from Calcutta. Thirty-three small pica lines of telegraphic news in a daily journal in a King's Capital of 170,000 inhabitants, is surely not an over-dose. Next, we have the pica heading, "News of the Day," under which the following facts are set forth: Prince Leopald is going on a visit to Vienna, six lines; Prince Arnulph is comming back from Russia, two lines; the Landtag will meet at 10 o'clock in the morning and consider an election law, three lines and one word over; a city government item, five and one-half lines; prices of tickets to the proposed grand Charity Ball, twenty-three lines,—for this one item occupies almost one-fourth of the entire first page; there is to be a wonderful Wagner concert in Frankfurst-on-the-Main, with an orchestra of one hundred and eight instruments, seven and one-half lines. That concludes the first page. Eighty-five lines, altogether, on that page, including three head-lines. About fifty of those lines, as one perceives, deal with local matters; so the reporters are not over-worked.

Exactly one-half of the second page is occupied with an opera-criticism, fifty-three lines (three of them being head-lines), and " Death Notices," ten lines.

The other half of the second page is made up of two paragraphs under the head of " Miscellaneous News." One of these paragraphs tells about a quarrel between the Czar of Russia and his eldest son, twenty-one and a half lines; and the other tells about the atrocious destruction of a peasant child by its parents, forty lines, or one-fifth of the total of the reading matter contained in the paper.

Consider what a fifth part of the reading matter of an American daily paper issued in a city of 170,000 inhabitants amounts to! Think what a mass it is. Would any one suppose I could so snugly tuck away such a mass in a chapter of this book that it would be difficult to find it again if the reader lost his place? Surely not. I will translate that child-murder word for word, to give the reader a realizing sense of what a fifth part of the reading matter of a Munich daily actually is when it comes under measurement of the eye:

"From Oberkreuzberg, January 21, the *Donan Zeitung* receives a long account of a crime, which we shorten as follows: In Rametuach, a village near Eppenschlag, lived a young married couple with two children, one of which, a boy aged five, was born three years before the marriage. For this reason, and also because a relative at Iggensbach had bequeathed M400 ($100) to the boy, the heartless father considered him in the way; so the unnatural parents determined to sacrifice him in the cruelest possible manner. They proceeded to starve him slowly to death, meantime frightfully maltreating him,—as the village people now make known, when it is too late. The boy was shut up in a hole, and when people passed by he cried, and implored them to give him bread. His long-continued tortures and deprivations destroyed him at last, on the third of January. The sudden (*sic*) death of the child created suspicion, the more so as the body was immediately clothed and laid upon the bier. Therefore, the coroner gave notice, and an inquest was held on the 6th. What a pitiful spectacle was disclosed then! The body was a complete skeleton. The stomach and intestines were utterly empty, they contained nothing whatever. The flesh on the corpse was not as thick as the back of a knife, and incisions in it brought not a drop of blood. There was not a piece of sound skin the size of a dollar on the whole body; wounds, scars, bruises, discolored extravasated blood, everywhere,—even on the soles of the feet there were wounds. The cruel parents asserted that the boy had been so bad that they had been obliged to use severe punishments, and that he finally fell over a bench and broke his neck. However, they were arrested two weeks after the inquest and put in the prison at Deggendorf."

Yes, they were arrested "two weeks after the inquest." What

a home-sound that has. That kind of police briskness rather more reminds me of my native land than German journalism does.

I think a German daily journal doesn't do any good to speak of, but at the same time it doesn't do any harm. That is a very large merit, and should not be lightly weighed, nor lightly thought of.

The German humorous papers are beautifully printed, upon fine paper, and the illustrations are finely drawn, finely engraved, and are not vapidly funny, but deliciously so. So also, generally speaking, are the two or three terse sentences which accompany the pictures. I remember one of these pictures: a most dilapidated tramp is ruefully contemplating some coins which lie in his open palm; he says, "Well, begging is getting played out. Only about 5 marks ($1.25) for the whole day; many an official makes more!" And I call to mind a picture of a commercial traveler who is about to unroll his samples:

Merchant.—(pettishly) No, don't. I don't want to buy anything!

Drummer.—If you please, I was only going to show you—

Merchant.—But I don't wish to see them!

Drummer.—(after a pause, pleadingly)—But do you mind letting me look at them?—I haven't seen them for three weeks!

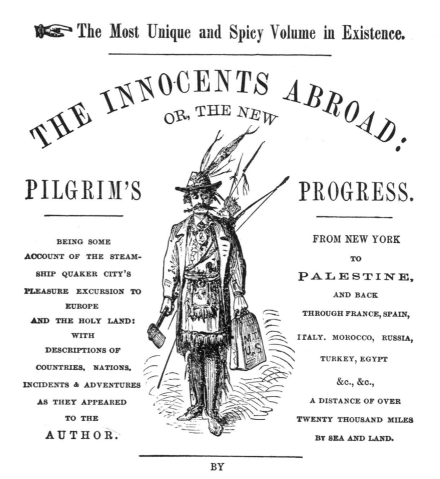

THE INNOCENTS ABROAD:

OR, THE NEW

PILGRIM'S PROGRESS.

BEING SOME
ACCOUNT OF THE STEAM-
SHIP QUAKER CITY'S
PLEASURE EXCURSION TO
EUROPE
AND THE HOLY LAND:
WITH
DESCRIPTIONS OF
COUNTRIES, NATIONS,
INCIDENTS & ADVENTURES
AS THEY APPEARED
TO THE
AUTHOR.

FROM NEW YORK
TO
PALESTINE,
AND BACK
THROUGH FRANCE, SPAIN,
ITALY. MOROCCO, RUSSIA,
TURKEY, EGYPT
&c., &c.,
A DISTANCE OF OVER
TWENTY THOUSAND MILES
BY SEA AND LAND.

BY

MARK TWAIN.

ONE LARGE AND EXCEEDINGLY HANDSOME VOLUME

OF

Over 650 Octavo Pages,

PROFUSELY ADORNED

WITH 234 BEAUTIFUL, SPIRITED, AND APPROPRIATE ENGRAVINGS,

EXECUTED BY SOME OF THE MOST NOTED ARTISTS IN THE LAND; FULLY ILLUS-
TRATING THE DESCRIPTIONS GIVEN OF COUNTRIES, NATIONS, INCIDENTS,
ADVENTURES, CHARACTERS, ETC., MET WITH BY THE PARTY WHOSE
(TO THEM) MOST REMARKABLE PILGRIMAGE THE AUTHOR IN
THESE PAGES HAS CHARACTERISTICALLY RECORDED.

AFTERWORD

James S. Leonard

In April 1878, publication contract in hand, Sam Clemens set out from New York aboard the liner *Holsatia* to sojourn for a year or so in Europe and generate material for a travel book. He hoped the book would reprise both the glory and the financial gain of its predecessor, *The Innocents Abroad*, published nine years earlier, and reverse the trend of declining sales for his more recent works, including a highly disappointing debut for *The Adventures of Tom Sawyer* (1876). Clemens blamed the slippage principally on Elisha Bliss, head of the American Publishing Company (of which Clemens himself was part owner). The company, with its subscription-sales marketing methods, had succeeded spectacularly with *The Innocents Abroad*; but when it came to *Tom Sawyer*, which in the long run (i.e., the twentieth century) would be Mark Twain's most popular book, the publication was a miserably botched affair. The mishandling so disaffected Clemens/Twain that when he originally contracted for the publication of *A Tramp Abroad*, it was not with the elder Bliss but with his son Frank, who was in the process of starting up a rival publishing firm. However, Frank's independent venture soon fell through, and the American Publishing Company's star author returned to the fold.

It requires a bit of imagination and practical rumination — taking into account the differences in transportation and communication between that time and this — to comprehend from a late-twentieth-century perspective the sales potential of travel books in Mark Twain's era. These books were a way of traveling equivalent to the method used to climb Mont Blanc in chapter 44 of *A Tramp Abroad*. There Twain follows the progress of a climbing expedition by means of a telescope and experiences in spirit the exhilaration of their ascent. He vicariously confronts the dangers and triumphs — without actual risk to life and limb. This vignette inverts the way Mark Twain himself served as the climbing party in his travel books — our man on the slopes — while America (and a substantial European readership as well) followed him, as it were, by means of the telescopic view his descriptions provided.

In *The Innocents Abroad*, Mark Twain had proven himself a master of the travel narrative. He was the consummately amusing traveling companion, full of droll anecdotes from back home and sharp judgments about the cultures he encountered. He was a skeptic in the self-reliant American style, yet careful to express the wonders both natural and of human making that he discovered along the way. Negotiating this polarity, he made his readers feel that he shared their ambivalences and uncertainties about things foreign, even as he charged ahead with an admirable bravado that asserted his and their undauntedness in the face of cultural phenomena which might elude his full comprehension but never (or almost never) left him without a rejoinder. Most of all, he believed exuberantly in the American way of doing things. He was, in a word, provincial. The travel books exploited this provincialism unabashedly, high-spiritedly, and for the most part good-humoredly, with a double edge of celebration and satire — but without so much of the latter as to cause his readers any real doubt about his allegiance to their way of life.

No wonder, then, that at this juncture, when Twain needed a success to restore him to the high eminence that seemed in danger of slipping away, he turned to the travel book as a proven formula, even choosing a title that consciously echoed its predecessor's. The title *A Tramp Abroad* punningly plays on the denotations of "a walk in distant territories" and "a vagabond (somewhat less than innocent) away from home." At the same time, though, it stamps the book as a sequel, unmistakably trading on the reputation of *The Innocents Abroad*. But of course, there was only one *Innocents Abroad*. The blessing of the *Tramp*'s heritage must also have seemed burdensome as Twain tried to work out a format for narrating his European adventure.

Contrary to the impression given by *A Tramp Abroad*, the European trip was a family excursion that included not only Clemens' wife, Livy, and daughters Susy (age six) and Clara (nearly four), but also Livy's friend Clara Spaulding and two servants, nursemaid Rosina Hay and butler George Griffin. By Clemens' testimony, an impetus for going to Europe (in addition to working on the travel book) was to reduce the family's outflow of money. Their lifestyle in Hartford was so socially active and otherwise extravagant that they believed they could save money by leaving their own home and living instead in European hotels. Joseph Twichell, who was to serve rather vaguely as the model for Mr. Harris, Mark Twain's "agent" in the book, would join the expedition (at Clemens' expense) about three months after their arrival in Germany. Twichell, pastor of the Asylum Hill Congregational Church in Hartford (which Clemens, a member of Thomas K. Beecher's Park Church in Elmira, New York, attended regularly but did not join), was perhaps Clemens' closest friend, and was certainly his favorite walking companion. The two, in fact, had a history of long "tramps" together. They had once set out from Hartford to walk to Boston, though in the end they made most of the trip by train — a real-life instance of the sort of detour that occurs often in the predominantly fictive journeying of *A Tramp Abroad*. And their walking tour of Bermuda together in May 1877 had served as the basis for "Some Rambling Notes of an Idle Excursion," published later that year in the *Atlantic Monthly*.

In terms of his own writing, Mark Twain had already been wandering a bit even before leaving home, beginning one project, then switching to another, only to move on to yet another. Among the unfinished efforts left in suspension by the departure for Europe and its resultant focus on the new travel narrative was a children's tale of Renaissance England, which he would return to after the completion of *A Tramp Abroad* and finally publish in 1882 as *The Prince and the Pauper*. Also left unfinished (with about sixteen chapters written) was "Huck Finn's Autobiography," which would eventually emerge (in 1884–85) as Mark Twain's masterwork, *Adventures of Huckleberry Finn*. And there was the Mississippi River narrative-travelogue that began with "Old Times on the Mississippi" (*Atlantic Monthly* serialization in 1875) and would later be expanded to form *Life on the Mississippi* (1883).

This, then, was a time of promising but problematic beginnings. Twain was the author of several successful books and was also an extremely popular lecturer (a less ambitious man with a smaller appetite for lavish expenditure might have been satisfied with that career alone). And as we look back now, we see that the projects he had recently begun and set aside would bear fruit in the years to come; he was, in fact, in the early stages of his greatest creative outpouring. But with the faltering sales of the recent past and the uncertain direction of current efforts, it must have looked a bit different to Sam Clemens in 1878.

What sets *A Tramp Abroad* apart from Clemens' other major projects of the time was that he stayed with it — in spite of frustrations, false starts, self-doubt, and bouts of illness — until he finished it. And it is a large book. As with his previous books produced by the American Publishing Company, it was sold to subscribers, and one of the things a subscription purchaser looked for was length; another was illustrations. *A Tramp Abroad* provided plenty of both: 631 pages of length, with 328 illustrations — a few of which were actually drawn (not very well) by Mark Twain himself in keeping with the book's running joke that its narrator, along with Harris, was in Europe partly to study art. Clemens also played a larger role than he had for previous books in lining up the other illustrators — a part of his growing sophistication and self-reliance with respect to the total production of books. This trend, no doubt rooted in his early experience as a typesetter (and possibly spurred by the marketing failure of *Tom Sawyer*), would lead to Clemens' founding (1884) of the publishing firm Charles L. Webster and Company, which brought out *Huckleberry Finn* and *A Connecticut Yankee in King Arthur's Court* (as well as *Personal Memoirs of U.S. Grant*), and to his gigantic investment in the Paige typesetting machine — will-o'-the-wisp misadventures (especially the latter) that he would pursue to the brink of financial ruin. However, if he feared ruin as he set out for Europe and set his sights on the sequel to *The Innocents Abroad*, the focus of his distracting concern, considering the accumulation of unfinished work, may have been as much creative as financial.

The Clemens family, without Joseph Twichell at this point, arrived in Hamburg in late April 1878, rested there, then journeyed via Frankfurt to Heidelberg, where they remained for several months. Clemens began writing and before long had amassed a large amount of manuscript — though as yet no viable organizing principle had emerged. In *The Innocents Abroad* Mark Twain had been a mainly passive passenger, along for the ride and the chance to comment as he saw fit. That trip's itinerary and the strongly focused intentions of the pilgrims had established a shape for the excursion and something of an agenda for the commentary. The problem with the 1878–79 "tramp" through Europe was that it was free-form, without predefined trajectory and with no stable context for conversation like that provided by the pilgrims aboard the *Quaker City* in the earlier book. Thus, although Clemens wrote a great deal for his new manuscript, he also had to discard a great deal.

What saved the day, in Clemens' view, was Twichell's arrival in Germany at the beginning of August. Twichell accompanied Clemens for six weeks of touring and talking together in Germany and Switzerland during August and September, before departing again for Hartford. This was only a small portion of Clemens' 1878–79 stay in Europe, yet it provided a badly needed core for the work in progress, which now came to be more firmly conceived as recounting "a journey through Europe on foot." Mark Twain, as narrator, declares himself "a person fitted to furnish to mankind this spectacle" and hires "Mr. Harris" as "the right sort of person to accompany me in the capacity of agent" (17). Exactly what "the capacity of agent" means in this narrative remains undefined, and Clemens' high regard for Twichell perhaps caused him to treat Harris, Twichell's fictional stand-in, so gently that Harris's comic potential is not thoroughly mined. Nonetheless, Twichell's company energized Clemens — at heart more the conversationalist than the solitary creator.

As for format, with no purposeful itinerary and no clear issues on the table, Twain decided to rely on running jokes to bolster the pedestrian plot. In addition to his study of art and his ongoing struggle with the German language, there was the notion of the "tramp" as ruse. While Twain claimed in the book to be making a walking tour of Europe (which he certainly was not doing in actuality), the gag was that every time he and Harris started off on what was intended to be a long walk, they would very soon decide to take some sort of conveyance — rail, wagon, raft, etc. — instead. One could speculate that this Harris-Twain stratagem plays on a wishful pursuit of shortcuts in the author's trudge through the writing process itself, especially in view of all those stalled projects.

However that may be, the course of the book is digressive from the start, frequently relying in the early chapters on side trips into German legends, some of which are repeated straightforwardly while others are spurious concoctions often seeming to be practical jokes on the reader. Mark Twain was a shameless borrower of material, quite willing to incorporate long passages from other authors, a technique highly visible in *A Tramp Abroad* and freely used in such later major works as *Life on the Mississippi* and *A Connecticut Yankee*; and he was expert at humorously blurring distinctions between the authentic and the spurious. Regional legends, functioning both as filler and as elements of local color, fit nicely into the wandering scheme of Twain's narrative as he seems simply to "bump into" the stories during his forays.

He inaugurates this motif as the narration passes through Frankfurt (en route from Hamburg to Heidelberg), scarcely a page into the book, with the story of Charlemagne's naming of that city. Even as he introduces the story (in which Charlemagne, leader of the Franks, finds a ford across a river by following a deer), he undermines it by stating that "Frankfort [Twain's spelling] is one of the sixteen cities which have the distinction of being the place where the following incident occurred," but then redeems it in the end by pointing out that although the other cities present themselves as sites of the alleged occurrence, Frankfurt is the only one for which the incident resulted in its naming. Then only half mockingly: "This is good evidence that Frankfort was the first place it occurred at" (18). This seems to verify Frankfurt's claim vis-à-vis the other cities; but simultaneously it calls the entirety into question by suggesting not that the incident happened in one place rather than the others but that it occurred in many places (and therefore nowhere?), Frankfurt being merely "the first." Instead of either disbelieving all the accounts or believing one to the exclusion of the others, Twain ingeniously (and with remarkable unobtrusiveness) evades the horns of the actual dilemma, finding a means to believe all the accounts at once while still giving priority to the claim of Frankfurt. This is one of the defining points of Mark Twain as narrator in his ironic relation to Sam Clemens. Mark Twain the narrator gives us the information we need to draw a sophisticated, skeptically informed conclusion, but he himself draws a different one. Thus we enjoy the story in its own right, place it in a context of rational belief and disbelief, and then enjoy it a second time as a joke based in the narrator's hasty conclusion. Twain, as he so often does, manages to have it both ways. This is a technique important to Mark Twain's narrative art — and a crucial aspect of the first-person narration used so effectively in *Huckleberry Finn* and *A Connecticut Yankee*.

But German legends are not the only detours. Possibly concerned that a cold plunge into the foreignness of German culture might leave Americans bewildered, Twain softens the entry by circling around a bit of transplanted Americana in the form of "Baker's Blue-Jay Yarn" (introduced in chapter 2 and then recounted in chapter 3). Here the telescope may seem turned the wrong way. How did a story from the genre of the Western American tall tale end up in a travel narrative set in Germany? It is a surprising digression, following the "that reminds me of" route of textual organization. In this case Twain manages it by telling a story about being accosted by talkative ravens in the woods near Heidelberg; the birds, he is convinced, say things to one another that include disturbingly demeaning references to himself. He then moves into Jim Baker's story (which he actually heard from Jim Gillis, brother of his close friend Steve Gillis, in a mining camp in California) by asserting, "Animals talk to each other, of course" (36) — a nicely jimmied hinge point opening the door to any and every spatiotemporal possibility. And if the yarn is geographically out of place in the forest near Heidelberg, it is nonetheless told in masterful style. This is the Mark Twain whose tales and sketches had by the time of *A Tramp Abroad* achieved a popularity rivaling even that of his travel narratives. Few writers could succeed with such digression; but through the strength of Twain's persona and the deftness of the telling, the anecdote does succeed. And its effectiveness helps to legitimize from the outset the somewhat miscellaneous quality of the book's meandering structure. We soon learn (or rediscover) that the pleasure of strolling with Mark Twain renders the question of destination (and particular mode of conveyance?) unimportant.

In fact, the bulk of the pre-Twichell portion of our tour of Europe (chapters 1–10) remains, geographically, rather stationary, taking its "shortcuts" mostly in the vicinity of Heidelberg. Its centerpiece is Twain's description of the well-organized, carefully orchestrated duels between members of the "corps" of university students (chapters 5–7). Here the narrator assumes the persona of a fascinated onlooker meticulously recording a strange event for his friends (i.e., readers) in America. There is little humor in this. The tone alternates among awe, respect, disgust, and enthusiasm; overall the effect is culture shock. Here the metaphor of the travel book as telescope is clearly applicable. Although we are in the room with Mark Twain and he gives us minute details of the proceedings, the duels are presented with such a sense of their strangeness that they seem to remain at a great remove. The reader feels that he or she has enjoyed a rare opportunity — an effect heightened by Twain's description of himself as lone (?) invited guest — to view something esoteric and, if somewhat brutal, also forcefully transporting.

Harris as viable traveling companion comes into the picture ten chapters into *A Tramp Abroad*, coinciding with Twichell's arrival in Germany. But Twain would have us believe that his agent is not newly arriving — that he has been with us all along, though we've scarcely noticed him until now. Harris's presence is mentioned on the first page and periodically thereafter, and is even validated by an illustration on page 99 titled "Harris Attending the Opera." However, Twain's "agent" begins to seem fully present, and the "expedition" of *A Tramp Abroad* really under way, in chapter 11 (at roughly the time when Sam Clemens began his actual excursions with Twichell). More precisely, the expedition begins to show *promise* of really getting under way as Twain and Harris plan "a pedestrian tour . . . up the shores of the beautiful Neckar to Heilbronn" (102). They are outfitted and on the move but don't manage to get out of Heidelberg before they decide (in keeping with the narrative's running joke about the infinite deferral of pedestrian activity) to take the train to Heilbronn instead, "because it would be just as enjoyable to walk *down* the Neckar as up it, and it could not be needful to walk both ways." Once they are at Heilbronn, having completed the journey in a cart "drawn by a small cow and a smaller donkey yoked together" (105) — i.e., anything to avoid the advertised ambulation — the narrative progress is sidetracked first by sightseeing, then by another legend, then by the story of Twain's search in the dark for a missing sock while Harris is sleeping (apparently based on an incident that actually occurred with Livy before Twichell's arrival in Europe).

For the trip back to Heidelberg (the now long-anticipated "walk *down* the Neckar"), Mark Twain, in Harris's company, again "pulls a fast one" — chartering a raft and crew (an imaginary incident based in part on a boat trip that Clemens and Twichell took on the Neckar in August 1878). Making the turn to the raft curiouser still is the way in which this river-bound venturing merges with scenes in the temporarily shelved *Huckleberry Finn* as the raft on the Neckar bears its riders out into a timeless serenity — an idyll of peaceful escape from life's complicating, often contradictory demands — scarcely distinguishable from that enjoyed by Huck Finn and Jim on the Mississippi.

> The motion of a raft is the needful motion; it is gentle, and gliding and smooth, and noiseless; it calms down all feverish activities, it soothes to sleep all nervous hurry and impatience; under its restful influence all the troubles and vexations and sorrows that harass the mind vanish away, and existence becomes a dream, a charm, a deep and tranquil ecstacy. (126)

"Needful," serving as keystone in this passage, ironically revises the remark that "it could not be needful to walk both ways" — now, either way. As in *Huckleberry Finn*, the rafting produces a moment of quiet and serious meditation on what is needful and what is not — the implication being that a significant portion of human activity falls into the latter category. Such paradisical glimpses, occurring here and at other points in *A Tramp Abroad* (as they do in many of Twain's extended narratives), form a mostly submerged thematic strand of protest against the philistinism and charlatanism comprising so much of life's experience.

Like Huck and Jim's, the "paradise" that Twain and Harris enjoy is violated by harsh intrusions (including a violent, life-threatening thunderstorm and a final crash reminiscent of the raft's being struck by a steamboat in *Huckleberry Finn*), but the broader irony in *A Tramp Abroad* is that the narrator himself, while articulating a longing for some incorruptible refuge, regularly exhibits — even flaunts — chicanery (think of the "walks") and crass materialism. In this respect the Mark Twain who tells the story of the "tramp" through Europe is a forerunner of Hank Morgan, the narrator-protagonist of *A Connecticut Yankee*. The spirit of Hank Morgan presides most conspicuously in the chapters that detail the ascent of the Riffelberg by Twain, Harris, and 152 hired assistants of various sorts (plus 51 animals). This burlesque of mountaineering, adventuring in general, and who knows what else is related in swashbuckling prose so exaggerated that Twain and Twichell's actual climb hardly shows through the tall-tale demeanor that meets the reader's eye. Besides the imposing size of the party, the trek is hugely overequipped with apparatus that includes — in addition to 143 pairs of crutches and a bale of lint — 154 umbrellas. Twain and Harris, noting the crowd gathered to watch the departure, decide that the party should make the ascent in evening dress, and as the climb begins, they order all 154 umbrellas raised at once. This is just the sort of "effect" that captivates Hank Morgan.

More tellingly, there is the incident in which a mule accidentally ignites some nitroglycerin, fortuitously removing an enormous boulder that has been in the way of the ascent. As for the mule, "an hour and a half afterward, many citizens of that town were knocked down and quite seriously injured by descending portions of mule meat, frozen solid" (429). This grisly joke, straight out of Mark Twain's grounding in the rough-and-tumble of Southwestern humor, re-forms in *A Connecticut Yankee* (chapter 27) when Hank Morgan blows up two knights: "Yes, it was a neat thing, very neat and pretty to see. It resembled a steamboat explosion on the Mississippi; and during the next fifteen minutes we stood under a steady drizzle of microscopic fragments of knights and hardware and horse-flesh." The light narrative tone of both passages is brutally out of tune with the gruesome events they relate, for the moment widening the gap between the author and his fictional stand-in. Such disparities, creating a duality in the telling, again let Mark Twain have it both ways: high-spirited humor, but with an undertone of *memento mori*.

The eye-catching ascent of the Riffelberg combines two of the *Tramp*'s continuing motifs: (1) the self-centeredly comic indifference of Twain the narrator to the misfortunes of others, extending at times even to enjoyment when the misfortunes are perceived to enrich the narrative, and (2) a display of obscene expenditure of a sort which in the mid-twentieth century became known as the "ugly American" mode of travel. The latter can, of course, be seen as a kind of self-conscious subterfuge covering the relation of the trip to a concern with family finances. The former may be a subterfuge as well, as indicated by its alternations with highly sentimental passages. The two together have the effect of turning the telescope (or microscope) back on the narrator himself, and by extension on the American culture he so flamboyantly represents. The satire is again double-edged, often casting a jaundiced eye on the cultures that Mark Twain encounters, but also frequently reflecting back on him and his "typically American" values.

On the whole, this fictionally constituted typical American seems moderately comfortable with the German people and their institutions. He hates the language (or does he?) but seems fond of those (ravens aside) who speak it. The tone becomes less positive, though, when the "tramp" moves into Switzerland. Perhaps the terrain makes him feel unsafe. Certainly the chapters devoted to Switzerland are filled with descriptions of disasters and near-disasters (mainly the former) that have befallen climbers, residents, and tourists in the Swiss mountains. To fill space and add drama, Twain dredges up what must have been every available heartrending tale of woe, as if warding off the dangers of mere sightseeing.

In Italy (following the actual course of the Clemens family's travels), the irritability of the narration (perhaps aggravated by the departure of Twichell) increases as Mark Twain launches into diatribes on manners, justice, art, religion, and even coffee. In fact, he draws a comparison between the last two of these: "You can get what the European hotel keeper thinks is coffee, but it resembles the real thing as hypocrisy resembles holiness" (571). But he does truly seem to admire St. Mark's Cathedral in Turin. "Too many of the world's famous buildings," he says, are "a methodless mixture of the ugly and the beautiful." St. Mark's, however, is "masterfully ugly"; its ugliness is "soul-satisfying" (567). This could be the beginning of an aesthetic theory worth elaborating, but one which hardly fits Twain's narrative instinct for the "mixture [achieved through varying degrees of methodlessness] of the ugly and the beautiful."

After Italy, the Clemens family returned to Germany, this time to Munich, to spend the winter while Sam tried to hammer and chisel the mass of accumulated material into a suitable shape. He expressed his frustration with this task when he wrote to William Dean Howells on January 30, 1879.

> I wish I *could* give those sharp satires on European life which you mention, but of course a man can't write successful satire except he be in a calm judicial good-humor — whereas I *hate* travel, & I *hate* hotels, & I *hate* the opera, & I *hate* the Old Masters — in truth I don't ever seem to be in a good enough humor with anything to *satirize* it; no, I want to stand up before it & *curse* it, & foam at the mouth, — or take a club & pound it to rags & pulp.[1]

But three months later, after the family had moved its quarters from Munich to Paris, he seemed much more sanguine as he told an interviewer about the book: "It talks about anything and everything, and always drops a subject the moment my interest in it begins to slacken. . . . In a word, it is a book written by one loafer for a brother loafer to read."[2]

In fine Twainian fashion, this puts the best face on the situation, presenting what he feared was the book's shapelessness as a matter of design rather than intractability. With respect to "loafing," it also interestingly redeploys the language of a letter he wrote (from Munich) to Twichell (in the United States) on January 26, 1879: "I haven't the slightest desire to loaf, but a consuming desire to work, ever since I got back my swing. And you see this book is either going to be compared with The Innocents Abroad, or be *contrasted* with it, to my disadvantage."[3] Though surely not loafing, he didn't finish the book during the winter in Munich or the spring in Paris. Even after his return to the United States in early September 1879, there remained several months' work ahead before publication. But when it finally appeared in March 1880, it was immediately the success he had hoped for. The American Publishing Company did its job well this time; in the first year *A Tramp Abroad* sold 62,000 copies in the United States, ending the downward slide in his books' sales. It also sold very well in England, as did all his works; over the course of Twain's lifetime *Tramp* was his most popular book there — perhaps suggesting the degree to which the English were receptive to satire at the expense of their continental neighbors. It was also quickly translated into Danish and German, and soon thereafter into Dutch and Swedish.

Clemens was right, of course, about its being compared to *The Innocents Abroad*, but for the most part the comparisons were not to the disadvantage of the sequel. Howells, always a staunch supporter of Mark Twain, reviewed the book anonymously in the *Atlantic Monthly* (of which he was editor in chief), finding that while it had "not the fresh frolicsomeness of the *Innocents Abroad*," that loss was amply compensated by a gain in wisdom: "His humor springs from a certain intensity of common sense, a passionate love of justice, and a generous scorn of what is petty and mean; and . . . these qualities . . . have never been more conspicuous than in this last book of his."[4] William Ernest Henley, in an unsigned review for the *Athenaeum*, praised Twain for, among other things, his genuine Americanness, declaring that "he shares with Walt Whitman the honour of being the most strictly American writer of what is called American literature."[5] Another unsigned notice (possibly attributable to Sir Leslie Stephen), for the *Saturday Review*, was more ambivalent, finding the book "dull" in places and hardly suitable for "reading straight through," yet conceding that "there are also plenty of passages, stories, bits of observation, scraps of character and conversation, and so forth, which are delightfully bright and clever. And a practised reader can always skip the dull parts."[6]

This is the approach most commonly used by the book's readers (and editors) today — taking advantage of the fragmented structure to select particular episodes, omitting others. The most popular targets for such browsing are "Baker's Blue-Jay Yarn" (chapter 3) and "The Awful German Language" (Appendix D). But while this method of reading fits with our desire for quick access (shortcuts) to the most potent material, it also loses a great deal. What it loses most of all is Mark Twain as host, conducting us on his tour with all of *its* shortcuts, in the odd order and at the eccentric pace he has arranged. Harris was Mark Twain's agent; Mark Twain is ours — our *agent provocateur/provocatif*.

NOTES

1. Henry Nash Smith and William M. Gibson (with the assistance of Frederick Anderson), eds., *Mark Twain–Howells Letters: The Correspondence of Samuel L. Clemens and William Dean Howells, 1872–1910* (Cambridge, Mass.: Belknap Press, 1960) 1:248–49.

2. Horst H. Kruse, "Tramp Abroad, A," *The Mark Twain Encyclopedia*, ed. J. R. LeMaster and James D. Wilson (New York: Garland, 1993) 743.

3. Albert Bigelow Paine, ed., *Mark Twain's Letters* (New York: Harper and Brothers, 1917) 1:350.

4. Frederick Anderson (with the assistance of Kenneth Sanderson), ed., *Mark Twain: The Critical Heritage* (New York: Barnes and Noble, 1971) 82.

5. Anderson 73.

6. Anderson 76–77.

FOR FURTHER READING

James S. Leonard

Samuel Clemens took copious notes in preparation for writing *A Tramp Abroad*. These notes, which give a fascinating behind-the-scenes look at the composition process, are reproduced in volume 2 of *Mark Twain's Notebooks and Journals* (ed. Frederick Anderson, Lin Salamo, and Bernard L. Stein). One has to be patient, though, in sorting out factual notations from ideas for the fictionalized narrative. There are also numerous secondary accounts of the Clemens family's 1878–79 travels in Europe and the writing of *A Tramp Abroad*. The most extensive of these appears in Robert M. Rodney's *Mark Twain Overseas*, but its reliability is sometimes compromised by inattention to distinctions between the actual trip and the fictional one. Briefer accounts, though rich in detail and commentary, can be found in Everett Emerson's *The Authentic Mark Twain*, Richard Bridgman's *Traveling in Mark Twain*, Walter Blair's *Mark Twain and Huck Finn*, Arthur L. Scott's *Mark Twain at Large*, and Horst Kruse's "*A Tramp Abroad*" entry in *The Mark Twain Encyclopedia*. The early reviews of the book reprinted in Frederick Anderson's *Mark Twain: The Critical Heritage* also are well worth reading.

ILLUSTRATORS AND ILLUSTRATIONS
IN MARK TWAIN'S FIRST AMERICAN EDITIONS

Beverly R. David & Ray Sapirstein

From the "gorgeous gold frog" stamped into the cover of *The Celebrated Jumping Frog of Calaveras County* in 1867 to the comet-riding captain on the frontispiece of *Extract from Captain Stormfield's Visit to Heaven* in 1909, illustrators and illustrations were an integral part of Mark Twain's first editions.

Twain marketed most of his major works by subscription, and illustration functioned as an important sales tool. Subscription books were packed with pictures of every type and size and were bound in brassy gold-stamped covers. The books were sold by agents who flipped through a prospectus filled with lively illustrations, selected text, and binding samples. Illustrations quickly conveyed a sense of the story, condensing the proverbial "thousand words" and outlining the scope and tone of the work, making an impression on the potential purchaser even before the full text had been printed. Book canvassers were rewarded with up to 50 percent of the selling price, which started at $3.50 and ranged as high as $7.00 for more ornate bindings. The books themselves were seldom produced until a substantial number of customers had placed orders. To justify the relatively high price and to reassure buyers that they were getting their money's worth, books published by subscription had to offer sensational volume and apparent substance. As Frank Bliss of the American Publishing Company observed, these consumers "would not pay for blank paper and wide margins. They wanted everything filled up with type or pictures." While authors of trade books generally tolerated lighter sales, gratified by attracting a "better class of readers," as Hamlin Hill put it, authors of subscription books sacrificed literary respectability for popular appeal and considerable profit.[1]

The humorist George Ade remembered Twain's books vividly, offering us a child's-eye view of the nineteenth-century subscription book market.

Just when front-room literature seemed at its lowest ebb, so far as the American boy was concerned, along came Mark Twain. His books looked at a distance, just like the other distended, diluted, and altogether tasteless volumes that had been used for several decades to balance the ends of the center table . . . so thick and heavy and emblazoned with gold that [they] could keep company with the bulky and high-priced Bible. . . . The publisher knew his public, so he gave a pound of book for every fifty cents, and crowded in plenty of wood-cuts and stamped the outside with golden bouquets and put in a steel engraving of the author, with a tissue paper veil over it, and "sicked" his multitude of broken-down clergymen, maiden ladies, grass widows, and college students on the great American public.

Can you see the boy, Sunday morning prisoner, approach the book with a dull sense of foreboding, expecting a dose of Tupper's *Proverbial Philosophy*? Can you see him a few minutes later when he finds himself linked arm-in-arm with Mulberry Sellers or Buck Fanshaw or the convulsing idiot who wanted to know if Christopher Columbus was sure-enough dead? No wonder he curled up on the hair-cloth sofa and hugged the thing to his bosom and lost all interest in Sunday school. *Innocents Abroad* was the most enthralling book ever printed until *Roughing It* appeared. Then along came *The Gilded Age, Life on the Mississippi*, and *Tom Sawyer*. . . . While waiting for a new one we read the old ones all over again.[2]

Publishers, editors, and Twain himself spent a good deal of time on design — choosing the most talented artists, directing their interpretations of text, selecting from the final prints, and at times removing material they deemed unfit for illustration.[3]

With the exception of *Following the Equator* (1897), books released in the twilight of Twain's career were not sold by subscription. Twain's later books, published for the trade market by Harper and Brothers, seldom contained more than a frontispiece and a dozen or so tasteful illustrations, rather than the hundreds of illustrations per volume that subscription publishing demanded. Illustration, however, remained a major component of Twain's later work in two important cases: *Extracts from Adam's Diary*, illustrated by Fred

Strothmann in 1904, and *Eve's Diary*, illustrated by Lester Ralph in 1906.

The stories behind the illustrators and illustrations of Mark Twain's first editions abound in back-room intrigue. The besotted or negligent lapses of some of the artists and the procrastinations of the engravers are legendary. The consequent production delays, mistimed releases, and copyright infringements all implied a lack of competent supervision that frequently infuriated Twain and ultimately encouraged him to launch his own publishing company.

In many cases, Twain took illustrations into account as he wrote and edited his text, using them as counterpoint and accompaniment to his words, often allowing them to inform his general narrative strategy and to influence the amount of detail he felt necessary to include in his written descriptions. In the most artful and carefully considered illustrated works, an analysis of the relationships between author and illustrator and between text and pictures illuminates key dimensions of Twain's writings and the responses they have elicited from readers. Examinations of even the most straightforward examples of decorative imagery yield insights into the publishing history of Twain's books and his attitudes toward the production process.

The original illustrations in Twain's works have often been replaced in the twentieth century by subsequent visual interpretations. But while Norman Rockwell's well-known nostalgic renderings of *Tom Sawyer* and *Huckleberry Finn* may tell us much about 1930s sensibilities, we would do well to reacquaint ourselves with the first American editions and the artwork they contained if we want to understand the books Twain wrote and the world they affected.

Illustrated books, like the illustrated weekly magazines that first appeared in the 1860s, were a significant source of visual images entering nineteenth-century homes. Because of their widespread popularity and the relative paucity of other sources of visual information, Twain's books helped to define America's perceptions of remote people, exotic scenes, and historic events. In addition to being an essential element of Mark Twain's body of work, illustrations are a documentary source in their own right, a window into Twain's world and our own.

NOTES

1. For background on subscription book publishing, see Hamlin Hill, *Mark Twain and Elisha Bliss* (Columbia: University of Missouri Press, 1964), chapter 1. See also R. Kent Rasmussen, "Subscription-book publishing" entry, *Mark Twain A to Z: The Essential Reference to His Life and Writings* (New York: Facts on File, 1995), p. 448.

2. George Ade, "Mark Twain and the Old-Time Subscription Book," *Review of Reviews* 61 (June 10, 1910): 703–4; reprinted in Frederick Anderson, ed., *Mark Twain: The Critical Heritage* (London: Routledge and Kegan Paul, 1971), pp. 337–39.

3. Beverly R. David, *Mark Twain and His Illustrators, Volume 1 (1869–1875)* (Troy, N.Y.: Whitston Publishing Company, 1986), discusses in detail Twain's involvement in the production of his early books.

READING THE ILLUSTRATIONS IN *A TRAMP ABROAD*

Beverly R. David & Ray Sapirstein

Following the mismanaged and financially disastrous release of *The Adventures of Tom Sawyer* (1876), Mark Twain sought the profit promised by his usual subscription book formula, a travel narrative loaded with comic anecdotes, tall tales, curiosities, and vivid and uproarious images. With this project in mind, Twain collected scraps of oddities and ephemera during his travels across the Atlantic in 1878–79, using legends, travel guides, and picture postcards to kindle his creative recall and inspire his narrative as he put pen to paper. While roaming through Germany and Switzerland, he picked up reference materials that the artists would later find useful: for example, an album featuring picturesque Heidelberg scenes by French artists and a brochure with engravings of a monumental wine cask, "Das Grasse Fass," drawn by a German artist. During his trip down the Neckar and his excursion in the Alps, he rummaged through tourist shops for old photos and postcards.

A young American art student, Walter Francis Brown (1853–1929), was one of Twain's incidental discoveries in Europe. Brown, a sometime contributor to *St. Nicholas* and *Harper's Weekly* magazines, had resolved, at least in theory, to give up illustration for more serious artistic pursuits; he was in Europe to study with the eminent French painter Jean Léon Gérôme. Shortly after meeting Brown in May 1879, Twain offered him the chance to illustrate the book and proposed that he oversee the engravers and the production of the plates. Brown accepted the commission.

In the past, Twain had frequently ascribed his commercial failures to shoddy, inaccurate illustrations and lack of overall supervision, the basis of many of his complaints against Elisha Bliss's American Publishing Company in Hartford, which had brought out all but one of his six books to date. Before he set off for Europe, Twain secretly made a contract for his new travel book with Elisha's son Frank, who had left his father's firm to form a publishing company of his own. Twain convinced a skeptical Frank Bliss that producing most of the illustrations in Europe made economic sense.

However he justified the arrangement, Twain saw to it that he retained close control over the product by personally selecting, approving, and editing all of Brown's sketches.[1] He eventually relinquished some control, agreeing that Brown should leave space for cuts by other artists, to be completed in Hartford, and after having a few plates made in Europe, he said that Bliss's people could engrave the remainder of Brown's images.[2] While he let some of the supervision of the engraving process slip into Bliss's hands, Twain made most of the creative decisions about the content of the engravings, initially letting Bliss handle only the technical translation of Brown's images from drawings into ink-ready printing plates.

Months before hiring Brown, as he began working on the manuscript, Twain had proposed making

> from 10 to 20 illustrations for my own book with my own (almighty rude and crude) pencil, and [I] shall say in the title page that some of the pictures in the book are from original drawings by the author. I have already made two or three which suit me. It gives me a belly-ache to look at them.[3]

Twain was intrigued with the marketability of a work in which he would act as both author and illustrator, exploiting the comic potential of his notoriously unorthodox artistic technique. In a letter to Frank Bliss, he wrote, "I propose to give several pages of space to *my own* pictures," adding, "I won't charge you anything for artist's work, although I've had a good deal of trouble with these things and thrown a world of mighty poor talent into them." Twain further reported, "Brown agrees to submit all pictures to me and re-draw them till I approve of them. He also agrees to superintend the process business and see that the work is properly done."[4]

In addition, Twain persuaded his close friend and traveling companion on the trip, the Reverend Joseph Twichell — "Harris" in the book — to try his hand at a couple of drawings. Both men contributed intentionally sophomoric drawings: thirteen by Twain and three by "Harris." Twichell's work received no notice on the title page; the first edition acknowledged only "three or four pictures made by the author of this book, without outside help." As few of Twain's images are identified in the list of illustrations, it is worth itemizing them here. Besides the frontispiece, they include "Piece of Sword" (68), which Twain assures us he has drawn "life-size"; "The Tower" (105), which he "composed from two points of view"; "Leaving Heilbronn" (123), a horse and carriage running down the page at two different speeds; a full page of diagrams, "Rafting on the Neckar" (139); "Dilsburg" (172), alleged in the list of illustrations to appear on the previous page; three biting satires of connoisseurship, "Etruscan Tear-Jug," "Henri II Plate," and "Old Blue China (185–86); two joint efforts with Brown, "Beauty at the Bath" (199) and "New and Old Style" houses (324); the sketchy view titled "The Jungfrau by M.T." (346); and the irreverently feeble "Lion of St. Mark" (562). "Harris" contributed "Our Start" (103), "The Unknown Knight" (151), and "Our Advance on Dilsburg" (172).

During his travels through Switzerland, Twain read in his handy *Baedeker* guidebook the story of the unfortunate accident on the Matterhorn in 1865 that had taken the lives of "a young English Lord, a young clergyman, and 3 guides."[5] Realizing that this was still the major event in the small town of Zermatt, he became fascinated with the saga and acquired a book written and illustrated by one of the survivors, Edward Whymper. Whymper's book eventually supplied a full chapter and seven illustrations for the Swiss section of *A Tramp Abroad*. Two of the sketches prominently displayed Whymper's signature. Twain added a crude cutout of a donkey to one of Whymper's prints, obliterating the reverent image of the awe-inspiring Matterhorn (448). In a note at the bottom of the page, Twain gave his rationale for the "collaboration": "It was my purpose to draw this photograph all by myself . . . but [I] was obliged to put the mountain part of it into the hands of the professional artist because I found I could not do landscape well." Twain named the appropriated image "My Picture of the Matterhorn."

While still in Europe, Twain produced a parody of Paul (Hippolyte) Delaroche's "Moses in the Ark of Bulrushes" for the frontispiece of the book.[6] Writing to Bliss, he explained, "It is a thing which I *manufactured* by pasting a popular comic picture into the middle of a celebrated Biblical one — shall attribute it to Titian" (he titled it "Titian's Moses").[7] Twain altered Delaroche's image himself and sent it out to a "master" engraver in Europe to be transformed into a printing plate, one of the few actually made in Europe according to the initial plan.

Ironically, although he was frequently exasperated by artists' inattention to his words, Twain seems to have encouraged Brown to stray from the text in one instance, perhaps to exploit the comic potential of the discrepancy. In a footnote following his description of age-old ruts worn into the cobblestones by the swinging feet of barefoot children, Twain highlights the inaccuracy of the illustration: "I certainly thought them barefooted, but evidently the artist has had doubts" (113). In addition to Brown's signature, the image bears the inscription of the engraver, Pannemaker, the same name that appears on the frontispiece (and on "Mouth of the Cavern" on page 135, also engraved in Europe). Either Brown's lapse was intentional or Twain chose not to correct an unintentional error, since Brown had agreed to redraw any image he did not find satisfactory. As the engraving was completed in Europe at his expense, Twain had ample opportunity and motivation to make sure the drawing was "properly done" before being permanently transferred to a printing plate. He would not have gone to the trouble of having a plate made without being certain he would use the image.

To supplement the European drawings, Frank Bliss — now at the helm of the American Publishing Company in place of his ailing father, his own firm having failed — hired the workhorse True Williams (1839–1897), an illustrator for each of Twain's books for the company since The *Innocents Abroad* (1869), whose success he hoped to duplicate.[8] Bliss also hired Ben H. Day (1838–1916), principally an artist for *Vanity Fair* magazine, to complete a few cuts. According to the title page, the book was illustrated with the help of "Other Artists" as well. One was William Wallace Denslow (1856–1915), whose initials appear in several images in chapter 47. Denslow is best known for his work for Frank Baum, including the illustrations for *The Wizard of Oz* (1900).[9] Artists not cited on the title page also included the pioneer Civil War combat artist and reporter Alfred Waud, a staff illustrator at *Harper's Weekly*;

Roswell Shurtleff, who helped illustrate *Innocents Abroad*; and James Beard, whose work was pirated in *Roughing It*, and whose brother Dan would be the illustrator of *A Connecticut Yankee in King Arthur's Court* (1889). Waud, Shurtleff, and Beard were probably unwitting collaborators; their prints were originally created for other American Publishing Company titles, and the ready-made plates were merely inserted into *A Tramp Abroad* in an appropriate spot.

Consistent with subscription publishing practices, Frank Bliss waited until he had 48,000 advance orders for *A Tramp Abroad* before he started the presses. The production of the second frontispiece, however, a steel engraving of the author, delayed the release of the book because "the original plate showed 'spots' during the course of printing and it became necessary to re-engrave it."[10] Despite the minor setback, Twain's book found a ready market and instant success.

Although the illustrations are central to Twain's comic art-school subplot, and although a number of images were drawn by Twain himself, more than appear in any of his other books, this is the first time *A Tramp Abroad* has been published with the original illustrations since the nineteenth century.[11]

NOTES

1. S. L. Clemens to Frank Bliss, May 10, 1879, in *Mark Twain's Letters to His Publishers, 1867–1894*, Hamlin Hill, ed. (Berkeley: University of California Press, 1967), pp. 114–15.

2. S. L. Clemens to Frank Bliss, June 10, 1879, in *Mark Twain's Letters to His Publishers*, p. 117.

3. Mark [SLC] to Joe [Twichell], January 23, 1879, in *Mark Twain's Letters to His Publishers*, pp. 110–11.

4. S. L. Clemens to Frank Bliss, May 10, 1879, in *Mark Twain's Letters to His Publishers*, p. 115.

5. *Mark Twain's Notebooks and Journals, Volume 2 (1877–1883)*, Frederick Anderson, Lin Salamo, and Bernard L. Stein, eds. (Berkeley: University of California Press, 1975), p. 163, n. 11.

6. *Mark Twain Journal* 27, no. 1 (Spring 1989): back cover.

7. S. L. Clemens to Frank Bliss, June 10, 1879, in *Mark Twain's Letters to His Publishers*, p. 116.

8. Nathan M. Wood, "True Williams, Pen Drew Literary Giant of Old," *Watertown [N.Y.] Daily Times*, August 30, 1938, p. 11. Until recently, very little biographical information on Williams has been available. Unearthed by Barbara Schmidt, instructional media coordinator at Tarleton State University in Stephenville, Texas, and a regular contributor to the Mark Twain Forum on the Internet, this article provides significant biographical information, including his dates and publishing history. We are indebted to Barbara Schmidt for generously sharing this reference and her pioneering research on Williams' later career, which she is working on for a forthcoming article. Biographical information on Williams is presented in greater detail in this series in "Reading the Illustrations in Tom Sawyer," in *The Adventures of Tom Sawyer*, The Oxford Mark Twain (New York: Oxford University Press, 1996).

9. See R. Kent Rasmussen, "Denslow, William Wallace" entry, *Mark Twain A to Z: The Essential Reference to His Life and Writings* (New York: Facts on File, 1995), pp. 109–10.

10. Merle Johnson, *A Bibliography of the Works of Mark Twain*, rev. ed. (New York: Harper and Brothers, 1935), pp. 34–35.

11. Thanks to Kent Rasmussen for raising this important point.

A NOTE ON THE TEXT

Robert H. Hirst

This text of *A Tramp Abroad* is a photographic facsimile of a copy of the first American edition dated 1880 on the title page. Although books printed from the first edition plates were manufactured until at least 1899, the earliest copies of the first edition came from the bindery in late February and early March 1880. Jacob Blanck reported a copy inscribed by its owner on March 3, and two copies were deposited with the Copyright Office on March 13. The copy reproduced here is an example of Blanck's state C, with the caption 'TITIAN'S MOSES' instead of the earlier 'MOSES' for the frontispiece (*BAL* 3386). It also corresponds to William M. McBride's "Copy 13" (*Mark Twain: A Bibliography,* p. 60). Neither Blanck nor McBride has reported any variants in the text proper. Although not the earliest possible state, this copy was still among the 62,000 copies printed and bound in the first year of publication. The original volume is in the collection of the Mark Twain House in Hartford, Connecticut (810/C625tr/1880/c. 2).

THE MARK TWAIN HOUSE

The Mark Twain House is a museum and research center dedicated to the study of Mark Twain, his works, and his times. The museum is located in the nineteen-room mansion in Hartford, Connecticut, built for and lived in by Samuel L. Clemens, his wife, and their three children, from 1874 to 1891. The Picturesque Gothic-style residence, with interior design by the firm of Louis Comfort Tiffany and Associated Artists, is one of the premier examples of domestic Victorian architecture in America. Clemens wrote *Adventures of Huckleberry Finn*, *The Adventures of Tom Sawyer*, *A Connecticut Yankee in King Arthur's Court*, *The Prince and the Pauper*, and *Life on the Mississippi* while living in Hartford.

The Mark Twain House is open year-round. In addition to tours of the house, the educational programs of the Mark Twain House include symposia, lectures, and teacher training seminars that focus on the contemporary relevance of Twain's legacy. Past programs have featured discussions of literary censorship with playwright Arthur Miller and writer William Styron; of the power of language with journalist Clarence Page, comedian Dick Gregory, and writer Gloria Naylor; and of the challenges of teaching *Adventures of Huckleberry Finn* amidst charges of racism.

CONTRIBUTORS

Russell Banks is author of twelve works of fiction, including *Family Life* (1975), *Hamilton Stark* (1978), *The Book of Jamaica* (1980), *The Relation of My Imprisonment*(1984), *Continental Drift* (1985), *Affliction* (1989*), The Sweet Hereafter* (1991), and *Rule of the Bone* (1995). He has also written poetry and short stories. He is a member of the American Academy of Arts and Sciences, and has received numerous prizes and awards for his work, including the O. Henry and Best American Short Story awards, the John Dos Passos Prize (1985), and the Literature Award from the American Academy of Arts and Letters (1985). He lives in upstate New York and Princeton, New Jersey, and is the Howard G. B. Clark University Professor at Princeton University.

Beverly R. David is professor emerita of humanities and theater at Western Michigan University in Kalamazoo. She is currently working on volume 2 of *Mark Twain and His Illustrators*, and on a Mark Twain mystery entitled *Murder at the Matterhorn*. She has written a number of sections on illustration for the *Mark Twain Encyclopedia* and her *Mark Twain and His Illustrators, Volume 1 (1869–1875)* was published in 1989. Dr. David resides in Allegan, Michigan, in the summer and Green Valley, Arizona, in the winter.

Shelley Fisher Fishkin, professor of American Studies and English at the University of Texas at Austin, is the author of the award-winning books *Was Huck Black? Mark Twain and African-American Voices* (1993) and *From Fact to Fiction: Journalism and Imaginative Writing in America* (1985). Her most recent book is *Lighting Out for the Territory: Reflections on Mark Twain and American Culture* (1996). She holds a Ph.D. in American Studies from Yale University, has lectured on Mark Twain in Belgium, England, France, Israel, Italy, Mexico, the Netherlands, and Turkey, as well as throughout the United States, and is president-elect of the Mark Twain Circle of America.

Robert H. Hirst is the General Editor of the Mark Twain Project at The Bancroft Library, University of California in Berkeley. Apart from that, he has no other known eccentricities.

James S. Leonard is professor of English at The Citadel in Charleston, South Carolina. He is co-author of *The Fluent Mundo: Wallace Stevens and the Structure of Reality* (1988), and co-editor of *Satire or Evasion? Black Perspectives on Huckleberry Finn* (1992) and *Author-ity and Textuality: Current Views of Collaborative Writing* (1994). Editor of the *Mark Twain Circular* since 1987, he lives in Charleston.

Ray Sapirstein is a doctoral student in the American Civilization Program at the University of Texas at Austin. He curated the 1993 exhibition *Another Side of Huckleberry Finn: Mark Twain and Images of African Americans* at the Harry Ransom Humanities Research Center at the University of Texas at Austin. He is currently completing a dissertation on the photographic illustrations in several volumes of Paul Laurence Dunbar's poetry.

ACKNOWLEDGMENTS

There are a number of people without whom The Oxford Mark Twain would not have happened. I am indebted to Laura Brown, senior vice president and trade publisher, Oxford University Press, for suggesting that I edit an "Oxford Mark Twain," and for being so enthusiastic when I proposed that it take the present form. Her guidance and vision have informed the entire undertaking.

Crucial as well, from the earliest to the final stages, was the help of John Boyer, executive director of the Mark Twain House, who recognized the importance of the project and gave it his wholehearted support.

My father, Milton Fisher, believed in this project from the start and helped nurture it every step of the way, as did my stepmother, Carol Plaine Fisher. Their encouragement and support made it all possible. The memory of my mother, Renée B. Fisher, sustained me throughout.

I am enormously grateful to all the contributors to The Oxford Mark Twain for the effort they put into their essays, and for having been such fine, collegial collaborators. Each came through, just as I'd hoped, with fresh insights and lively prose. It was a privilege and a pleasure to work with them, and I value the friendships that we forged in the process.

In addition to writing his fine afterword, Louis J. Budd provided invaluable advice and support, even going so far as to read each of the essays for accuracy. All of us involved in this project are greatly in his debt. Both his knowledge of Mark Twain's work and his generosity as a colleague are legendary and unsurpassed.

Elizabeth Maguire's commitment to The Oxford Mark Twain during her time as senior editor at Oxford was exemplary. When the project proved to be more ambitious and complicated than any of us had expected, Liz helped make it not only manageable, but fun. Assistant editor Elda Rotor's wonderful help in coordinating all aspects of The Oxford Mark Twain, along with literature editor T. Susan Chang's enthusiastic involvement with the project in its final stages, helped bring it all to fruition.

I am extremely grateful to Joy Johannessen for her astute and sensitive copyediting, and for having been such a pleasure to work with. And I appreciate the conscientiousness and good humor with which Kathy Kuhtz Campbell heroically supervised all aspects of the set's production. Oxford president Edward Barry, vice president and editorial director Helen McInnis, marketing director Amy Roberts, publicity director Susan Rotermund, art director David Tran, trade editorial, design and production manager Adam Bohannon, trade advertising and promotion manager Woody Gilmartin, director of manufacturing Benjamin Lee, and the entire staff at Oxford were as supportive a team as any editor could desire.

The staff of the Mark Twain House provided superb assistance as well. I would like to thank Marianne Curling, curator, Debra Petke, education director, Beverly Zell, curator of photography, Britt Gustafson, assistant director of education, Beth Ann McPherson, assistant curator, and Pam Collins, administrative assistant, for all their generous help, and for allowing us to reproduce books and photographs from the Mark Twain House collection. One could not ask for more congenial or helpful partners in publishing.

G. Thomas Tanselle, vice president of the John Simon Guggenheim Memorial Foundation, and an expert on the history of the book, offered essential advice about how to create as responsible a facsimile edition as possible. I appreciate his very knowledgeable counsel.

I am deeply indebted to Robert H. Hirst, general editor of the Mark Twain Project at The Bancroft Library in Berkeley, for bringing his outstanding knowledge of Twain editions to bear on the selection of the books photographed for the facsimiles, for giving generous assistance all along the way, and for providing his meticulous notes on the text. The set is the richer for his advice. I would also like to express my gratitude to the Mark Twain Project, not only for making texts and photographs from their collection available to us, but also for nurturing Mark Twain studies with a steady infusion of matchless, important publications.

I would like to thank Jeffrey Kaimowitz, curator of the Watkinson Library at Trinity College, Hartford (where the Mark Twain House collection is kept), along with his colleagues Peter Knapp and Alesandra M. Schmidt, for having been instrumental in Robert Hirst's search for first editions that could be safely reproduced. Victor Fischer, Harriet Elinor Smith, and especially Kenneth M. Sanderson, associate editors with the Mark Twain Project, reviewed the note on the text in each volume with cheerful vigilance. Thanks are also due to Mark Twain Project associate editor Michael Frank and administrative assistant Brenda J. Bailey for their help at various stages.

I am grateful to Helen K. Copley for granting permission to publish photographs in the Mark Twain Collection of the James S. Copley Library in La Jolla, California, and to Carol Beales and Ron Vanderhye of the Copley Library for making my research trip to their institution so productive and enjoyable.

Several contributors — David Bradley, Louis J. Budd, Beverly R. David, Robert Hirst, Fred Kaplan, James S. Leonard, Toni Morrison, Lillian S. Robinson, Jeffrey Rubin-Dorsky, Ray Sapirstein, and David L. Smith — were particularly helpful in the early stages of the project, brainstorming about the cast of writers and scholars who could make it work. Others who participated in that process were John Boyer, James Cox, Robert Crunden, Joel Dinerstein, William Goetzmann, Calvin and Maria Johnson, Jim Magnuson, Arnold Rampersad, Siva Vaidhyanathan, Steve and Louise Weinberg, and Richard Yarborough.

Kevin Bochynski, famous among Twain scholars as an "angel" who is gifted at finding methods of making their research run more smoothly, was helpful in more ways than I can count. He did an outstanding job in his official capacity as production consultant to The Oxford Mark Twain, supervising the photography of the facsimiles. I am also grateful to him for having put me in touch via e-mail with Kent Rasmussen, author of the magisterial *Mark Twain A to Z*, who was tremendously helpful as the project proceeded, sharing insights on obscure illustrators and other points, and generously being "on call" for all sorts of unforeseen contingencies.

I am indebted to Siva Vaidhyanathan of the American Studies Program of the University of Texas at Austin for having been such a superb research assistant. It would be hard to imagine The Oxford Mark Twain without the benefit of his insights and energy. A fine scholar and writer in his own right, he was crucial to making this project happen.

Georgia Barnhill, the Andrew W. Mellon Curator of Graphic Arts at the American Antiquarian Society in Worcester, Massachusetts, Tom Staley, director of the Harry Ransom Humanities Research Center at the University of Texas at Austin, and Joan Grant, director of collection services at the Elmer Holmes Bobst Library of New York University, granted us access to their collections and assisted us in the reproduction of several volumes of The Oxford Mark Twain. I would also like to thank Kenneth Craven, Sally Leach, and Richard Oram of the Harry Ransom Humanities Research Center for their help in making HRC materials available, and Jay and John Crowley, of Jay's Publishers Services in Rockland, Massachusetts, for their efforts to photograph the books carefully and attentively.

I would like to express my gratitude for the grant I was awarded by the University Research Institute of the University of Texas at Austin to defray some of the costs of researching The Oxford Mark Twain. I am also grateful to American Studies director Robert Abzug and the University of Texas for the computer that facilitated my work on this project (and to UT systems analyst Steve Alemán, who tried his best to repair the damage when it crashed). Thanks also to American Studies administrative assistant Janice Bradley and graduate coordinator Melanie Livingston for their always generous and thoughtful help.

The Oxford Mark Twain would not have happened without the unstinting, wholehearted support of my husband, Jim Fishkin, who went way beyond the proverbial call of duty more times than I'm sure he cares to remember as he shared me unselfishly with that other man in my life, Mark Twain. I am also grateful to my family—to my sons Joey and Bobby, who cheered me on all along the way, as did Fannie Fishkin, David Fishkin, Gennie Gordon, Mildred Hope Witkin, and Leonard, Gillis, and Moss

Plaine — and to honorary family member Margaret Osborne, who did the same.

My greatest debt is to the man who set all this in motion. Only a figure as rich and complicated as Mark Twain could have sustained such energy and interest on the part of so many people for so long. Never boring, never dull, Mark Twain repays our attention again and again and again. It is a privilege to be able to honor his memory with The Oxford Mark Twain.

Shelley Fisher Fishkin
Austin, Texas
April 1996